POWER AND CHOICE
An Introduction to Political Science

Power and Choice
An Introduction to Political Science

Second Edition

W. Phillips Shively
University of Minnesota

McGRAW-HILL, INC.

New York St. Louis San Francisco Auckland Bogotá Caracas
Hamburg Lisbon London Madrid Mexico Milan Montreal New Delhi
Paris San Juan São Paulo Singapore Sydney Tokyo Toronto

This book was set in Caledonia by the College Composition Unit
in cooperation with Ruttle Shaw & Wetherill, Inc.
The editors were Bert Lummus and Tom Holton;
the production supervisor was Leroy A. Young.
The cover was designed by Charles A. Carson.
R. R. Donnelley & Sons Company was printer and binder.

POWER AND CHOICE

An Introduction to Political Science

Copyright © 1991, 1987 by McGraw-Hill, Inc. All rights reserved. Printed in the United States of America. Except as permitted under the United States Copyright Act of 1976, no part of this publication may be reproduced or distributed in any form or by any means, or stored in a data base or retrieval system, without the prior written permission of the publisher.

2 3 4 5 6 7 8 9 0 DOC DOC 9 5 4 3 2 1

ISBN 0-07-056992-4

Library of Congress Cataloging-in-Publication Data

Shively, W. Phillips, (date).
    Power and choice: an introduction to political science / W. Phillips Shively.—2nd ed.
        p.   cm.
    Includes bibliographical references (p.) and index.
    ISBN 0-07-056992-4
    1. Political science.   I. Title
JA66.S47   1991
320—dc20   90-6188

About the Author

W. PHILLIPS SHIVELY is Professor of Political Science at the University of Minnesota, where he moved in 1971 after teaching at the University of Oregon and Yale University. He has also served as Visiting Professor at the University of Oslo in Norway. His research, which has appeared in numerous articles, deals with the comparative study of elections, and he has written *The Craft of Political Research*, an introduction to research techniques. He has also had practical political experience as a lobbyist in Minnesota, and his true love is bird-watching.

To Ruth Phillips Shively
and
Arthur W. Shively

Contents

PREFACE   xv

PART I: INTRODUCTION

Chapter 1   Politics: Setting the Stage   3

Politics   4
Politics as the Making of Common Decisions   4
Politics as the Exercise of Power   6
Implicit and Manifest Power   7
Politics and Power   10
Power and Choice   11
Politics of the State   13
Political Science   14

PART II: THE STATE AND PUBLIC POLICY

Chapter 2   The Modern State   19

The Development of the Modern State   21
The Origin of States   24
Nationalism   25
Government and the State   27
"State" and "Nation"   28
Political Organization beyond the State?   32
The West, the East, and the Third World   35

  EXAMPLE: *State Building in Nigeria*   35

  EXAMPLE: *State Building in the European Community*   37

Chapter 3   Modern Ideologies and Political Philosophy   42

American Ideologies   43
Liberalism   45
The Conservative Reaction   48
The Socialist Alternative   51
Communism and Socialism   55
Fascism   55

The Great Ideologies in the Late Twentieth Century   56
America: Land of Liberalism   58
Political Philosophy through the Ages   59

Chapter 4   Policies of the State   63

What Do Governments Do?   66
Defense Policy   70
Education   73
Research and Development   74
Health and Social Welfare   74
Redistribution of Income   77
Economic Development   78
The Place of Power in Policy Analysis   80

    EXAMPLE: *Norway's Program to Encourage Norwegian-Language Publications*   81

    EXAMPLE: *A Village in Sri Lanka*   82

Chapter 5   Political Choices: The Problems of Fairness and Efficiency   85

Fairness and the Problem of Justice   85
Other Aspects of Fairness   88
Efficiency   91
Modes of Decision: Incremental vs. Radical   93
Modes of Decision: Authority vs. the Market   95
Conclusion   100

    EXAMPLES: *Political Choice*   101

PART III: THE APPARATUS OF GOVERNANCE

Chapter 6   Authority and Legitimacy: The State and the Citizen   107

Legitimacy and Authority   109
Sources of Legitimacy   109
The "Democratic Citizen"   113
How Well Are These Requirements Met?   114
Political Socialization   119

    EXAMPLE: *Building Authority and Legitimacy in West Germany*   121

    EXAMPLE: *Declining Democratic Legitimacy in the United States*   124

Chapter 7   Constitutions and the Design of Government   127

Variations in Formality   128
The Virtue of Vagueness   129
Other Principles of Constitutional Design   130
The Geographic Concentration of Power   134
"Federal" and "Unitary" States   135
The Distinction between "Unitary" and "Centralized" States   136
How Much Centralization Is Good?   139
"Constitutionalism"   140

    EXAMPLE: *Constitutional Government in Great Britain*   141

    EXAMPLE: *Constitutional Government in the Soviet Union*   144

Chapter 8   Elections   147

Elections as a Means of Building Support   147
Elections as a Means of Selecting Leaders and Policies   151
Electoral Systems   152
Referendums   156
Electoral Participation   157
The Paradox of Participation   158
The Bases of Electoral Choice   161

    EXAMPLE: *Proportional Representation Elections in Italy*   163

    EXAMPLE: *Elections in Nigeria*   165

Chapter 9   Parties: A Linking and Leading Mechanism in Politics   169

The Political Party   169
Origins of the Modern Party   170
Political Parties and the Mobilization of the Masses   172
Political Parties and the Recruitment and Socialization of Leaders   173
Political Parties as a Source of Political Identity   175
Political Parties as a Channel of Control   179
Party Organization   180
Party Finance   182
Political Party Systems   184
Conclusion   187

    EXAMPLE: *The Communist Party of the Soviet Union*   188

    EXAMPLE: *Mexico's Dominant Party System*   190

Chapter 10   Structured Conflict: Interest Groups and Politics   195

Interest Groups and Representation   196
Types of Interest Groups   201
Tactics of Interest Groups   204
Patterns of Interest-Group Activity   209
Pluralism   210
Neocorporatism   211

    EXAMPLE: *Interest Groups in France*   213

Chapter 11   National Decision-Making Institutions: Parliamentary Government   217

Cabinet Control   219
What Does a Parliament Do?   220
The Life of a Member of Parliament   224
Parliamentary Committees   225
Exceptions to Parliamentary Supremacy   227
Parliaments in Nondemocratic Systems   228
Conclusion   229

    EXAMPLE: *Parliamentary Government in India*   229

    EXAMPLE: *Parliamentary Government in West Germany*   233

Chapter 12   National Decision-Making Institutions: Presidential Government   237

Presidential and Parliamentary Systems Compared   239
Governmental Responsibility   240
Presidential Systems and Comprehensive Policy   241
Recruitment of Executive Leaders   242
Review and Control of the Executive   244
The Split Executive of Parliamentary Systems   244
Constitutional Review and the Fragmentation of Power   246
Why Aren't All Democracies Parliamentary Systems?   249
A Note on Constitutions and Power   250

    EXAMPLE: *Presidential Government in France*   252

    EXAMPLE: *Presidential Government in Mexico*   255

Chapter 13   Nondemocratic Government   258

Military Government   261
Why Aren't There More Military Governments?   263
One-Party States   265
"Court Politics"   267

"Power and Choice" Again   268
Conclusion   268

    EXAMPLE: *Civilian Participation in Nigeria's First Military Regime*   869

    EXAMPLE: *"Court Politics" in Nazi Germany*   271

Chapter 14   Bureaucracy and the Public Sector   276

Public Administration as a Political Problem   277
Characteristics of Good Public Administration   279
"Bureaucracy": A Reform of the Last Century   280
Bureaucracy vs. Flexibility   282
The Problem of Protected Incompetence   283
Adjustments to Bureaucracy   283
Social Representativeness of Public Administration   286
Conclusion   287

    EXAMPLE: *The French Bureaucracy*   287

    EXAMPLE: *The Saudi Arabian Bureaucracy*   289

    EXAMPLE: *Battling the Bureaucracy in Brazil*   291

PART IV: INTERNATIONAL POLITICS

Chapter 15   Politics Among States   297

The Evolution of the International System since World War II   297
International Politics   302
The Absence of Central Authority   302
Fiduciary Political Roles and International Morality   304
Impediments to International Communication   305
Power and International Politics   306
Power and Choice in International Politics   309
Conclusion   310

Appendix: Principles of Political Analysis   312

Falsifiability   312
What Makes a Statement Interesting?   313
Causation and Explanation   315
Historical Explanation   316
A Few Common Pitfalls in Analysis   317

GLOSSARY   **320**

BIBLIOGRAPHY   **327**

INDEX   **337**

Preface

This book provides a general, comparative introduction to the major concepts and themes of political science. For a number of years I had taught a course that attempted to accomplish this aim, and that experience had shown me how badly we need a text that is conceptually alive and that engages students with concrete examples of analysis without losing them in a clutter of definitional minutiae. That is what I aimed for when I first wrote this book, and I've been most pleased at the response it has elicited.

The title of the book, *Power and Choice*, indicates a subsidiary theme that recurs at intervals. Politics may be seen as (1) the use of power or (2) the production of a public choice. Often one or the other is heavily emphasized in approaching the subject. Marxism emphasizes politics as the use of power, while pluralism and much formal modeling work emphasize the emergence of public choices. For our present purpose, I have defined politics as the use of power to make common decisions for a group of people, a definition that obviously demands that one hold both perspectives simultaneously. At various stages of my presentation I note instances in which an emphasis on just one of the two halves of the definition may yield a distorted interpretation.

Behind this subsidiary theme lies a broader theme that remains largely implicit—that political analysis is best conducted eclectically, rather than being straitjacketed into a single approach. My own research is squarely in the "behavioral" realm, for instance, but I found as I was working on this book that necessities of exposition and understanding pulled me toward a greater emphasis on policy and institutions than I had originally intended. Similarly, the state as an organizer of politics thrust itself more to the fore than I had anticipated. Distinctions that provide useful boundaries for research proved unhelpful in my efforts to build an understanding of politics among students; I think this is a healthy sign.

Material in the book is presented topically rather than on a country-by-country basis; but in order to add the sort of detailed contextual grounding that students gain from a country presentation I have included within each substantive chapter a couple of extended examples from countries that particularly display the conceptual material of that chapter. For instance, Chapter 2, which deals with the state, concludes with detailed sections on the European Community and on the establishment and maintenance of the Nigerian state. Similarly, Chapter 14 (Bureaucracy and the Public Sector) gives detailed treatment to France, Saudi Arabia, and Brazil.

Topical organization of the book is not unusual. After a basic conceptual introduction in Chapter 1, Chapters 2 through 5 present the state, and empirical and normative questions about public policy. Chapters 6 through 14 present the apparatus of governance. The primary, but not sole, emphasis of these sections is on democratic processes; a separate chapter (13) deals more particularly with questions of nondemocratic politics. The book concludes with a chapter on international politics, and an appendix introduces some basic methodological issues about evidence and the design of argument. The latter material appears in an appendix because instructors might have varying ideas about its order of presentation in the course; placement in an appendix makes it easier to take up the topic whenever one prefers.

In the second edition, aside from a pervasive updating of topical material I have made the treatment of political ideology more clear, and have added new material on a number of questions, including the semiautonomous state, redemocratization, and the so-called "end of history."

Many people have helped me as I have worked on this book. McGraw-Hill and I would like to thank the following reviewers for their many helpful comments and suggestions: Marcus E. Ethridge, University of Wisconsin–Milwaukee; Victor Gibean, University of Alabama; Margaret Kahn, University of Michigan–Flint; Orville Menard, University of Nebraska–Omaha; Alwyn R. Rouyer, University of Idaho; and Patricia Ruffin, Howard University. I would especially like to thank Tom Holton, Stuart Johnson, Bertrand Lummus, and above all, my wife, Barbara Shively. Writing this book proved to be a (prolonged) educational experience for me. I hope that you will enjoy using it as much as I enjoyed the writing.

W. Phillips Shively

Permissions Acknowledgments

POWER AND CHOICE
An Introduction to Political Science

Part I

INTRODUCTION

Chapter 1

Politics: Setting the Stage

Everyone knows something about politics, and many people know a great deal about it. It is an interesting, amusing, and moving spectacle that ranks not too far behind professional sports in the eyes of many. Political scientists, however, *study* politics and *analyze* it. This involves doing pretty much the same sorts of things that other people do who follow politics; we read the newspapers and listen to press conferences, take part in political campaigns, and so on. But we also do some things differently. We usually try to see both sides of any question and to keep our emotions in low key, because emotions can cloud judgment. We borrow deliberately from other disciplines—such as economics, history, sociology, psychology, and philosophy—to help us understand what is going on politically. And above all, as you will see later in this chapter, we try to be precise about the meanings of the words we use. Many words having to do with politics—such as "liberal," "represent," and even "politics" itself—are quite complex, but most people use them unthinkingly. Political scientists are careful to analyze the varied meanings of such words and to use them precisely, partly because it is important to know exactly what we mean by the words we use and partly because careful examination of a richly complex word may teach us a lot about the things it describes.

What do political scientists study? Recently we have seen work in which political scientists:

- Measured just how much it actually costs a country to lose a war
- Devised a new system of voting in primaries that might have led to a different set of candidates for the most recent presidential election
- Analyzed and explained the various styles that members of the U.S. Congress adopt in dealing with their constituents
- Studied the spread of pension reforms across the states
- Showed how West Germans over the last two decades have developed a deeper support for democracy than existed after Hitler's defeat
- Analyzed Mao Tse-tung's ideas about representation
- Showed why most nations will ignore warnings about surprise military action by hostile nations

These are the sorts of things political scientists do. In this book you will be introduced to the broad principles of what we have learned about politics, especially about the politics of democracies like the United States. We hope the study will sharpen and enrich the more general understanding of politics that you already have.

This first chapter, in particular, involves the precise definition of several words with which you are already somewhat familiar. We must examine these definitions because you should start your study with some basic terms in place. You may also find it intriguing to see complexity in words, such as "politics," that have probably not struck you before as being particularly complicated.

POLITICS

What is politics? What is it that makes an act political? Consider the following questions, all of which seem to involve political circumstances. What do these have in common?

- How was Hitler able to take power through a series of supposedly democratic elections?
- Why does the U.S. Congress so often disagree with the president in framing energy policies?
- Why should workers sort letters the way their boss directs if they know a more efficient way?
- Why were southern blacks denied the vote and placed in segregated schools throughout the 1950s while their housing was not as segregated as that in the North?
- Should communists be barred from teaching in the schools?
- Should Nazis be barred from teaching in the schools?
- Why does the United States have only two major political parties when most democracies have more?
- Should state and local governments have the right to force landholders to sell them land that is needed for public purposes?
- Was Harry Truman right to bomb Hiroshima and Nagasaki?
- Why do people so often feel guilty about not doing what their parents want them to do?

These questions all deal with politics. The questions about bosses and parents may not have looked to you as if they belonged in this group, but their connection with politics should become clearer by the end of this chapter.

What is it that all these questions have in common? There are two main things, and both have often been used as the defining characteristics of politics. First, all the questions involve *the making of a common decision for a group of people*, that is, a uniform decision applying in the same way to all members of the group. Second, all the questions involve *the use of power* by one person or a group of people to affect the behavior of another person or group of people. Let us look at both of these in more detail.

POLITICS AS THE MAKING OF COMMON DECISIONS

Any group of people must often make decisions that will apply to all of them in common, as a group. A family must decide where to live, what sorts of rules to set for children, how to balance a budget, and so on. A class in a college or university must decide what reading material to require, how students are to be graded by the instructor, how bright the light should be in the classrooms. A country must decide where to locate parks, what allies to seek out in case of war, how to raise revenue by taxing its citizens, how to care for the helpless, and many other things. Each of these requires the setting of some sort of common policy for the group, a single decision that affects all members of the group.

Not all human actions, of course, involve the making of a common policy for a group. When one brother teases another, he is not carrying out a family policy, nor is a family member who decides to write the great American novel. A student who decides to read extra material on one section of the course (or, perhaps, to skip a bit of the reading) is not executing a policy of the class. A person's decision to build a new house is not part of any common national policy, although his country may have policies—on interest rates, the regulation of building, land use and zoning and so on—that affect this person's decision. Ford Motor Company's decisions on new-car styling are not part of a common national policy.

Those actions that contribute to the making of a common policy for a group of people constitute politics, and questions about those policies and the making of those policies are political questions. The political/nonpolitical distinction is not always easy to draw. The example of the Ford Motor Company, above, is tricky because Ford is so large that its decisions verge on being common policy for the whole United States, even though the company has no formal role in the nation's government. In other words, one might argue that because the U.S. government tolerates the concentration of our automobile industry among three giant corporations and because (as a result of this) the decisions of any one of the three bulk so large in American life, those decisions have a quasipublic character and are "sort of" political. In 1980 the quasipublic nature of large corporations was underlined when the government found that it had to become intimately involved in Chrysler Corporation's financing in order to prevent Chrysler from going out of business. Chrysler was so large that the economic health of the country was unavoidably bound to its economic decisions; therefore the government decided it had no choice but to support Chrysler's loans. In this sense, decisions made by the management of Chrysler were to a degree binding on the country as a whole and became, to some extent, U.S. political decisions.

Another tricky aspect of the "political/nonpolitical" distinction is that it is partly a matter of perspective. Ford's design decisions are not (except via Ford's quasipublic nature) political decisions for the *United States*; but they *are* political decisions for Ford's stockholders, managers, and workers, inasmuch as they set a common policy for the company. A family's decision to build a house is not a political decision for the *country*, but it is a political decision for the *family* as a group inasmuch as it involves a common policy for the family. "Company politics" is involved in Ford's decision and "family politics" is involved in the family's decision. Neither, however, is a national political decision. Society consists of groups within groups within groups. Ford Motor Company is a group within the United States, and a family may be a group within the larger group of those dependent on Ford. Politics exists within any of these groups whenever a decision that will apply to all the members of the group is made. So depending on which group you are thinking of, a given decision—the decision of the Clauski family to build a house—may be treated either as political or nonpolitical. The Clauski decision is political for the family as a group but not political for the nation.

POLITICS AS THE EXERCISE OF POWER

A second characteristic of politics, one that runs through all the questions at the start of this chapter, is that politics always involves the exercise of *power* by one person or persons over another person or persons. "Power" is the ability of one person to cause another to do what the first wishes, *by whatever means*. Politics always involves this: one person causing others to do what that person wants either by forcing or convincing them to do so. Looking back to our list of questions, we note that Hitler rose to high office by convincing many Germans to vote for him; the U.S. Congress disagrees with the president so often about energy policy because the president does not have much power either to force or to convince Congress to go along with his wishes in that area; and so on. In such ways, each of these questions involves the power of one person or persons over another or others.

The two defining characteristics of politics, then, are (1) politics always involves the making of common decisions for groups of people *and* (2) those decisions are made by some members of the group exercising power over other members of the group. Power can consist of a wide variety of tools that help one person affect the actions of another. Power may be stark, as when a police officer stops a demonstrator from marching up the street; or it may be subtle, as when a group of poor people, by their very misery, elicit positive governmental action on their behalf.

Power may be exercised as *coercion* when we force a person to do something he or she did not want to do, as *persuasion* when we convince someone that that is what she or he really wishes to do, or as the *construction of incentives* when we make the alternative look so unattractive that only one reasonable option remains. The ability to exercise any of these forms of power may be based on all sorts of things—money, affection, physical strength, legal status (the power of a police officer to direct traffic, for instance), the possession of important information, a winning smile, strong allies, determination, desperation (which helped Vietnam to defeat the United States in the 1960s), and many more. Any of these can help some people get other people to act as they wish.

It is not necessary to learn the specific bases of power listed above. They are meant to provide a sense of the variety and complexity of power, not as an exhaustive list of all its important sources. The point is that all politics involves the use of power, and such power may take varied forms.

A business planning session. These people are conducting politics—using power to reach collective decisions.

(Beringer/Dratch/The Image Works)

IMPLICIT AND MANIFEST POWER

In fact, power need not consist of any observable link between the people or groups involved. Scholars distinguish between *manifest* power and *implicit* power. Manifest power is based on an observable action by A that leads B to do what A wants. A police officer's signal that causes a driver to stop and wait is an example of manifest power. In the case of implicit power, B does what A desires not because of anything A says or does but because (1) B senses that A wants something done and (2) for any of a variety of reasons, B wishes to do what A wants done. Many examples of implicit power are found in families, whose members are so attuned to one another that there is often no observable communication between members of the family who yet manage to "read" and comply with one another's wishes. A father may toss the car keys to his daughter on Saturday morning completely unprompted except by his knowledge of her habits and his desire to comply with her wishes. As she drives, the daughter may obey the 55-miles-per-hour speed limit because she knows that her parents feel strongly about it. In neither case is there any overt signal from one family member to the other.

A famous example of implicit power in a broader sphere of politics comes from the reign of King Henry II of England. The king had been involved in a series of disputes with Thomas à Becket, the Archbishop of Canterbury. Henry exclaimed one day, "Will no one rid me of this man?" Four of his knights over-heard what the king said and proceeded to murder Becket. Historians still dis-pute whether the king really wished to have Becket killed. Frequent examples of implicit power occur in modern politics. Many issues never get raised in Congress, for example, simply because their proponents know they would have no chance. We never *see* the power that has led to the quashing of such proposals, but it is nonetheless real.

What is most important and interesting about implicit power is that an ob-server would have a hard time deciding whether or not such power has been exercised in any particular instance. The source of implicit power may lie far away from its exercise. To understand why the daughter drives 55 miles per hour, for instance, we might have to look back to her early childhood, to ob-serve the hugs and admonitions she received years before. Power can be an-alyzed easily in the case of one country telling another "Cede the province Anemone to us or we'll invade you." It cannot be so easily analyzed if the re-sources on which it is based are varied and complex, as in the power of a de-feated Germany to draw economic aid from the United States after World War II; or if it is in whole or in part implicit, as in the king's muttered remark in the presence of his soldiers.

An Example of the Difficulty of Analyzing Power

Because power is so important to politics and because it is so difficult to mea-sure precisely how and when power is exercised, there are recurrent disputes within political science about how much power various groups have. One such dispute centers on American cities, about which the following question is asked: "Is there a small group of people [the "downtown people," the political bosses, or what have you] who run things in American cities?" This might seem to be a simple question, but it has been difficult for political scientists to answer.

In a study of Atlanta, Georgia, Floyd Hunter attempted to answer the question by asking journalists, officials, business leaders, and others who the most important people in the city were.[1] When all his varied sources named roughly the same set of leaders, he concluded that Atlanta was run by a small group of "insiders."

In response, however, Robert Dahl observed that all Hunter's respondents might be mistaken in the same way—they might all *think* that the downtown corporate elite ran Atlanta because that idea was part of the conventional wis-dom about the city, but they might all be wrong. That the downtown people had a *reputation* for power did not prove to Dahl's satisfaction that they really

---

[1]Floyd Hunter, *Community Power Structure* (Chapel Hill: University of North Carolina Press, 1953). Note that the politics of Atlanta today is very different from that which Hunter described in 1953. The most obvious difference is that Atlanta has now had a black mayor for a number of years; the power structure Hunter described was all white.

had power; rather, he said, we must actually see power being used. As a response to the earlier Atlanta study, he performed a new study of his own based on New Haven, Connecticut.[2] He chose a set of major issues that faced the community—education, urban renewal, and so on—and recorded who actually participated in making decisions on each type of issue. Since he was restricting himself to observable power, he had to ignore the possibility of implicit power; other than that, his procedure was straightforward. He found that quite different groups of people were active on the different issues. Parents and "society people" were especially involved in education, for example, while downtown people were especially involved in urban renewal. He concluded that New Haven was not run by a single group of insiders but that all sorts of groups were involved.

Still a third position was then staked out in the dispute. Two scholars criticizing Dahl's study of New Haven noted that it is not enough just to see who was active in various kinds of decisions but that we must also investigate why particular issues get raised in the first place.[3] Perhaps the really important decision is the one that governs which issues will be brought before the public. For instance, during the period Dahl studied, New Haven did not consider any policies for taking over utilities and running them publicly, for breaking up the residential racial segregation of the city, or for cutting property taxes sharply. At this level, decisions may or may not be controlled by a small "power elite"; we simply cannot tell from a study such as Dahl's.

Notice how complex the question of power in American cities has become as we have proceeded through these studies. Hunter gave us a very straightforward assessment of Atlanta. Dahl complicated the issue by pointing out that in New Haven different types of people had dominant power with respect to different kinds of issues. Bachrach and Baratz finally left us with the realization that we must also consider who decides which issues will come before the public in the first place. In the end, it is difficult to say anything general and conclusive about the concentration of power in our cities because it is difficult to study what might have been—what issues might have entered public discussion but did not. This series of studies clearly illustrates the inherent complexity of power.

Although these studies certainly show that there are few blanket truths about power, one should not therefore conclude that power is impossible to study. Rather, an understanding of the complexity of power and the difficulty of measuring it can lead us to detailed examinations of very specific instances of power. In response to the Bachrach and Baratz article, for instance, several interesting studies have appeared on the setting of agendas in American politics. These are a direct result of the argument that the most important power is that which decides what issues will be up for debate.

[2]Robert Dahl, *Who Governs?* (New Haven: Yale University Press, 1961).
[3]Peter Bachrach and Morton S. Baratz, "The Two Faces of Power," *American Political Science Review* 56 (1962): 947–953.

POLITICS AND POWER

Despite the complexity and elusiveness of power, we *can* say that all politics is based on some form of power and that its sources may be highly varied. For most questions about politics, however, it is not necessary to specify in detail exactly what sort of power is involved. For all political analysis, it is helpful to bear in mind that you are dealing with power of one sort or another; but that realization may often serve best as a background or setting for your analysis. For instance, most of the questions posed at the opening of this chapter can be addressed without conducting precise analyses of the power relationships that form contexts for the questions.

Before we leave our consideration of power in politics, we might draw attention to the surprising universality of the use of power to determine common decisions for groups of people. People around the world vary remarkably little in physical strength and intelligence; they are also more or less equal in their basic talents. Yet millions of them will fear and obey another person whose intrinsic capacities are little superior to theirs.

Because of the weakness and inexperience of children, it is understandable that this should be so within families. The adult members of a family are stronger than the children, and it' is perhaps natural that they should be able to control them. But it is astounding that large numbers of adults will grant this

"Congratulations, keep moving, please. Congratulations, keep moving please. Congratulations..."

(Drawing by B. Tobey; © 1974 The New Yorker Magazine Inc.)

sort of control over their own actions to a military officer, a member of Congress, a dictator, or a religious leader. How is it that political power is so universal and often so concentrated in small numbers of people?[4]

Simply posing the question in this way demonstrates once again that the bases of power must be varied and complex. Physical compulsion alone would not be sufficient to ensure the obedience that people all over the world give to their political leaders.

POWER AND CHOICE

Politics, then, consists of the making of common decisions for a group through the use of power. Though the concept involves some complexity, it will usually be clear to everyone concerned whether a given action is or is not political in this sense. There are two very basic ways of looking at the making of such common policies, and people often use one or the other of these in evaluating any particular political action. In so doing, they may fail to consider how their viewpoint colors their conclusions. The two alternative viewpoints are as follows:

1. Political action may be interpreted as a way to work out rationally the best common solution to a common problem—or at least a way to work out a reasonable common solution. That is, politics consists of *public choice*. (Note that even though this perspective emphasizes the cooperative aspect of decisions, power will still be involved in the making of choices; if nothing else, the power to persuade will be involved.)
2. Political action may be interpreted as a way to justify the domination of some people by other people. That is, politics consists simply of the use of *power*. Here power is primarily thought of as power through coercion.

In other words, two people who observe the same political action from these opposing viewpoints will each have a different idea of it. For instance, a person operating from the "public choice" viewpoint might look at the large number of people who fail to vote in American presidential elections and conclude that this is a reasonably healthy situation, because if such a large number of people have chosen not to bother voting, they must be tolerably satisfied with things as they are. Someone else, operating from the "power" viewpoint, might look at that same large number of nonvoters and conclude that American elections are a sham, that they are meant to give the appearance of popular choice without providing the voter with significantly different options (i.e., many voters do not bother to vote because their choices have been restricted).

Most often, *both* viewpoints are partly accurate. Politics generally involves considering at least the broad needs of the group for whom policy is being made: pure tyranny is rare and is difficult to maintain. At the same time, the making of common policy generally means that one part of a group will be

---

[4]R. M. McIver, *The Web of Government* (New York: Macmillan, 1947), chap. 1.

dominating another part to at least some extent. In the presidential voting example above, both characterizations probably have some truth to them.

It is good to bear these two perspectives in mind, because we may then be able to avoid misjudging a particular political situation as being all one or the other. For example, a college or university class is a group for which common policies must be made and in which a single person (the instructor) is formally charged with responsibility. Thus the group's politics will largely consist of domination of the students by the instructor. However, it is not solely or simply a system of domination because there are a number of informal mechanisms by which students participate in decision making, and these should not be overlooked. In short, the politics of a classroom also includes aspects of a rational working out of solutions to common problems. Such questions as the timing of tests, whether or not doors should be closed or the lights on, or the nature of special projects and examinations are often decided by the instructor in consultation with the students. In less direct ways, students—by their expressions of interest—often influence the very content of a class. Thus, although the politics of a classroom consists primarily of domination, there is also a considerable element of a common search for solutions to common problems. This might be overlooked if one were not alert to the two sides of politics.

It is especially important to bear these two points of view in mind when we consider political actions about which we have strong feelings and about which we may expect to be prejudiced. Until the recent opening up of partially democratic elections in the Soviet Union, for instance, Americans tended to dismiss elections in communist countries as fraudulent. Yet, as you will see in Chapter 8, there is evident in the elections of most such countries a surprising element of broad participation in a search for common solutions. For instance, during the period of noncompetitive elections, 28 percent of Soviet citizens reported that they had at one time or another attempted to persuade others to vote as they did; 19 percent had even contacted a state or national government official about some problem.[5] "The weeks preceding the election see the formation of countless study circles, discussion groups, campaign meetings, door-to-door canvassing, rallies, demonstrations and speeches."[6] Thus there appears to have been more to the Soviet Union's uncontested elections in some ways than we have commonly been able to see. Bearing in mind that it is rare, if not impossible, for a political choice to consist solely of the use of power can help us to remain alert to such possibilities even when we know we are strongly prejudiced about a subject.

To sum up this section of the chapter: Politics consists of the making of a common decision for a group of people through the use of power. Any act of politics may be viewed from either of two perspectives, either as a cooperative search for an answer to common problems or as an act by which some members of a group impose their will on other members of the group. It is impor-

---

[5]Richard D. Little, "Mass Political Participation in the U.S. and the U.S.S.R.," *Comparative Political Studies* (January 8, 1976), p. 439.

[6]Ibid., p. 439.

tant to remember that generally both viewpoints are valid, especially when we might be prejudiced about the subject at hand, because keeping both viewpoints in mind can help us to avoid thinking about the subject in narrow, prejudiced ways. Power and choice, the two major themes by which we organize our views of politics, have provided the title of this book. And they will recur in succeeding chapters as we examine various aspects of politics.

POLITICS OF THE STATE

One thing that has probably seemed odd to you in this chapter, right from the set of questions on page 4, is that things we do not always think of as "politics" have been described under this heading. There is some variation in common usage of the word. Family, workplace, church, and so on are not often thought of as political places, though they are *sometimes* thought of in that way. When we refer to "office politics," "campus politics," and "church politics," we mean activities that fit under the definition of politics presented in this chapter: the use of power to make common decisions for groups of people. When Kate Millett wrote a book about the relations between men and women, she titled it *Sexual Politics* explicitly to underscore her claim that men use various sorts of power to dominate the making of common decisions involving women:

> ...a disinterested examination of our system of sexual relationship must point out that the situation between the sexes now, and throughout history, is a case of that phenomenon Max Weber defined as *herrschaft*, a relationship of dominance and subordinance. What goes largely unexamined, often even unacknowledged (yet is institutionalized nonetheless) in our social order, is the birthright priority whereby males rule females.... The fact is evident at once if one recalls that the military, industry, technology, universities, science, political office, and finance—in short, every avenue of power within the society, including the coercive force of the police, is entirely in male hands. As the essence of politics is power, such realization cannot fail to carry impact.[7]

This broad usage of the word "politics" fits the general definition presented in this chapter, but a much more common usage of the word is slightly narrower. If we say, "Frank went into politics," or "I'm fascinated by politics," we are not thinking of the family or corporation or church. In this sense of the word we are referring only to the kind of politics that has to do with government of the state.

"State" has a special meaning in political science. It is not the same thing as the states of the United States; instead, it is what we commonly call a country. The United States is a state in this sense, as are France, the Soviet Union, Algeria, Mexico, and so on.

In the next chapter we will look at the state in more detail, but for now it

[7]Kate Millett, *Sexual Politics* (Garden City, N.Y.: Doubleday, 1970), pp. 24, 25. Note that Millett approaches politics almost exclusively from the standpoint of power.

is enough to note that the state is a particular kind of social group. Over the last few centuries, people have focused more and more on the state of which they are citizens, and the state has determined more and more of what goes on in their lives. Several centuries ago, most people were almost unaware of the state in which they lived; they only noticed it if the king's soldiers marched through their fields. In fact, at that time, many large geographic areas could hardly be said to have been organized as states at all. Gradually states have become more thoroughly organized and have demanded more and more from us. First, states became the prime focus of peace and war, maintaining peace within their borders and waging war with other states. Then, states became the organizers of commerce and industry within their borders, regulating prices and the quality of products, constructing roads and canals, and so on. Only for the last several decades has the state generally been expected by its citizens to maintain stability in the economy, guarantee employment, and keep the value of currency stable. A century or so ago events in the economy were treated as "acts of God," and the state was not involved in them, but today the state is generally held responsible for economic conditions. The responsibilities of the state continue to grow. In the future might the weather, which is now treated as an "act of God," become part of the responsibility of the state?

For better or worse, the state has become critically important to us, and its politics has taken on great importance. In fact, when we say "politics" today, we usually mean by it simply "politics of the state." Political science shares this general preoccupation with politics of the state. Though we will occasionally look at other sorts of politics in this book, most of our attention will be directed to the politics of the state. It is good to remember the more general meaning of "politics," however, and to remember that we will be looking at politics only in its most important, most complex form.

POLITICAL SCIENCE

Political science is the academic field that takes as its sole and general task the analysis of politics, especially the politics of the state. There has been continuing debate over how "scientific" political science should be. Some political scientists think that politics is so complex and involves such basic personal values that we should not try to pin it down to exact regularities. Rather, we should interpret each political event and idea more or less in and of itself, in a personal, subjective way. Such political scientists would model themselves upon historians, who interpret a particular sequence of events more or less in and of itself, seeking to retain the richness of its detail while making a general patterned interpretation of what process unfolded through the events.

Other political scientists think that their discipline should be more scientific than this, seeking out the basic essence of regularities across a whole set of events, even though this means sacrificing some of the rich detail with which each single event is laden. They think that the only way we will be able to explain and predict what happens in politics is to emphasize the underlying processes that a number of disparate events may have in common. These political scientists would model themselves on other social scientists such as economists, who analyze events simply as instances of general processes, which they treat in the abstract. Economists, for instance, prefer to deal abstractly with supply-and-demand theories rather than analyze specifically what happens in a given used-car lot.

The first kind of political scientists are sometimes called "traditionalists," the latter "behavioralists." Traditionalist political scientists are most likely to deal in historical and philosophical aspects of politics and to seek detailed, nonnumerical information on a few cases. Behavioralists lean more to abstract, mechanical theories of politics and to statistical analyses of numerical information. They find numerical information especially attractive because it distills a set of complex details down into something very simple and basic—a number. Thus, since behavioralists are looking for simple descriptions of basic processes, they see it as more useful to summarize party competition in many congressional districts with a single index number for each district than to try to digest masses of biography, newspaper accounts, and so on from a few congressional races.

This picture should not be seen as starkly black and white. Political science does not consist of two warring camps, and most political scientists combine some element of "traditionalism" with some element of "behavioralism." However, there are nevertheless different *degrees* of these among political scientists, which adds greatly to the variety of materials available in the field.

For practical purposes of curriculum and organization, the field is divided into subfields according to the subjects in which political scientists specialize. The major subfields are:

- *American political behavior:* The study of individuals and nongovernmental organizations involved in politics and of why they do what they do. Studies of public opinion, elections, interest groups, and political parties would fall under this heading.
- *American political institutions:* The study of national governmental bodies, the Congress, the presidency, the bureaucracy, and—in part—the courts.
- *American public law:* The study of legal reasoning and of why courts hand down the decisions they do.
- *American public policy:* The analysis of the product of politics, the kinds of policies that are laid down.
- *American state and local politics:* The study of all of the above, but at the level of "states" (such as California or Minnesota) and localities rather than the nation as a whole.
- *Comparative politics:* The study of all of the above in any place *but* the United States. To lump all aspects of politics outside of the United States together is obviously parochial, but that is what is usually done. In other countries, political scientists may differentiate their own politics and lump that of the United States together with the rest as "comparative."
- *International politics:* The studies of politics *between* states—the making of common decisions for a group of states through wars, diplomacy, and so on. All of the subfields listed above deal with politics within states.
- *Political theory:* The history of ideas about politics and critical discussion of political values.

This book reviews the general findings of political science but blends U.S. politics and "comparative politics," treating the politics of all parts of the world (including the United States) comparatively.

SUMMARY

Politics consists of the use of power to make common decisions for groups of people. It always involves the use of power by some members of the group, but power is so varied and complex that it may be difficult to analyze precisely.

Two general points of view compete for our attention in assessing any political situation. We may think of such a situation as a matter of public choice or as one of domination. It is important to remember that both points of view always apply.

Politics as treated in this chapter is a broad concept, embracing the making of common decisions for the family, the corporation, the state, and so on. However, common usage generally refers only to the politics of the state, which is increasingly important to us and is distinctively formal and complex. For the rest of this book we will deal almost solely with the politics of the state.

FURTHER READING

Politics and Power

Dahl, Robert. *Modern Political Analysis*. 4th ed. New York: Prentice-Hall, 1984. Chaps. 3 & 4.

Lasswell, Harold D., and Kaplan, Abraham. *Power and Society*. Yale Law School Studies. Vol. 2. New Haven, Conn.: Yale University Press, 1950.

Maier, Charles S., ed. *Changing Boundaries of the Political*. New York: Cambridge University Press, 1987.

McIver, R. M. *The Web of Government*. Rev. ed. New York: Free Press, 1965.

Nagel, Jack H. *The Descriptive Analysis of Power*. New Haven, Conn.: Yale University Press, 1975.

"Power," in *International Encyclopedia of the Social Sciences*.

Wrong, Dennis. *Power*. New York: Harper & Row, 1979.

Political Science

Fenno, Richard. *Home Style: House Members in Their Districts*. Boston: Little, Brown, 1978. (The appendix to this book provides a good argument for qualitative social science.)

Lave, Charles A., and March, James G. *An Introduction to Models in the Social Sciences*. New York: Harper & Row, 1975. (Chaps. 1–3 provide a good, nontechnical argument for quantitative social science.)

"Political Science," in *International Encyclopedia of the Social Sciences*.

Wiarda, Howard, ed. *New Directions in Comparative Politics*. Boulder, Colo.: Westview Press, 1985.

Part II

THE STATE AND PUBLIC POLICY

Chapter 2

The Modern State

In this book, we have chosen to focus on the politics of the *state*—rather than on "office politics," the politics in the family, and so on—simply because the state has come to play such a central role in modern politics.[1]

The extent to which the state has come to dominate our attention is evident even in the way we treat individuals. When we think about a person who comes from a different country, we are likely to think of him or her primarily in terms of this—to the exclusion of other characteristics that may actually have more to do with what the person is like. If you knew a Danish engineer named Ole, for instance, and were asked to say quickly, in one word, what Ole is, you would be very likely to say "a Dane." The other likely answer would be "a man"; gender has not given way even to the state in the amount of attention we give it. Ole is an engineer, and that should say a lot about him; but not many people would choose that over his nationality as a label for him. He may be a Lutheran or a Jew, pious or apathetic, tall or short, a charmer or a clod— still, most people who know him would characterize him first as a Dane. This does not really make much sense, since almost all the other things mentioned would have told you more about Ole's personality or person than does the fact that he is a Dane. It is a result not of logic but of our modern fixation on nationality and the state.

If you have ever lived abroad, you will have noticed this phenomenon in a particularly striking way. Most of us do not ordinarily think of ourselves in terms of the state to which we belong. But let us reside in a different state, and suddenly our native state becomes a most important aspect of our identity. Canadians living in the United States or Europe begin to think of themselves much more as Canadians than they ever have before, Nigerians studying or working in the United States suddenly begin to think of themselves as Nigerians, Americans living in Europe or Asia suddenly feel themselves to be vividly American, and so on.

Our fixation on the state goes beyond what reason would dictate. We have seen that we could really say more about Ole if we characterized him as tall or university educated than merely as a Dane, as most people would nevertheless begin by doing. Another paradoxical result of our fixation on the state is that most people pay a good deal more attention to the national government, which is remote and inaccessible to them, than they do to their relatively more ac-

---

[1] As noted in Chapter 1, the word "state" as used here does not refer to a place like California or Pennsylvania. Rather, it means approximately what is often called a "country," such as Canada, Nigeria, or the United States of America.

(Drawing by S. Harris; © 1981 The New Yorker Magazine Inc.)

cessible local governments. In America, politics and attention to politics reach a peak every four years at the election of a new president. This national event so seizes our attention that enrollment in political science courses at American universities generally follows a four-year cycle, rising 10 or 20 percent in a presidential election year! Americans turn out to vote in considerably larger numbers at presidential than at local elections.

The paradox in this attention to national politics is that in a country as large as the United States, which has so many voters, an individual voter has virtually no chance of affecting the outcome of a national election. As a character in Skinner's *Walden Two* remarks to his friend,

> "How is the people's will ascertained? In an election. But what a travesty! In a small committee meeting, or even a town hall, I can see some point in voting, especially on a yes-or-no question. But fifty million voters choosing a president—that's quite another thing."
>
> "I can't see that the number of voters changes the principle," said Castle.
>
> "The chance that one man's vote will decide the issue in a national election,"

said Frazier, speaking very deliberately, "is less than the chance that he will be killed on his way to the polls."[2]

By contrast, an individual voter in a modest-sized city has a small but significant chance of casting the deciding vote in a local election, where perhaps ten or twenty thousand other people will vote in the same election. One can also reasonably argue that the policies of local government are just as important as the policies of the national government. It is true that foreign policy and issues of war or peace, the state of the national economy, and the broad issues of social policy—all the purview of the national government—are extremely important to people's lives. But the policies of local government are also important. The public schools, the condition of the street in front of your house, the purity and taste of your drinking water, how you are treated by police officers—all these and more are decided by your local government.

How odd, then, that most people pay so much more attention to their national than to their local government! This is just another proof that our focus on the state and its operations goes beyond the demands of reason.

The people of the world have not always been so thoroughly organized into states. In the remainder of this chapter, we shall look at the history of how the modern system of states arose; we shall then consider the relationship between the modern state and "nationalism"; finally, we shall look at emerging political forms that might serve as alternatives to the state.

THE DEVELOPMENT OF THE MODERN STATE

The invention of this thing to which we pay so much attention, the state, is fairly recent. Just six or seven hundred years ago people simply did not think of themselves as belonging to a state or nation as we know it today. Most people lived on subsistence farms, intimately concerned with the village in which they lived but not caring much about the world beyond. Armies sometimes raided the village, but it did not make much difference to the villagers whether the army was hired by the king of France, by the pope, or by the Inca king. Barbara Tuchman's picture of what we now call "France" in the fourteenth century depicts a geographic region carved into various political divisions that might be controlled now by the English king, now by the French, and whose populations did not seem to care much which of these was their ruler.[3]

In the fourteenth and fifteenth centuries, as European kings began to claim greater powers and to tighten their control over large territories, these shifting political divisions began to coalesce into states. Even in Europe, however, it

[2]B. F. Skinner, *Walden Two* (New York: Macmillan, 1948), pp. 220–221.

[3]Barbara W. Tuchman, *A Distant Mirror: The Calamitous Fourteenth Century* (New York: Knopf, 1978).

was not until the early nineteenth century that states were well established in the form we now know.

Throughout the early period of state building in Europe, populations continued to be largely indifferent about the state to which they belonged. During the early stages of its formation, for example, the state of Prussia was spread in little smears and droplets all over the map of northern Europe (see Figure 2–1), and this did not especially concern the Prussians. Some of these regions had been acquired for the crown by royal marriages, others by settlements of war or debt, and the people living in them were simply transferred like property from one ruler to another.

If ordinary people did not care much about the state, the leaders and the educated elite also saw it more as a convenience than as something special. This was particularly true early in its formation, but to some extent it remained true even as late as the eighteenth century. At the beginning of the period of state building, most members of the elite, if they could write at all, wrote in Latin rather than in their local tongue. Although daring writers such as Dante were breaking out in their local languages by the fourteenth century, most

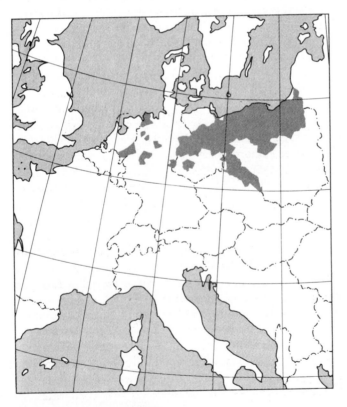

Figure 2–1   Prussia in 1789.

writers still tended to think of themselves well into the seventeenth century as belonging primarily to a cosmopolitan, European literary world rather than to a local English, French, or Spanish community.

The kings who were creating these new states often had family ties or other interests that took priority over their state. As late as 1714, a German line of kings whose members could not even speak English for the first generation or so came to power in England. Later, during World War I (after Britain and Germany had evolved into modern states), it would prove an embarrassment to the British royal house that the kaiser of Germany was their cousin—so much so that they changed their name from Hanover to Windsor.

Even military affairs were not as clearly divided by state through much of this period as they were at the end. Foreign mercenaries were an important part of most wars: For example, bands of English soldiers could be hired by the French king to fight the English, and vice versa. In the American Revolution, the king of England hired German troops (the Hessian soldiers) to do some of the fighting in America.

It was not until the early nineteenth century that the state as we know it today could be seen—a relatively large territory with stable boundaries, whose people were bound together by intricate political ties and who thought of themselves distinctively in terms of the state to which they belonged.

The invention of modern states in Europe may be said to have been completed by Napoleon from 1800 to 1815. In France, he created one of the first recognizably modern states by joining the excitement and the passions of the French Revolution to an active and efficient bureaucracy and army. The resulting state was nearly invincible and succeeded in conquering most of Europe. Its power rested partly on the first European army whose members fought not only for what they themselves might gain but for their nation—*France*. The modern state had finally emerged. Even after Napoleon eventually overreached himself and was defeated, things could never be the same. He had demonstrated what could be accomplished by a full-fledged state, and the new or remaining states that emerged after 1815 tried, some eagerly, and some with more hesitation, to emulate his method of organization.

Although the modern state had finally been invented in Europe and North America by the early nineteenth century, most other peoples of the world still lived under a variety of other arrangements. But a great surge of European colonial expansion during the eighteenth and nineteenth centuries had divided the rest of the world into colonies organized somewhat as subsidiary states. When, in the twentieth century, European power waned as a result of two disastrous world wars, these colonies were able to break away and establish themselves as independent. Then their new leaders, almost all of whom had been educated in Europe, adopted the state as their own form of political organization. Thus the modern state became the universal form of political organization.

THE ORIGIN OF STATES

What was it that led to the invention of the state over the last several centuries? Perhaps an exploration of this question will help us to better understand the nature of the state. There is a vigorous debate among scholars as to why states developed in Europe.[4] However, one thing is clear: The modern state developed there along with the coming of industry and of complicated commercial arrangements. Large-scale industry and commerce could be carried on most easily among large populations whose members could be held together with minimal difficulty and who were willing to have their economic activities coordinated. As long as most economic activity consisted of subsistence farming, cottage weaving, coastal fishing from small boats, and so on, almost any form of political organization would do. But as larger-scale, more complicated economic operations developed, something like the state offered important advantages.

With the development of the state, merchants and industrialists could draw on a large, uniformly treated population as their pool of laborers, and they could sell their products across a large market subject to a single set of laws. Goods could be transported readily, without being subject to special taxes or duties as they passed from one part of the state to another. On the greater scale made possible by the modern state, large factories and ships could be built, and these could be involved in complex nets of transactions. Industry and commerce thus benefited from the development of the state.

In this sense, then, modern industry and commerce *needed* something like the state, and this partly explains why it developed when it did. But modern industry and commerce also made the state *possible* by providing the hardware, the technology, and above all the ease of communication by which a large, widespread population could be readily controlled by an army. Before the coming of modern communications, it was difficult for the government of a state of even moderate size to control the population with any exactness. As late as the early nineteenth century, it took a stagecoach three days to cross southern England. Under those circumstances, the government's control was necessarily loose. But with the coming of the railroad and the telegraph in the nineteenth century, governments could keep an instantaneous check on what was happening throughout their realm and could move troops rapidly to any trouble spot.

We can see that the relationship between the modern state and modern commerce and industry can be interpreted in two ways. On the one hand, commerce and industry needed something like the state, so the state was invented. It emerged because it was an appropriate choice. On the other hand, modern commerce and industry made it easier to control people and seize taxes from them, so the state was able to develop. Governments were able to

---

[4] A good introduction to this debate may be found in Charles Tilly, ed., *The Formation of National States in Western Europe* (Princeton, N.J.: Princeton University Press, 1975). See especially Tilly's introductory chapter.

The Marxist Theory of the State

In this chapter the state has been interpreted partly as being made possible by modern military technology and communications and partly as required by modern commerce and industry. Another way of interpreting the rise of the state is offered by Marxist socialism. (A fuller treatment of Marx and of socialism is offered in Chapter 3.)

Marx thought that modern society consisted of one class (the capitalists) dominating another (the workers). Because of the tensions caused by this domination, the workers had to be controlled, and for this the state was needed. The state keeps the workers under control partly by repression (the police) and partly by integrating them into the prevailing system by convincing them, in school and by other means, that their current situation is good.

Marx thought that eventually the workers would revolt and set up a socialist system in which one class would no longer dominate another. Then the state would have become unnecessary and would wither away through disuse.

Note that this theory sees the state solely as an instrument of power and that it does not analyze public choice at all. As you will see in Chapter 3, this is generally true of Marxist socialism, which sees politics solely as a matter of power.

Further readings in the Marxist theory of the state are: Ernest Mandel, *Late Capitalism* (London: NLB, 1975), chap. 15; and V. I. Lenin, "State and Revolution," in *Sources in Twentieth-Century Political Thought*, ed. Henry Kariel (New York: Free Press, 1964).

spread their power more widely. Probably both explanations carry part of the truth. These interpretations embody "power" and "choice," the two sides of politics introduced in Chapter 1. To the extent that one believes the state emerged because it was made necessary by the modern economy, its invention represents politics as choice. To the extent that one believes it developed because people could now be controlled more easily, it represents politics as power.[5] Different scholars will lean more to one or another of these points of view. In extreme cases, like that noted in the box headed "The Marxist Theory of the State," some may hold that one of the viewpoints is totally false; but to go wholly one way or another is probably a distortion.

NATIONALISM

One striking and disturbing thing about the modern state is the way it has been able to enlist its people in its cause. Citizens of a state generally identify themselves strongly with it and will defend it with passion. This passionate

[5]Tilly takes somewhat more the viewpoint of politics as choice. For a view that emphasizes politics as power, see John H. Herz, *The Nation-State and the Crisis of World Politics* (New York: McKay, 1976), especially the third and eighth essays.

identification with the state is called "nationalism" and, like any passion, it can make people either noble or base. Some have performed great acts of courage and self-sacrifice under the influence of this sentiment, and others have carried out cowardly assassinations and brutal massacres under the same influence. Whether it makes people noble or ignoble, nationalism is undeniably convenient for governments. It predisposes a large and varied population to obey the single government of the state; and if the state is attacked from outside, nationalist passion makes the defending soldiers a much more formidable force than they would otherwise be. Therefore all governments try to encourage nationalism—not necessarily a hate of others, but at least a national pride—by holding parades, using national symbols like the flag, presenting the state's history to schoolchildren, and so on.[6]

We have always been ambivalent about nationalism. Consider the two sides of it presented in the following quotations. The first is Sir Walter Scott's celebration of patriotism in his *Lay of the Last Minstrel:*

> Breathes there the man, with soul so dead,
> Who never to himself hath said,
>   This is my own, my native land!
> Whose heart hath ne'er within him burned,
> As home his footsteps he hath turned,
>   From wandering on a foreign strand!
> [Such a man] concentered all in self,
> Living, shall forfeit fair renown,
> And, doubly dying, shall go down
> To the vile dust, from whence he sprung,
> Unwept, unhonoured, and unsung.[7]

The second gives the view of a cynical spy, portrayed in a novel by Eric Ambler:

> Love of country! There's a curious phrase. Love of a particular patch of earth? Scarcely. Put a German down in a field in Northern France, tell him that it is Hannover, and he cannot contradict you. Love of fellow-countrymen? Surely not. A man will like some of them and dislike others. Love of the country's culture? The men who know most of their countries' cultures are usually the most intelligent and the least patriotic. Love of the country's government? But governments are usually disliked by the people they govern. Love of the country, we see, is merely a sloppy mysticism based on ignorance and fear. It has its uses, of course. When a ruling class wishes a people to do something which that people does not want to do, it appeals to patriotism. And, of course, one of the things that people dislike most is allowing themselves to be killed.[8]

---

[6]There is considerable room for disagreement as to what causes nationalism and how nationalist sentiments are maintained. A good review of the debate on these questions may be found in Chong-do Hah and Jeffrey Martin, "Towards a Synthesis of Conflict and Integration Theories of Nationalism," *World Politics* 27 (April 1975): 361–386.

[7]Walter Scott, *The Lay of the Last Minstrel*, canto 6, 1807.

[8]Eric Ambler, *Journey Into Fear* (New York: Knopf, 1943; rpt. Bantam), p. 166.

GOVERNMENT AND THE STATE

Who is the state? We have talked here about the state acting in various ways. (Look back to the opening sentence of the preceding section, "Nationalism," for example.) But, who in fact does the acting?

A *government* is a group of people within the state who have the ultimate authority to act on behalf of the state (see below, p. 108). They are a unique group in the state; they, and only they, have the right to make decisions that everyone in the state has a duty to accept and obey. An influential current of thought in political science has sought to sensitize us over the last several years to the fact that governments and their bureaucracies are often self-starters in questions of policy—that they may actively develop a problem and seek a solution to it, rather than waiting for the population to come to them with problems. To understand politics properly, according to this current of thought, we must think of the government and bureaucracy itself as a participant and claimant in politics, rather than as a kind of adjudicator over a political process which comes from outside it; this is often referred to as the theory of the "autonomous state."[9] That is, the idea is that the state apparatus may itself participate autonomously in political conflict and decision making.

There is a creative ambiguity here, because this theory treats the government and bureaucracy as if they *were* the "state." Actually, the government/bureaucracy acts on behalf of the state, but the state obviously consists of more than just the government and bureaucracy. However, recognizing the ambiguity at least helps us to address the inherent vagueness in our notion that the "state" acts, does things. The first sentence in "Nationalism" above is inevitably fuzzy, because it refers to the state "enlisting its people in its cause." But, this sounds as if the state is doing something to itself, since in the most usual sense, the people *are* the state. In this case the actions of the state in fostering nationalism come largely from government and bureaucracy (in outlawing burning of the flag, for instance), but also to some extent from a broader group including television announcers, religious leaders, teachers and writers (as in the quotation from Sir Walter Scott). The theory of the autonomous state helps sensitize us to this problem, but it cannot answer it finally, because there is an inherent ambiguity in whom we mean when we refer to the state as acting.

Another good thing about the theory of the autonomous state is that it does emphasize for us the fact that the government and bureaucracy often may participate in politics directly, as claimants on their own behalf.[10] Especially in new states where diverse populations have been thrown together into a state, and where there is little consensus about proper directions to take, the state apparatus may be forced to (or, find itself free to) govern in an authoritarian

---

[9]P. B. Evans, D. Rueschmayer, and Theda Skocpol, eds., *Bringing the State Back In* (Cambridge, England: Cambridge University Press, 1985).

[10]This is especially relevant to the discussion of "pluralism" below, p. 210.

Opening ceremonies, 1984 Olympics, Los Angeles, California
(Douglas Kirkland/Sygma)

way.[11] Under these circumstances, free from the constraint of shared traditions
and norms, governments sometimes pursue policies benefiting their own personal or class interests in a fairly direct way, which simply adds further to the
problems of the new state. This is part of what is going on in the example of
Nigeria at the end of this chapter. Another, more dramatic example is the Phil-
ippine government's charge that Ferdinand Marcos stole several billion dollars
from the government during the period of his rule.

"STATE" AND "NATION"

Up to this point the word "state" has not been defined precisely, although we
have considered the modern state, its development, and its characteristics at
some length.

We must distinguish between "nation" and "state." We often use these
terms loosely as synonyms, along with the more common word "country," and
they are clearly related. As one example of the relationship between the two,

---

[11]Here is another nice contrasting example of alternative "choice" and "power" interpretations of
a political situation. Note in this sentence that I was uncertain whether to characterize the government as "forced" to govern in an authoritarian way (which would suggest that they were simply
seeking the best public outcome and that circumstances forced them into authoritarian rule: a
choice perspective), or to characterize them as "free" to govern in an authoritarian way (which
would suggest that they were self-seeking, and took advantage of the chance that was available to
them to initiate authoritarian rule: a power perspective).

we have earlier in this chapter labeled as "nationalism" a passionate identification with the state. In fact, in ordinary conversation, most people use the words "state," "nation," and "country" interchangeably.

But "nation" and "state" have more precise meanings for political scientists. A nation is *a large group of people who are bound together, and recognize a similarity among themselves, because of a common culture; in particular, a common language seems important in creating nationhood.* A state, on the other hand, is *a political unit that has ultimate sovereignty—that is, a political unit that has ultimate responsibility for the conduct of its own affairs.* France is a state, Brazil is a state, the United States of America is a state. The Jewish people do not make up a state, since they are not a political unit, but

Figure 2–2 Linguistic map of Europe.

SOURCE: Norman J. G. Pounds and Robert C. Kingsbury, *An Atlas of European Affairs* (New York: Praeger, 1964), p. 23.

Israel is a state. General Motors and Exxon are not states, though they are very large organizations. Chicago is not a state; although it is a political unit, it lacks sovereignty (the ultimate responsibility for the conduct of its own affairs) because another government, represented by the Supreme Court and the U.S. Army, has the right to intervene and force decisions on Chicago should that be necessary. A nation is a *cultural* and especially a linguistic grouping of people who feel they belong together; a state is a *political* unit.

Nations do not necessarily coincide with the political boundaries of states. Figure 2–2 shows a linguistic map of Europe. Notice that some apparent nations spread across the boundaries of states. For instance, the German language and culture spread well beyond the boundaries even of East and West Germany combined. Austria, a large part of Switzerland, and a small part of Italy are German, and there are pockets of German population across eastern Europe. The Basques are spread across northwest Spain and southwest France. The states of Yugoslavia and Switzerland both encompass a variety of linguistic groups that might qualify as nations.

Correspondence between nation and state is particularly loose in Africa and Asia. The boundaries of many African and Asian states are left over from the older colonial era, when they were drawn by the colonizing powers to suit their own convenience.[12] Thus a crazy quilt of boundaries was superimposed on the land, with little regard for the culturally coherent groups of people living there. Once they regained their independence, of course, those people inherited these peculiar boundaries. The map of Nigeria in Figure 2–3 illustrates the loose correspondence between nation and state that exists in much of Africa today. Turkey, Iraq, and Iran are all home to some of the Kurdish people, who are a minority in each of these countries and have made attempts to break away and form their own unified state. India includes fifteen official linguistic groups. And many other former colonies exhibit similar mixtures of state and nation.

With the modern importance of nationalism, we have come to think it a right of people, if they feel that they have a common nationality, to have a state to match that nationality. This "right" has become a constant source of political tension and conflict for two reasons. As just pointed out, many state boundaries do not coincide with the geographic distribution of nations. But beyond this, the sense of nationhood is a subjective thing. It is a feeling on the part of a group of people that may be stimulated or laid to rest by persuasive leaders and which is therefore liable to change. Even if state boundaries could ever at any one time be brought into a perfect fit with the distribution of nations, this benign situation could not last, because new nations would gradually be invented and some old ones would fade and be forgotten. The once influential

---

[12]The correspondence between state and nation is reasonably close in South and Central America, for an unhappy reason: Here the native population was often largely exterminated or enslaved, to be replaced by a reasonably coherent population of settlers from Europe.

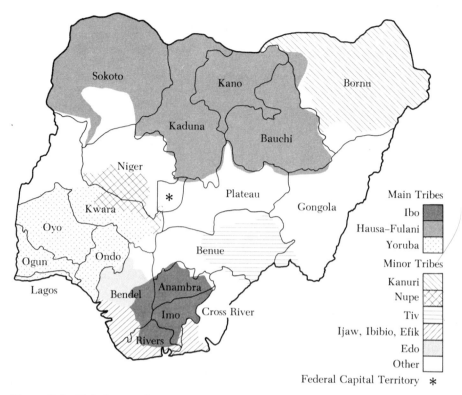

Figure 2–3   Tribal map of Nigeria.

SOURCE: Pauline H. Baker, "Lurching Toward Unity," *Wilson Quarterly* 4 (Winter 1980): 78.

although small black nationalist movement in the United States is just one example of an attempt to arouse a "nation" (the nation of blacks) among a people who had not generally thought of themselves as belonging to a separate nation.

At any given time, then, the system of states will not coincide with the system of nations. Points at which state and nation fail to coincide are likely to be hot spots politically; indeed, a great many intense political struggles of recent years have resulted from such situations. The movement to separate Quebec from the rest of Canada; the war between East and West Pakistan, which resulted in the formation of a new state, Bangladesh; the Basque nationalist movement in Spain; the conflict between French- and Dutch-speaking Belgians; the civil war in Nigeria in 1967; the activities of the Palestine Liberation Organization, which embodies the desire of Palestinians for a state of their own; the chronic unrest among Kurds in Iraq and Iran—these are only a few examples of hot political conflicts occasioned by a disparity between state boundaries and people's sense of nationhood.

POLITICAL ORGANIZATION BEYOND THE STATE?

For many years writers and thinkers have dreamed of ways to replace the present political organization of the world—the system by which the world is divided into distinct states—with something better. The state has always been associated with wars and a military establishment. It grew up with the development of modern military techniques, and probably the best simple definition of states' sovereignty is a military one. Many people think that the system of states is a dangerous thing, made even more dangerous by the age of nuclear war.

How might the system of states become less dangerous? There are many proposals for wholesale revisions of the system—the anarchist movement, the World Federalist Movement, some versions of socialism, and so on—but they would require too much space for consideration here. However, four trends are currently at work that might (or might not) eventually modify the present system of states by gradually making them more and more dependent on each other, so that at some point we might say that this was no longer a system of states. Since "sovereignty" is a relative thing, this might occur almost imperceptibly. In fact, it may already be happening—the United States, China, Nigeria, Paraguay, the Soviet Union, Italy, Egypt, and all other states today are less isolated from the rest of the world than they were forty years ago, and they find it more necessary now than they did then to coordinate their policies with those of their neighbors. It is arguable that a time could come when no single part of the world would be allowed "ultimate responsibility for the conduct of its own affairs." The causes of this could include the following trends:

1. Regional Integration

Many regions in the world have attempted to establish regional organizations that would have at least limited power to overrule and coordinate the actions of their member states. The Organization of American States in North and South America, the African unity movement, occasional attempts at economic union in Central America, and several abortive attempts to form a united Arab republic all attest to this wish, though none of these have succeeded very well. The European Community, which includes most of western Europe, has had considerable success at integrating the politics of its member states, so much so that one can at least conceive of a time at which one might ask whether its members were still sovereign states. (The European Community is discussed in greater detail below.)

At its best, regional integration would only represent a consolidation of the system of states into a smaller number of larger states. But this might represent progress in its own right, and the process by which states were brought to yield up portions of their sovereignty voluntarily to a higher organization might teach us much about how the world system as a whole could begin to coordinate its members' activities.

2. The United Nations

There does exist an organization of almost all states of the world which is supposed to stand above them and lead them into peaceful coordination of their activities. The United Nations has little power to force states to cooperate, but it does have considerable persuasive power and has helped at least modestly to defuse several crises that could have led to war. The United Nations is discussed in more detail in Chapter 15.

3. Communications and a "World Culture"

As electronic communication makes it possible to send messages easily from one end of the world to another, as people travel more widely and observe cultures that are new to them, the world is beginning to develop a more common set of attitudes. Different nations are becoming slightly less distinctive in their points of view. Blue jeans have become almost an international uniform of young people, and English has become an almost universal second language in which business is conducted among strangers. Much cultural richness may be lost in this homogenization, but it may become easier for populations of different states to understand each other's point of view. Too much faith should not be placed in this, since conflicts may as easily arise from understanding as from misunderstanding; still, it may be a hopeful sign.

4. Increasing Economic Interdependence

This is probably the most potent force bringing us together. Today the United States tries not to damage the fragile political structures of oil-producing countries; and the oil producers must be careful not to damage the economy of the United States, which is an important customer and in which a large part of their wealth is invested. The Soviet Union must be concerned not to endanger its supply of grain from the United States; and the countries of western Europe must be concerned for the economic well-being of the Soviet Union, which is an increasingly important customer for their manufacturers. The United States, Japan, and western Europe are bound by ties of trade and by the existence of companies that spread across their borders, a net of connections it would now be almost unthinkable to disrupt. Huge multinational corporations have arisen, such as Exxon and ITT, that do not belong to any particular state; all states have a common interest in monitoring these corporations and in coordinating their responses to them.[13]

None of these four trends will lead us tomorrow to a system beyond the system of states, but taken together they have already given the term "sovereignty" a bit of an old-fashioned flavor, smacking of an earlier period in which states were "really" independent. These trends are now working to make states more dependent on each other, and they might at some point imperceptibly alter the system in such a way that we will suddenly say, "But this is not a system of states!" We must leave to the future, however, our question as to what that brave new world might look like.

---

[13]A good review of arguments about the processes described here may be found in James E. Dougherty and Robert L. Pfalzgraff, Jr., *Contending Theories of International Relations*, 2nd ed. (New York: Harper & Row, 1981), especially chap. 10.

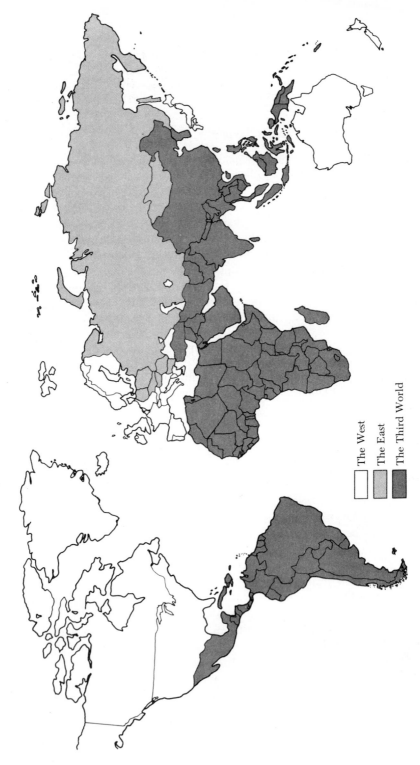

Figure 2–4 The West, the East, and the Third World.

The West

The East

The Third World

THE WEST, THE EAST, AND THE THIRD WORLD

The states of the world are generally grouped into three broad regions: the West, the East, and the Third World, the three regions indicated on the map in Figure 2–4. The "West" comprises the industrialized states of North American and western Europe, plus Australia, New Zealand, and (probably) Japan. These are economically prosperous states, with a moderate degree of governmental direction in their economies, linked in a more or less common foreign and military policy behind the leadership of the United States. The "East" comprises the Soviet Union and its east European satellites. These states are also prosperous (though generally not so well off as the West). They are marked by massive governmental direction in their economies, and they join in a more or less common foreign policy under Soviet leadership.

These two regions make a good deal of sense, in that the states in each have a good deal in common with each other and are different in important ways from the world's other states. The remaining region, the "Third World," is something of a catch-all region, as its name suggests. It is "none of the above"; the thing that distinguishes its members is that they are neither of the West nor of the East. This is important enough in itself, but beyond that these states have nothing uniquely in common.

Over two-thirds of the world's population lives in the Third World. Politically, the region ranges from communist states like Cuba to conservative monarchies like Saudi Arabia. Western culture is relatively new to most of the region, except that many Latin American states have made active cultural contributions for centuries. Most Third World states are poor, but a number of them have great mineral wealth (like Saudi Arabia and other oil-producing countries), and some have become rather heavily industrialized (like Argentina, Brazil, Singapore, and South Korea). Most Third World states have rather new political structures, and their populations are generally not broadly involved in politics.

EXAMPLE: STATE BUILDING IN NIGERIA

No state's experience has been "typical," but it is useful to look at some examples in order to flesh out the concepts and analyses you have read so far in this chapter. In this section we will take a brief look at how the Nigerian state was established; in the next section, we will consider the European Community and how it is drawing a number of west European states into something new, which is a bit like a much broader "state."

Nigeria is a populous state on the west coast of Africa, with a population (as of 1986) of 99 million. One out of five Africans lives in Nigeria, and its gross national product is second on the continent only to that of South Africa. The country is rich in oil, but it has so many people to feed that the average Nigerian is not especially well-off; in 1985, the average annual income was $800 per person.

Until 1960, Nigeria was a British colony; like most colonies, it was not constructed for internal coherence. Over 250 different languages and dialects are spoken within its borders, and there is also an important religious split, as the north is primarily Muslim and the south is primarily Christian or animist. After World War II, Britain experimented with various ways of handling this diversity. The plan eventually adopted was a decentralized system under which Nigeria was divided into three regions, each centered on one of the three main tribes (see Figure 2–3): (1) the northern region, based on the Hausa-Fulani tribe, (2) the western region, based on the Yorubas, and (3) the eastern region, based on the Ibos. These regions were administratively distinct, each having its own budget.

This arrangement continued in the initial democratic structure set up in 1960. The central government of the new state left many functions under the control of regional governments, in what is called a "federal" system. The situation was unstable, however, because tensions soon developed among the regions. The simple democratic procedures that were written into Nigeria's constitution favored the north, because it was the most populous region, and the north quickly established political control under the first prime minister, a northern Muslim named Abubakar Balewa.

However, the Ibos in the eastern region—a restless, economically active, and well-educated minority—felt stifled by the political domination of the north. Ibos all over Nigeria were disproportionately urban and held many technical and administrative positions. Three-quarters of Nigeria's diplomats were from the eastern region, as were about half the students who graduated from Nigerian universities in 1966.[14]

In 1966 a coup by Ibo officers toppled the democratic government and put an Ibo general at the head of the state. Six months later Muslim soldiers struck back and a new government under Yakubu Gowon, a northerner but a Christian, was installed. At this point the eastern region seceded from Nigeria and proclaimed itself the state of Biafra. The federal government refused to accept Biafra's right to secede, and there followed a bloody civil war lasting 2½ years, in which over a million people died. Eventually the Ibos were starved out and had to give up on secession. Gowon wisely followed a generous, conciliatory policy toward the defeated province and its leaders, one calculated to make it easy for them to rejoin the rest of the country.

Gowon had promised an eventual return to democracy, but he proved slow to deliver and was ousted in yet another military coup in 1975. He was replaced by General Olusegun Obasanjo, a Yoruba Christian who proceeded carefully to build the basis for a return to democracy. Elected local governments were established, and a new constitution was designed under which re-

---

[14]Pauline H. Baker, "Lurching Toward Unity," *Wilson Quarterly* 4 (Winter 1980): 76.

gional diversity would be respected in local affairs and no one region could dominate the central government. The state was divided into nineteen federal districts that, to some extent, broke down the old Hausa-Fulani, Yoruba, and Ibo regions. In order to be elected president, one had not only to receive at least one-third of the total popular vote but also at least one-fourth of the vote in two-thirds of the nineteen regions. Finally, power was divided between the president and a congress, so that regions that had not supported the president had a chance to defend themselves in the congress.

The first presidential election was held in 1979, and a northerner, Sheliu Shagari, was elected. His main area of strength was obviously in the north, but he could not have won if he had not also had considerable support in the east. He was reelected strongly in 1983, with at least one-quarter of the vote in sixteen of the country's nineteen regions, although the election was marred by opposition charges that it had been rigged.[15] Within a few months of the election, the civilian government was once again overthrown by the military, who charged it with massive corruption. Currently a military government rules (itself the product of another coup in 1985), but it proposes to reestablish civilian rule in 1992.

All in all, Nigeria in its first decades as a state appears to have held together successfully in spite of its diversity and has at least made efforts to govern itself democratically. The state has faced great economic difficulties and many other problems associated with rapid social change. Certainly Nigeria's ways of approaching the problem of regional diversity compare with those of the United States in the early decades of its history. On the broader question of whether Nigeria will be able to reestablish a stable democratic government, however, the jury is still out.

EXAMPLE: STATE BUILDING IN THE EUROPEAN COMMUNITY

The European Community is an association of twelve states in western Europe that have agreed to coordinate much of their economic policy and some other policy areas; toward this end, they have set up a weak governmental structure that has some limited power over the governments of the member states.[16] The Community is of particular interest to political scientists because it represents the most serious experiment to date in getting states to give up some of their sovereignty voluntarily.

There had been mutterings about the need to unify Europe throughout the

---

[15]See Chapter 8, pp. 156–158.

nineteenth and early twentieth centuries, but the first real push to do so came after World War II. Many people thought that France and Germany, which had twice in the century fought disastrously against one another, should be bound together in such a way that war between them would be inconceivable. Also, the advantages of operating as a large economic unit, with a single free market open to all, were obvious to those who were trying to rebuild Europe after the war.

With encouragement and some pressure from the American side, the European Community was established in 1956. A French administrator, Jean Monnet, was a key figure in this. He had led several European states through earlier cooperative efforts in coordinating their policies on coal, steel, and nuclear power to a point at which they were willing to merge much of their economic policymaking. Initially, only six states were members—West Germany, France, Italy, and the Low Countries. To Monnet's great disappointment, Great Britain refused at that time to join.

The main economic agreement among the initial members was that all trade would flow freely within their borders. That is, no member could place a tariff on imports of a product from another member in order to discourage local people from buying it. All the combined populations of the six member states were freely available as customers to any producer in any member state. Also, the member states soon coordinated their agricultural policy, giving up control of most agricultural policy within their borders to the governmental structure of the Community. It is the Community government that decides how high price supports will be for a given commodity, what will be charged for that commodity abroad, and so on. The Common Agricultural Policy was a breakthrough in regional integration, although it has proved in practice to be cumbersome and expensive, leading to large production surpluses and to high prices for consumers.

Currently the Community is in a state of ferment. In 1985 it decided to institute an entirely free internal market by 1992. This turned out to require hundreds of specific changes, some of them rather drastic, such as the establishment of something approaching common tax rates in all countries. Initially many observers thought the resolution was a hollow gesture, but the prospect of real economic union seized the imagination of many people, and the Community now seems bent on accomplishing at least most of the 1992 objectives; a substantial amount of national independence will have to be given up in the process.

The original six members set up a governmental structure for the Community, which stands more or less unchanged today. The two most important parts of the Community government are the Commission and the Council of Ministers, which make most of the rules and carry out executive functions. Two other parts are the Parliament and the Court of Justice. These have lesser powers but are still important.

The European Commission consists of seventeen appointed commissioners who head a bureaucracy of about 10,000 people. Commissioners are appointed by their home governments for a term of four years, but they must swear an oath to act on a European basis rather than in the interests of their home country. In practice the Commission has been the focal point of broad European interests, as opposed to national interests. In this it has been cheered on by its thousands of bureaucrats, whose lives and careers are obviously bound up in the Community. The Commission has consistently pushed for a blending of states in the Community and has frequently been opposed in this by one or more member states fearful of giving up too much sovereignty.

The Commission has a great deal of power. On its own it sets most of the Community budget ($56 billion in 1989) and makes many rules. As the only permanent part of the executive branch of the Community's government, it also takes the lead in initiating new proposals for policy.

The other part of the executive is the Council of Ministers, in which national interests are represented. It consists of the foreign ministers of the member states; these meet together several times a year to consider proposals from the Commission. Any major policy proposal must be approved by the Council of Ministers before it can go into effect. The Council votes on proposals, with large states getting extra votes, but a practice has also developed over the years of letting any member state veto a proposal if the proposal affects what the state considers to be a "vital national interest." The status of this practice is not entirely clear, since in 1983, both Greece and Britain were overruled when they tried to apply vetoes of this sort. In general, however, no policy can be initiated if any member state feels strongly threatened by it. While the Council of Ministers has thus tended to retard the blending of the Community, it has probably also made possible such blending as has occurred. Without this haven for the individual interests of member states, the Community might have fallen apart long ago.

The Community also has a parliament, but this does not have great legislative power. Policies of the Commission and Council of Ministers are debated and criticized in the parliament, but the parliament does not have the final say over most decisions. For instance, it has final authority over only about 17 percent of the Community's budget. A change made in 1979, however, may add to the power of the European Parliament in the future. Before 1979, members of the European Parliament were chosen by the parliaments of their home countries, but since then the members have been directly elected by voters in their countries. While this is not a change that directly gives the European Parliament any new powers, it may, indirectly, eventually do a great deal. The members of the European Parliament are now the only officials of the Community who are elected, who are there because some ordinary people wanted them to be there. This gives them an advantage in prestige and "standing" and also has attracted more able, vigorous members. (In the earlier period, membership in the European Parliament was sometimes a way for a country's parties to kick their more tired members upstairs.) Since 1979 the European Parliament has used this new vigor to push for a greater role in the Community's decisions, and recent years have been marked by considerable squabbling between this body and the Council and Commission. Eventually the European Parliament may develop into a more powerful body than it is today.

Finally, the European Court of Justice is a court of twelve justices serving six-year terms. It rules on disputes over the treaties that the states signed on joining the Community. Most cases that come before the Court involve trade problems, but it also decides disputes among the governing institutions of the Community and about the individual rights of citizens in the member states. Over the years, the Court has pretty well established itself as dominant over the states' governments, although it has had to tread cautiously in order to avoid stepping on any government's feet. From 1956 to 1983, the Court ruled in only forty or so cases involving individual rights, but some of these cases demonstrated an astonishing willingness on the part of member states to subordinate themselves to the Community's laws. Court decisions have included such questions as whether British teachers could legally whip their students, how soldiers could be disciplined in the Netherlands, and the conditions under which people could be put in prison to await trial in West Germany.

The original six members of the Community prospered economically after 1956, and gradually other states joined, until the Community reached its present size of twelve states. Together, the members of the European Community have great strength. As seen in Table 2–1, the members of the Community combined have a population greater than that of the United States; they have more people under arms, and their combined gross national products nearly equals ours. If they could pursue a unified foreign policy and developed a full-scale strategic nuclear force, they would be a superpower similar to the United States or the Soviet Union.

How close is the European Community to being something like a state? Clearly the member states have given up a good deal of their sovereignty to the Community. The Community has independent taxing powers, collecting a sales tax of a bit over 1 percent to finance its operation. It sets its members' tariff and trade policies as well as their policies on agricultural price supports. The European Court of Justice has successfully imposed surprisingly political judgments on member states. On the other hand, military control is the real core of statehood; in that area, the Community has not developed any control over its members. Most but not all members of the Community are also mem-

TABLE 2–1   European Community Compared with the United States and the Soviet Union

	Total Population	Total Armed Forces (1989)	1987 Total Gross Domestic Product (Billions of Dollars)	1987 Defense Expenditures (Billions of Dollars)
U.S.A.	245,320,000	2,163,000	$4461	$291.6
U.S.S.R.	284,819,000	5,096,000	$1800–2310 (est.)	cannot be estimated
E.C.	323,246,000	2,483,400	$4209	$133.8

SOURCE: *The Military Balance 1988–1989* (London: International Institute for Strategic Studies, 1989).

bers of the NATO alliance, but even NATO has not been very successful at coordinating its members' military policies. (It has been difficult for NATO even to establish a standard caliber for rifle bullets, so that its members could exchange ammunition in time of war.)

The European Community illustrates nicely the gray area in which it becomes difficult to distinguish clearly when a state is a state. But without a military core, it is still something less than a state.

FURTHER READING

Deutsch, Karl. *Nationalism and Social Communication*. Cambridge, Mass.: MIT Press, 1953.

Evans, P. B., Rueschmayer, D., and Skocpol, Theda, eds. *Bringing the State Back In*. Cambridge, England: Cambridge University Press, 1985.

Hah, Chong-do, and Martin, Jeffrey. "Toward a Synthesis of Conflict and Integration Theories of Nationalism." *World Politics* 27 (April 1975): 361–386.

Herz, John H. *The Nation-State and the Crisis of World Politics*. New York: McKay, 1976.

Mandel, Ernest. *Late Capitalism*. London: NLB, 1975. Chap. 15.

Nettl, J. P. "The State as a Conceptual Variable." *World Politics* 20 (July 1968): 559–592.

Skocpol, Theda. *States and Social Revolutions*. Cambridge, England: Cambridge University Press, 1979.

Smith, Anthony B. *Theories of Nationalism*. New York: Harper & Row, 1971.

Tilly, Charles, ed. *The Formation of National States in Western Europe*. Princeton, N.J.: Princeton University Press, 1975.

Wallerstein, Immanuel. *The Capitalist World Economy*. Cambridge, England: Cambridge University Press, 1979.

Chapter 3

Modern Ideologies and Political Philosophy

Most people approach politics through an *ideology*—a set of related ideas that modify one another, or an *organized set of ideas*. For instance, one person may believe that everyone is basically selfish, that politicians are all crooks, that a citizen owes nothing to the state, that it is all right to cheat on one's taxes, that gun control is a bad thing because it keeps us from protecting ourselves, and so on. This is an ideology—a set of ideas about politics, all of which are related to one another and that modify and support each other. The belief that everyone is basically selfish helps provide a justification for the need to carry a gun, the wish to cheat on taxes helps make one comfortable in the belief that the citizen owes nothing to the state, and so on. Another person may believe that individual freedom is terribly important, that government should regulate people as little as possible, that the United States should try to protect any people whose government is oppressing them, and that the U.S. government should not tell people whether or not they may carry guns. This is also an ideology, an organized set of ideas that modify and support each other. In this second example, the high value placed on individual freedom supports both a wish to protect human rights around the world and a reluctance to have the government regulate the ownership of guns.

Ideologies are useful to people, both for their own personal ease and satisfaction and for their public political activities. From the *personal* point of view, an ideology helps us to make sense reasonably easily and quickly of the varied political questions that come to our attention. In any given week, the newspaper will raise questions about the control or deregulation of oil prices, the busing of schoolchildren to improve racial balance, the level of support for retired people in the social security system, the size of the military budget, federal acquisition of land for parks and wildlife refuges, and so forth. If we had to consider each of these issues anew, starting from scratch, we would have an awesome task. But if we approach each from the standpoint of a general ideology that we have developed over time, the job is much simpler. Most issues will turn out to be instances of more general principles that can quickly be settled by applying the principles.

The new issues may also modify our ideology, since an ideology is not graven in stone. For instance, devout Catholics who believe that the government should regulate people as little as possible may find themselves torn over the issue of legalized abortion and may modify some of their more general ideas about politics in light of the new issue. An ideology, then, is a continually developing, organized set of ideas about politics that helps us to make sense of the myriad of political questions that face us.[1]

An ideology also has *public* uses. In politics, we are normally concerned to convince others that a policy we favor is the right one. We usually have personal reasons for favoring the policy—we may want taxes to be cut because we are wealthy, oppose gun control because we like to collect guns, or favor national health insurance because we are poor—but these personal reasons are not usually good *public* reasons. People distrust a self-interested argument. Also, arguing for a policy by giving one's personal reasons for it would not win many allies; only those who are also rich could be convinced by the argument "I'm wealthy, therefore I want to see taxes cut." In political argument, we usually try to attract as many allies as possible to our position, so personal reasons will not make good arguments. *Ideologies*, however, can serve this purpose very well. The wealthy person who argues, "Government spending and taxation hamper individual initiative," may appeal to a great many people who for various reasons favor individual initiative.

Ideologies are developed and maintained both because of their usefulness to individuals in responding to events and their utility in public political argument. This is not a conscious, cynical process in which we deliberately frame an ideology so as to enlist allies in some cause or another. Rather, we are all comfortable with ideology and generally, over time, work out ideologies that fit our particular needs. Too, ideologies are not simply the creation of those who hold them; they tend to take on a life of their own and guide their holders' political views in unanticipated ways. A business leader who feels that government should regulate as little as possible (for what we may think are obvious reasons) may find that this ideology also leads to positions—not particularly connected to self-interest—on the censorship of books in public libraries or the regulation of handguns.

An ideology is an organized set of ideas that helps us both to make sense out of politics for ourselves and to present arguments effectively in public. We obviously develop our ideologies in such a way that they fit our needs and predispositions, reflecting what we want; but they also take on a life of their own and *guide* our decisions.

AMERICAN IDEOLOGIES

All of us have some sort of ideology, in the sense that our various ideas about politics bear some sort of relationship one to another. But not every ideology is equally neat and tidy, nor is every ideology worked out in equally full detail.

[1]A review of the literature on ideology and an interesting, fresh approach are offered by Pamela Johnston Conover and Stanley Feldman, "Belief System Organization in the American Electorate," in *The Electorate Reconsidered*, ed. John Pierce and John L. Sullivan (Beverly Hills, Calif.: Sage, 1980).

Americans' ideologies tend to be more loosely organized than those of other peoples. In fact, Americans tend to admit exceptions and inconsistencies into their ideologies rather cheerfully.

Two main ideologies are found among Americans: "American liberalism" and "American conservatism." The former is characterized in the following ways. Compared to American conservatism, it is:

- More concerned about inequality (between the poor and the well-off, between blacks and whites, between women and men).
- Less hesitant to use the power of the government to make conditions for people more equal. Thus, American liberals are willing to see a larger government, supplied by higher taxes, than are American conservatives. And they are willing to see the government intervene through such devices as forced integration of schools and a graduated income tax in order to alleviate inequalities.
- More concerned to maintain freedom of expression and the separation of church and state.
- Less concerned about the maintenance of morality, at least in the sense of prescribed rules of conduct, and opposed to the use of state power to ban the "victimless crimes" of prostitution, drug use, and gambling. Similarly, it opposes laws to ban abortion.
- More reluctant to maintain a large military force and to intervene militarily abroad.

American conservatism represents the other side of all these comparisons.

American liberalism and American conservatism are not neat ideologies. It is hard to see, for instance, what logical connections exist among the various attitudes detailed above. In fact, it frequently happens that an American political figure is "liberal" on some of these issues and "conservative" on others. American labor unions, for example, have generally been quite concerned about issues of equality but have not been equally eager to defend freedom of expression.

As we shall see below, both American liberalism and American conservatism are variants of a more general and well worked out ideology known simply as *liberalism*. "American liberalism" and "American conservatism" are simply differing versions that have sprung up in a predominantly liberal society, to unite under the loose term "liberal" (American version) the weaker parts of society (the poor, those who were discriminated against, those whose moral values went against the dominant grain, those with unpopular ideas) against the stronger and more dominant parts, whose interests were represented by "conservatism" (American version). Both ideologies are thus hodgepodges, representing marriages of political convenience, and it is difficult to find internal coherence among the various parts of either one.

However, even though the American ideologies are untidy, they have still been of some influence. American labor leaders have probably been more concerned than they might otherwise have been with freedom of expression because of this issue's association with the redistribution of income in American liberalism. And Americans concerned about high taxes may have picked up more concern than they might otherwise have had for questions of official morality because of the juxtaposition of these positions in American conservatism.

LIBERALISM

The two American ideologies are actually variants of *liberalism,* one of the three great ideologies that developed in Europe in the eighteenth and nineteenth centuries. These ideologies—liberalism, conservatism, and socialism—have provided the framework for most political debate throughout the world since then.

To understand their development, we must remember that the medieval social order in Europe was one in which people were bound together in patterns of rather strict domination, with mutual responsibilities between those who were dominated and those who dominated them, between "top dogs" and "bottom dogs." Farmers often lived in a condition of near-slavery, subject to a local church official or a member of the nobility. A farmer paid heavy taxes to his local patron and had to provide him with specified periods of labor for road building, war, and so on. In many parts of Europe, the farmer was not allowed to leave his land and move elsewhere without the permission of his patron. Further, farmers were required to offer the patron formal social respect and deference. In return, the patron was supposed to provide his farmers with protection and with help in times of illness or want. Such industry as existed was organized in guilds, which laid down strict rules as to how an item was to be manufactured, how many such items were to be produced, and what was to be charged for them. Trade in many items was subject to ancient rules: The king might have a monopoly on trade in a commodity such as salt, for instance, or a particular town might have the enduring right to receive all imports of some specific item. Jews were a pariah group, banned from many occupations and generally forbidden to own land. The church maintained a stern control over proper belief (a striking example of this occurred when, in 1616, the church forced the great astronomer Galileo to state, contrary to his true convictions, that he did not believe the earth orbited around the sun). To transport goods from one end of a country to another could be a complex affair, in which the carrier of the goods was required to pay taxes, fees, and tributes to various local personages at all stages of the journey. Politics was the province of the king, the nobility, and the church.

For our present purposes, two things are important about these arrangements: (1) people were bound to each other in complex and cumbersome systems of domination and (2) the arrangements were rather static, difficult to change. Ownership of the land, feudal privileges, the rights of the church, the political role of the king and nobility, the power of the guilds—all were granted in perpetuity and could only evolve slowly over time.

Onto this setting—faintly in the fifteenth and sixteenth centuries, in crescendo through the seventeenth and eighteenth centuries, and with a deafening crash in the nineteenth century—came modern large-scale commerce and industry. The new commercial and industrial leaders chafed under the static restrictions of medieval society. In order to carry on large-scale trade and manufacture, it was often necessary to move commodities over great distances; laborers had to be gathered together at large factories, which often involved moving people from one end of the country to another; canals and roads had to be built, which would run through many different patrons' domains; prices and the nature of goods often had to be adjusted to reflect changing needs and technology; science and invention had to be free to pursue truth wherever they found it, regardless of orthodoxy. All these requirements collided with the organization of preindustrial medieval society. The new and increasingly powerful commercial and industrial elite cast about for ways to make society more fluid and manageable. One helpful solution, as we saw in the preceding chapter, was the invention of the modern state. Another was the appearance of liberalism.

Liberalism was not introduced by the commercial and industrial leaders themselves. Rather, it was invented by intellectuals who were moved by the general artistic and scientific restlessness of the age. But it suited the new economic leaders, and they warmed to it. It gave them a view of politics that could make sense to them in light of their needs, and it allowed them to argue for their causes in ways that were less crass than simply saying, "We wish to limit the power of the nobility, the guilds, and the church because we want to make money."

Liberalism posits as the highest good of society *the ability of the members of that society to develop their individual capacities to the fullest extent*. That is, in a good society, all individuals should be able to develop their minds, musical talents, athletic abilities, or any other gift as much as possible. This requires, according to liberalism, that people be maximally responsible for their own actions, rather than having someone else do things for them or tell them what to do. It is only by acting and feeling the consequences of such action that we can develop our capacity to act.

This is the central assumption of liberalism, from which a number of consequences flow. For instance, in his essay *On Representative Government*, John Stuart Mill based his argument in favor of democratic government on liberal premises, as follows: The chief end of politics is to allow people to become responsible and mature. They can do this only if they take part in decisions affecting their own lives. Therefore, even though a wise and benevolent despot or monarch might actually make better decisions on behalf of the people than they could make for themselves, democracy is better, since under it the people make their own decisions, mistakes and all. Therefore some form of democracy is the best kind of government.

By the same sorts of argument, the following elements follow from the basic liberal premise; together, they constitute the liberal ideology:

- Democracy of some sort is the proper form of government.
- People should have full intellectual freedom, including freedom of speech, freedom of religion, and freedom of the press. (They should have responsibility for their own values, so that they will develop the ability to judge values.)

John Stuart Mill and Liberalism

John Stuart Mill (1806–1873) was a major figure in liberal thought. His father, James Mill, himself an important figure in the history of British philosophy, educated young John himself, following an incredible regimen: John was reading Greek at age three, and by the time he reached maturity he probably knew more of science and literature than anyone else in Britain. He spent his adult years in a sinecure with the British East India company, which allowed him plenty of time to write. His main contribution to liberal thought was to reconcile, in a fairly tight logical system, individual freedom with the general good of society. Curiously for his time, John Stuart Mill was a strong feminist and advocated women's suffrage. Some have ascribed this to the influence of his wife, Harriet Taylor Mill, while others simply believe his logic pushed him to this conclusion.

- Government should remain minimal and should regulate people's lives very little. (As few decisions as possible should be made *for* people, so that they learn to make decisions for themselves.)
- In particular, people should be free to regulate their own economic activity. (As above.)
- Power of one person over another is a bad thing; hence government should be organized so as to guard against abuses of power. (Again, one person should not make decisions for another.)

Liberalism flourished especially in Great Britain and her colonies, perhaps because Britain was the first country to industrialize. In Britain, liberal forces first gained control of the House of Commons and the cabinet in 1832; through the nineteenth century, political control of the country seesawed back and forth between liberals and conservatives. (See below for a discussion of conservatism.) In the United States, the new Constitution of 1789, with its precautions against a concentration of power in any one part of the government and its guarantees of various individual freedoms, clearly signified the ascendance of liberalism. On the continent of Europe, liberalism was a potent force throughout the nineteenth century, but it was nowhere as strong as in Britain and her former colonies. Most western European countries had liberal constitutions by the end of World War I, but by that time liberalism was fading quickly.

Note that with regard to the distinction between the "choice" and "power" perspectives, liberals will strongly favor a view of politics as choice. To liberals, power is simply a bad thing that should be limited as much as possible. Power allows some people to force choices on others, which flies directly in the face of liberal principles. To a liberal, politics should properly consist of public choices in the making of which each person shares equally. And further, as many choices as possible should be kept private. That is, the sphere of politics itself should be limited.

THE CONSERVATIVE REACTION

When liberalism arose to challenge the existing social arrangements, the defenders of those arrangements needed an ideology to counteract the persuasive power of liberalism. Conservatism was developed in response to this need.

Conservatism in the European sense is unfamiliar to Americans, since it is quite different from American conservatism. Defenders of existing arrangements in Europe pointed out quite properly that liberalism is an individualistic doctrine; that is, liberalism looks on society as simply consisting of the individuals constituting it. To liberals, the whole of society equals the sum of its component parts, so that society is happiest in which the total of individuals' happiness is greatest. This is implied in the basic premise of liberalism, that the goodness of a society is to be judged by the extent to which its members individually are able to develop their capacities.

In opposition to this, conservatism holds that societies and other groups of people are *more* than just the sums of their parts, that a group of people creates greater happiness through its existence and maintenance as a group than its members could individually produce for themselves. Liberalism, conservatives say, is a lonely and selfish philosophy whose ultimate result would be a group of people resolved to better themselves with no regard for the people around them.

Conservatives regard it as important that their society should have order and structure and that this structure should be stable enough to let people know where they stand with regard to each other. Most important, an ordered group develops and maintains religion and standards of morality. People gain greater happiness as members of a family, members of a church, and members of society than they could possibly gain individually. This is what conservatives see as the highest good of society: *the maintenance of ordered community and of common values.*

In such a society, it is silly to try to keep one person from doing things for another or to keep one individual from exercising power over another. The whole point of "community" is that people are important as members, not as individuals. What matters is how they fit into the web of mutual responsibilities.

Since the structure of the community should be relatively stable and predictable so that all may easily fit into their place in it, there is nothing wrong with assigning power to people by even such arbitrary devices as heredity if those people can be expected to use their power wisely. Patterns of domination that have evolved gradually over time should not be changed casually, since what has grown slowly is at least familiar to us and must have had some virtue to have lasted so long. Conservatism is an ideology that accepts and welcomes power; conservatives believe that appropriate arrangements for power will ensure good treatment for everyone.

It is obvious why this philosophy based on ordered community was useful to the aristocracy, the established church, and others who were trying to maintain their positions against the liberal challenge. But ideologies take on a life of

Edmund Burke and Conservatism

Edmund Burke (1729–1797) is perhaps the most important figure in the development of conservative thought, at least in Britain. He was born and educated in Dublin, Ireland, the son of a lawyer. Although he was a professional politician and a great orator in the House of Commons, he was too intellectual and independent to rise to a major position in his party. As a philosopher, he was not abstract and did not deal in logical systems. Rather, he drew pragmatically from experience. What was already a well-developed conservative ideology was sharpened for him by what he saw as the excesses of the French Revolution.

their own, and conservatism stresses another theme that might not otherwise have come so naturally to the defenders of the status quo: the responsibilities of power. Where liberalism is suspicious of power and seeks to limit it, conservatism sees power as binding and shaping its holder in good ways. Conservatives do not see a powerful monarch or president as one who is in a position to treat people capriciously. Rather, they see such an official as one who is in a position of awesome responsibility, with generally very little choice as to courses of action. Conservatism stresses the responsibility of the powerful in a community to help the weak, a position opposed to the view of liberals that the weak should be given responsibility for their own affairs. Because of this side of conservatism, European conservatives have not been especially reluctant to help the poor or to develop the welfare state. In the late eighteenth century in Britain, under the conservative regime, there was already a system of guaranteed minimal income for anyone in Britain—a floor below which no one was to be allowed to fall. *Abolishing* this system was one of the first tasks of the liberals when they took power in 1832. To take another example, when Otto von Bismarck, the conservative chancellor of Germany from 1871 to 1890, introduced the world's first systems of unemployment insurance, workers' compensation, and social security, he had no apparent sense that he was doing something out of character.

We have noted that conservatism is unfamiliar to Americans. This is because, to the extent that the early immigrants had any ideas about politics at all, America was founded by liberals and populated largely by liberals. Most of the early settlers, after all, were trying to escape the rigidities of the old order in Europe. But also, our more fluid society has had few ordered systems of domination; conservatism, which is a defense of such systems, has therefore been largely irrelevant.[2]

Recently, however, one of our few ordered systems of domination has come under liberal attack and something rather like conservatism has arisen as a defense. The feminist attack on men's domination of women has often been

---

[2]Louis Hartz, *The Liberal Tradition in America* (New York: Harcourt, Brace, 1955).

framed as a classic statement of liberal argument. Women should be free to take on all sorts of responsibility, according to feminists, so that they can develop their capacities to the fullest. Protective laws (limiting the hours women may work, barring them from certain dangerous jobs, and so on) are wrong because in being protected from unpleasantness people are made weak and dependent. Feminists do not want women put "on a pedestal."

Opponents of feminism have often responded in ways that are akin to conservatism. The traditional family is a good thing in its own right, they say, especially if children are involved. It is the family we should be thinking of, not the individuals who make it up. And families work better, children are raised better, everyone is in the end happier, if there is a clear structure of authority in the family rather than a situation in which each member is striving individually.

Conservatism was a strong force throughout Europe in the nineteenth and early twentieth centuries. With the massive changes brought by World War II and its aftermath, European conservatism changed. The nobility were generally destroyed or discredited, the church was in ferment, and most countries had introduced a sweeping expansion of taxation and social services, the "welfare state," in order to make people more equal. After the huge destruction of the war, it was not always clear that there was a social order for conservatism to defend.

But conservatism adapted fairly rapidly to these changed circumstances. Their traditional emphasis on the responsibility of the powerful to help the poor and weak, together with a willingness (in contrast to the position of liberals) to see power concentrated, made it fairly easy for conservatives to accept the welfare state. Also, conservatism welcomes active encouragement of religion by the state, whereas liberalism is suspicious of it; large numbers of Europeans after the war apparently felt a need for a stability of values offered by religion, although among the youngest recent generations religious practice has dropped off sharply. While liberalism has declined in Europe throughout the twentieth century, conservatism has lived on healthily. Its adherents have accepted the welfare state but urged that it be built in ways that are consistent with traditional moral values and that it should not lead to a leveling of society. In other words, conservatives feel that some structure should remain by which one part of society can lead the rest. In Britain, the Liberal party declined during the 1920s and 1930s, until it is quite weak today; but the Conservative party has remained as the chief opponent of the new Labour party. When Labour introduced the welfare state in 1945, the Conservatives accepted it within a few years and went on to dominate British politics over the following decades. On the continent of Europe, after the war, Christian Democratic parties arose in many countries; these adhere to an established church but are flexible and pragmatic with regard to taxes and social programs. They have been especially strong in Italy and Germany, while a somewhat similar movement, the Gaullist movement, dominated French politics from 1958 to 1981. One can safely characterize the politics of most west European states since World War II as having consisted of a conflict between socialism (described in the next section) and a modified conservatism.

In the Third World, liberalism generally is weak (poor countries that are trying to develop their economies apparently find that they cannot afford to limit and restrain concentrations of power) and conservatism is rather strong. Traditional religious leaders and the aristocracy, as in Saudi Arabia and Iran, or new elites of business leaders, as in Japan or Brazil, can often maintain a strong political movement to keep the political leadership of the state in their hands. Frequently, the two groups join forces in a conservative movement.

Unfortunately, there is often a strong element of direction from the military in such movements as well, as in the conservative regime of South Korea. While by no means all military governments are conservative, there is often an affinity between military leaders and conservative political parties. Military organization requires an ordered structure of command in which certain members of the military direct the activities of other members. This is rather similar to the conservative view of society as a whole and may help to make military leaders comfortable with conservatism.[3]

THE SOCIALIST ALTERNATIVE

When liberalism first arose to challenge the established order, it drew considerable support from the "working class," the workers and their families who were beginning to congregate in the growing cities. Workers especially liked the assumption that all people were equal and should have an equal opportunity to develop their talents. And they liked the liberal doctrine of democracy, which would give them a share in political power. In 1848 a wave of attempted revolutions by liberals swept across the continent of Europe; in most of these, skilled workers played a leading part, along with shopkeepers and other small businessmen. In Britain, the leaders of most labor unions were active in the Liberal party as late as 1900.

But through the latter part of the nineteenth century, the enthusiasm of the working class for liberalism weakened. Liberalism implied not only that people should be politically equal but that they should be regulated and helped by the government as little as possible. Workers were in a weak position socially and economically, and they often found that they would like to have help from the government in ways that were inconsistent with liberalism. Governmental protection against unemployment and sickness, governmental regulation of working hours and of safety in the factories, governmental prohibition of child labor—these and similar wishes of labor were inconsistent with liberal principles. Naturally, compromises and accommodations could be reached within the movement, and labor was not left totally out in the cold, but the fact remained that labor often found that it had to buck the basic philosophy of the movement of which it was a part. When a new ideology ap-

---

[3]However, see the more detailed discussion of military governments in Chapter 13.

peared that was more congenial to labor, workers moved to it fairly readily. This ideology was socialism.

Socialism retained the assumption of liberalism that all persons deserve equal treatment by the state and should have equal opportunities to develop themselves; but unlike liberalism it did not posit that people could develop individually, and it was not as suspicious as liberalism of the concentration of power and of positive action by the state. Karl Marx (1818–1883) was the greatest socialist writer, and socialism since Marx has been heavily influenced by his views. Marx thought that society consisted not of individuals but of *classes*. A class is a group of people who share the same relationship to the means of production and who therefore develop a distinctive view of themselves and of the world. Marx thought that the most important thing about us is our work, that this is what creates for us most of our view of the world; people who share similar work (a similar "relationship to the means of production") form the natural basis for a class. The aristocracy had been such a class, intellectuals were such a class, the industrialists were such a class, and now a new class—the working class—was appearing in Europe. To Marx, people did not develop themselves individually—in a vacuum, as it were—but of and through the class to which they belonged. According to this view, individuals do not form their own values, their own ideas about politics, their own sense of their needs; rather they and the people they associate with form these things communally in ways that are difficult to specify. A person may contribute to these values and ideas, but so do all of the other members of his or her class. And each member draws much more from the class than he or she or any other single member contributes to it.

For Marx, then, the basic unit of concern was the class. As he saw it, the working class was oppressed; it was made to give up its members' labor to feed the rich capitalist class. But this was wrong, because the working class were numerically much larger than the capitalist class and their oppression bred

---

Karl Marx and Socialism

Karl Marx (1818–1883) was raised at first in Bonn, Germany, and later in Berlin. After graduating from the university, Marx and his close friend Friedrich Engels (1820–1895) worked as journalists for the left-wing press. In 1848 they wrote the *Communist Manifesto* and, in the aftermath of unsuccessful revolutions in Germany in that year, were forced to flee Germany. They settled in London, where Engels's family had connections and Engels could take care of Marx. Marx did not return to Germany until shortly before his death. In London he worked as a correspondent for the *New York Tribune* and wrote his massive, major work, *Das Kapital*. Marx combined a sweeping view of history with an astonishing appetite for the minutiae of economics. At its most basic level, his theory of politics, as of all other human activity, was that it is determined solely by economic processes and can be understood by economic analysis.

Karl Marx, architect of socialist ideology.

(UPI/Bettmann Newsphotos)

great misery. Therefore the working class should take over control of the government and the government should take over all industry, so that the workers themselves, through their government, would control the industries in which they worked. This would ensure fair treatment for everyone.

The writings of Marx and other socialists derived their energy and moral force from the writers' awareness of the truly miserable conditions under which workers lived in the nineteenth century. Marx's friend and collaborator Friedrich Engels, in his study of the living conditions of English workers, quoted an Anglican priest's account in 1844 of conditions in his parish:

> It contains 1,400 houses, inhabited by 2,795 families, comprising a population of 12,000. The space within which this large amount of population are living is less than 400 yards square, and it is no uncommon thing for a man and his wife, with four or five children, and sometimes the grandfather and grandmother, to be found living in a room from ten to twelve feet square, and which serves them for eating and working in. . . . There is not one father of a family in ten throughout the entire district that possesses any clothes but his working dress, and that too commonly in the worst tattered condition; and with many this wretched clothing form their only covering at night, with nothing better than a bag of straw or shavings to lie upon.[4]

Engels goes on to describe his own investigation of the living conditions of the working class in the city of Manchester:

[4]Friedrich Engels, *The Condition of the Working Class in England,* tr. by W. O. Henderson and W. H. Chaloner (Oxford, England: Basil Blackwell, 1958), pp. 35 and 36.

One walks along a very rough path on the river bank, in between clothesposts and washing lines to reach a chaotic group of little, one-storied, one-roomed cabins. Most of them have earth floors, and working, living and sleeping all take place in the one room. In such a hole, barely six feet long and five feet wide, I saw two beds—and what beds and bedding!—which filled the room, except for the fireplace and the doorstep. Several of these huts, as far as I could see, were completely empty, although the door was open and the inhabitants were leaning against the door posts. In front of the doors filth and garbage abounded. I could not see the pavement, but from time to time, I felt it was there because my feet scraped it.[5]

Marx developed a theory of history arguing that a revolution of the working class was not only appropriate but inevitable. According to Marx's *dialectical* theory, all history has consisted of a successive unfolding of domination by one group, leading to revolution against that group, followed by domination by a new group (the group that had led the successful revolution), leading to yet another revolution, and so on. Thus, Europe in the Middle Ages was dominated by the nobility, but there was an internal contradiction in their rule—they needed the services of bankers and traders but were barred by their social codes from undertaking this work themselves. Thus they created a new class, the capitalist class, which (as we have seen above) eventually overthrew them in the industrial revolution and with the coming of liberalism. The capitalist class now dominated Europe, said Marx, but there was an internal contradiction in their rule as well, which would eventually lead to their overthrow. The capitalists had had to create a new class, the working class, to serve their needs. But because capitalists are forced by their code to seek ever-greater profits, they would have to grind the working class nearer and nearer to starvation, until at last the situation would be intolerable and there would be a revolution. Note that this theory of politics is based almost solely on the use of power.

Marx thought that the process of history would have worked itself out with the victory of the working class, because now for the first time the dominant class would not be a minority but would include almost the whole population. His theory of history and revolution was powerfully attractive to workers. It told them that their unhappy plight was not their own fault as individuals but rather a condition imposed on all of them as a class by the working out of a broad historical process. Further, it prophesied that they must, in the end, prevail over the capitalists because that is the way history works. Finally, it assured them that once they had prevailed a brave new world would be created in which the cycle of revolutions was no longer necessary. In the words of a favorite British working class hymn:

> I will not cease from mental fight,
> Nor shall my sword sleep in my hand,
> Till we have built Jerusalem
> In England's green and pleasant land.
> (originally from WILLIAM BLAKE'S *Milton*)

[5]Ibid., p. 61.

Socialism burst explosively on Europe. In 1850 there were only a few socialists on the continent. By the early 1900s the Social Democratic party was the largest party in Germany and was growing fast; socialism was growing just as rapidly in other western European countries.

COMMUNISM AND SOCIALISM

In 1917, a key event occurred in the development of socialism when Lenin's Bolsheviks succeeded in seizing control of the Russian Empire and transforming it into a socialist state renamed the Union of Soviet Socialist Republics (U.S.S.R.). Marx and Engels had never fully settled whether they thought the working class should take control of the state peacefully through electoral victory or violently through revolution. Many socialists thought revolution was the only answer, while others believed deeply in democracy. Lenin's successful revolution galvanized those who wanted to take the route of revolution, and over the years after 1917 they tried to dominate the socialist movement. They argued that the one state that had now successfully become socialist, the U.S.S.R., should lead all socialists in the world. The attempt to commit socialism to a revolutionary strategy led to a split in the socialist movement in the 1920s. The revolutionists set themselves up as Communist parties, while the democratic socialists continued to call themselves Socialist or sometimes Democratic Socialist parties.

The split has endured, so that there are today two branches of socialism. Communists have generally held to a revolutionary strategy, although with the passage of time they have grown a good deal less emphatic about it. Socialists have been much more willing to settle for a portion of power within an only partially socialist system, and they have generally worked within a democratic framework. Socialists have also been more willing than communists to settle for partial improvements for workers, rather than holding out for a total change.

In the period after World War II, most of eastern Europe was governed by communists, with some help from the U.S.S.R.; as Poland, Czechoslovakia, and other eastern European states moved away from communism in 1990, they tended to look to democratic socialism as a model. Socialists have participated strongly in the governments of almost all western European states, and they took the lead in bringing the modern welfare state to western Europe. Communism and socialism have both been strong forces in the Third World. China, Cuba, and Vietnam have communist governments, while scores of Third World states have socialist governments.

FASCISM

Fascism is not really much of an ideology, but I shall treat it here because it is often discussed as if it were. In the 1930s three European dictators arose who had a similar style that came to be known as "fascism." Adolf Hitler in Germany, Benito Mussolini in Italy, and Francisco Franco in Spain all set up regimes that were antisocialist but nonconservative in that they did not so much wish to defend a particular social order as to tear all existing order apart and replace it with mass adulation of a single leader. This was accomplished by making the leader a cult figure, the center of a showy mass of ritual and pageantry. (The word "fascism" derives from Mussolini's adoption of the fasces, a symbol of the ancient Roman Empire, as his own symbol, and Hitler's Nuremberg rallies were notable for their Hollywood-style, pseudopagan splendor.) The state was supposed to be strong and active militarily in order to achieve its role of historic greatness. Communism was a great enemy, to be opposed and suppressed.

This, then, is fascism: a romantic type of nationalism with a great deal of showmanship thrown in. It was not really an ideology in the sense that it connected a set of ideas. To the extent that it had any philosophical core, it was the idea that the state should attain greatness. This should be accomplished by the Leader, supported by the mass of people, whom he should energize by appeals to their emotions.

The details of fascism actually varied a good deal from one place to another. The Nazi party of Germany attacked the existing social system, including the churches, more actively than most. It had a strong element of anti-Semitic racism that was not present in Italian or Spanish fascism and which ultimately led to the murder of millions of Jews. Spanish fascism identified with conservative church leadership and supported the church. Italian fascism was marked by an attempt to reorganize the economy into "corporations"—guilds of employers and workers in each industry. Such variations in fascist policy again underscore the fact that fascism was more a political style than a system of ideas.

Fascism appealed particularly to the middle class, who found that neither conservatism nor socialism offered them much and who may have found liberalism a bit dull and shopworn. Fascism also attracted a certain number of disillusioned socialists (Mussolini had been a left-wing socialist, and the British fascist Oswald Mosely had earlier been a leading figure in the left wing of the Labour party), and once fascist parties became strong, they also gained opportunistic support from industrialists and other conservatives who saw in them a good way to fight communism.

Fascist parties were active not only in the three fascist-ruled countries but in many other European countries at the time. It is tragic that such misery—the Holocaust, World War II—was caused by movements that did not even offer their peoples much in the way of an idea, only emotion and show.

THE GREAT IDEOLOGIES IN THE LATE TWENTIETH CENTURY

With the long period of general peace in Europe and among other industrialized states since World War II, some of the edge has worn off the conflict among the great modern ideologies. As modern society has become more firmly established, the old grievances do not seem to move people as strongly as they once did.

Many leaders of parties, especially those which hold responsibility for the government of a state, have begun to modify their ideologies in light of practical experience. The most dramatic example of this is provided by Mikhail Gorbachev's campaigns for *glasnost* ("openness") and *perestroika* (economic reform) in the Soviet Union. Faced with a limping economy under the traditional communist regime, he has introduced sweeping changes that bear little resemblance to communist ideology. And, encouraged by his example, other communist regimes such as Hungary, Poland, Czechoslovakia, and East Germany have gone considerably further than the Soviet Union.

Other leaders show more and more a compromised blend of ideologies. Britain's Margaret Thatcher is the leader of the Conservative party, which among other things emphasizes close ties to the Anglican Church and the monarchy. But her personal ideology combines these conservative elements with a set of very liberal economic policies calling for a great shrinkage of the state's role in the economy, marked by the "privatisation" (sale to private owners) of many government enterprises. On the other side of the spectrum, some socialists such as Premier Felipe Gonzalez of Spain have so blended their socialism with concerns for efficiency and stable economic growth that it is scarcely recognizable as a doctrine of conflict between classes.

However, ideological conflict is not dead in the late twentieth century. A set of issues are currently raised in Europe by new "green" parties, which established leaders, accustomed to the old ideologies, have found hard to absorb into their debates. These issues, labeled "post-industrial issues" by Ronald Inglehart, include feminism, protection of the environment, and open and spontaneous styles of life.[6] In part, they have been represented by totally new parties (among others, the Greens); in part they have found their way into established Socialist parties where they often represent a minority voice. In Socialist parties, the new mood has especially produced interest in direct participation by workers in the management of their industries.[7]

History, and the development of ideologies, does not stop. The great modern ideologies were a product of the tension between Europe's industrialization and the static institutions Europe had inherited from its feudal past. As that tension now recedes other sources of ideological development have come to the fore, in a sometimes confusing mix of forces and tensions: the practical economic experiences of the Soviet Union and the United States; the increasing problem of degradation of the environment; the resurgence of militant Islam; the discovery of youth and women as classes, even though Marxist socialism saw classes as based solely on economic position; and the increasingly clear

---

[6]Ronald Inglehart, *The Silent Revolution: Changing Values and Political Styles Among Western Publics* (Princeton, N.J.: Princeton University Press, 1977).
[7]See, for example, W. Rand Smith, "Toward 'Autogestion' in Socialist France? The Impact of Industrial Relations Reform." *West European Politics* 10 (no. 1, January 1987): 46–62.

division of interests between rich states and poor states—the "North" and the "South."

AMERICA: LAND OF LIBERALISM

From this review of the great modern ideologies we can see that the only one that is much in evidence in American politics is liberalism. Conservatism has only rarely appeared in American politics because there have been few traditional ordered systems of domination to defend. The feminist attack on the domination of women by men has provoked a conservative response, as we have seen. And the 1950s defense of the system by which southern blacks were kept in a dependent position ("Our Negroes are happy here, we take care of them when they're old or sick") also had tones of conservatism to it. But these examples are unusual. American politics has more often consisted of arguments between varying kinds of liberals—about freedom and opportunities and rights and about the dangers of concentrated power.

If conservatism never prospered in America because there were few traditional systems of ordered domination to require a conservative defense, why is it that socialism has not been established either? Certainly there have been workers and poor people who have felt they needed things from the government that strict liberalism would not provide.

In a sense, socialism *has* been established, since what we have called American liberalism represents a compromise between liberalism and some elements of socialism. American liberalism has held firmly to the traditional concern of liberalism for freedom of expression, but it has been open to compromise on economic regulation. In order to address problems of poverty and inequality, American liberalism has been willing to see the government grow and intervene in people's economic activity. Thus there are some elements of socialism in American liberalism.

Still, this is a very modest and compromised socialism. Why is it that America has not seen a full-fledged socialist movement? Why was it that Eugene Debs, who ran several times as the Socialist candidate for president, was never able to get more than 900,000 votes, or 6 percent of the total (in 1912)? The answer is probably complex. First of all, Americans have by and large been rather well off economically, though there have been great differences among them. Second, for reasons which will be explored in Chapter 8, it is more difficult in the United States than in other countries to start a new political movement. Finally, it was not only economic inequality but a desire for full political rights that added fuel to the socialist movements of Europe. Workers did not have full voting rights in Germany in 1918. In the United States, full political rights, at least for white males, came easily and were universal by the early 1800s. In this sense, America's lack of a feudal past (which kept European workers subordinated to the aristocracy) may have been partly responsible for the absence of a socialist movement, just as it was responsible for the absence of a conservative movement. This is the thesis of Louis Hartz, who characterizes the United States as having been "born free" because it had no feudal past.[8] Slavery was America's only quasifeudal institution, and abolishing it was trauma enough.

To consider the view of an expert, here is a letter from Engels to a friend in America, offering his explanation as to why America did not have a major socialist movement at that time (1893):

> ...First, the Constitution, based as in England upon party government, which causes every vote for any candidate not put up by one of the two governing parties to appear to be lost. And the American, like the Englishman, wants to influence his state; he does not throw his vote away.
>
> Then, and more especially, immigration, which divides the workers into two groups: the native-born and the foreigners, and the latter in turn into (1) the Irish, (2) the Germans, (3) the many small groups, each of which understands only itself: Czechs, Poles, Italians, Scandinavians, etc. And then the Negroes. To form a single part out of these requires quite unusually powerful incentives. Often there is a sudden violent élan, but the bourgeois need only wait passively and the dissimilar elements of the working class fall apart again.
>
> Third, through the protective tariff system and the steadily growing domestic market the workers must have been exposed to a prosperity no trace of which has been seen here in Europe for years now (except in Russia, where, however, the bourgeois profit by it and not the workers).[9]

POLITICAL PHILOSOPHY THROUGH THE AGES

In this chapter we have followed the development of modern ideologies, approximately since the eighteenth century. But great minds throughout the ages have been concerned with the question of how politics should properly be conducted. Let us consider briefly the development of political philosophy up to the modern period.

The Greeks were the first great political philosophers, especially the Greeks of Athens a few centuries before the birth of Christ. They were especially concerned with the nature of justice and with the question of what sort of constitution would produce the best political community. Plato (428–347 B.C.) was the greatest of the Athenian philosophers. In *The Republic*, he describes a utopian political community in which good, gifted people are selected as infants to be the leaders ("guardians") and are carefully trained (their reading censored, their minds honed by the study of mathematics) so that they will be able to rule wisely and autocratically. His was an ideal world, not likely to be accomplished in fact. It is reminiscent of modern conservatism.

While Plato sought for the ideal, Aristotle (384–322 B.C.), another great Athenian, restricted himself more to observations of the world around him.

---

[8]Hartz, op. cit., n. 2.

[9]Karl Marx and Frederick Engels, *Basic Writings on Politics and Philosophy*, ed. Lewis S. Feuer (Garden City, N.Y.: Doubleday, 1959).

Analytic Political Philosophy

Much work in the study of political philosophy is of the sort presented in this chapter—a history of the development of political ideas, with critical commentary on them. An alternative way of approaching the study draws its inspiration from the modern school of "analytic philosophy," which concerns itself especially with the meaning of words.

This approach, called "analytic political philosophy," does not primarily concern itself with the history of political ideas or with critical argument about them at a general level. Rather, its practitioners feel that they can contribute most to our understanding of politics by clarifying the language we use when we talk about politics. Certainly, a problem of muddled language lies behind many political arguments. The United States calls itself a "democracy," and so does the Soviet Union. The two mean quite different things by the word, but this is often forgotten in red-faced arguments along the lines of "We're a democracy!" "Are not!" "Are!" "Aren't!"

Some questions commonly dealt with by analytic political philosophers are: What is the state? (You already had a taste of the complexities of this question in Chapter 2); and more important: What are our *obligations* to the state? What is the "public interest"? What should be considered "rights," as in "human rights"? What should be meant by "equality"? And so on.

One excellent example of work in the mode of analytic political philosophy is Hannah Pitkin's study, *The Concept of Representation*, in which the author examines all of the varied ways in which, over the last several centuries, the word "representation" has been used, in order to make clear what *general, central* meaning it has.[1] A useful collection of analytic works is *Political Philosophy*, edited by Anthony Quinton.[2]

[1]Hannah Pitkin, *The Concept of Representation* (Berkeley: University of California Press, 1967).

[2]Anthony Quinton, ed., *Political Philosophy* (Oxford, England: Oxford University Press, 1967).

Aristotle thought that if people could be trusted to rule unselfishly, the very best constitution was one in which a single person ruled; the next best was aristocracy, the rule of the few; and the least good was rule by a large number of people. In practice, however, people were selfish, and Aristotle argued that—since the perversion of the best leads to the worst—selfish rule by a single person was worse than selfish rule by a large number. So in the end he argued for something like democracy.

With their concerns about the proper role of citizens, about the nature of justice, and about what sort of constitution produces a good community and good people, the Greeks laid the foundation for all Western political philosophy that followed. During the Roman Empire relatively little was done in this area, the Romans tending simply to rely on what the Greeks had already done. With the coming of the Christian church in the first centuries after Christ, however, a new period of activity began. The development of a church that claimed allegiance from people all over Europe raised to the forefront the question of just what obligation people bore to their *earthly* rulers. If they were ruled by God in Christ, why should they do what their king told them to do? What should they do, for instance, if ordered by their king to do something that was a sin?

Much of the development of political philosophy for a thousand years or so centered on this question, and the answers shifted as the relative power of the church and of secular rulers waxed and waned. Early Christian writers, perhaps reflecting the weakness of the young church, claimed a rather modest role for the church in the affairs of this world. The greatest of these writers was Saint Augustine (354–430), who argued that government was made necessary by humanity's sinfulness and that only once we were without sin could we be ruled by God. To Augustine, government was a necessary evil (*made* necessary, in fact, by evil), which at least produced internal order for sinful humanity.

As the church grew in power, popes sought to assert more authority over secular rulers. By the Middle Ages, Saint Thomas Aquinas (1225–1274) was asserting that the church was responsible for people's spiritual well-being and rulers were responsible for their physical well-being; since the spiritual was more important than the physical, however, rulers must be guided by the church whenever the church held that spiritual needs were involved.

The church was not without opposition in this thrust, of course, especially as it weakened in later centuries. A curious and famous response to it was that of Niccoló Machiavelli (1469–1527), who wished to help kings resist the church and wrote *The Prince*, a primer of how to be a successful king, to help them. In it he argued that a king should be ruthless and pragmatic, not swayed by sentiment or morality.

Toward the end of the Middle Ages, and as Europe entered the modern period, kings grew stronger and the church weakened. This became particularly clear during the Reformation, when the historic Catholic church was replaced in much of northern Europe by local Protestant churches established by local kings. The pendulum of political philosophy now swung back against the church, as in the writings of Martin Luther (1483–1546), who returned to Saint Augustine's doctrine that government is a necessity to which even faithful Christians should submit.

As kings now became more powerful, questions of political philosophy shifted to what obligations people in general bore to *them*. This question was brought to a head in the English Civil War (1647–1649), in which a diverse group of opponents to the king succeeded in deposing him and set up a republic that lasted for a bit over a decade. This successful challenge to royal authority focused attention on the question of the duties owed to kings and eventually led to the development of liberalism, discussed above.

One particularly important writer who participated in this debate was Thomas Hobbes (1588–1679), author of *Leviathan*—a strangely modern defense of authority. (Hobbes does not specify whether that authority must be vested in a king.) His argument is as follows: All people are selfish; in the absence of authority they will turn on each other, and life will be "solitary, poor, nasty, brutish, and short." To avoid this, people voluntarily band together into states and contract to give their rights to a sovereign, who will rule autocratically to provide peace and order for all. Hobbes's theory was intended primarily to justify the rule of kings, but it could be used to justify any sort of dictatorship. Of their free wills, by a cooperative decision, the people set up a power to dominate them for the common good.

With the questioning of royal authority at this time, the stage was set for the development of liberalism and of the other modern ideologies responding to liberalism; the bulk of this chapter has dealt with these ideologies.

FURTHER READING

Berlin, Isaiah. "Does Political Theory Still Exist?" In *Philosophy, Politics, and Society*, 2nd series. Ed. P. Laslett and W. G. Runciman. Oxford, England: Basil Blackwell, 1962.

Bronowski, Jacob, and Mazlish, Bruce. *The Western Intellectual Tradition*. New York: Harper & Row, 1960.

Conover, Pamela Johnston, and Feldman, Stanley. "Belief System Organization in the American Electorate: An Alternate Approach." In *The Electorate Reconsidered*. Ed. John C. Pierce and John L. Sullivan. Beverly Hills, Calif: Sage, 1980.

Converse, Philip E. "The Nature of Belief Systems in Mass Publics." In *Ideology and Discontent*. Ed. David E. Apter. New York: Free Press, 1964.

Dahl, Robert. *A Preface to Democratic Theory*. Chicago: University of Chicago Press, 1956.

Ebenstein, William, and Fogelman, Edwin. *Today's Isms: Communism, Fascism, Capitalism, Socialism*, 9th ed. Englewood Cliffs, N.J.: Prentice-Hall, 1985.

Plamenatz, J. "The Uses of Political Theory." *Political Studies* 8 (1960): 37–47.

Riker, William. *Liberalism Against Populism*. San Francisco: Freeman, 1982.

Sibley, Mulford Q. *Political Ideas and Ideologies*. New York: Harper & Row, 1970.

Strauss, Leo. "What is Political Philosophy?" *Journal of Politics* 19 (August 1957): 343–368.

Wolin, Sheldon S. *Politics and Vision*. Boston: Little, Brown, 1960.

Chapter 4

Policies of the State

In Chapter 2 we saw that the modern state is a relatively recent invention. It developed fairly gradually over the last several centuries and is developing still, as people come to expect the state to take care of more and more aspects of their lives and as military operations—the special purview of the state—become more complex and expensive. In this chapter we shall survey some of the most important policies of modern states in order to consider the variety of things the state does today.

Figure 4–1 charts the growth of state activity since the nineteenth century for Great Britain, Italy, Sweden, and the United States.

The most interesting thing about the figure is that these four countries have developed in much the same way, though they have had quite different kinds of governments and their experiences during the twentieth century have varied a great deal. Italy had a fascist government from 1922 to 1943. Britain had a socialist government from 1945 to 1951 and intermittently from then on. Sweden was ruled uninterruptedly by a socialist party from 1932 to 1976 and is well-known for its wide-ranging welfare state. The United States, on the other hand, has never had a socialist government, though the New Deal after 1932 was strongly oriented toward reform and the expansion of social programs. Despite these political and historical differences, the four countries show a rather similar expansion of state activity. During the latter part of the nineteenth century and into the early twentieth, all four devoted a stable and relatively small percentage of their wealth to the government. Government spending accounted for 5 percent of all economic activity in Britain, Sweden, and the United States and for a bit over 10 percent in Italy. Starting at about the time of World War I, however, governmental spending began to take up more and more of the economy, until by 1969 it accounted for anything from 19 percent (Italy) to 34 percent (United States) of all economic activity.

The two great world wars appear to have had something to do with this growth. Britain, Italy, and the United States showed great jumps in their governments' roles in the economy at these wars, and when the governments' roles subsided again after the war, they generally did not go back down as far as they had been before. This pattern is most pronounced in the British case, but it is evident in the other two as well. The lasting expansion of government as a result of these wars is probably due not only to the actual expenditures in the wars but also to the fact that in the "total warfare" of the twentieth century, governments have become accustomed to controlling the lives of their people rather directly—rationing the goods they may buy, telling them what jobs they

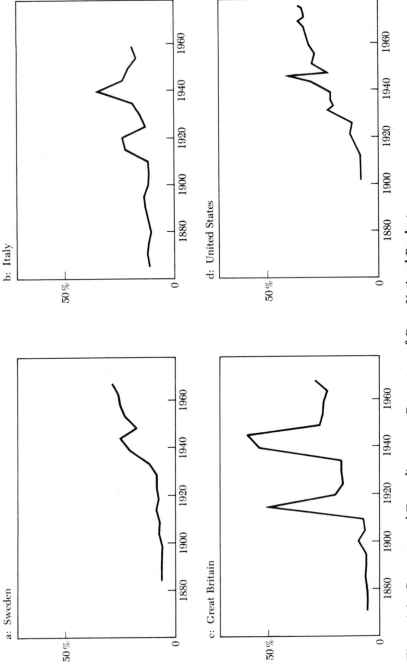

Figure 4–1 Governmental Expenditures as a Percentage of Gross National Product.

SOURCE U.S. Department of Commerce, *Historical Statistics of the United States*; Brian R. Mitchell, *European Historical Statistics, 1750–1970* (New York: Columbia University Press, 1975).

NOTE Figures for the United States are for federal, state, and local governments combined. Figures for the other three countries are for the central government only. Local governments in Britain, Italy, and Sweden have few independent resources, but this still means that the U.S. figures are somewhat high relative to the others.

may work at, and so on. After the wars, the governments intervened actively in people's lives and acted this way on behalf of other causes as well.

Sweden was neutral during both wars, so they did not have the same effect on her as they had on Britain, Italy, and the United States. But Sweden, too, left behind the stable, low level of expenditure that had characterized her in the earlier part of the period and, with a socialist government, began in the 1930s a steady increase in the government's share of the economy. By the 1950s, this had brought Sweden up to the same levels as the other three countries.

A heavy governmental role in society appears to be typical of industrialized democracies late in the twentieth century. When we note that 35 percent of the U.S. gross national product consisted of governmental expenditures, this means that slightly over one-third of all purchasing of goods and services was done by the government.

There seems to be a strong pressure in industrialized democracies to expand the role of the state. This was well illustrated by Sweden in the late 1970s. In 1976 a nonsocialist government replaced the Socialists, who had been in power almost continuously since 1932. This new government had pledged to avoid expanding the role of government, but as Sweden entered a period of economic difficulty and businesses looked as though they might fail, the government felt it had to take over some of them and keep them going so as to prevent unemployment. Thus the *non*socialist government ended up nationalizing a number of industries, including the country's largest shipbuilding firm.

As a result of such pressures, to which all industrialized democracies seem to be subject, the industrialized democracies do not vary a great deal with regard to the degree of governmental involvement in society and the economy. In all of them the governmental role has expanded greatly during the twentieth century and is now very large.

In addition to this expansion of the government's role in the industrialized democracies, an even more marked expansion of this kind occurred with the establishment of communist governments in sixteen countries during the twentieth century. We cannot present figures to measure the role of the state in communist societies, as we did for industrialized democracies in Figure 4–1, because the state is so closely enmeshed in a communist economy that we cannot clearly delineate where state spending ends and private spending begins. It is enough for our purposes here to realize that in communist systems, the state plays a dominant role. But it is also worth remembering that even in the communist systems the state does not control everything that happens, either in the economy or in other affairs. In all the communist systems there is some private economic activity. For instance, about 25 percent of agricultural production in the Soviet Union comes from small plots (accounting for only 2 percent of the arable land!) that the peasants are allowed to farm for profit. And in Poland, almost all farms are privately owned. Apart from such exceptions, however, the fact remains that the coming of communism has inevitably meant a massive expansion of the role of government. As of this writing there is much interest among communist systems, especially Hungary, in experimenting with an expansion of private economic activity.

If the industrialized democracies are all pretty similar with regard to the extent of governmental activity and if the communist systems are also pretty similar to one another, the picture is different among Third World states. Here there is a wider range of governmental activity, and governmental involvement is generally lower than it is in the industrialized democracies. Table 4–1 gives a few examples.

As we have seen, "Third World" is a bit of a catch-all category, and the politics of the countries grouped in this category varies greatly. The extent of governmental activity in the economy varies just as greatly, and it is hard to come up with explanations for this. It is perhaps no surprise that the primitive dictatorship of Paraguay does not have an especially active government, but then why does the democratic Dominican Republic have a similarly low governmental profile?

Whereas the politics of industrialized democracies involves a rather standard set of pressures from business, interest groups, and the international community—which result in a similar level of governmental activity from one such country to the next—politics in the Third World is much more variable, less developed, and more fluid. Thus it is more difficult to generalize about Third World politics than about the politics either of industrialized democracies or communist systems.

WHAT DO GOVERNMENTS DO?

We have seen that governments generally have gotten much larger in the twentieth century. What is it that these governments do? In general, their activities fall under four main headings: transfer of resources, subsidies with strings attached, regulation, and development and administration.

Table 4–1   Governmental Revenues as a Percentage of the Gross Domestic Product in Selected Third World States

Country	Government's Percent of Economic Activity	Location	Governmental Form
Zaire	25%	Africa	dictatorship
Thailand	17%	Asia	military dominated partial democracy
Egypt	41%	Middle East	one-party state
Israel	49%	Middle East	democracy
Dominican Republic	15%	South America	democracy
Paraguay	10%	South America	dictatorship
India	20%	Asia	democracy

SOURCE: International Monetary Fund, *Government Finance Statistics Yearbook*, 1988.

1. Transfer of Resources

A government often takes resources from some people and gives them to others without offering much direction as to what the transferred resources are to be used for. An American example of this is the social security system, which taxes employers and their workers, and gives the proceeds of the tax to retired people, the disabled, and the survivors of wage earners who have died young.

2. Subsidies with Strings Attached

As a somewhat more active form of intervention, the government may provide money to some of the people, but with the requirement that it be used in certain ways. The U.S. government voted a series of subsidies to Chrysler Corporation in the early 1980s, for instance, but with the requirement that Chrysler cut its costs, hold down wage increases, and so on. With its liberal tradition, the United States has been a bit reluctant to impose such state guidance, but in many other countries, the practice is quite pervasive. In the Scandinavian countries, for example, complex sets of purposive subsidies direct most aspects of the economy. Just to give one example, the Norwegian government—as part of a general campaign over the postwar period to keep the population from concentrating in the southeast, in the vicinity of Oslo—has provided a state subsidy on all milk produced in the western part of the country. This has had the two desired effects: (1) milk prices have stayed low for the

'HOW D'YA LIKE THAT? MOSCOW SAYS TO FORGET ABOUT COMMUNISM – THEY WERE JUST KIDDING.'

consumer and (2) the dairy industry in the east was destroyed, helping to keep the population more evenly distributed. Note that such governmental intervention is not free—tax money is used to pay the subsidy, and many dairy farmers in the east suffered from the change.

Frequently, government subsidies occur not as direct payments but as *tax expenditures*, reductions in taxes for people who use their money in certain approved ways. In the United States, taxpayers have been encouraged by targeted reductions in their taxes to do such things as buy municipal bonds, invest in oil companies, and make their homes energy efficient.

3. Regulation

The government may also directly lay down rules telling people how to conduct their affairs. Traditional areas of regulation prohibit crimes such as murder, theft, or extortion. The twentieth century has seen an explosion of regulatory activity beyond this traditional sphere everywhere; many countries now regulate the way in which foods may be prepared or packaged, what sorts of things may be printed in books or newspapers, what type of access the handicapped must have to business premises, how many pollutants may be emitted into the air, and so on.

As regulatory activity has increased, regulations have rectified many abuses. In many countries today the air is cleaner, children are safer, food is more accurately labeled, workers are less vulnerable to injury—all because of government regulation. But regulation, too, is not free. It does not cost the government a great deal to set and administer regulations, but critics charge that the complicated mass of regulations that exists in many countries channels too much of the people's effort into keeping records, paying for lawyers and courts, and so on.

A rough measure of the growth of regulatory activity in recent decades in the United States is the number of pages in the annual *Federal Register*. This is a publication of the General Services Administration which updates rules and regulations set by the federal government. Table 4–2 presents the number of pages published in the *Federal Register* during selected years. Note espe-

Table 4–2   Pages Contained in Selected Years of the *Federal Register*

1936	2,355
1946	14,528
1956	10,528
1966	16,850
1975	60,221
1984	50,997
1988	53,375

SOURCE: Morris P. Fiorina, *Congress: Keystone of the Washington Establishment* (New Haven, Conn.: Yale University Press, 1977), p. 93; *The Federal Register* for 1984, 1988.

cially the huge growth in regulatory activity from 1966 to 1975 and the slight reduction under the Reagan administration by 1984.

4. Development and Administration

Finally, the government is not restricted to merely supervising how other people conduct their affairs but may step in and do the job itself. Defense and diplomacy are obvious areas where the government must do this, and education is another activity in which governments have felt they must be active. (In the latter case, however, they have not generally felt the need to have a monopoly. In the United States, for instance, significant numbers of children are educated in private or parochial schools.)

There are other, more controversial areas in which some governments have chosen to develop and administer programs themselves. Especially notable here is nationalization, by which a government takes over one or another industry—the trains, the steel industry, auto manufacturing, or what have you—and runs it. The intent is that the industry should then be operated for the general public good rather than for private gain, but the performance of nationalized industries has been mixed. Critics charge, on the one hand, that nationalization makes the management of the industry cumbersome and inefficient, and, on the other hand, that the civil servants who run the nationalized industries do not in fact do things all that differently than the old "selfish" managers did. Following a flurry of nationalization after socialist parties came to power (generally after World War II in Europe, or on the establishment of national independence in the Third World), nationalization has gone rather out of vogue. In the late 1970s and early 1980s, however, many European countries felt that they had to nationalize numerous industries in order to keep them from going bankrupt and putting their employees out of work. This is generally a shortsighted policy, since it means that inefficient businesses are kept in operation with the public absorbing their losses; but it is understandable that governments would not want to see large numbers of workers lose their jobs all at once.

Most countries have more of their industry nationalized than the United States does. In the communist states, of course, all major industries, with the sole exception of agriculture in a few countries, are nationalized. Most Third World countries have significantly nationalized industries. And in western Europe, most countries have many more of their industries nationalized than does the United States. In France, for example, the following industries are wholly or largely operated by the state: insurance, banking, automobile manufacturing, air transport, the railroads, natural gas, electricity, and coal.

These, then, are the four main forms of governmental activity: transfer of resources, subsidies with strings attached, regulation, and the development and administration of programs. In the next chapter we shall look more closely at whether one or another of these forms of activity is preferable. For the remainder of this chapter, let us look a bit more closely at some selected areas of

Why Are the World's States Expanding?

Almost all states in the world today are expanding in the degree to which they intervene in their people's lives. Why this is so is a challenging puzzle for political scientists. David Cameron ("The Expansion of the Public Economy: A Comparative Analysis," *American Political Science Review* 72 [December 1978]: 1243–1261) reviews five main explanations that have been advanced:

1. As people become more prosperous, they may want more and more done for them and are willing to pay for it. Thus, as industrialization makes people more prosperous, the state naturally grows.
2. As governments have become more clever at using "hidden taxes" such as excise taxes and payroll withholding of income taxes, they can get away with taxing people more heavily, and the state grows.
3. Electoral democracy results in a "bidding up" of the state's operations as parties compete to see which can promise more services to the voters.
4. Once governmental bureaucracies are established, they develop internal pressures for expansion. Inevitably, they succeed in slowly ratcheting upward the scope of their operations.
5. As world trade grows and states' economies become more and more subject to disruption by events in the international economy, their governments are less and less able to control what is happening in the state. The governments must then grow in order to compensate for the greater difficulty they find in functioning.

The jury is out, and will stay out for a long time, as to which among these explanations are valid. For examinations of evidence on the subject, see Cameron's article and also David Lowery and William D. Berry, "The Growth of Government in the United States," *American Journal of Political Science* 27 (November 1983): 665–694.

Note, incidentally, that of the five proposed explanations, numbers 1 and 5 are based on the perspective of politics as choice, numbers 2 and 4 are based on the perspective of politics as power, and number 3 is ambiguous.

policy in order to see what sort of attention various governments have paid to them.

DEFENSE POLICY

This is the one area of policy in which governments have almost without exception proceeded by developing and administering programs themselves and have insisted on holding a monopoly with regard to the policy. Private schools, private hospitals, and so on are sometimes tolerated by governments, but this is practically never true of private armies!

As Table 4–3 shows, states vary a great deal in the effort they expend on defense. Generally speaking, communist states spend heavily in this area. The U.S.S.R. shows up as high in Table 4–3 and, on the average in 1986, all communist states (including those not appearing in Table 4–3) spent 5.6 percent of their gross national product on defense.[1] The industrialized democracies generally did not spend so much. Canada, the United States, and Britain all have volunteer armies, and none of the industrialized democracies in Table 4–3 spent more on defense than the United States did (6.4 percent of the gross national product in 1987). On the average, in 1987 all industrialized democracies (including those not appearing in Table 4–3) spent 2.9 percent of their gross national product on defense.[2]

Third World countries vary tremendously in their military expenditures. Algeria, Colombia, Paraguay, and Tanzania show up as fairly low in Table 4–3, but Israel and South Korea are quite high. Some parts of the Third World have been the scene of continuing tensions in recent decades, with frequent threats of war, and some countries in those regions spend shocking sums on defense.

Table 4–3   Defense Preparations for Selected States

	Military Service	Percent of Population in Active Military	Percent of GNP Spent on Defense
U.S.S.R. (C)*	2 years	1.8	15 to 25
China (C)	selective; 3–5 years	0.3	4.1
Canada (I)	voluntary	0.3	2.1
France (I)	1 year	0.8	4.0
West Germany (I)	18 months	0.8	3.1
Great Britain (I)	voluntary	0.6	4.9
United States (I)	voluntary	0.9	6.4
Algeria (T)	2 years	0.6	1.7
Colombia (T)	1–2 years	0.3	2.2
Israel (T)	men, 3 years; women, 2 years	3.2	21.0
Paraguay (T)	1.5–2 years	0.4	1.2
South Korea (T)	2.5–3 years	1.5	5.0
Tanzania (T)	2 years	0.2	3.1

*C = communist state; I = industrialized democracy; T = Third World

SOURCES: International Institute for Strategic Studies, *The Military Balance, 1988–89* (London: Adlard & Son, 1989); Stockholm International Peace Research Institute, *World Armaments and Disarmament: SIPRI Yearbook 1988* (Oxford, England: Oxford University Press, 1988).

[1] International Institute for Strategic Studies, *The Military Balance, 1988–89* (London: Adlard & Son, 1989).
[2] Ibid.

Peruvian schoolchildren
(PAUL CONKLIN)

In East Africa, the Middle East, and Central America, many countries spend as much as 10 percent or more of their gross national product on defense. This is tragic, since defense spending neither feeds people nor furthers economic development. Outside of those "hot spot" regions, Third World countries on the average spent 3.3 percent of their gross national product on defense in 1986.[3]

The actual use to which this investment in the military is put varies a great deal from one country to another. The two superpowers, the United States and the U.S.S.R., invest substantially in nuclear weapons and missiles. Beyond this, the U.S.S.R. has emphasized the development of a large land army, since it has long borders with potential enemies in China and Europe. The United States, with its peaceful borders, has emphasized more the development of its navy, so that it can keep in touch with its allies around the world and support them.

The military often play a special role in Third World states, simply because they are often the most "modern," best-organized group. They may figure importantly in the politics of the state, as we shall see in Chapter 13. But beyond this, they may serve as an important modernizing force. An organization through which thousands of young men pass each year, in which they are

[3]Ibid.

Table 4–4   Educational Effort for Selected States

	Percent of GNP Spent on Education	Percent of Eligible Youth Enrolled in High School	Adult Literacy Rate (percent)
U.S.S.R. (C)*	6.8	—	99
China (C)	2.7	42	65
Canada (I)	7.4	92	98
France (I)	6.0	86	98
West Germany (I)	4.6	70	99
Great Britain (I)	5.4	81	99
United States (I)	6.7	90	99
Algeria (T)	6.1	45	45
Costa Rica (T)	5.2	36	95
Israel (T)	10.2	79	88
Haiti (T)	1.2	18	35
India (T)	3.6	35	41
Tanzania (T)	5.9	3	46

*C = communist state; I = industrialized democracy; T = Third World
SOURCE: UNESCO, *Statistical Yearbook, 1988*.

taught disciplined methods of sanitation and organization, in which they learn how to use machinery, and so on—and from which they often return to their home villages—can be an important educational force as well as serving to defend the state.[4]

EDUCATION

The most basic service that most governments are expected to offer their people is education. This is a prerequisite of economic development for the country as a whole, and it greatly expands the world of the individuals who are educated. Many Third World nations, whose populations were largely illiterate at the time independence was acquired, have had an uphill fight in bringing education to their peoples.

As Table 4–4 shows, most countries invest a substantial effort in this area of policy and most Third World countries have already accomplished a good deal along these lines. Others have had to overcome great difficulties. One of these, Tanzania, clearly exemplifies the problems faced by a poor Third World state in attempting to educate its people. It takes over 4 percent of Tanzania's gross national product simply to make a good stab at education. Even at that, not

[4]See for example John J. Johnson, ed., *The Role of the Military in Underdeveloped Countries* (Princeton, N.J.: Princeton University Press, 1962).

many "frills" are possible; only 3 percent of youths between the ages of fourteen and seventeen were enrolled in school in 1982. And progress takes time; only 46 percent of adults could read in 1982, though this represented a dramatic improvement over the 10 percent adult literacy rate of 1960.

RESEARCH AND DEVELOPMENT

If Third World states must concentrate on spreading basic education throughout their populations, the more highly developed economies of the industrialized democracies and of communist systems depend on continuing technological development to give them a competitive edge in making "high-tech" goods (computers, electrical machinery, aircraft, etc.) for export. In most of these developed economies, labor costs are too high to allow basic industries such as the manufacture of clothing or of simple plastic goods to be competitive internationally. Third World states can produce such goods much more cheaply. The special province of the developed economies is in the production of high-tech goods and services, where their scientific and technological capacities allow them to outperform everyone else.[5]

Table 4–5 shows how dependent the industrialized democracies, in particular, are on high-tech industry for their trade with other states. Over half of all United States exports were high-tech goods. When we consider that about an additional 20 percent of United States exports were products of agriculture, we can see that the United States functions in the economic world almost entirely as a producer of foodstuffs and of high-tech goods.

In all countries, the technology that makes this sort of industry possible is provided partly by government-sponsored research, partly by research carried on directly by the industries involved, and partly by basic research conducted in universities and other institutions of higher education. A good idea of the general level of such activity in a country may be gained by observing the number of scientists and engineers in the population. This figure is displayed for several states in the second column of Table 4–5, which gives the number of scientists and engineers engaged in research and development.

HEALTH AND SOCIAL WELFARE

Most modern states have accepted some responsibility for maintaining their people in reasonable health, in adequate housing, with financial security in their old age, and with some security against disability or disaster. Generally speaking, developed economies, whether communist or democratic, devote considerable resources to these purposes, while Third World states generally

[5]This idea, and its implications for economic policy, are developed in Andrew Shonfield, *Modern Capitalism* (Oxford, England: Oxford University Press, 1965). See also Robert Teich, *The Next American Frontier* (New York: Times Books, 1983).

Table 4–5   Involvement of Selected States in Research & Development

	Percent of All Exports That Are "High-Tech" Goods (machinery, electronic equipment, precision instruments, weapons, etc.)	Number of Scientists & Engineers Engaged in Research & Development (thousands)	Governmental Spending on Research & Development as a Percent of GNP	Percent of Public Education Operating Budget Expended on Higher Education
U.S.S.R. (C)*	12.1	1,501	5.1	12.6
Canada (I)	43.0	38	1.5	28.8
France (I)	40.1	102	2.3	12.3
West Germany (I)	52.8	133	2.5	20.8
Great Britain (I)	44.4	87	2.2	21.4
United States (I)	54.5	787	2.8	38.3
Japan (I)	76.5	575	2.8	21.4
Egypt (T)	0.6	21	0.2	32.7
Central African Republic (T)	0.0	0	0.2	18.8
Israel (T)	21.1	39	2.5	19.3
Brazil (T)	14.3	33	0.7	19.6
South Korea (T)	36.8	47	1.8	10.3
India (T)	7.5	100	0.9	18.7

*C = communist state; I = industrialized democracy; T = Third World

SOURCES: United Nations, *Yearbook of International Trade Statistics, 1982*; UNESCO, *Statistical Yearbook, 1988*.

do not do as much. For the people of many Third World states, daily life is a series of catastrophes, and it is all they can do to deal with those, much less prepare for future ones. Third World governments must often use any surplus funds they have to develop systems of basic education or to build industrial plants for future economic growth. Finally, as we have already seen, many Third World states are burdened with large military budgets. All these circumstances put such strains on the economies of Third World states that social programs are put on a back burner. Israel is perhaps an extreme case of this because of its exposed military position, but it illustrates the point nicely, if with a bit of exaggeration. Military spending and interest payments on its debts and a development budget (for dams, irrigation, etc.) took 65 percent of the national budget for 1987–88. That Israel devoted 23.9 percent out of the remaining 35 percent to social programs is actually evidence of a great devotion to social welfare, though the amount is small compared to what is spent in the developed economies.

This pattern is evident in the first column of Table 4–6, which lists the proportion of national budgets devoted to such items as health, recreation, unemployment insurance, pension systems, housing, and so on. These figures must

Table 4–6   Social Welfare Activity by Selected Governments

	Percent of National Budget Spent on Health, Welfare, Housing, Pensions, etc.	Percent of New Housing Built by Government or Semipublic Agencies
Czechoslovakia (C)*	N.A.†	30.8
Canada (I)	41.1	N.A.
Sweden (I)	N.A.	28.2
France (I)	N.A.	18.4
West Germany (I)	N.A.	1.5
Great Britain (I)	42.8	21.7
United States (I)	42.6	0.1
Japan (I)	24.2	6.6
Bolivia (T)	21.3	35.0
Israel (T)	23.9	25.5
Morocco (T)	9.4	4.0
Papua New Guinea (T)	11.6	66.4
Kenya (T)	6.9	N.A.
South Korea (T)	N.A.	58.2
Syria (T)	N.A.	13.2
Lesotho (T)	8.3	N.A.

*C = communist state; I = industrialized democracy; T = Third World
†Not available.
SOURCES: *Europa Yearbook 1988* (London: Europa, 1988); United Nations, *Construction Statistics Yearbook 1985*.

be treated with caution, since spending by local governments is not included, and it is often difficult to tell exactly what the label on a budget item means. The broad pattern, however, is clear: The governments of developed economic systems make a considerable effort to ensure social welfare, whereas the governments of Third World systems do not.

What sorts of things do governments do in order to promote social welfare? A vast number of programs have been used in one country or another for this purpose. To name a few: Governments may provide child-care centers for working parents, psychiatric counseling for emotionally troubled people, medical care for their citizens—as the British government does and as the United States does for poor people and for all people over age sixty-five; governments may build residential housing and offer it at inexpensive rates; governments may give grants of money to all families with children, to help them with the costs of child rearing (most European governments do this); governments may provide some sort of minimal national pension for people too old to work; and so on. There is a bewildering array of programs, and countries vary widely in the extent to which they give one or another kind of aid. The second column of Table 4–6 illustrates this diversity in one area of social welfare policy, the provision of residential housing. The activity of governments listed in the table varies from Papua New Guinea, where the government constructs 66 percent of all housing, to the United States, where the government constructs less than 1 percent.

REDISTRIBUTION OF INCOME

In all states of the world, incomes are distributed unequally—that is, some people make a good deal more money than others. Many governments make some effort to ease these differences in income by taking money from those who are better-off and redistributing it to those who are poorer.

Such efforts are of two types: (1) special subsidies and aids for the poor and (2) systems of "progressive taxation." A progressive tax is one that takes a greater percentage of income from a person who is relatively well-off and a smaller percentage from one who is not doing so well. Graduated income taxes are designed to be progressive, though they are often filled with loopholes that benefit the rich. This, of course, makes the tax less progressive. For instance, if an income tax is set up so that a person earning $5,000 a year pays no tax, a person earning $20,000 a year pays $2,000 (or 10 percent of that income), and a person earning $50,000 pays $10,000 (or 20 percent of that income), then the tax is progressive.

Not all taxes are progressive. Many are "regressive" in that they take a higher percentage of poor people's income than they do of the income of those who are better-off. The social security tax in the United States is an example. In 1989, workers in the United States had to pay 7.5 percent of their income, up to a maximum income of $48,000, to social security. Any income over this amount was untaxed; thus a person earning $10,000 a year paid 7.5 of that in social security taxes, whereas a person earning $60,000 a year paid only 6.0 percent.

In the United States over recent years, taking all sorts of levies into account, the progressive and regressive taxes have just about canceled one another out, so that people's relative incomes have been about the same before and after taxes.

Governments have not been very active in redistributing incomes, because those who have high incomes also usually have a good deal of political clout and are able to defend themselves vigorously. Table 4–7 displays income inequalities in a number of countries. In the table, the percentage of all income that goes to the poorest 20 percent is compared to the percentage of all income that goes to the richest 20 percent of the population. The greater this difference is, the more unequally incomes are distributed.

Three things are apparent in this table. First of all, Third World states are often burdened with considerably greater inequality of incomes than are developed economies. It is paradoxical that in the midst of the poverty, especially of Asian and Latin American Third World states, there may be found a small group of people who are quite rich. Modern development—with its widespread education, mobility of populations, trade unions, and so on—alleviates inequality somewhat, but for a country with a backward economy, deep inequalities may remain.

Table 4–7   Income Inequality in Selected States

	Percent of National Income Earned by Poorest 20% of Population	Percent of National Income Earned by Richest 20% of Population	Difference
Yugoslavia (C)*	6.6	38.7	32.1
Hungary (C)	6.9	35.8	28.9
Canada (I)	5.3	40.0	34.7
Great Britain (I)	7.0	39.7	32.7
United States (I)	5.3	39.9	34.6
Sweden (I)	7.4	41.7	34.3
Israel (T)	6.0	39.9	33.9
India (T)	7.0	49.4	42.4
Philippines (T)	5.2	52.5	47.3
Ivory Coast (T)	2.4	61.4	59.0
Mexico (T)	2.9	57.7	54.8

*C = communist state; I = independent democracy; T = Third World

SOURCE: World Bank, *World Development Report, 1987*.

The table also shows that if governments make an effort to do so, they can redistribute incomes somewhat. The two communist systems, at the top, are among the least unequal states. Among industrialized democracies, Great Britain and Sweden have made special efforts to redistribute income; both have large and steeply progressive income taxes. And these two countries, along with the two communist systems, are among the least unequal, although the differences between them and the other industrialized states are small.

The clearest message of this table is that incomes are unequal in *all* systems. Even strenuous governmental efforts have relatively little effect.

ECONOMIC DEVELOPMENT

This item has been left to the last not because it is unimportant but because every other act of government we have considered depends on this one, so it seems to fall logically at the end. Except for actually keeping the boundaries of the state intact, there is probably nothing that citizens demand of their governments more urgently than this—that the economy grow so that people will be better-off from one year to the next.

The best way to measure the growth of economies is to compare the change in per capita real income from one year to the next—that is, the annual change in the people's average income adjusted to take the effects of inflation into account.

Figure 4–2 shows on a map of the world the average annual growth, 1960 to 1986, in per capita real income for each country.

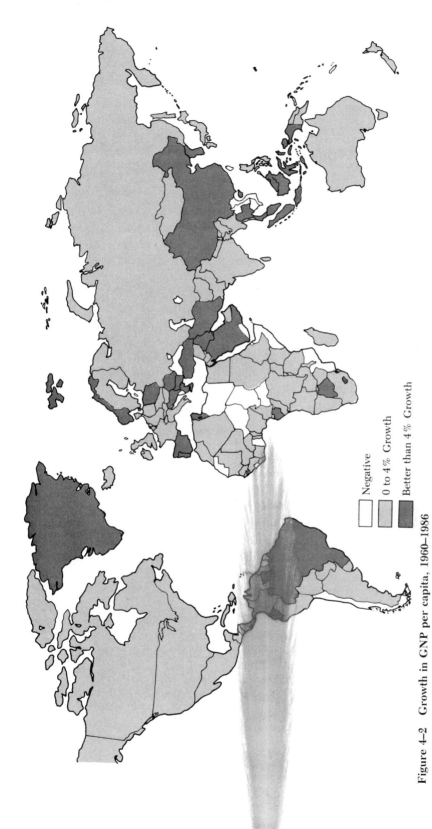

Figure 4–2 Growth in GNP per capita, 1960–1986

SOURCE United Nations Conference on Trade and Development. *Handbook of International Trade and Development Statistics, Supplement,* 1987.

Negative

0 to 4% Growth

Better than 4% Growth

One thing to note from the map is that this was a period of economic progress for most of the world. In 111 out of 133 countries, average per capita real income grew from 1960 to 1986. While the world generally did well, however, there was a good deal of variation from one state to another. How might we explain such variations?

In what must be a frustrating aspect of this map from the standpoint of politicians, one is forced to the conclusion that politics—that is, what governments do—had rather little to do with how rapidly their states' economies grew at this time. Communist Bulgaria and Romania grew at a faster rate than democratic western Europe, but the noncommunist eastern European states (Greece, Austria, Finland) grew rapidly as well, and conservative, noncommunist Japan was one of the great economic growth stories worldwide. The communist People's Republic of China and noncommunist Republic of China (Taiwan) grew at about the same rates. And the oil-rich states of the Persian Gulf grew almost no matter what sort of governments they had. Strategic position with regard to markets; availability of cheap, competent labor; the possession of natural resources—these, rather than political factors, seem to have dominated in determining economic growth. One sad fact is that the poorest states became still poorer over the period, at least "poorer" compared to the rest of the world. The average annual growth rate of these poorest states was only .70 percent. And during this period of generally increasing prosperity around the world, per capita income *declined* in fifteen states, all but one of which were poor to start with. On the other hand, most of the star performers (Romania, Bulgaria, Malta, Hong Kong, South Korea, Singapore, and Botswana), all of which grew at rates over 6 percent annually over the whole twenty-six-year period, all started from a poor base. Obviously the range of possible outcomes is greater for a poor country. Established industrial countries will not vary greatly in their performance. For poor countries, however, leadership and luck can make huge differences.

THE PLACE OF POWER IN POLICY ANALYSIS

Since we have been looking in this chapter at policies, which are the product of the state, it is easy to lapse into an almost pure "choice" perspective. We are, after all, looking at a variety of choices that states have made, and it is easy to forget the interchanges of power lying behind the states' decisions.

This is indeed a common failing of specialists in the study of policy. Since they deal with the policies that states have adopted, it is easy for them to begin to treat states as unitary actors, as "black boxes" that produce policy. If they lose the habit of looking inside the black box to see why a particular policy came out, they may lose touch with reality in their analysis of policy. Good policy analysis will not only assess the objective merits of a policy but will also take into account the political constraints under which the policy must work. For instance, any reasonable assessment of U.S. policy in banning the use of

marijuana should take into account the difficulty of enforcing that law, the con-
nivance of local governments with marijuana farmers, and so on. Once again,
we see that even when our subject matter pulls us rather strongly toward one
of the poles of power and choice, good analysis requires that we retain both
perspectives to at least some extent.

EXAMPLE: NORWAY'S PROGRAM TO ENCOURAGE NORWEGIAN-LANGUAGE PUBLICATIONS

As an example of how a state may address a problem
through governmental policy, consider the plight of writers and publishers in Norway. Norway has a population of
only about 4 million, roughly that of the state of Iowa.
Few people outside of Norway can read Norwegian, so an
author who publishes a book written in Norwegian is limited to a relatively small potential market. By contrast, the
potential worldwide market of an author writing in En-
glish is over 500 million, that of a Spanish author is about 250 million, and
that of a Japanese author is over 100 million. How can a publishing house
whose potential market is limited to just 4 million do enough business to
survive? Left to its own devices, it would be forced to charge such high
prices that no one could afford to buy its books. The Norwegian government—which, like most Scandinavian governments, is not shy about inter-
posing itself in social choices in order to accomplish what it sees as worthy
goals—has developed a complex set of policies to help publishers of materials written in Norwegian.

First of all, in Norway, the normal sales tax of 20 percent is not charged on
books, which lowers their cost substantially (and artificially) compared with
other things consumers may choose to spend their money on. In addition, the
government buys the first 1,000 copies of every new Norwegian-language book
of fiction, drama, or poetry and then donates them to public libraries. As a
result, a publisher can be certain that sales on such books will never be less
than 1,000 copies.

To lower the price of books further, the government also helps with the
publisher's payment of royalties to authors. Norwegian authors receive a royalty of 20 percent of the sales price on each copy of their book, but the government contributes half of that to the publisher on the first 3,000 books sold
and one-fourth of the royalty for the next 2,000 books. This means that the cost
to the publishers is lower and that they can charge their customers lower
prices.

There are additional special subsidies for types of books the government
especially wishes to see published: classic Norwegian works, illustrated children's books, and books written in minority dialects.

Finally, all booksellers are required by law to keep any new Norwegian title in stock for three years after it appears, whether people wish to buy it or not, in order to give it a fair chance.

As you can see, the state intervenes directly and in very precise detail to encourage publication in the Norwegian language. In this way, it can help to keep the language alive and protect it from being displaced by neighboring languages such as German or English.

EXAMPLE: A VILLAGE IN SRI LANKA

 Below, a correspondent for *The Economist* describes how governmental policies affected the people's lives in a village of Sri Lanka in 1981:

The villagers ask: "What are we going to do?" The predicament of Makandana, a small village 30 miles east of Colombo where your correspondent recently spent some days, is that successive oil shocks have put a bare subsistence diet beyond almost every family's means. It is one of Sri Lanka's new villages, settled in 1976. Each of its 122 families was given a meagre eighth of an acre of land on an expropriated rubber estate. The country's farmers, who own on average three acres, grow most of their own food; it is the landless, or the nearly-landless, who make up 40–45% of Sri Lanka's people, who are running out of food and hope.

Even faced with hunger, there is warmth and colour to rural Sri Lanka. The meanest hut will have a garden and the coconuts, bamboo, bananas and paddy, like the island's rubber and tea plantations, deceptively promise abundance. Long years of free universal education and health care mean an 88% literacy rate and a life expectancy of 67 among a remarkably gentle, tolerant and cheerful people.

Until lately there was a new sense of dynamism. President Jayawardene, who in 1977 took over from the socialist governments that had run Sri Lanka for the previous 20 years, has concentrated spending on agricultural productivity. He is trying to draw private and foreign investment into export industries. Fifteen months ago Mr. Jayawardene abolished the food rationing system which, for almost 40 years, had provided Sri Lanka's people (now 15.4m) with free or subsidised rice, sugar and kerosene. The poorest, with monthly incomes of $15 or less, still get food stamps.

Will Mr. Jayawardene's prescription work in time? In Makandana village, it seems not. Food prices trebled last year. Then, in October, the government, under pressure from soaring oil costs, raised bus and train fares 80%.

Except for the cassava, coconuts, and fruit they grow in their gardens, nearly three-quarters of the village's men depend on $1-a-day field labour, when they can get it. Only eight men from the village work in Colombo; since bus fares doubled to $1 a round trip, half of what they earn goes on the journey. The fishmonger and other peddlars bringing goods from Colombo have raised their prices too. It used to take about $37 a month to feed the average household of seven; now it takes $50 and nobody makes that much. Village women tap rubber trees, make lace or weave baskets, making 30–50 cents daily. Others try to sell batiks to tourists, but lack designing skills.

Worst off are two ex-mechanics, members of a group of 60,000–80,000 who were sacked last July from government jobs for taking part in an attempted general strike to demand higher wages. Now nobody will give them a job. Best off is a carpenter back from six months in Saudi Arabia, one of about 50,000 Sri Lankans working temporarily in the Gulf states who together sent home remittances of about $80m last year; he has $1,250 in the bank.

Asked who is to blame for their troubles, the villagers invariably answer, "the government". Officially, Sri Lanka's number of unemployed is about 800,000; inflation in 1980 was estimated 32%. In Makandana, only a few of the 854 people had full-time jobs and inflation was closer to 200–300%; there is gross malnutrition.

Immediate help has come only from Sri Lanka's *Sarvodaya* ("awakening") movement for village self-development, which has spread to 4,000 of the island's 23,000 villages in the past few years. Operating on a $1.6m budget contributed by west European voluntary agencies, mostly Dutch, German and British, the movement came to Makandana two years ago when several thousand young volunteers spent three days building the village's first access road. It has since set up a preschool children's centre, various community groups, and has hired skilled carpenters and masons to teach the villagers how to build new brick and tile-roofed houses to replace Makandana's thatched mud huts. The basic thrust is to find the villagers jobs.[6]

FURTHER READING

General Studies of Policy:

Heclo, Hugh. *Modern Social Politics in Britain and Sweden*. New Haven, Conn.: Yale University Press, 1974.

Heidenheimer, Arnold J., Heclo, Hugh, and Adams, Carolyn. *Comparative Public Policy*. 3rd ed. New York: St. Martin's, 1990.

Shonfield, Andrew. *Modern Capitalism*. Oxford, England: Oxford University Press, 1965.

Studies of Particular Areas of Policy, Mostly American:

Alford, Robert R. *Health Care Politics*. Chicago: University of Chicago Press, 1975.

Coulter, Philip B. *Measuring Inequality*. Boulder, Colo.: Westview Press, 1989.

Lange, P., and Garrett, G. "The Politics of Growth: Strategic Interaction and Economic Performance in the Advanced Industrial Democracies, 1974–1980." *Journal of Politics* 47 (August 1985): 792–827.

Page, Benjamin I. *Who Gets What from Government*. Berkeley: University of California Press, 1983.

[6]*The Economist*, March 21, 1981, pp. 46–47.

Pechman, Joseph A., ed. *Setting National Priorities: The 1984 Budget*. Washington, D.C.: Brookings, 1983.

Peterson, Paul. *City Limits*. Chicago: University of Chicago Press, 1981.

Piven, Frances Fox, and Cloward, Richard A. *Regulating the Poor*. New York: Pantheon, 1971.

Russett, Bruce. *What Price Vigilance?* New Haven, Conn.: Yale University Press, 1970.

Chapter 5

Political Choices: The Problems of Fairness and Efficiency [1]

In the preceding chapter we reviewed the varying functions that governments do (or do not do) on behalf of their people. What are the considerations that lie behind these policies? What things must the leaders and their people think about in considering what the state should do? If you were the leader of a state, what sorts of policies would you opt for? On the "choice" side of "power and choice," how should a group of people choose?

There seem to be two broad characteristics that almost everyone wants to see in state policies: (1) the policies should be "fair"—that is, people in the state should be treated in the way they deserve—and (2) the policies should be "efficient," producing the greatest good at the least cost. As you might expect, the problem with these criteria is that both are multifaceted and hard to pin down. In addition, even these two broad criteria sometimes come into conflict, since what is most "fair" may not be most "efficient," and vice versa. Sorting out the various factors that make one policy "good" and another "bad" is more an art than a science, and people of goodwill may frequently come up with differing conclusions regarding a policy. In this chapter, we shall look at some of the things that go to make a policy "fair" or "efficient" and also, perhaps, come to see how complex the final evaluation of a policy must be.

FAIRNESS AND THE PROBLEM OF JUSTICE

What do we mean by "fairness," by the notion that people should be treated "as they deserve"? One important element of fairness is our idea of *justice*, the idea that people should be treated *justly*. But what does this mean?

Does justice consist of treating everyone equally? Surely not, since we can think of many instances in which treating everyone equally would seem quite unjust. If you had worked especially hard on a paper but your instructor decided to give everyone in the class the same grade, this would seem unjust.

---

[1] Any author of an introductory book owes debts to many people, but in this chapter a special debt is owed to Charles Anderson, whose splendid book *Statecraft* (New York: Wiley, 1977) pursues similar themes in more detail and with greater elegance than we have done here.

You had worked hard, while others sloughed off, yet all got the same reward. *Different members of the class had contributed different amounts, and justice would seem to require that they be rewarded accordingly.* A rather different consideration appears in the following example: Suppose six people were waiting on a corner on a cold, rainy day, and one of the six was suffering from asthma. Suppose further that a car came along that could take only one additional passenger. Equal treatment would require that the six draw lots to see who should get to go in the car. But would not justice require that the other five defer to the asthma victim, who was suffering more from the rain than they were? In this case, justice would seem to require that the person whose *needs* were greatest should get special treatment.

Should justice, then, be based solely on the weight of contributions or solely on need? Neither of these can provide a sufficient basis for justice, though obviously both are part of the picture.

There are many problems with the "weight of contributions." People's contributions are frequently as much a matter of luck as of virtue, and we are often a bit queasy when rewards are based solely on such "lucky" contributions. To continue with the example of grades, what if you worked very hard on your paper but a friend, who happened to have been born very intelligent, dashed off a brilliant piece in one evening while drinking beer and got a better grade than you did? You would probably have mixed feelings about the justice of the grades. Or, to follow the same line of thought, is it just that Kirby Puckett should have been paid such a high salary simply because his shoulders and back happened to be so constructed as to help him hit the long ball? Or, is it just that a worker living in West Virginia should have so few opportunities to find a job as compared with a worker living in California? Contribution alone, then, cannot provide a sufficient criterion for determining justice. Contribution may often involve elements of luck, so that we are uncertain how much it should be rewarded. And looking only at contributions would cause us to ignore questions of need; even if four of the six people on the rainy corner had managed to stop a cab (thus contributing more than the other two), we might think it "just" if one of them were excluded to make a place for the asthma victim.

Similar problems arise if need alone is used as a criterion for justice. Like "contribution," "need" is a tricky thing, and we are not always sure that it should be rewarded. If some members of an office staff are having a hard time economically because of bad luck (or bad judgment) in the houses they bought and the debts they've run up, should they get bigger raises than members of the staff who are not in trouble economically? Should parents get better pay because they have children to support? Would this be unjust to single people who are doing the same work as the parents are doing? And again, if need alone were used as a criterion, this would mean that contribution would have to be ignored. To return finally to the example of grades, how would you feel if the papers were graded solely on the instructor's assessment of each student's need for a "positive self-image"?

Justice, then, is a complex issue. It involves a number of things that are often in conflict and need to be balanced—the contributions people have made, their varying needs, and even some further sense that people should not be treated *too* unequally. Not only do these things have to be balanced, but each of them is itself ambiguous and hard to pin down.

This does not mean that justice is an unworkable concept but simply that it is a difficult one. We all have a strong sense for the justice or injustice of certain things, and there is a good deal of agreement among us about these. If this were not so, the examples used above could not be expected to mean roughly the same thing to each reader. It is when we judge a question of justice differently, though, that we must tackle the problem of working out our disagreement. Different people will weigh contribution, need, and the necessity of equality differently, and they will also disagree on precisely what sort of need or what sort of contribution exists, or on just what sorts of things need to be equal. Many might see no injustice in Kirby Puckett's high salary. One could argue that the amount of pleasure he gave millions of people merited this sort of pay, or one could see a certain kind of justice in the fact that a black made so much money, or one could note the short period of earnings Puckett had open to him before he retired in his thirties.

Fairness? On June 7, 1976 officials in a small town in Pennsylvania notified a Mr. Selby that he would have to tear down a backyard tree house because he had not obtained a permit and the house exceeded the 40-foot height restriction. Mr. Selby ignored the notice, and the following month two police cars, a dump truck, and a power-line truck with a cherry picker returned to the tree house and demolished it.

(AUTH, by Tony Auth. Copyright, 1976, Philadelphia Inquirer. Reprinted with permission of Universal Press Syndicate. All Rights Reserved.)

Justice is a complex question, but one on which we can talk productively. By bringing out and examining the differing ways people evaluate contribution, need, and the necessity for equality and by examining the differing weights people place on each, we may at least *clarify* disagreements about the justice of a policy.

OTHER ASPECTS OF FAIRNESS

We entered into this long discussion of justice because justice is the primary component of "fairness"—the somewhat broader and vaguer term that designates one of this chapter's themes. We are concerned about how to judge when a policy is or is not "fair." Whether the policy is *just* is the most important part of this judgment, but it is not the only thing that enters in. Other things that may also make us see a policy as fair or unfair are: *(1) whether governmental action is "arbitrary," (2) whether special basic rights are violated, and (3) whether special overriding social needs are present.*

Arbitrary Policies and Due Process

Governmental action is *arbitrary* if decisions are made and communicated capriciously, that is, if the people affected by a decision do not know what to expect before the decision is made and do not learn on what grounds it was made. Decisions that single out particular individuals for punishment or reward are arbitrary decisions. For instance, highway patrols sometimes appear to be especially strict in enforcing speed limits and other regulations on "hot-looking" souped-up cars just because of the cars' appearance. This is arbitrary action. Librarians are acting arbitrarily when they allow people owing fines to escape without paying provided that they are "properly sorry about having been late." In some dictatorships such as Nazi Germany or Idi Amin's Uganda, a person could be executed simply because someone in the government bore a grudge against him or her. This was the worst sort of arbitrary terror.

Note that the question of arbitrariness is not exactly the same as the question of justice. A policy we regard as unjust might be reached by means we admit are not arbitrary. And arbitrary means might even produce results we considered just![2] Regardless of the justice of the result, however, arbitrariness lessens the fairness of a policy.

The notion of *due process* has evolved to help control arbitrary decision making. This is the idea that certain standard procedures must always be followed in making some policies, and that if those procedures were not followed in making a given policy, then the policy should be void. This prevents

---

[2]This often produces uneasiness about legal processes in the United States and other countries with protections against arbitrary criminal investigation. If the police had stopped a "souped-up" car and found a bloody ax in the back seat, justice would require that the driver be investigated for murder. However, the initial search was arbitrary, and a court might well dismiss the evidence on the grounds that it had been obtained unfairly. Citizens frequently find it difficult to appreciate these distinctions.

policymakers from acting arbitrarily, since they obviously want to see their policies stick. To keep from having their policies voided, they stay within the standard set of procedures in making policy.

This sort of standardization involves some costs in that it lessens governmental flexibility. Generally it is not set up for all areas of policymaking. Britain, the United States, and Canada especially emphasize due process in criminal trials, because historically those countries have been especially concerned to protect their citizens from unfair prosecution by the government. In criminal trials in English-speaking countries, due process generally consists of the following:

1. People may not be accused of crimes unless they could have learned of the existence and meaning of the law before they committed their acts.
2. When people are accused of crimes, they are entitled to know what crimes are charged, they are entitled to know on what evidence the charges are based, and they are entitled to gather and present their own evidence to rebut the charges.
3. Judges must be disinterested, unbiased, and attentive.
4. Once a judgment has been made, some means for later reconsideration must be available. If any of these conditions has been violated in an American, Canadian, or British court except under certain special circumstances, the trial is ruled invalid.[3]

In other areas of policy, such as the setting of regulations, assignment of people to schools, levying of taxes, and so on, the general spirit of due process is still supposed to be followed—that is, policymaking is not to be arbitrary— but there are usually not such precise and strict rules to safeguard due process.

Special Basic Rights

Another added factor that enters into considerations of fairness is the existence of certain basic rights whose violation is thought to be unfair in and of itself. Such rights have a special status in that only extraordinary circumstances would make it appropriate for policymakers to violate them for anyone. Although almost everyone would think that some such rights exist, it is not always possible to get people to agree on exactly which rights have this status. Three rights that have frequently been held to have the special status are:

1. *The right to survive:* It can be argued that since death negates all other rights, the right not to be killed should be kept almost absolute. Opposition to capital punishment is often based on this idea, as is opposition to abortion.
2. *The right of free speech:* It can be argued that since politics itself depends on the exchange of ideas, policymakers should be especially reluctant to regulate the expression of ideas, because decreasing the flow of ideas decreases politics itself.

---

[3]To some extent this is an idealization of what happens. In fact, American courts, at least, are badly overworked and many shortcuts are tolerated to move the business through. For instance, in "plea bargaining," a deal is struck between the accused, the prosecutor, and the judge by which the accused pleads guilty to a lesser charge, the prosecutor's original charge is withdrawn, and the trial ends. Thus many of the theoretical protections listed above are avoided.

3. *The right to privacy:* It can be argued that if one's very personality is to exist, there must be some space that can be called one's own, where no one else may peek in, and that governments must if at all possible respect those boundaries. It is for this reason that in British, Canadian, and American law people may not be compelled to speak about themselves in court and wives or husbands may not be compelled to testify against their spouses.

Few people, if any, would hold any of these special rights to be *absolute*. Most people would agree that it would have been good if Hitler had been assassinated in 1942, even those who believe strongly in the right to survive. Almost everyone recognizes that the special right of free speech must have some restrictions, as well; the classic example is that no one should have the right to yell "Fire!" in a crowded theater. Similarly, there must also be some ultimate limits to the right to privacy.

Thus "special rights" are not absolute. But to the extent that the idea of special rights is accepted, a society sets aside those rights as having a top priority, so that it would take something unusual for us to compromise them. Fairness, under these circumstances, may require that justice, or even due process, might have to be tempered in the interests of one or another special right. As one example of this, many people have opposed the establishment of a central, computerized data file of information about Americans because they are concerned about the potential abuses of people's right to privacy that could result if all official information about a person—military record, tax returns, criminal record, health information, record in school, and so on—were brought together and made easily accessible. Those opposing the file grant that justice might be better served if such a file existed, since tax fraud and other crimes would be easier to detect, but they think that the right to privacy is more important than these needs of justice.

Overriding Social Needs

Finally, fairness in a broad sense may require that in order to be fair to most of the people, the state must be less fair to some people. That is, there may be overriding social needs which enter into considerations of fairness. The best example is the military draft. In many countries, young men (and at least in Israel, women) are required to serve a fixed period of time in the military, whether they wish to do so or not. The reasoning behind this is that the people of the state need to have a strong army, but it is difficult to get people to serve in an army of their own free will. Therefore some people must be compelled to do so for the greater general good. Similarly, affirmative action programs for employment in the United States often require that minorities and women should be given a slightly better than even break in hiring decisions (even though an even break would be the "just" decision) to help overcome historic patterns of unjust decisions going the opposite way. The argument is that society will benefit from an integrated work force and that at least modest levels of individual injustice during the transition period are not too great a price to pay.

Another example of this sort of consideration is seen during wars. When they are at war, most countries subordinate almost everything else to winning the war. Among the subordinated things is a concern for individual justice, due process, and special individual rights. Governments are often given extraordinary powers during wars, and they are not expected to be primarily concerned with fairness to individuals. Sometimes governments do things during war that they later regret. The internment of hundreds of thousands of Japanese-Americans in prison camps during World War II, simply because of their national origin, is a shameful piece of America's past that occurred under the stress of war.

Revolutionary governments often justify suspensions of due process and justice because of the great good that will eventually result from the revolution. Thousands of British sympathizers were driven into Canada at the end of the American Revolution; aristocrats and many others were beheaded during the French Revolution; and millions of farmers were executed or deported to forced-labor camps in the Soviet Union in the 1930s.

Each of the examples given here—the draft, affirmative action, wartime civil liberties, the needs of a revolution—in fact, any claim to an overriding social need, is based on an assumption that ends can justify means. This assumption should not be too easily accepted *nor* too readily rejected. It would be wrong to read into the assumption an exaggerated claim that means can be ignored. Clearly, there are many means that cannot be justified by many ends. The internment of Japanese-Americans by the U.S. government during World War II did nothing to help the American war effort; even if it had helped in small ways, the enormity of the injustice would not have been worth it. That internment was unjustified. Similarly, even though many Soviet citizens have benefited greatly from the Russian Revolution, the immense human suffering during that revolution and the continuing limitation of free speech in the Soviet Union were and are unjustified.

But if we should not accept too easily the notion that ends can justify means, neither should we reject it totally. Some social ends, such as an integrated work force or secure national borders, may be worth modest degrees of individual injustice. *Some* ends can clearly justify *some* means—as anyone must agree who has ever told a "little white lie"!

In the end, then, we see that "fairness" is a mix of several things: justice (which is itself a mix of concerns for contribution, need, and equality); governmental action that is not arbitrary; consideration of special rights; and the possibility of overriding social needs. It is because so many things are involved that people can honestly disagree on whether a policy is fair. At the same time, being aware of what goes into "fairness" can help us to understand and work out such disagreements.

EFFICIENCY

We have seen that one question for the policymaker is whether a policy is *fair*, both to individuals and to society as a whole. The other basic question is whether the policy is *efficient*. An efficient policy is *one that gives the state and the people of the state the greatest benefits at the least cost*. The trick in dealing with efficiency is that often neither the benefits nor the costs of a policy are easy to calculate.

First, many of the effects of a policy are difficult to measure and compare. They bring up the old problem of "apples and oranges" in its severest form. How can we compare the amount of recreational value gained by building a dam and the value of the protection against flooding that is gained by building it against the cost of pain and inconvenience of those who have to leave their homes to make way for it, the economic loss of farm production on the flooded lands, and the government's cost in constructing it? There is no common unit by which to measure recreational value, protection against flooding, pain and inconvenience, and agricultural loss, so it is difficult to say whether in this case the gains are greater than the costs.

A second reason why the costs and benefits of a policy are not always clear is that policies always have a variety of effects, many of which one cannot anticipate when the policy is set up. These are often referred to as the *unanticipated consequences* of a policy.

As one example of such an unanticipated consequence, consider the following: A study of phosphate pollution of Lake Erie—which had at one time killed off almost all life in the lake—yielded the surprising finding that in the 1960s the level of phosphates in the lake had jumped sharply and had remained at that high level thereafter. It appeared that some massive new source of pollution had appeared on the scene at the time of the jump in phosphate levels, but no such new source could be found. On investigation it turned out that at the time of the jump, the state of Michigan had ordered Michigan steel mills to stop dumping waste acid into the lake. The acid had been combining with phosphates in the water to form a solid, which then dropped to the bottom of the lake. In other words, the acid had been cleaning phosphates out of the lake water, and when, in the name of *pollution control*, the source of acid was shut off, phosphate levels in the water shot up!

This is only one of the numerous incidental costs and benefits of stopping the dumping of acid into Lake Erie, many of which may not have been anticipated. As another example of the varied effects that a policy may have, consider the social security program of the United States. This is a fairly simple program. As of 1989, all employed workers except government employees paid a tax of 7.5 percent of their salary (up to a maximum salary of $48,000), and their employers paid a matching tax of the same amount. From the proceeds of this tax, pensions are paid to people of age sixty-five and above who have retired; also, support payments are paid to disabled workers and to children of workers who have died young. The direct purpose of the program is to provide a national system of pensions and catastrophe insurance. Among the many *side* effects of the program, some good and some bad, are the following:

1. People with low salaries are taxed relatively more heavily than people with high salaries (see page 77). Thus, the distribution of incomes in the state is made less equal.

2. Retired people have been made less dependent economically on their families. This has surely been a good thing for them, but it may also have helped to lessen the ties of the extended family, which are already weak in our highly mobile society.
3. The age of retirement has been made more or less standard nationally.
4. Because people are encouraged to retire at age sixty-five rather than at a later age, the overall production of goods and services has been reduced for the country and all the people are economically somewhat less well-off than they would otherwise be.
5. But conversely, the policy has allowed many who wish to stop working at age sixty-five to do so without being forced by economic need to work on beyond that age.
6. The payroll tax on employers takes a higher percentage of the payroll for low-pay employees than for high-pay employees. For example, the employer pays a tax of 7.5 percent of the salary of an employee who earns $30,000 a year but 4.0 percent of the salary of an employee who earns $90,000 a year. Thus the policy encourages industries like the electronics and computer industries, which have highly paid work forces, while it discriminates against industries like steel and automobile manufacturing, which employ large numbers of workers at lower pay. This encourages the development of clean industries with a great deal of potential for export sales, but it also hurts the economically weak industrial areas of the northeastern United States.

As this example shows, even a fairly simple program like social security has many effects beyond those for which it was originally designed. Some of these were not anticipated by the designers and have probably not yet even been noticed by scholars. Certainly the above list does not include all the consequences of the social security plan.

As a final example of the unintended consequences of policy, some studies have suggested that stiffer penalties for those caught driving while intoxicated may have led to an increase in hit-and-run accidents, as drunk drivers flee the scene of accidents in order to avoid the stiffened punishment for driving while intoxicated.

Any judgment as to the *efficiency* of a policy must take into account *all* its costs and benefits—insofar as we can guess what these are—not just the *intended* costs and benefits. It is often hard to put a price tag on these, as we have seen in the example of social security; we are usually comparing apples, oranges, bananas, and grapefruit. And many of the consequences may be difficult to foresee. As a result, it is just as much an art to judge the efficiency of a policy as to judge its fairness. There is nothing terrible in recognizing that policymaking is not an exact science; it is simply a good thing to realize that policy choices are neither simple nor direct.

MODES OF DECISION: INCREMENTAL VS. RADICAL

How do policymakers react to the complex and difficult decisions they must make? One important way in which they may differ is in style. A decision maker may, to varying degrees, take an *incremental* or a *radical* approach to the making of policy.

A decision maker who operates more *incrementally* will make only a small change in policy at any one time, wait to see what the results of that change are, then make another small change, and so on. A person who is worried about all the uncertainty in devising policies—and about the possibility of making big, costly mistakes—will tend to be an incrementalist. As we have seen above, it is often very difficult to assess all the costs and benefits of a policy; therefore an incrementalist stance is certainly not unreasonable.

A *radical* decision maker, on the other hand, is more concerned about lost opportunities than about the possibility of costly errors. A radical is likely to feel that while the incrementalist is creeping up on a decision, a chance for a decisive breakthrough may be lost. Sometimes, says the radical, bold action may accomplish something that could never be done in small steps. A decision maker of relatively radical mood might hasten to buy up land for a state park all at once, before land prices rise to prohibitive heights, rather than announce a ten-year plan for gradual land acquisition.

Neither one of these styles is necessarily preferable. Partly, the choice is a matter of individual personality, as some people are more averse to risk than others. The incrementalist's caution in the face of uncertainty and complexity makes a lot of sense, and so does the radical's worry that opportunities may be lost through slow, cautious movement.

Some types of policy seem to lend themselves better to one style of decision making than to the other. Anything based on age and generational change is probably best handled incrementally, for instance, because we know well in advance what is coming and all change is rather slow. Closing of schools or the expansion of school systems in response to changes in the number of school-age children can be managed incrementally, because we know years in advance what we can expect simply from local birthrates.

Military policies, on the other hand, often require boldness because even the difference of an hour can change a situation totally, as armies change position, attacks are launched, and so on. History's great generals—Napoleon, Robert E. Lee, and others—have been gamblers. During World War II, Winston Churchill constantly complained that his generals were too cautious, as in this memo to the first sea lord:

> It is now three weeks since I vetoed the proposal to evacuate the Eastern Mediterranean and bring Admiral Cunningham's fleet to Gibraltar. I hope there will be no return to that project. Anyone can see the risk from an attack which we run in the Central Mediterranean. From time to time and for sufficient objects this risk will have to be faced. Warships are meant to go under fire.[4]

So one would not wish to say that one or the other of these stances is *the* right one. Which mix of the two is best depends on circumstances and on the

---

[4]Winston Churchill, *The Second World War*, vol. 2 (Boston: Houghton Mifflin, 1949), p. 443.

character of the decision maker. What *is* true, though, is that modern politics tilts things heavily in favor of incrementalism. In fact, other than in revolutions themselves, radical policy changes are quite rare. Partly this is because in our complex and active societies a group will arise to protest vociferously against almost any change; such groups can usually force a compromise which is, in effect, an incremental change. The other reason for the predominance of incremental change is that officials and bureaucrats are rarely punished for a continuously unsatisfactory state of affairs, but they know that they *will* be punished for any dramatic failure. This leads some of them to be timid.

MODES OF DECISION: AUTHORITY VS. THE MARKET

Another very basic choice about policy is whether we want to rely more on *governmental authority* or on *market mechanisms* to carry it out. "Governmental authority" is just what it sounds like. Under governmental authority, policy is made by the government telling people what they may or may not do, how much they may spend on X, how much the country is to invest in Y, and so on. Many policies with which you are familiar are matters of governmental authority. The public school system, in which the government fixes a minimum number of years of education that each child must receive and sets up free public schools to provide that education, is an instance of policy provided by governmental authority. The system of highways and streets, in which the government decides where streets should run and then uses public money to build and maintain them, is another example. So is the nationalized coal industry of Great Britain, in which the government owns all coal mines and decides how much coal is to be mined, what sort of equipment is to be built, how much the miners are to be paid, and how much the coal will cost.

Under a "market mechanism," the government leaves the choice as to what people are to do, what goods they are to receive, and so on up to the people to choose for themselves. The government depends on the *costs* of action, of goods, and so on to restrain people in their choices so that they will end up choosing to do or buy only those things they most want (or can afford). In the coal industry of the United States, which is not nationalized, the choice as to how much coal is to be produced is a matter for a number of mine operators to decide on the basis of their operating costs; their decision is strongly affected by the choices of millions of customers as to how much coal they will buy at a given price. The policy decision—how much coal is to be produced—which in Britain is made directly by the government, is made in the United States by the interplay of a large number of individual decisions.

In a modification of the market mechanism, a government may leave a policy to be settled by the market but may intervene to structure the individual decisions that go to make up the market choice.[5] Almost every country, for

---

[5]See above, pp. 67–68.

Incrementalism: Normative and Empirical Analysis

Analysis in political science may be of either the normative sort or the empirical. Normative analysis deals with values: What should be? Empirical analysis deals with observation: What is? Incrementalism offers an interesting example of how a given thing may be dealt with either normatively or empirically.

In an influential normative book in the mid-1960s, Charles Lindblom argued that central direction of policy could not work but that a variety of decision makers, each operating incrementally, could produce good policies (*The Intelligence of Democracy* [New York: The Free Press, 1965]). In this sense, incrementalism can be held up as a normative guide to how policies should be made.

But incrementalism has also functioned importantly as a descriptive category, to help empirical students of politics understand how politics actually happens. In their pioneer study of how governments design budgets, Davis, Dempster, and Wildavsky concluded that the budgetary decisions of the president and Congress could be described as simple incremental decisions. Agencies were rarely created or disbanded; rather, each year each agency received a budgetary increase of some small percent—an incremental way of designing the budget ("A Theory of the Budgetary Process," *American Political Science Review* 60 [September 1966]: 529–547). Here, then, "incrementalism" is not a *value* to be debated, but a descriptive category that is applied to U.S. budgetary politics.

instance, taxes liquor and tobacco products heavily so as to raise their prices and make it less likely that people will choose to consume such unhealthy substances rather than, say, meat and vegetables. The choice as to what to consume is still the customer's, but the government has taken steps to help determine what that choice will be. By contrast, in banning the consumption of heroin, the U.S. government is relying on governmental authority rather than on a market mechanism to determine the level of consumption of a dangerous substance.

Whether authority or a market mechanism is a better way of making policy is a continual subject of debate. Is it better for the government to nationalize railroads, airlines, and such and run them in the public interest? Or is it better to leave decisions on scheduling, allocation of investment, salaries, and so on in these industries to be worked out by management, workers, and customers through their individual choices? In an energy shortage, should gasoline be rationed (with a set number of gallons allocated per family), or should the price be allowed to shoot up, so that those who do not need gasoline as much as others or who cannot afford it as readily will reduce their driving? Either policy would reduce consumption to meet the short supply, but they would have different side effects. *Both* types of policy—authority and the market—have considerable disadvantages.

(Sidney Harris)

The two main problems with authority as a means of policy are: (1) authority does not generally get things to the people who will value them most—that is, it does not allocate optimally, and (2) authority-based policy does not generally use resources as efficiently as they might be used. (Note that these are the twin problems of "fairness" and "efficiency" with which we introduced this chapter.)

Regarding the first of these problems, it stands to reason that if government officials make a choice on behalf of all the people, they cannot very well take into account the infinitely varying needs of those people. They might write a thousand exceptions and special conditions into their decision, but it would still be a clumsy instrument for deciding who is to get how much of what. Consider the example of gasoline rationing. If the government states that each family may receive 42 gallons of gasoline a month, should they not allow rural families more than that because of the long distances they must drive? But then, what about an urban resident who must drive to a job 20 miles away? Perhaps the government should allow less gas to those living near a bus line. How about people with weak hearts? Should they receive extra gasoline? How about people with small children? People who own a vacation house 40 miles out of town? This can go on forever, and even if the government writes terribly complicated rules, there will still be many people who do not receive gasoline in proportion to their desire and need for gasoline. As Lindblom has put it, authority systems have "strong thumbs, no fingers."[6]

The second main problem with policy made by authority is that it generally does not lead to a very efficient use of resources. When the government decides how much is to be invested in what ways in schools, highways, coal mining, or whatever, the government officials responsible do not *personally* gain much of anything from a wise decision or lose much of anything from an unwise one. Under a market arrangement, however, the people making such decisions save money directly from wise decisions and lose money directly from unwise ones. Even with the best intentions in the world, it is natural that, in systems of authority, decision makers should be more careless with resources than they would be under a market system. As a fairly extreme example of the sort of inefficiency that can result, the Soviet Union allows its farmers to manage small plots themselves and to sell their produce in competitive markets, though most Soviet agricultural products come from large, government-managed collective farms. On the private plots, on the average, it takes 4 pounds of feed grain to produce a pound of meat; on the collective farms, it takes up to 13 pounds of feed grain to produce a pound of meat.[7]

Given these two very serious problems, why would anyone ever use authority? Why don't governments simply leave all decisions to market mechanisms? The reason is that market mechanisms themselves suffer from several serious defects; we shall consider three of them here.[8]

First, as we saw in Chapter 4, wealth and income are distributed unequally in all societies, with some people poor and others better-off. When decisions are left to the market, goods and opportunities flow to those who can afford them, and these will not necessarily be the people who need them most. If medical care is allocated by letting the price rise, for instance, poor people who needed surgery to avoid being crippled might have to do without, while richer people might be able to afford casual cosmetic surgery. Where a need is especially important, the government may step in to make certain that justice is done in a way that cannot be guaranteed by a market mechanism. This is part of the motivation behind systems of free public education, socialized medicine (such as the national medical care programs that serve people of all ages in Britain, Canada, and many European states, or Medicare, which serves those over age sixty-five in the United States), and the rationing of food during shortages.

A second problem with market mechanisms is that they are not very effec-

---

[6]Charles Lindblom, *Politics and Markets* (New York: Basic Books, 1977).

[7]*The Economist*, February 7, 1981, p. 14.

[8]For a more thorough discussion, see Lindblom, *op. cit.*, chap. 6, n. 6.

tive in producing *collective goods*. A "collective good" is something that benefits all members of the community and that no one can be prevented from using; every member of the community can enjoy the benefits of it whether that person has helped pay for it or not. Some examples of collective goods are national defense, medical research, weather forecasting, and public health programs to control the spread of disease. All members of the community benefit from such programs, whether or not they have helped pay for them. An army, for instance, cannot defend just those people who have helped pay for it; it defends a territory and unavoidably defends everyone in that territory. Left to the market, such collective goods would be terribly difficult to finance. Each individual could quite sensibly think, "If I don't pay my share, the army will still be there, and I'll get all the benefits of it; why should I pay?" As a result, no one would pay to finance the army, there would be no army, and all would lose out. Rather than let such paradoxical failures occur, governments often decide not to rely on the voluntary choices of a market mechanism. Instead, they force the people to pay taxes, and they use those taxes to provide the collective good that all (or most) desire.

A third problem with market mechanisms is that they do not take into account *externalities* of individual transactions. An "externality" exists when there are social costs or benefits beyond the individual costs and benefits between two individuals. For example, let us say that a couple contract with a trash company to dump refuse on their land. The trash company presumably has greater benefits than costs from the deal. For the landowners, the benefit is the money paid by the trash company; the cost is the odor and sight of the trash plus the fact that a portion of the land is occupied by the trash. Presumably the landowners are satisfied with the deal (the benefit outweighs the costs), or there would have been no deal. So, the trash company and the landowners are happy, and according to market practices the deal will be struck. But there is an externality here. All of the landowners' neighbors, including a nursing home and a day-care center, must also suffer the sight and smell of the trash. They receive no benefits, so there is a large *social cost* that should be taken into account but does not enter into market calculations. This is the problem of externalities, a problem in which governmental authority is often brought to bear to make certain that the broader social costs and benefits—as well as the narrower individual costs and benefits—are taken into account in transactions. The most obvious externalities are negative ones—pollution, the setting up of ugly structures, and so on. But there can also be *positive externalities*, in which there are positive social benefits that would not be taken into account in individual transactions and that government may step in to guarantee. Two examples are the preservation of historic buildings and the requirement that every member of society acquire a basic education. (The notion in the latter case is that society as a whole benefits from general literacy above and beyond the benefit any single individual gains from being literate.)

Governmental authority and market mechanisms, then, are two general modes for the making of policy. There are problems with each, so it is hard to argue an absolute case for one as opposed to the other, and personal prefer-

Factories and their neighbors in South Boston, Massachusetts. A strong example of "externalities."
(Ellis Herwig/The Picture Cube)

ences will play a role. Furthermore, it is clear that certain areas of policy lend themselves better to one mode than to the other. Defense is always provided by governmental authority, not by a market mechanism, probably because it is so difficult to provide collective goods through a market mechanism. Art and science seem to flourish best when left to a "marketplace of ideas" rather than being made to conform to decisions of governmental authority. Many other policy areas—industrial production, health care, and others—seem susceptible to either mode of decision, and examples of both modes from numerous countries can be found.

CONCLUSION

At this point you may think that the general message of this chapter is "Policymaking is awfully complicated." This is understandable. We have seen that the question of "fairness" is complex and subjective, and that reckoning "efficiency" is similarly tricky—that it is difficult to count accurately the costs and benefits of a policy in order to choose the one that gives the greatest benefits at the least cost. It should by now be obvious that the making of policy is an art, not a science.

Unfortunately, a description of the complexity of policy decisions could lead some people to give up in discouragement. If it is so difficult to decide what policy is most fair and most efficient, why bother to try? Carried too far, an appreciation of complexity can be paralyzing.

We must always carry on a difficult balancing act between recognizing that our decisions are fallible, and therefore require continual reexamination, yet being able to act decisively on our best judgment at any given time. It is the duty of those who recognize the complexity of decisions to hold themselves always ready to act in spite of their knowledge that their choices may be wrong. Otherwise, the only people to act would be those who did not understand the complexity of policy choices, and the world would be ruled by simpletons.

EXAMPLES: POLITICAL CHOICE

Here are three examples of policy questions that have recently concerned governmental decision makers. In each instance the policy issue is stated; this is followed by some of the questions that those making a decision on the issue must consider:

1. *The problem of need-based scholarships:* Most systems for providing college scholarships are based on some definition of financial need, with scholarships generally being given only to those students who most need financial help in order to attend school.

   Is need, rather than academic ability, the best basis on which to choose those students who are to be encouraged to attend college?

   • Which way of choosing who gets aid is the more just?
   • Which is the more efficient? Is the overall educational level of society increased more by giving financial aid to bright students or to needy students? Presumably the aid offers more leverage to needy students, since they all need the money in order to attend college, whereas many of the bright students would attend college in any case. But is a smaller number of bright students the more important addition?

   Assuming we wish to use need as a basis, how do we determine "need"?

   • Is need a function of parents' income? What, then, do we do about children of wealthy parents who are living independently of them and get no aid from them? Should they be punished for their parents' wealth? But if they are given aid, won't all students, in order to get aid, claim to be independent of their parents?
   • Is need solely a matter of family income, or shouldn't we take a family's financial obligations into account? Doesn't it make more sense to give aid to someone whose parents must put eight children through school than to someone from a family of four with the same income? But in a possibly parallel situation, should a family that carries big mortgages on two large homes get preference simply because they don't have much money left to spend on college? (Many scholarship systems do count mortgage payments as contributing to need.)

Does doing this merely reward imprudence? Is there a difference between the case of the eight children and the case of the large mortgage?

- How should parents who are not married but are living together and supporting their children jointly be counted? Most systems allow just one of the parents to be counted as the "supporter," and if the one who earns less is so designated, the family will show up as more "needy" than most people would consider them to be. Is this fair to married couples? Does it discourage marriage? If it is not allowed, how can one address the problem of separated couples where one of the parents does not pay a fair share of support? In this case, the single responsible parent and children would appear as *less* needy than they really are. Whichever way you decide to define need in the case of unmarried parents, how can you police the system?

2. *The problem of water pollution:* Most states have laws to limit the pollutants that can be dumped into the water.

- How do we decide which pollutants to ban? Should we ban primarily those that are dangerous to human health? Those, such as phosphates or DDT, that have especially bad effects on fish, birds, and mammals? Those that discolor the water? Those that stink?
- Who is to bear the cost of cleaning up the water?
- Is it better to use a flat ban on pollution or to charge people and corporations a stiff fee for polluting? The main argument against doing the latter is that it puts the government in the position of saying that pollution is acceptable (or at least legal) as long as one can pay the fee. The main argument for it is that it adds flexibility to the law. Cleaning up pollution always carries costs and may lead to plant closings, higher prices for consumers, and other socially undesirable consequences. The fee system would allow some continued pollution where the cost of cleaning up would be prohibitive. Where the cost is not so high, people would choose to clean up rather than pay the fee. Thus, the system would be made more efficient, but at the expense of losing some of the moral and symbolic vigor of the law. Which is the better course?

3. *The problem of gender-based pension payments:* Almost all insurance companies have varying insurance rates for low- and high-risk categories of people. Many companies give lower insurance rates to students who maintain a B average, for instance, on the assumption that those students drive better (or less often) than others and thus will have fewer accidents. Similarly, young drivers carry higher rates for auto insurance, nonsmokers have lower rates for life insurance with many companies, almost all companies give lower life insurance rates to women because women live longer than men, and so on. In the same spirit, until recently most insurance-based pension plans have paid women who retired at age seventy a lower monthly pension than men who retired at that age because, since women have a longer life expectancy, the companies can reasonably expect to make payments to the women for a greater length of time.

- Is it fair that a woman who has worked as hard as a man should not enjoy as comfortable a retirement as the man does?
- On the other hand, if payments are made equal, a man who has worked just as

hard as a woman can expect to draw out a smaller total amount of retirement income before he dies. Is this fair?

- If the system is changed to give equal payments, will men reinvest their retirement savings in other ways that allow them to draw out their retirement income in whatever way they wish? This could result in an insurance-based scheme with only female clients, thus defeating the purpose of the change.
- Why should gender be singled out as a basis for this distinction? People who live in Iowa live longer, on the average, than people from Rhode Island. If we're to be consistent, shouldn't Iowans draw a smaller pension than Rhode Islanders? How about people who exercise regularly, people who don't smoke, slender people, and so on?

FURTHER READING

Anderson, Charles. *Statecraft*. New York: Wiley, 1977, especially chaps. 1–6.

Ascher, William. *Forecasting: An Appraisal for Policy-Makers and Planners*. Baltimore: Johns Hopkins University Press, 1978.

Axelrod, Robert, Bobrow, Davis B., Eulau, Heinz, Jones, Charles O., and Landau, Martin. "The Place of Policy Analysis in Political Science." *American Journal of Political Science* 21 (May 1977): 415–433.

Heidenheimer, Arnold J., et al., eds. *Political Corruption: A Handbook*. 2nd ed. New Brunswick, N.J.: Transaction Books, 1988.

Lindblom, Charles. *Politics and Markets*. New York: Basic Books, 1977.

Sabatier, Paul, and Mazmanian, Dan. "The Implementation of Public Policy: A Framework of Analysis." *Policy Studies Journal* 8 (special issue, no. 2, 1980): 538–559.

Schulman, Paul R. "Nonincremental Policy Making: Notes Toward an Alternative Paradigm." *American Political Science Review* 69 (December 1975): 1354–1370.

Wildavsky, Aaron B. *Speaking Truth to Power*. New Brunswick, N.J.: Transaction Books, 1987.

Part III

THE APPARATUS
OF GOVERNANCE

Chapter 6

Authority and Legitimacy: The State and the Citizen

In the preceding section we looked at the state and at questions that go into the setting of state policies. But how does "the state"—which comprises many different people—choose a particular set of policies? What goes on within a state that determines the policies it will pursue? It is not a simple decision-making mechanism, since its complex organizational structure strongly influences the processes of political choice. In the next two sections—Chapters 6 through 10 and 11 through 14—we will look at those internal structures.

In this chapter we shall consider the relationship between the state and its citizens. Every state has some sort of government, which sets its policies. A "government," when you think about it, is an unusual body within the state. It is the only group of people entitled to make decisions that everyone in the state has a duty to accept and obey. There are many groups of people who have power over others, in that they can force others to do what they wish; for example, General Motors may induce a local government to give it a special tax break in return for locating a plant in the town, or a union may force an employer to increase wages.[1] But the government has a different kind of power, which we call *authority*. (We discussed this also in the preceding chapter, as an alternative to market mechanisms for making public choices.)

If General Motors tries to convince a family to sell it their house and the family refuses, that is all there is to it. The family may have made a wise or an unwise decision, but whether they sold or not, the decision was theirs to make, and either decision is socially acceptable. If the school bully tells another child to eat dirt and the child runs away or fights the bully, no one faults the child for not doing what the bully commanded. General Motors does not have authority to make someone sell a house, and the bully does not have authority to make anyone eat dirt.

Authority is power based on a general agreement (1) that a person or group has the right to issue certain sorts of commands and (2) that those commands should be obeyed. If a person fails to obey authority, that failure is socially unacceptable, since the authority itself is based on a general acceptance of its exercise.

Various individuals or groups in a society have limited sorts of authority that extend over specific ranges of behavior. A parent has authority to tell chil-

---

[1] See Chapter 1 for a fuller discussion of power.

dren of a certain age when they should go to bed, with whom they should play, and so on, but as the child grows older the range of activities over which a parent has authority dwindles until it finally disappears entirely. A teacher in a classroom has the authority to tell students how they should prepare for classes, but the teacher cannot tell them whom they may date or what political candidate to support. A General Motors supervisor has the authority to tell an assembly-line worker which bolts to tighten, but he or she cannot tell the worker how to spend coffee breaks; and when the worker resigns, the supervisor has no authority at all.

A *government* is unique in society in that all of its power involves authority and, at least potentially, there is no limit to the range of activities over which it may exercise authority. Most governments themselves impose some limits on their authority; for instance, the U.S. government, in its Constitution, rules out the exercise of authority over what religion people are to follow, what people are to say to each other, and so on. But these limitations are self-imposed and not necessarily "natural" to governments. Many governments around the world, at one time or another, have claimed authority to tell people what religion they should follow, what they should or should not say to one another, what sort of sexual activity they were permitted, what they might eat or drink, or what sorts of sports and recreation they could take part in. It is safe to say that there is no area of human activity over which some government or another has not at some time exercised authority. "Government," then, is set apart from all other groups in society by the fact that all of its power is based on authority and that, at least potentially, there is no limit to the range of activities over which it may exercise authority.

Authority is a particularly efficient kind of power. It may be backed up ultimately by the threat of coercion (the police will haul you off and punish you physically if you do not do what those in authority tell you to do), or it may be backed up ultimately by persuasion (if you keep your well clean, as the government tells you to do, you will be sick less often). But if people simply do what the government tells them to do, without having to be coerced or persuaded, everything goes more smoothly and—at least from the government's point of view—more satisfactorily. In general, authority does not require the actual use of coercion or persuasion to any great extent. No one has to stand at streetcorners to *force* cars to stop at red lights, and no one has to stand there to *persuade* them to do so. One of the things that makes the modern state such an efficient form of political organization is the very fact that the state has *authority*, and thus can ensure that people will comply with its commands with a minimum of expensive and time-consuming coercion or persuasion.

People do obey the authority of the state. Because actions against authority are by definition "outlaw" behavior and are by definition extraordinary, we can think of many vivid examples of refusals to obey authority—burglary, speeding on the highways, tax evasion, and so on. But the startling thing, when you think about it, is that few people steal things even when it would be safe to do so, most people drive at or near speed limit even though only a sprinkling of police are available to monitor what they are doing, and most people pay the taxes they owe.

It is authority that makes this system of commands and obedience work as smoothly as it does, and this makes the modern state appear to us to be the most natural form of political organization. But authority is not a simple thing that is either present or absent. Rather, it is a matter of degree. Remember that authority exists because it is "generally agreed on," that is, most people believe it exists. There will probably never be a state in which every single person agrees on the existence and range of the state's authority. Often, when a state issues certain commands, a portion of the people do not accept its authority to do so. If enough people deny the authority of the state, the state has a problem. In the early twentieth century, the government of the United States attempted to command people not to drink alcohol. So many people denied the authority of the state in this area that enforcement proved impossible and the law was eventually abandoned. More seriously, in the 1860s the whole southern region of the United States denied that the national government had any authority over them at all. They set up their own new government instead, and it took a long and bloody Civil War to reestablish the authority of the U.S. government over them.

LEGITIMACY AND AUTHORITY

The crux of the state then, and of its ability to function effectively, is the government's wide-ranging authority to organize the lives of its people. But paradoxically, this authority exists only because the people in general believe it to exist and to be appropriate. If authority were to fail, it might still be possible for a government to organize its people by coercion and persuasion, but at such great cost that this approach probably could not be sustained over the long haul. A pure tyranny, existing without the benefit of at least some degree of authority, probably could not last long.

Thus it is crucial to a government that large numbers of its people should believe that it has authority and that it properly *should* have that authority. We call the existence of this sort of feeling, to the extent that it does exist, the *legitimacy* of the government. Legitimacy, like authority itself, is a matter of degree. Not everyone in a state will necessarily always agree that its government is legitimate or that a given kind of governmental act is legitimate. Much of the violence of politics in Iran in the early 1980s, for instance, resulted from a failure to agree on what sort of government could be legitimate.

SOURCES OF LEGITIMACY

How does a government achieve a reasonable degree of legitimacy? There are many ways by which the people's allegiance may be bound to a government so that it is generally considered legitimate:

1. Legitimacy by Results

First and foremost, a government may gain and retain legitimacy from its people by providing for them the things they most want: security against physical assault, security of their country's borders against invasion, pride in their nation, economic security, and so on. If the government can provide these things, its legitimacy will be greatly strengthened. If it cannot, its legitimacy is likely to be called into question.

A good case in point of "legitimacy by results" is the rule of Adolf Hitler in Germany in the 1930s. In 1933, Hitler took power legally, but through dubious maneuvers and with at most a bare majority of support. The most votes the Nazi party had received in a fully free election was 37 percent—enough to make it the largest party in the country, but hardly a mandate for dictatorship. Once in power, he could initially count on the free support of only about one-third of the Germans, and powerful forces were arrayed against him—the labor unions, the Catholic church, much of the army's general staff. What solidified Hitler's hold on Germany and gave him a high degree of legitimacy by the end of the 1930s was the *results* of his early policies. He reduced unemployment by large-scale deficit spending; by some audacious bluffs, he outmaneuvered France and England and reestablished Germany as a great power; he built the autobahn system of superhighways; and he pioneered the Volkswagen "bug" automobile. In spite of his suppression of free speech, his oppression of Jews, and the vulgar behavior of his party comrades, these accomplishments brought him widespread and deep support from the German people. By the late 1930s

Adolf Hitler dedicating his latest project, the Volkswagen! Fallersleben, Germany 1938.

(The Bettmann Archive)

it would probably have been impossible for anyone to seek to overthrow his rule. It was not until 1944, when he had obviously lost World War II, that a group of generals were able to muster sufficient strength to try to depose him; and even then, the attempt failed.

2. Legitimacy by Habit

Once a government has been around for a while, people become accustomed generally to obeying its laws. People expect to operate under some government or other, so whatever government is in place and has been obeyed in the past it is likely to be regarded as legitimate—unless a particular crisis arises or some force (another state, perhaps) intervenes from outside. In other words, once a particular government has been in place for a while, so that the people have developed the habit of obeying it, it no longer has to perpetually justify its existence. Rather, the burden of proof lies with whoever would propose an alternative government. The existing government remains legitimate unless and until a compelling alternative comes along. We should not underestimate the importance of simple habit in maintaining governments in power.[2]

3. Legitimacy by Historical, Religious, or Ethnic Identity

Many governments enhance their legitimacy by the ties that exist between themselves and the people because of the government leaders' past accomplishments (their historic role) or because of the religious and/or ethnic similarity between the government leaders and the people.

This may be especially important in a new state, in which the government has not yet been in place long enough for the people to have developed the *habit* of treating it as legitimate and in which the many economic and social problems that plague most new states make it difficult for the government to achieve legitimacy by *results*.

Many governments of new states are able to buy time by virtue of the status they acquired in leading the state into independence in the first place. George Washington was revered as the "father of his country" after his success as commander of the Revolutionary Army. He and his associates enjoyed a couple of decades in which the people of the United States regarded them as their natural government, and this time allowed them to get the Constitution into place and to establish among the people the habit of obeying it. Similarly, the Labor party in Israel, the Congress party in India, the party of Julius Nyerere in Tanzania, and the National Liberation Front in Algeria all had a breathing space in which their governments were accepted, simply because they had led the independence movements which had established their states

---

[2]Also, a government that is in place is usually able to foster a supportive mythology. For some examples of this in the case of the United States, see Dan Nimmo and James Combs, *Subliminal Politics: Myths and Mythmakers in America* (Englewood Cliffs, N.J.: Prentice-Hall, 1980).

in the first place. Religious or ethnic ties may also be used by a government to enhance its legitimacy. In Iran, the regime of the Ayatollah Khomeini and his successors has used its ties to the dominant Shiite Muslim sect and has played on antagonisms between the Persian majority in the country and the Arab populations in the rest of the Mideast to strengthen its legitimacy. Similarly, the government of South Africa has used whites' fears of blacks to strengthen its legitimacy among the white population.

4. Legitimacy by Procedures

Finally, a state may strengthen the legitimacy of its government by following certain procedures in setting itself up—procedures in which many people have confidence, so that they will start off with a fund of trust for any government that has been established along these lines.

The best example of this is democracy—a state in which all the citizens participate in selecting their leaders and perhaps also in determining the state's policies. Typically, democratic governments are chosen by competitive elections in which all citizens vote to decide which of various alternative leadership teams are to govern. Because the resulting government has won broader support than any alternative, it gains a strong base of legitimacy. It is the government "of the people."

The *procedures* of democratic election are what give such a government a good part of its legitimacy. One may dislike particular leaders or think their policies unwise, but it is hard to argue with their right to govern as long as they have been selected by the proper procedures.

Democratic government is the preeminent example today of legitimacy by procedures—so preeminent, in fact, that democratic procedures are often imitated through staged elections in dictatorships. But at other times, other procedures have served as the basis for legitimacy; all that is important is that the procedure be generally accepted as appropriate. Until a few centuries ago, for instance, it was generally accepted that political leadership was most properly passed on by inheritance. One king ruled; when he died, his heir became the new king. This procedure was so important as a basis of legitimacy that great care was taken to lay out precise rules of inheritance; if no clear heir was available, the result was sometimes civil war.

Authority, then, through the legitimacy on which it is based, depends on the relation between the state and its citizens. A particularly interesting problem in authority and legitimacy is posed by modern democracy. A "democracy" is a state in which all fully qualified citizens vote at regular intervals to choose, among alternative candidates, the people who will be in charge of developing the state's policies. It is in one sense an odd sort of state, since the government has power over the citizens (it makes the laws), but the citizens also have power over the government (they can vote it out of office). What sort of relationship between state and citizens is best in a democracy?

THE "DEMOCRATIC CITIZEN"

The one most special thing about the relationship between a democratic state and its citizens is that democracy requires citizens who will do more than simply obey and follow the government. In our discussion above, it was more or less sufficient, in order for authority to exist, that the people regard the actions of the government as legitimate. This would ensure obedience to the laws.

Some nondemocratic states go a step further and try to generate *enthusiastic* support for the government. Hitler—through his pageantry, his rallies, and his network of youth organizations, sports clubs, and so on—tried to generate enthusiastic support for Nazism that would help him to build a powerful German military force more rapidly. The Soviet Union and other communist countries have always tried similarly to build enthusiastic support through rallies, discussion groups, parades, and strenuous campaigning even when their elections were restricted to a single party.

But democracy goes yet a step further than this. In a democracy, it is hoped not only that people will obey the laws and be enthusiastic citizens but that they will also and at the same time be *critical* citizens. Democratic citizens are expected to walk a difficult line along which they support the authority of their government leaders but, at the same time, are critical enough of those leaders that they might readily vote them out of office at the next election. This requires a complex and sophisticated view of politics. It is not easy to be a citizen of a democracy.

What characteristics would we look for in a "democratic citizen"?

1. *Tolerance.* If varied groups are to support those opinions, it is necessary that the people in general have a reasonable tolerance for diversity. If people could be prevented from setting forth unpopular ideas, then the democracy would not function well. Thus, citizens must generally be at least minimally tolerant of different races, different social behaviors, different religions, and political beliefs that may depart sharply from their own. At the very least, most citizens in a democracy must be willing to allow these various groups to present their cases freely. If they are not, then there is a danger that the voters will not be allowed a full range of options from which to choose.

2. *Active Participation.* Democracy requires more than just that citizens obey the laws the government lays down. Since authority in a democracy is a two-way street, the citizens must take concrete political actions to exercise their authority over the government. At the very least, they should vote in elections. Better yet, they should maintain frequent contact with the government by writing to their representatives, serving on citizen committees, and so on. If the citizens do not do this, a state simply cannot be a democracy. Its government will have authority over its citizens, *but not vice versa.*

3. *High Level of Interest and Information.* But it is not enough that citizens participate actively. If they do not know what is going on, they can be as active as they wish but they will have little effect on what the government does. Action based on no interest or understanding would simply be aimless, and one

"I'M HEDGEPATH, FROM THE C.I.A., AND I'D LIKE TO CONFIRM YOUR SUSPICIONS. WE ARE BOMBARDING YOUR HOME WITH NUCLEAR RADIATION."

(Sidney Harris)

person's act would tend to cancel the other's out. If the citizens' active participation is to be constructive, democracy requires also that those citizens be well informed.

4. *Support for the State.* Finally, while the three characteristics noted above are required, if the people are to maintain authority over the government, democracy requires also that the government maintain authority over the people. This is difficult, since the people are required to remain skeptical about the holders of government positions and must stand ready to vote them out of office if that is necessary. What is necessary, if this balancing trick is to work, is that citizens retain an abstract support for the state—and for the democratic procedures that place certain individuals into positions in the government—even while they remain skeptical about the particular individuals currently holding those positions.

HOW WELL ARE THESE REQUIREMENTS MET?

As you see, it takes work to be a citizen in a democracy. How well do the citizens of modern democracies measure up? In particular, how do citizens of the United States measure up?

1. Tolerance

The citizens of most democracies will readily agree with abstract statements guaranteeing minorities the right to express their opinions freely. However, concrete applications of this principle may be another matter. First of all, there is often not much support for any kind of participation beyond "conventional" acts such as running for office and voting in elections. A survey of the Italian public in 1975 showed that only 75 percent approved of people participating in peaceful demonstrations and that only 36 percent would themselves be willing to participate in a demonstration; further, only 49 percent approved of people signing petitions and only 27 percent would be willing to do so themselves.[3]

Second, people often think that even conventional political participation should be banned for those who they think are wrong or dangerous. In a 1978 study in the United States, people were asked to name the political group they liked the least (29 percent picked communists; 24 percent the John Birch Society; 8 percent atheists; 8 percent the Symbionese Liberation Army, a radical left group; 6 percent the Black Panthers; 5 percent fascists; 4 percent pro-abortionists; 2 percent antiabortionists; and the rest scattered among other groups). They were then asked several questions about what rights that group should have to participate in politics. Only 16 percent thought that members of the group they disliked should be allowed to serve as president if elected, only 19 percent thought that members of that group should be allowed to teach in the public schools, and only 29 percent thought the group should not be outlawed.[4] A related study in Israel in 1980 showed Israelis to be even less tolerant in these ways than Americans.[5]

2. Active Participation

At the very least, citizens in a democracy should vote regularly in elections. As we shall see in Chapter 8, even this cannot be taken for granted. However, it is also necessary, if the democracy is to function well, that good numbers of citizens go beyond voting to involve themselves in more demanding tasks such as writing or phoning officials, organizing neighborhood groups, working in political campaigns, and so on.

Table 6–1 presents the results of a survey of the American public in the 1960s, in which people were asked whether they participated in a variety of ways. (Other studies suggest that these things have not changed markedly since the 1960s except for a drop-off in the percentage of people voting in elections and an increase in the percentage writing letters to officials.) In looking at

[3]Sartori and Marradi, cited by Giacomo Sani in Gabriel Almond and Sidney Verba, eds., *The Civic Culture Revisited* (Boston: Little, Brown, 1980), p. 312.

[4]John L. Sullivan, James Piereson, and George E. Marcus, "An Alternative Conceptualization of Political Tolerance: Illusory Increases 1950s to 1970s," *American Political Science Review* 73 (September 1979): 781–794.

[5]Michael Shamir and John Sullivan, "The Political Context of Tolerance: The United States and Israel," *American Political Science Review* 77 (December 1983): 911–928.

Table 6–1   Percentage of Americans Engaging in Twelve Different Acts of Political Participation

Type of Political Participation	Percentage
Report regularly voting in presidential elections	72
Report always voting in local elections	47
Active in at least one organization involved in community problems	32
Have worked with others in trying to solve some community problems	30
Have attempted to persuade others to vote as they were	28
Have ever actively worked for a party or candidates during an election	26
Have ever contacted a local government official about some issue or problem	20
Have attended at least one political meeting or rally in last three years	19
Have ever contacted a state or national government official about some issue or problem	18
Have ever formed a group or organization to attempt to solve some local community problem	14
Have ever given money to a party or candidate during an election campaign	13
Presently a member of a political club or organization	8

SOURCE: Sidney Verba and Norman H. Nie, *Participation in America* (New York: Harper & Row, 1972), p. 31.

this table, you must bear in mind that people usually tell pollsters that they are more active than they truly are; actual turnout in the 1960 and 1964 presidential elections was 64 percent and 62 percent, for instance, although 72 percent of the people polled said that they voted regularly in presidential elections. Still, the figures here give a rough idea of the relative frequency with which people participate in these various ways.

Do the people depicted here participate a lot or a little? Political science is often the science of the half-filled glass. (Is it half full or is it half empty?) Against a standard of what a democracy *should* be, these citizens obviously fall short. Only 20 percent of them (or fewer, if some were exaggerating) have ever contacted a local government official about a problem. On the other hand, against a standard of what we might feel we could realistically expect, these figures show considerable activity. To turn the earlier sentence around, fully 20 percent of the people polled had at one time or another contacted a local official about a problem.

By way of comparison, Table 6–2 presents similar information on Austria, Japan, and Nigeria. Overall, the citizens of these states seem to be about as active as U.S. citizens, although there are interesting variations from one state to another in the *ways* in which citizens participate.

Table 6–2   Political Participation in Four Countries: Percent Who Say Yes or
Perform Act Regularly

	Austria (Percent)	India (Percent)	Japan (Percent)	United States (Percent)
Vote in national election	96	59	72	72
Ever worked for a party	10	25	25	26
Attended political rallies	27	14	50	19
Member of a political club	28	6	4	8
Active member of an organization engaged in solving community problems	9	7	11	14
Contacted local official on a social problem	5	4	11	14

SOURCE: Adapted from Sidney Verba, Norman H. Nie, and Jae-on Kim, *Participation and Political Equality* (London: Cambridge University Press, 1978), p. 58.

3. Interest and Information

Of course, people who regularly turn out and vote in elections might know little or nothing about the candidates among whom they were choosing; in that case, they would contribute little to the working of democracy. How interested are citizens of democracies in what goes on politically, and how accurately informed are they? Voters in the United States are rather interested in politics, according to most studies. For instance, a poll of Americans in 1976 showed that 38 percent said they followed what was going on in government and public affairs most of the time, 31 percent said they followed it some of the time, 18 percent now and then, and 12 percent hardly at all.[6]

Of course, most people will exaggerate to a stranger how much they do something as virtuous as following public affairs. How well informed are these virtuous people? Not very. Only 46 percent of a national survey of American adults could name their representative in Congress, and only 41 percent could tell the representative's party. Only 39 percent could name both of the senators from their state.[7]

In a study of the 1976 presidential election in two U.S. cities, Thomas E. Patterson found that even by October surprisingly few voters could accurately state the positions of the two candidates, Gerald Ford and Jimmy Carter. As seen in Table 6–3, in only two of eight instances could more than half of the voters accurately state a candidate's position on an issue.

[6]Warren E. Miller, Arthur H. Miller, and Edward J. Schneider, *American National Election Studies Data Sourcebook, 1952–1978* (Cambridge, Mass.: Harvard University Press, 1980).

[7]U.S. Senate, Committee on Governmental Operations, *Confidence and Concern: Citizens View American Government* (Washington, D.C.: Government Printing Office, 1973), p. 244.

6–3   Percent Accurately Stating Candidate's Position

	Issue			
	Public Works Jobs	*Defense Spending*	*Welfare Spending*	*Tax Burden*
Ford	35	57	43	22
Carter	54	29	22	40

SOURCE: Adapted from Thomas E. Patterson, *The Mass Media Election* (New York: Praeger, 1980), p. 154. The percentages reported include a correction for guessing.

4. Support for the State

You will recall that what is needed here is a general abstract support for the state and for its democratic form of government, which can coexist with skepticism about the qualities of individual officeholders. Many democracies seem to be fairly successful at commanding this kind of respect from their people.

In a survey in 1959, Americans were asked, "Generally speaking, what are the things about this country that you are most proud of?" They could mention anything they wished to, including religious values, the wealth of the country, landscape, culture, and so on. Over 60 percent of the things mentioned were aspects of government and politics.[8] At about the same time, in a survey in 1958, 73 percent of those polled said that they trusted the government in Washington to do what was right either "most of the time" or "just about always."[9] As we shall see later in this chapter, there has been a steady erosion since then of this sort of confidence and support of their government by the American people. The point is, such support was maintained at a time when, in the same study, Americans felt considerable skepticism about the *people* running the government. In 1958, 24 percent thought that "quite a lot" of the people running the government are crooked, 37 percent said that the people running the government did not usually know what they were doing, and 85 percent said that the people in government wasted "some" or "a lot" of the money they paid in taxes. At about this time also the American electorate repudiated their Republican President Eisenhower by giving the Democrats a landslide victory in the congressional election of 1958.

This balance between support for state institutions and skepticism about officials is hard to maintain and many shaky democracies are rarely able to achieve it. As we shall see in examples below, one democracy, West Germany, has only now begun to achieve it, while another, the United States, has for now to a large extent lost it.

[8]Gabriel Almond and Sidney Verba, *The Civic Culture* (Princeton, N.J.: Princeton University Press, 1963), p. 102.

[9]University of Michigan, Center for Political Studies, 1958 National Election Study.

Political Culture

Political scientists have given the name "political culture" to the sorts of basic attitudes we deal with in this chapter. The political culture of a society consists of all attitudes and beliefs held communally by the people, which form the basis for their political behavior. We have borrowed the term from anthropology, in which the idea of "culture" forms a central organizing concept.

It is clear that political culture varies a good deal from one state to another and that it is responsible for major differences in how politics is conducted in the United States as compared, say, with Japan. For instance, political decisions are made in Japan much more on the basis of unanimous consent than by a vote (with one side losing) because of the value placed on consensus in the Japanese culture.

For all that we think it is important, however, political scientists have not been very successful at analyzing "political culture." It almost seems that such a big concept resists precision and invites fuzzy generalization. It is too easy to lapse into stereotyping of peoples: the lock-step, obedient, efficient Germans; the unflappable British; the breezy, pragmatic Americans; the hot-blooded Latins. While there is often a germ of truth in the stereotypes, it is often merely a germ, lost in a gross oversimplification. Even in the hands of careful scholars, the concept can lead us away from precision. The best work on political culture in recent decades (Gabriel Almond and Sidney Verba's *The Civic Culture* [Boston: Little, Brown, 1965]), came in for justified criticism because it rather casually assumed that the ideal culture for democracy was one which, not surprisingly, looked very much like Americans' culture.

The concept remains a challenge and a teaser to political scientists. On the one hand, we recognize that it is extremely important, but, on the other hand, we have not found safe ways to work with it and, in fact, rather little analysis of political culture is attempted these days.

POLITICAL SOCIALIZATION

The values and assumptions people hold about politics are acquired in a process we call *political socialization*, which simply means the learning of political values and factual assumptions.[10] This can in principle occur at any age and under any circumstances, but it tends to be concentrated at certain points of our lives.

Like most learning, political socialization apparently comes most easily and fully in our childhood, and diminishes as we grow older. However, explicit and detailed information about politics tends not to be picked up much before the

---

[10]Two good reviews of political socialization, though both are now a bit old, are Dean Jaros, *Socialization to Politics* (New York: Praeger, 1973), and Richard E. Dawson et al., *Political Socialization* (Boston: Little, Brown, 1977). See also Stanley W. Moore et al., *The Child's Political World* (New York: Praeger, 1985).

Table 6–4   **Development of Political Orientations Among Swedish Youth**

Age	*Percent Undecided as to Best Party*
11–12	73
13–15	66
16–18	55
19–21	47
22–24	32
25–27	35

SOURCE: Adapted from Herbert H. Hyman, *Political Socialization* (New York: The Free Press, 1959), p. 49.

teen years. Children learn in their families many basic social attitudes, such as trust in people and attitudes to authority, that will be important in shaping their later response to politics. But most children have only rather primitive ideas about what government is and how politics works. These things are primarily learned in adolescence and early adulthood and, of course, continue to be learned throughout adult life. For example, Table 6–4 shows the percent of Swedish youths of varying ages who were undecided as to which political party was the best. Among eleven- to twelve-year-olds, 73 percent did not have a preference among the parties. This indecision declined to 35 percent by early adulthood.

One of the concerns of political scientists studying socialization is to assess the varying roles of different *agents of socialization*. We must learn about politics *from* someone, and the various sources of learning are what we call the agents of socialization. Different agents operate in different ways and affect different areas of our values and assumptions about politics. Obviously, we learn about politics from an infinite variety of agents, but a few particularly important ones are our families, schools, and peer groups.

From our parents we acquire a number of general social values that will apply to politics just as they do to other aspects of our lives. It is also thought that we may gain expectations about how politics should occur in the state by extension from the way politics (the making of family decisions by the use of power) is conducted in the family; an authoritarian family may prepare one for an authoritarian state and a democratic family for a democratic state.[11] More specific political values and assumptions do not develop as much through the family as we might suppose. As noted above, they tend to be acquired during adolescence, a period when most children are trying to establish an independent identity.

[11]This is a controversial position; many scholars think it oversimplifies a complex process of the development of values. A good presentation of the position is Harry Eckstein and Ted Robert Gurr, *Patterns of Authority* (New York: Wiley, 1975).

Schools are of particular interest to students of political socialization because this is an agent of socialization that the state controls, and through which the leaders of the state can attempt to mold the citizenry. In all states there is some degree of guided socialization through the schools. Schools in the United States try to develop informed, patriotic citizens both directly through civics classes and salutes to the flag, and indirectly through class materials in history, literature, and other courses. Some states such as Cuba, China, and Nazi Germany have used the schools vigorously and directly to remake their citizens.

Peer groups are extremely influential in developing adolescents' tastes and their view of the world, but they vary considerably in their political impact. In most friendship groups of adolescents, politics does not figure importantly in the attention of the group. Where this is the case, the group will influence its members' choices in clothes or social behavior strongly but will leave their political identity to develop independently. However, youths who are already somewhat involved in politics may gravitate together as a friendship group, and when this happens, the group may have a profound impact on the political development of all its members.

EXAMPLE: BUILDING AUTHORITY AND LEGITIMACY IN WEST GERMANY

After the defeat of Germany in 1945, the Germans as a people were demoralized politically. They had bought a dream of greatness from Adolf Hitler, but he had brought them to defeat and international disgrace. They were hated throughout Europe, their country had been cut up on the map, and their industries and farms were in ruins. Germans who were fifty years old in 1945 could not be blamed if, having been dazzled by politics, they now withdrew from it. They had grown up under the kaiser's monarchy and had seen it overthrown in disgrace at the end of World War I, when they were in their early twenties. They then lived through fifteen years of a chaotic attempt at democracy which never really established its authority and legitimacy with the people and ended in Hitler's dictatorship. They were thirty-eight years old when Hitler came to power; in the next twelve years they saw Germany approach world conquest and then come close to total destruction. They could be pardoned if they were shy of politics after that.

In many ways, West Germany after 1945 has given political scientists much the same opportunity to observe an evolutionary development as a new volcanic island rising from the sea offers to biologists. When a new island is formed, biologists get a rare chance to observe which animals are the first to appear on it and see how long it takes a diverse flora and fauna to be established. Similarly, political scientists get few chances to see attitudes towards politics estab-

6–5   **Attitudes Toward the "Past," 1951–1970**

Q.: When in this century do you think Germany has been best off?

	Year			
	1951 *(percent)*	1959 *(percent)*	1963 *(percent)*	1970 *(percent)*
Federal Republic (present)	2	42	62	81
Under Hitler before the war (1933–1939)	42	18	10	5
Under the kaiser, before World War I	45	28	16	5

SOURCE: Adapted from David Conradt, "Changing German Political Culture," in Gabriel Almond and Sidney Verba, eds., *The Civic Culture Revisited* (Boston: Little, Brown, 1980), p. 226.

lish themselves among a people who initially have essentially no attitudes. Germany after the war did provide such a case.

For many years, political observers asked themselves whether democratic behavior and attitudes could possibly develop among Germans. Some said that the people who had put Hitler into office just could not develop into democrats. Others thought that if Germany were lucky enough to have a period of peace and economic stability, democracy would be able to establish itself. But no one could hazard a guess as to how long the process would take.

As we can see in Tables 6–5, 6–6, and 6–7, the optimists were correct; in fact, the development of democratic support occurred steadily and fairly rapidly. As we see in Table 6–5, during the first twenty years, the democratic regime established itself as the best arrangement Germany had known—better than Hitler's dictatorship or the kaiser's monarchy.

It was not simply that the country was economically well off either. The political institutions of democracy became more popular during this period. In 1959, in a survey similar to that mentioned earlier for the United States, Germans were asked what they were proud of their country for. Only 7 percent pointed to Germany's political institutions. In 1978 the question was repeated in a survey. By that time, 31 percent of things mentioned were aspects of government and politics.[12]

Support for democracy in the abstract also grew across the first few decades. In 1953, only a bit over 55 percent of Germans stated in the abstract that democracy was the best form of government.[13] By 1976, 90 percent answered yes to the same question.[14]

The sort of social relations among people that are required if a loose system of authority is to work were also developing. In a society where people are hostile and suspicious of each other, democracy cannot work well. As we see in

[12]Conradt, op. cit., p. 230.

[13]Kendall Baker, Russell Dalton, and Kai Hildebrandt, *Germany Transformed* (Cambridge, Mass.: Harvard University Press, 1981), p. 24.

[14]Conradt, op. cit., p. 234.

6–6　Trust and Hostility Among Germans, 1948–1976

a. Percent "trusting most people"

1948	1959	1967	1973	1976
9%	19%	26%	32%	39%

b. Percent thinking more people are evil minded than good minded

1949	1951	1953	1971	1976
46%	43%	34%	17%	16%

SOURCE: Adapted from David Conradt, "Changing German Political Culture," in Gabriel Almond and Sidney Verba, eds., *The Civic Culture Revisited* (Boston: Little, Brown, 1980), p. 226.

6–7　Frequency of Political Discussion, 1953–1972

	1953 (percent)	*1959 (percent)*	*1961 (percent)*	*1965 (percent)*	*1969 (percent)*	*1972 (percent)*
Daily	9	11	10	10	37	50
Occasionally	29	50	51	66	40	34
Never	63	39	39	25	23	16

SOURCE: Kendall Baker, Russell Dalton, and Kai Hildebrandt, *Germany Transformed* (Cambridge, Mass.: Harvard University Press, 1981), p. 40.

Table 6–6, trust grew steadily and social hostility decreased during this time.

Finally, it is necessary that the people begin to be active and interested citizens. As we see in Table 6–7, this also developed steadily.

West Germany has not necessarily become an ideal democracy, but it is interesting to see that there have been established, over just a couple of decades, patterns of behavior and support similar to those of such democracies as the United States or Great Britain. No one would have predicted this with any confidence in 1950, and it has been an eye opener for political scientists.

EXAMPLE: DECLINING DEMOCRATIC LEGITIMACY IN THE UNITED STATES

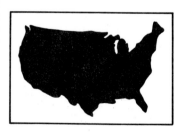

The story of the last couple of decades in the United States has been in some respects the opposite of what we have seen in Germany. Since about the mid-1960s, there has been a puzzling decline in people's confidence in officials and in the political system. It might not seem so strange that the political turmoil of the 1960s and

6–8   **Decline of Confidence, 1958–1980**

	1958	1964	1968	1972	1976	1980	1984	1986
Percent who trust the government to do what is right "most of the time" or "always"	73	76	61	53	33	25	45	39
Percent thinking the government is run for a few big interests	—	29	40	53	66	69	59	—
Percent thinking "quite a lot" of government people are crooked	24	29	25	36	42	46	33	—

SOURCE: University of Michigan, Center for Political Studies, National Elections Studies. Data made available by the Inter-University Consortium for Political and Social Research.

the Watergate scandal of 1973 shook people's faith, but there has appeared to be further erosion during the return to normality of the late 1970s and the 1980s.

Table 6–8 shows a steady downward trend in the percentage of Americans thinking that one can trust the government to do what is right most of the time or always and an upward trend in the percentage thinking that the government is run for the benefit of a few big interests and that quite a lot of people running the government are crooked. Although the figures for 1984 suggest a possible reversal of the trend, overall this is a dramatic loss in legitimacy both for the government as a whole and for the particular people in office. The steadiness of the trend across various events and various presidents makes it look as though it were not a response to particular disappointments, but political scientists are frankly at a loss to say just what *has* caused the decline.[15]

While this plunge in trust and legitimacy has been occurring, Americans have remained an attentive and reasonably active citizenry. As you can see in Figure 6–1, while turnout in elections has dropped somewhat, the decline is a fairly gentle one, from 59 percent of the electorate voting in the 1956 presidential election to 50 percent in 1988.

The number of people performing the more substantial act of writing to officials rose steadily, from 17 percent in 1964 to 20 percent in 1968, 27 percent in 1972, and 28 percent in 1976, the last year for which we have comparable figures.[16]

[15]Arthur Miller and Jack Citrin present an interesting interchange concerning the possible causes of the decline in "Political Issues and Trust in Government: 1964–70," *American Political Science Review* 68 (September 1974): 951–1001.

[16]University of Michigan, Center for Political Studies, National Election Studies. Data made available by the Inter-University Consortium for Political and Social Research.

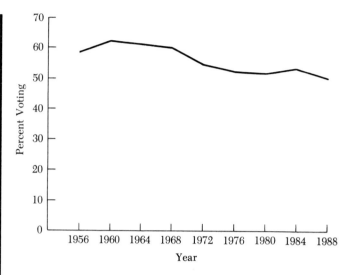

Figure 6–1   Percent of voting age population voting, U.S.A.

SOURCE U.S. Bureau of the Census, *Statistical Abstract of the United States*, 103rd ed., p. 489.

Finally, the percentage who state that they follow what is going on in government and public affairs some or most of the time has remained virtually unchanged: 63 percent said they did so in 1960 and 61 percent in 1986.[17]

The combination of a still fairly attentive citizenry who have dropped off sharply in their trust of the government is alarming and puzzling. It does not bode well for a continuation of stable, constructive democracy, and for this reason it is important that we find out the causes of the change. The first person who does so will have made an important contribution to our understanding of democracy.

FURTHER READING

Almond, Gabriel, and Verba, Sidney. *The Civic Culture*. Boston: Little, Brown, 1965.

Almond, Gabriel, and Verba, Sidney, eds. *The Civic Culture Revisited*. Boston: Little, Brown, 1980.

"Authority," in *International Encyclopedia of the Social Sciences*.

Barber, Benjamin. *Strong Democracy*. Berkeley: University of California Press, 1984.

Dahl, Robert. *Modern Political Analysis*, 4th ed. Englewood Cliffs, N.J.: Prentice-Hall, 1984.

[17]Ibid.

Dawson, Richard E., Prewitt, Kenneth, and Dawson, Karen S. *Political Socialization*, 2nd ed. Boston: Little, Brown, 1977.

Gellner, Ernest. *Culture, Identity, and Politics*. Cambridge, England: Cambridge University Press, 1987.

Graber, Doris. *Mass Media and American Politics*. Washington, D.C.: Congressional Quarterly Press, 1980.

Inglehart, Ronald. *Culture Shift in Advanced Industrial Society*. Princeton, N.J.: Princeton University Press, 1990.

Lane, Robert E. *Political Ideology: Why the American Common Man Believes What he Does*. New York: Free Press, 1962.

"Legitimacy," in *International Encyclopedia of the Social Sciences*..

McCloskey, Herbert. "Consensus and Ideology in American Politics." *American Political Science Review* 58 (June 1964): 361–382.

Mueller, John. *War, Presidents, and Public Opinion*. New York: Wiley, 1973.

Patterson, Thomas E. *The Mass Media Election*. New York: Praeger, 1980.

Sniderman, Paul. *Personality and Democratic Politics*. Berkeley: University of California Press, 1975.

Sullivan, John L., Piereson, James, and Marcus, George E. "An Alternative Conceptualization of Political Tolerance." *American Political Science Review* 73 (September 1979): 781–794.

Verba, Sidney, and Nie, Norman. *Participation in America*. New York: Harper & Row, 1972.

Chapter 7

Constitutions and the Design of Government

Every state—in fact, every political organization, club, or other group—has a constitution, or set of rules by which power is distributed among the members. Obviously no group of people engaged in politics could exist without rules of this kind.

We speak of such unwritten rules as a "constitution with a small 'c,'" meaning simply the generally understood rules by which power is distributed in any political group—rules that have come to be accepted informally, over time.

Most organizations and states, however, also have a formal set of central rules that outline the basic ways in which they conduct their affairs. The Constitution of the United States (note the *capital* "C") is such a document, as are Canada's Constitution Act of 1982, the Basic Law of West Germany, and the Constitution of the Soviet Union. Typically, such a document tells who is to carry out the major functions of politics (proposing, deciding on, and implementing laws); how the people holding those positions are to be chosen; who is to be in charge during an emergency; and by what procedures the constitution itself may be changed. Often there is also a section, such as the Bill of Rights in the U.S. Constitution, that sets out certain basic rights of the citizen or basic aims of the state. Thus, a constitution may state that all citizens are guaranteed the right of freedom of speech (U.S.A.), or that the state guarantees full employment (France), or that the state is socialist (Soviet Union).

No state can put *all* the rules governing the distribution of power into its formal constitution: Much must always be left to informal arrangements or to other documents. In the United States, the Constitution lays out a basic structure for politics. But the "constitution with a small 'c'" includes a great deal more than just the Constitution. It includes the stipulation that the U.S. Supreme Court may overturn an act of Congress—a rule not written into the Constitution but only developed later under the strong Chief Justice John Marshall. Further, it includes the tradition that presidents take a leading role in the making of foreign policy, and it includes much else besides. All these things are rules governing the distribution of power, which are not part of the Constitution but *are* part of our constitution.

So much is left out of the formal Constitution of the Soviet Union that a person reading it could misunderstand totally how Soviet politics works. The Constitution of the Soviet Union sets up a formal structure of government, with a parliament (the Supreme Soviet) whose members are elected by the citizens and which passes all laws of the state. From this description, one would expect that the Supreme Soviet was the dominant factor in the making of policy and that the people of the Soviet Union had fairly direct access to power by their right to select the members of the Supreme Soviet. But to understand Soviet politics one must also understand an important political force that is left out of the Constitution, the Communist party. As we shall see in more detail in Chapter 9, the Communist party has generally controlled both the politics and the economy of the Soviet Union by making certain that key actors in both spheres are party members who will obey party orders and see to it that rival centers of power do not develop. Until changes that started in 1989, members of the Supreme Soviet were part-time legislators who generally served only a single term before they were replaced; further, the Supreme Soviet met for only a few weeks each year; and finally, voters were not offered a choice of candidates in the election, but could only vote for the nominee or else spoil their ballots. Through these arrangements, *none of which were specified in the Constitution*, the Supreme Soviet was reduced to a group who met briefly amid considerable ceremony to ratify the laws that had been drawn up for them by the leaders of the state—in spite of the fact that the Constitution refers to the Supreme Soviet as the "highest organ of state power in the U.S.S.R."[1]

Under Mikhail Gorbachev's policy of *glasnost* ("openness"), elections to the Supreme Soviet were for the first time made competitive in 1989, and the Supreme Soviet has stirred itself to acquire some real political power. It now meets for eight months of the year, and in its first session it forced a couple of changes in the set of ministers Gorbachev appointed to his cabinet. However the body may evolve in the future, though, the point remains that at present its reality is still far different from the powerful body described in the Constitution.

Such disparities between formal rules and actual political power are not limited to the Soviet Union, and there is nothing necessarily "sneaky" about them. In the United States, a reading of the Constitution would lead one to think that the members of the electoral college had great power, since they are elected to meet and select a president; in fact, however, the practice and expectation have developed that the members of the electoral college simply ratify the vote of the citizens of their states, so that in practice it has essentially no political power at all. As another example of the frequent disparity between formal political power and actual power, consider the fact that no constitutions in Europe or North America mention the great political power of newspapers and television networks more than in passing.

VARIATIONS IN FORMALITY

Constitutions vary as to how much is set out formally in a central document and how much has gradually developed outside of it. Generally speaking, older

[1] John S. Reshetar, Jr., *The Soviet Polity*, 3rd ed. (New York: Harper & Row, 1989), p. 178.

constitutions put less into a central document; newer ones, more. Two of the oldest political bodies in the world, Great Britain and the Catholic church, have no central written constitution at all. Rather, the rules of politics for each are embodied in a variety of documents, traditions, and accepted practices. Each has a constitution (with a small "c"); people are aware of it and cite it frequently in British or church politics, but they are not referring to any single document when they do.

The United States is a relatively old state, and the original U.S. Constitution was approximately 4,300 words long; approximately 2,900 words have since been added in amendments. West Germany is a new state, and its Basic Law, written in 1949, is approximately 19,700 words long; this includes numerous amendments. France's most recent constitution, published in 1958 and amended only slightly since then, is about 9,100 words long. Perhaps constitutions that have been written in more recent years are longer because their writers are aware of the greater size and importance of the state today and have taken greater pains to protect the state's power from difficulties that might arise. A large part of West Germany's Basic Law is devoted to who is to govern during emergencies, though this is unusual. The one thing that is generally true of recent constitutions is that they are *specific* and complicated.

THE VIRTUE OF VAGUENESS

Such specificity is by no means always an advantage. Napoleon once said that a constitution should be short and obscure. If rules are stated very specifically, it becomes difficult to adapt a constitution to unforeseen or changing circumstances. Just as French generals in the period from 1919 to 1933 devised a marvelous fortification (the Maginot line) that would have served well for the trench warfare of World War I but was useless against the changed strategies of World War II, writers of constitutions often include in their design solutions to the problems with which *they* have become familiar. If these solutions are precise and inflexible, they are likely to produce new problems later on. Republican lawmakers in the United States were upset by the fact that Franklin Delano Roosevelt (a Democrat) had served more than the customary two terms as president. After his death, they wrote a stern amendment into the Constitution, limiting presidents to two terms of service. A few years later they were faced with Dwight Eisenhower, a popular Republican candidate whom they would have loved to nominate for a third term but who was now constitutionally barred from running again.

Similarly, the writers of the Basic Law of West Germany were preoccupied, after the war, with the fact that Hitler had been able to take over the democratic government of Germany peacefully and legally in 1933 and transform it into a dictatorship. In dozens of ways, they tried to make their new constitution "Hitlerproof." One of the many devices they added was a restriction on the ability of the parliament to unseat the chancellor and his cabinet. This power of parliament was hemmed about by numerous conditions, which led to an unpleasant comic opera when in 1972 the socialist-led government of Willy Brandt had lost so much support in the parliament that it could not even pass the national budget. Brandt and his cabinet wished to step down and call for a new election, since, under the circumstances, they could not govern effectively. But for six months no one could think of a way by which this could be arranged, under West Germany's complicated constitutional provisions, without the embarrassment of the socialists voting themselves out of office (which they were not willing to do). The point is that the authors' precise and detailed constitutional tinkering with the Basic Law, designed to "win the last war," led to unforeseen difficulties in governing West Germany.

Another example of misplaced specificity in writing constitutions comes from a regional political science association in the United States. This group publishes a scholarly journal, the editor of which is changed every three years. At one time, it was suggested that the term of the editor might be lengthened to four years, since it cost the association a few thousand dollars each time the editor was changed and the journal's operations had to be moved from one campus to another. This was not a big issue, but everyone agreed that the change would be a good idea since it would save some money and inconvenience. On looking at the association's Constitution, however, it found that the change could not be made easily. This document, instead of sensibly stating that the editor should serve a term to be determined by the association's council, plainly said that "The editor shall serve a term of three years. . . ." Since an amendment to the Constitution, tedious and difficult to arrange, would have been required in order to change the editor's term, the idea was dropped. One would think that the political scientists who wrote this document should have known better!

OTHER PRINCIPLES OF CONSTITUTIONAL DESIGN

Let us now assume that you are in a position to help design or amend a state's constitution. Are there any additional principles that might help guide you? Beyond the general principle that you should not try to be too specific, a few additional rules of thumb you might consider are as follows: (1) the constitution should preferably not break drastically with long-standing traditions of government, (2) the constitution should be relatively easy to change, and (3) "incentive compatibility" should be built in as much as possible, so that the holders of power will find it personally advantageous to do what society as a whole needs from them. Let us consider each of these in some detail.

The Importance of Long-standing Traditions

If a set of rules is to work, it must not be too far out of line with what most people in the state wish to do. One famous instance of a rule that did not work because it deviated too far from the people's wishes was the prohibition of liquor in the United States in the 1920s. In 1919, a constitutional amendment forbidding the possession or consumption of alcoholic beverages in the United States was passed. While many people had obviously supported this amendment (else it would not have been passed), many opposed it. The law was openly disobeyed, and criminals like Al Capone flourished on the illegal traffic in liquor. Eventually the state gave up and in 1933 the Constitution was amended to make alcoholic beverages legal once again.

It is not enough, either, just to set up rules that the people are willing to obey only reluctantly; something more is needed than bare acquiescence. As we saw in Chapter 6, it is important that a state have a reservoir of goodwill and positive support from its people to carry it over the occasional rough times. A good constitution will not only be one that people are *willing* to obey but also one that comes close enough to their preconceptions that they will be able to identify enthusiastically with the system. Many historians, for instance, think it is unfortunate that, when Germany lost World War I, the monarchy to which its people were accustomed was destroyed. The democratic constitution of 1919 did not provide for the sort of personal, emotional attachment that the monarch had always provided. Instead, the first president of the new system was a quiet man, the son of a lowly saddle maker, with no dash or glamour. Hitler was later able to exploit the people's hunger for an exciting focus of patriotic devotion. How much better if the constitution of 1919 could have made a less dramatic break with the past by including a powerless but handsomely dressed monarch. This of itself would not have solved all of Germany's problems, but it might have helped.

This is not to say that a constitution cannot depart at all from what the people expect. Many revolutionary states—such as China, for example—have imposed new systems of government and society that transformed their people's expectations. There has always been a great deal of tension associated with this, however, and such states have had to keep tight control of things, causing much human suffering, in order to ensure the state's stability. There is inevitably a price to be paid in instituting rules for which the people are not prepared; but in some instances this price may be worth paying.

The Importance of Amendability

If a new constitution must come reasonably close to reflecting the people's expectations, it must also be open to revision or amendment in response to changing needs over time. It is always a temptation, when writing a formal document, to "protect" it by making it difficult to change.

The U.S. Constitution, for example, was designed to be difficult to change. As a result, in the approximately two hundred years that it has been in force, only sixteen amendments beyond the original Bill of Rights have been added. Such inflexibility could have been dangerous, since the conditions of U.S. politics must obviously have changed immensely over two or more centuries. Fortunately, a new device for adaptation appeared when the Supreme Court took onto itself the power to interpret the Constitution with a certain amount of discretion. The Constitution itself was sufficiently "obscure," in Napoleon's sense, that the Court could adapt it with reasonable ease to changed circumstances. In 1954, for instance, the Court ruled that, in light of modern sociological theory, "separate but equal" schools for blacks and whites could not be taken to provide the equal protection under the laws that the Constitution guarantees. The Court ruled in this way despite the fact that in earlier decisions, without the benefit of such theory, it had ruled that segregated school systems *were* constitutional.[2] Allowing nine judges who are appointed for life the discretion to adapt the Constitution may not be the best or the most democratic way to proceed, but it has at least provided a flexibility that the authors of the Constitution were not originally wise enough to build in.

In many states provisions for adapting the constitution are much simpler. Often, a simple majority in the parliament is sufficient.

The Importance of Incentive Compatibility

In any political system, it is important that people in positions of power have personal incentives to do what society as a whole needs from them. That is, holders of power should find that they are personally rewarded when they do what society needs done and personally punished when they do not.

We may safely assume that when people find that what is good for them personally conflicts with what is good for the state, they will usually choose what is good for themselves. This is not to say that people are extremely selfish. Because the state and the individual are so different in size, it is easy for the individual to conclude that the damage to the state will be tiny compared to the benefit to him or her. As a result, people can usually make the "selfish" choice without feeling that they are doing much damage to the state. If a little cheating on my income tax can save me $300, what does that matter to a national budget of billions upon billions of dollars?

The problem, of course, is that if large numbers of people find themselves in a similar position, the result can be very serious indeed. Precisely this problem occurs in constitutions. The constitution—the set of rules determining who has what kinds of political power—places individuals in positions in which they will make certain choices that society needs to have made. Presidents and members of a congress or parliament are expected to make laws for the state, public health officials are expected to watch out for epidemics, judges are expected to settle legal disputes fairly, police officers are expected to keep order, members of town councils are expected to set rules within their towns, and so on.

But it is not enough simply to *say* what a person is to do in one of these positions. If costs and benefits are not set up so as to encourage officials to act in the intended manner, there is a good chance that they will act in ways that suit their personal interests rather than those of society.

---

[2]*Brown v. Board of Education,* 347 U.S. 483 (1954).

For instance, the U.S. Congress was set up to make rules for the country as a whole. However, members of Congress are rewarded or punished not by the country as a whole but by the voters of their districts. It is a well-known problem of American democracy that, if the two conflict, members of Congress will generally pursue the needs of their districts rather than those of the country as a whole. If the United States had stronger political parties, which could develop national programs and punish members of the Congress who did not support their party's program, then the personal incentives to members of the Congress would be different and we might expect to see them support national interests even when these conflicted with their own districts' interests. As we will see in Chapter 9, many states do have political parties of this sort, and there we do not find that members of the parliament place local needs over national ones.

As another example, consider the role of civil servants. Society needs to have civil servants develop programs creatively and administer them to the public efficiently—that is, at as low a cost as possible. However, in almost all countries civil servants are personally rewarded most highly if they are cautious about innovation (in this way they will avoid ever making a dramatic mistake) and always spend all the money that had been allocated to them (if they

"THE HECK WITH THE CONSTITUTION—
I'M GOING TO SHOUT 'FIRE'."

(Sidney Harris)

show that they can do the job for less money, they're likely to be given less money the next year). These rewards push civil servants toward uncreative, inefficient administration of programs.

Other examples could be drawn to show the importance of designing incentive structures so as to reward people for doing what the constitution intends them to do rather than for something else. It should be stressed that this is necessary *not* because holders of public office are especially greedy or cynical or selfish. Rather, just like the income tax cheater, they are faced with differences in scale such that very important things for them personally (security in their jobs, advancement) are balanced against almost trivial losses to the state. (What does it really matter if I vote for an inefficient project for my district? It is tiny compared with the overall budget. Is it really that important to the United States that my office—the transcribing division of the Southwest Regional Advisory Branch of the Weedgit Marketing and Regulatory Board— function at top form?) Just as with the problem of tax evasion, the problem here is that from the point of view of the single official, little damage is done to the state; but because there are thousands of officials like this, their combined impact may be grave indeed. We can expect most of these individuals to do what they are actually rewarded for doing, not necessarily what they are meant to do. Therefore we must try hard to design our constitution so that rewards follow for what officials are meant to do.

THE GEOGRAPHIC CONCENTRATION OF POWER

In later chapters we will look at a variety of questions on one aspect or another of constitutional design—how officials should be chosen, how laws should be passed, what the best way of administering policies is, and so on. But one very general question of constitutional design deserves treatment in this chapter.

That is the question of how much political power should be concentrated in the central government and how much should be distributed among the governments of cities, of "states" (as in the United "States"), or of regions. Some constitutions place almost all political power in the central government, with very little independent decision making left to localities or regions. Others create a relatively weak central government, with many political decisions being made at lower levels. And a variety of arrangements that fall between the two are possible.

What makes this a particularly important question is that all over the world, hot conflicts frequently rage between central governments and local groups. This is the single greatest cause of political conflict today—a more incendiary one, for instance, than the perennial conflict between "haves" and "have-nots" or any of the newer conflicts such as those associated with feminism or with protection of the environment. In Spain, separatists have for several years waged an intermittent campaign of terror on behalf of their claims for a separate Basque state or at least for a greater degree of local indepen-

dence in making political decisions. In 1981, Canada saw a divisive constitutional crisis which was set off by attempts of the central government to gain
greater control over oil production and pricing; there has also been a strong
movement in favor of separating the French-speaking province of Quebec from
the rest of the country. In Britain, a Scottish nationalist party has from time to
time been able to sweep most of the Scottish seats in the parliament with its
claim for greater independence for Scotland. India is divided into many districts speaking different languages; these districts operate fairly independently
of the central government, and disputes over language policies and job preferences for those speaking different languages are always hot political items.
The Soviet Union consists of fifteen governmental units called "republics" (one
of which is Russia); many of these have their own languages and there are frequent muted conflicts among them. Soviet troops had to be sent into Georgia,
Uzbekistan, Azerbaijan, and Armenia at various times in 1988 and 1989, while
at the same time the Baltic republics of Estonia and Latvia were pressing for
full economic autonomy. And when German troops invaded the Soviet Union
in 1941, tensions between the central government and the large southwestern
republic of the Ukraine were so great that initially the Germans were wel-
comed as liberators by many Ukranians; it was only after the Germans brutally
abused the occupied parts of the Ukraine that the Ukrainians turned against
them. In another part of the world, many parts of Africa have had intense
center-region conflicts; civil wars have been fought in Nigeria, Ethiopia, the
Sudan, and Zaire between the central government and one or more regions
that wished to break away. In the Mideast, Kurdish regions of Syria, Iraq, and
Iran have been a source of political tension for those countries for many years.
As one last example, remember that the one time that politics in the United
States heated up into civil war was in 1865, in a dispute between the central
government and the southern part of the country.

"FEDERAL" AND "UNITARY" STATES

The question of central versus local control is a hot item of politics; how is it
dealt with constitutionally? First of all, there is a formal distinction between
states that are "unitary" and those that are "federal." We shall look first at this
formal distinction (a characteristic of constitutions with a capital "C") and then
consider less formally (and more realistically) the division of power between
central governments and their local or regional units.

A *unitary state* is one in which no other governmental body but the central
government has any areas of policy that are exclusively under its control. In a
unitary state, local and regional political bodies may potentially be overruled
by the central government in any political decision they make. In a *federal
state*, by contrast, local governmental authorities of some sort are set up by the
constitution (usually for regions of the state, as in the "states" of the United
States or the "republics" of the Soviet Union), and these authorities are given

certain political decisions over which they have a legal monopoly of control.[3] In a *federation*, then—a federal state—two governments both control the same group of people but with regard to different political questions.

West Germany is an example of a federation. The regional governments, called Länder, have total control of education, television, and radio; the central government has total control of defense, diplomacy, currency and monetary policy, the postal service, railroads and air transport, and copyrights; the central government and Länder share responsibility for all other areas of policy.

A federal system often has been the result of a compromise by which reluctant members were induced to join together in a state; this is how the United States was originally formed, for instance. Generally, federal systems exist where there was some difficulty in uniting the state or where the state is so large or so culturally diverse that it is thought there may be problems holding it together. Small states are less likely to be federal systems than large ones simply because problems like these are more likely to have cropped up in large states with diverse populations.

As of 1989, a total of 20 states were federal systems while 153 were unitary. From this it might appear that the question of federalism is unimportant, since so few states are federal systems. However, the federal states tend to be the larger ones. Though these 20 states represent only 12 percent of the world's states, they contain 38 percent of the world's people and cover 51 percent of the world's land area. The 20 states are indicated on Figure 7–1.

THE DISTINCTION BETWEEN "UNITARY" AND "CENTRALIZED" STATES

A formal definition like that given on page 135 usually needs to be supplemented by an understanding of informal arrangements. We stated there that in a federal system, separate governmental units coexist on the same territory, each with its own, constitutionally set areas of policy. In a unitary system, by contrast, the central government is given the authority to make all policies, though it may deputize other governmental structures to act on its behalf. From this, we can see that in at least a *formal* sense, political power is more *centralized* (concentrated more on a central authority) in unitary systems than in federal ones.

However, politics is filled with surprises, and as usual there are many informal arrangements that modify the centralizing tendency of the unitary state and the opposite tendency of the federal state. First of all, actual control of money counts at least as much in politics as the formal authority to make decisions. "Who pays the piper, calls the tune," as they say. Table 7–1 shows the percentage of all governmental revenues collected and controlled by central, regional, or local governments in a variety of federal and unitary systems.

---

[3]William Riker, *Federalism: Origin, Operation, Significance* (Boston: Little, Brown, 1964), chap. 1.

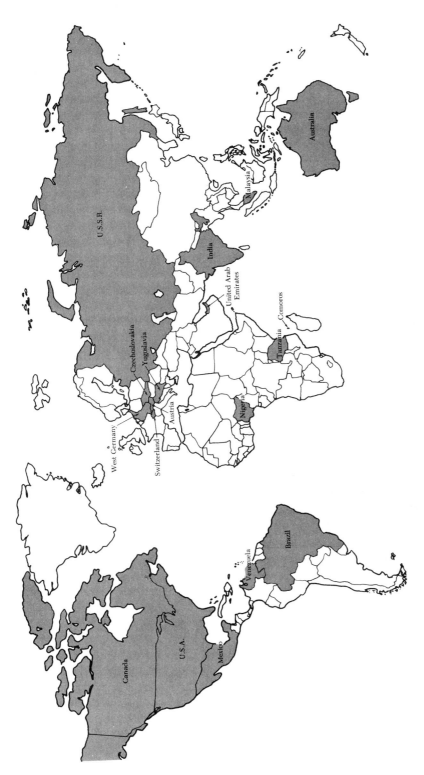

Figure 7–1 Federal systems (shaded areas) of the world.

7–1   **Percent of Revenue Collected by Different Levels of Government**

	Central Government	"States" or Regions	Local Governments
FEDERAL SYSTEMS			
Australia	83	11	6
U.S.A.	57	25	18
Canada	46	41	12
West Germany	39	37	24
Yugoslavia	36	44	20
UNITARY SYSTEMS			
Israel	97	0	3
Poland	96	—	4
Turkey	94	—	6
Great Britain	85	—	15
France	82	8	10
Netherlands	79	19	2
Sweden	68	—	32
Japan	52	23	25

SOURCE: Annual statistical yearbooks for each country.

While the central government controls more of the money in almost all unitary systems than in any of the federal systems, there is considerable variation within each category. The central government of Japan draws only 52 percent of the governmental revenues, less than the 83 percent drawn by the central government of Australia, the most centralized of the federal systems displayed here. Clearly, if we look at the control of cash, there is considerable variation in degrees of government centralization that goes beyond our crude distinction between "federal" and "unitary."

In other ways, less easily measured than revenues, states vary in their degree of centralization. France and Britain, for example, look fairly similar on Table 7–1. Both are unitary states, and the central government of France draws 82 percent of all revenues, while the central government of Great Britain draws 85 percent. But *how* authority and revenues are used is as important as *whether* they are used. In Britain, the central government has traditionally kept only a loose control over local governments' actions and expenditures. For instance, the choice of whether to shift to the modern, "comprehensive" high school was left entirely to localities. Or, as another example, consider that the British central government faced a serious difficulty in recent years in writing its budget—it had to provide money to local governments to pay their work force, but it did not know in advance how big the raises granted by local authorities to their civil servants would be. In effect, local authorities had control over the writing of a significant chunk of the national budget.

In France, on the other hand, power was for centuries lodged firmly in Paris. A minister of education in the late nineteenth century is said to have demonstrated this to a visitor, when, checking his watch, he looked up and said, "My friend, at this moment every third-grade pupil in France is reciting 'The Blue Bird.'" Power in France has become somewhat less centralized in the decades since then; but it was still true until recently that for almost any major decision—whether to build a new town hall or school, for instance—cities had to gain the approval of the government of Paris. In 1981 President Mitterand instituted a number of decentralizing reforms, devolving many functions on new regional and departmental councils, but the system remains on balance a tightly centralized one.[4]

As a final example of how important informal mechanisms of power may be, consider the Soviet Union. Here is a state which, constitutionally, is strongly federal. But as we will see in an example below, through the informal arrangement of discipline via the Communist party, party leaders associated with the central government were until recently able to direct straightforwardly what the leaders of the republic governments (who rank beneath them in the party apparatus) do.

To sum up, the degree of centralization in politics is greatly influenced by the formal constitutional choice between federalism and a unitary arrangement, but it is also strongly affected by all sorts of less formal arrangements.

HOW MUCH CENTRALIZATION IS GOOD?

Obviously, any country has to strike some balance between centralized and decentralized politics. With totally decentralized politics, the state would cease to exist; it would be broken up into many small independent states. And even short of this, strong decentralization might lead to uncoordinated policies and confusion. But great centralization, on the other hand, especially in a state that is at all large or geographically varied, would make for inflexible and insensitive government.

How much centralization is good will vary from state to state and with the circumstances the state faces. Generally, large and diverse states find it necessary to be less centralized than other states in order to meet varying local needs flexibly. Or if a given state is faced with an emergency, as in time of war, it may feel that all power must be pulled together centrally so that it will be able to concentrate its resources on the single goal of meeting the emergency. (Most decentralized systems do, in fact, give their central governments extraordinary temporary power during war.) There is no single level of centralization of politics that one should necessarily prescribe for all states at all times.

It is interesting to note, though, that at least the industrialized states of the world have shown signs over the last few decades of converging toward a fairly similar degree of centralization. Apparently the circumstances in which these states find themselves are sufficiently similar that a common level of centralization has seemed appropriate to the leaders of each.

[4]A good review is J. R. Frears, "The Decentralization Reforms in France," *Parliamentary Affairs* 36 (Winter 1983): 56–66.

Thus centralized states like France or the Soviet Union have attempted over the last decade to decrease the centralization of power. In the Soviet Union, managers of individual factories have been given more discretion over how much of a good to produce and how to produce it, instead of responding simply to directions from Moscow. In France, the government of President Mitterand has sharply decreased the powers of the "prefects," civil servants who used to be responsible for keeping Paris in control of what local governments were doing. On the other hand, in the decentralized United States, the last decade or so—despite recent attempts to reverse the trend—has been marked by an extension of power by the central government over the states and localities. This has been accomplished by aid grants from the central government to the state or local government that carry with them some control over how the money is to be spent. As one example of this, the central government today has the power to order school districts to supply certain services to handicapped students. This would have been unthinkable thirty years ago.

We cannot give a simple answer to the question of how much centralization of government is good. But we can note that all around the world, complex industrialized states are indicating by their own choices that they are most comfortable with a considerable but limited degree of centralization.

"CONSTITUTIONALISM"

A somewhat different question from the *nature* of constitutions is the question of "constitutionalism": Given that each state has a constitution, how faithful is a state to its constitution? That is, how fully do the leaders of the state honor the rules of politics in the state? "Constitutionalism" is the doctrine that states should be faithful to their constitutions because the rules so provided are all that can protect the citizens from arbitrary decisions by powerful people. There is also a notion in "constitutionalism" that constitutions themselves should be designed fairly, rather than to give undue advantage to one particular group.

Constitutionalism is strong in Britain, the United States, Canada, Australia, and New Zealand. In the United States, for example, the Supreme Court, which is rather insulated from political pressure, has the power to overturn any act of government if it finds that the act is unconstitutional. The Court has been particularly active in guarding the Bill of Rights, a list of personal freedoms from governmental action that is written into the Constitution. Britain, Australia, Canada, and New Zealand do not have a supreme court to enforce the formal constitution, but in all of them there is a long tradition of impartial obedience to the rules of politics and to the protection of individuals from arbitrary official action. Even in these five countries, however, constitutionalism is only *relatively* strong. It is not, and probably can never be, an absolute. Especially in times of national emergency, the governments of these countries have sometimes felt that it was necessary for them temporarily to suspend rights that they would ordinarily honor. Great Britain, for instance, held no elections for the duration of World War II, even though an election had been due in 1940; Churchill and the other party leaders thought that an election would be an unnecessary distraction during wartime, and they were critical of the United States for going ahead and holding its presidential election in 1944. Similarly, President Roosevelt ordered the internment of most Japanese-Americans during the war on the grounds that they were security risks. The president would never have had the power to do this in peacetime.

A country in which traditions of constitutionalism are a bit weaker is France. While individual rights are generally secure there, leaders' faithfulness to the rules of politics is a more fragile thing than in the United States, Canada, or Britain. In the last century, France has had four different constitutions, and it has had a total of nine different systems for holding elections. Election laws, in particular, are manipulated so as to benefit the party in power. Also, it is generally understood that the party in power will manipulate news reports on public television and radio to enhance its election chances, and French embassies abroad have often tried to manipulate absentee voting so as to help the party in power. Finally, aside from these cynical manipulations of the rules of electoral politics, French military leaders have, three times in this century, given up on democratic rules altogether and have tried to seize power; twice they have been successful.

If France is a bit weak in its constitutionalism, many states are far, far weaker than France. The majority of the world's people live in systems that give them only small protections against arbitrary power. In China from 1966 to 1976, over a million people were killed in the Cultural Revolution, which the state's leader, Mao Tse-tung, initiated in order to restore the Communist party to its original revolutionary zeal. A similar disregard for individuals was shown in the 1989 suppression of the student movement at Tiananmen Square. In *The Gulag Archipelago*, Alexander Solzhenitsyn described the network of concentration camps in the Soviet Union under Stalin; in these, several million Soviet citizens were arbitrarily confined, often without trial.[5] In the late 1970s, under a right-wing military regime, several thousand Argentinians "disappeared" when they were seized by the state police; they were never tried and were not seen again.

EXAMPLE: CONSTITUTIONAL GOVERNMENT IN GREAT BRITAIN

Great Britain is an unusual example of constitutional government in that there is no written constitution—no single document that claims to set out the central principles of the organization of power.

What does the British constitution consist of? Some of it is made up of statute, or acts that Parliament has passed. Much of it also consists of court precedent, decisions that

---

[5]Alexander Solzhenitsyn, *The Gulag Archipelago, 1918–1956* (New York: Harper & Row, 1974).

have been made by judges in cases of constitutional significance. And finally, many important parts of it simply consist of practice—behavior that has arisen in the day-to-day conduct of government and that is not written down anywhere. In all of this, Parliament is ultimately supreme, because a new statute passed by it would override decisions by any court and would, of course, override any practices that had grown up. In the absence of contrary action by the Parliament, however, court decisions or practices stand. And much of the British constitution consists exactly of this: Court precedent and practices that the Parliament has not chosen to change by statute.

The Magna Carta is one of the earliest parts of the British constitution. In 1215 an unpopular king (John) was forced by rebellious barons to sign a document limiting the king's authority over them in a number of ways. This document was later read into statute in 1295. Other important statutes have settled the system for determining who succeeds to the crown when a king or queen dies (Act of Settlement of 1701) and have laid out the powers of the two houses of Parliament (Parliament Acts of 1911 and 1949). Many smaller matters are also dealt with in statutes.

Court precedents have also contributed importantly to the constitution. For instance, the powers of the queen are largely determined by a long series of precedents from court cases over the centuries. And the definitions of individual rights—which in the United States are written into the Constitution as the Bill of Rights—evolved over centuries of court decisions in Britain.

Finally, and this is probably the most puzzling thing of all to non-British readers, important parts of the constitution are not written down in any document whatever but simply exist in practice. They are "what one does." For instance, the prime minister and cabinet are probably the most powerful single part of the process of government in Britain. All but a few of the bills considered by Parliament have been initiated by the cabinet, and the cabinet controls closely what happens in the Parliament. (You will see more about this in Chapter 11.) But nowhere in any statute or in the decision of any court is the cabinet set up or its powers defined. The only law that mentions the cabinet even indirectly is one setting the salaries of cabinet ministers.[6] All the rules governing the cabinet's behavior and defining its powers have arisen in practice and remain as unwritten understandings.

One might well ask how a constitution like this gets enforced. How do we make sure that people play by the rules if not all of the rules are even written down? For instance, the fact that the prime minister is dominant within the cabinet and can ask members to resign or to exchange posts is simply a matter of practice. What would happen if a prime minister fired a cabinet minister, but the cabinet minister did not leave? Or as another example, an important aspect of the British constitution is that a British monarch will always sign into law a bill passed by the Parliament. Without the signature, the bill does not

[6]Ministers of the Crown Act 1937, from S. B. Chrines, *English Constitutional History* (London: Oxford, 1947), p. 21.

become a law, so in principle the monarch has the right to veto acts of Parliament. In practice, however, this is not done. What would happen if a monarch were to try to exercise the right?

The British themselves puzzle over how a system like this can work. The authors of a recent British textbook write:

> Why have countries found it necessary to draw up [formal constitutions]? Three reasons can be advanced. First, they are needed when nations make a fresh start with their institutions, as when India, Pakistan, Ceylon, etc. gained their independence after World War II. Secondly, the country may contain groups of people distinct from each other through race, religion or language. In order to incorporate all

Queen Elizabeth II, the ceremonial head of state of the United Kingdom.

(Tim Graham/Sygma)

people within the nation, each group must be given some guarantee that its identity will be maintained. Thirdly, in large countries, people in different parts may have particular interests and needs which they feel cannot be adequately provided for by a government in a remote capital. Here some form of federalism is likely, the division of powers between federal and state authorities being laid down in a written constitution. None of these considerations applies to Britain.[7]

This does not ring true, however. Certainly, Britain has been subject to major stresses, especially the breaking away of Ireland in the early twentieth century and the continuing troubles in Northern Ireland today. It is not plausible that the British have simply been so peaceful that they have not needed a set of rules to govern them. In the end, one must conclude that the system depends on the goodwill of those who are involved in it. They must *want* to have the system work and see this as in their interest; otherwise it would not work. It may be that the very existence of an unwritten constitution pushes people to behave cooperatively. Where there is a formal set of rules, clever people may feel challenged to find loopholes. But where there is only a set of practices based on certain commonsense principles, clever people will find it necessary always to cite those central commonsense principles and to tailor their arguments and their behavior to them.

For good or bad, an "unwritten" constitution is not something a state can just decide to start up at any time. It must be received from the past, so it is unlikely that a state could deliberately imitate Britain and set up an unwritten constitution! However, we may draw the lesson from Britain that it is well to leave some aspects of our constitution to custom, if that is practical, rather than trying to write everything down.

EXAMPLE: CONSTITUTIONAL GOVERNMENT IN THE SOVIET UNION

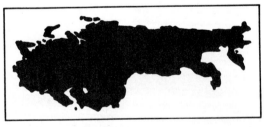

A reasonable general outline of the constitution of the Soviet Union could be given simply by noting that the Communist party is supreme in running the country. It gained its position of power in the Russian Revolution (1917), and it has maintained its control in a practical sense by carefully placing party members in key positions in the armed forces, universities, bureaucracies, and governmental structure.

In at least a formal, legal sense, however, the party does not rule directly;

[7]J. Harvey and L. Bather, *The British Constitution*, 3rd ed. (London: Macmillan, 1974), p. 510.

it exercises its control by directing the actions of a formal governmental structure that enacts into law measures the party apparatus has written.[8] The design of this governmental structure is laid down in an elaborate constitution. While the Soviet Union pays great attention to this document, it is seen as an expression of the political development of the party and the state, not as a set of rules regulating and restricting the behavior of governmental officials. The Soviet Union has had four different constitutions since 1917, with "obsolete" constitutions regularly replaced by newer ones. The most recent constitution was adopted in 1977. As John Reshetar describes the Soviet attitude to their constitutions:

> The instrumental nature of the Soviet constitution is seen in the assertion that "new constitutions are adopted when substantial changes occur in the relationship of class forces in the country." Thus a constitution is not regarded as a repository of certain sacrosanct political norms and principles but simply as a device designed to fulfill the alleged needs of a particular stage of historical development. The Soviet constitution has been amended with great ease (the 1977 Constitution, like that of 1936, has provided for amendment by a two-thirds majority of both chambers of the Supreme Soviet); amendment has been frequent and at times has even been initiated by executive decree. Soviet constitutions have little relationship to constitutionalism, for they have not effectively restrained the country's rulers.[9]

In addition to laying out the design of the governmental superstructure, the Constitution of 1977 guarantees a variety of social and economic rights to Soviet citizens, including the right to employment, housing, and a forty-one hour work week. Political rights such as freedom of speech are guaranteed, but always with the proviso that these rights may be exercised only to further communist goals.

The Constitution of 1977 continues the organization of the Soviet Union as a federation consisting of fifteen republics that are granted considerable formal autonomy—including the right to secede from the U.S.S.R.—but that are in fact kept under close control. They have no independent source of revenue other than the central government, and all their chief leaders are party members, subject to party discipline. By this contrast between *formal* provisions for autonomy but *actual* tight central control, the Soviet Union stands out among the world's federal systems.

What are we to make of a constitution like this? In one sense it seems to be mere decoration, setting up a pretty governmental structure to mask the actual working of politics. On the other hand, these arrangements are undoubtedly useful to the party. By ruling indirectly, the party is not forced into static arrangements but may keep quite fluid and informal its own power structure and

---

[8]The Soviet governmental structure will be described in more detail in later chapters; it will suffice for our purposes here to note that approximately 90 percent of the members of the Supreme Soviet (parliament) are members of the Communist party; that until 1989 it met for a total of only several days a year; and that all bills are passed by a show of hands.

[9]John S. Reshetar, Jr., *The Soviet Polity*, 3rd ed. (New York: Harper & Row, 1989), pp. 175–176.

the devices by which it maintains its control over the governmental structure. Also, the governmental superstructure *does* serve as a useful decoration, helping the system to look less alien to the leaders of western democracies. And finally, as we shall see in later chapters, the superstructure of government and elections serves certain useful functions of its own; for instance, it provides an added channel for communication between Soviet leaders and the general population.

As I am writing this second edition, Mikhail Gorbachev's program of reforms known as *glasnost* ("openness") has been under way for a couple of years. This is an attempt to change the way politics occurs in the U.S.S.R. by tolerating organized dissent, allowing a degree of competition in elections, giving some power to governmental organs such as the Supreme Soviet, and allowing a degree of autonomy to the federal republics. All of this adds up to a considerable diminution of the Communist party's monopoly of power, and of course it might proceed to be much more than that eventually. Even in its present, modest form it is a dramatic break with the tightly controlled system of the past. Interestingly, the *glasnost* changes have not required that the Constitution be redrawn, which indicates once again how loosely connected the Soviet Constitution is to realities of power.

FURTHER READING

Bakvis, Herman, and Chandler, William M. *Federalism and the Role of the State*. Toronto: University of Toronto Press, 1987.

"Constitutions and Constitutionalism," in *International Encyclopedia of the Social Sciences*.

Duchacek, Ivo D. *The Territorial Dimensions of Politics Within, Among and Across Nations*. Boulder, Colo.: Westview Press, 1986.

Finer, S. E., ed. *Five Constitutions*. Baltimore: Penguin, 1979.

Friedrich, Carl. *Limited Government: A Comparison*. Englewood Cliffs, N.J.: Prentice-Hall, 1974.

Goldwin, Robert A., Kaufman, Art, and Schambra, William A., eds. *Forging Unity Out of Diversity: The Approaches of Eight Nations*. Washington, D.C.: American Enterprise Institute, 1989.

Harvey, Jack, and Bather, L. *The British Constitution*, 3rd ed. London: Macmillan, 1974.

Jennings, W. Ivor. *The British Constitution*, 3rd ed. Cambridge, England: Cambridge University Press, 1950.

Riker, William. *Federalism: Origin, Operation, Significance*. Boston: Little, Brown, 1964.

Schlesinger, Joseph. *Ambition and Politics: Political Careers in the United States*. Chicago: Rand McNally, 1966 (especially with regard to incentive compatibility).

Wheare, K. D. *Federal Government*, 4th ed. London: Oxford University Press, 1963.

Chapter 8

Elections

In the long swing of history, elections with broad mass participation are rather new. Such elections originated with democratic government, which means that they came along at the end of the eighteenth century and the beginning of the nineteenth. Today elections are widespread around the world, even though most of the world's states are not democracies. Many nondemocratic states, such as the Soviet Union, hold them regularly. Why are elections so much in vogue?

Part of the answer, of course, is that "democracy" is a word that purrs with respectability. Even states that are not democratic wish to appear democratic, and holding elections is one of the easiest ways to follow some of the *forms* of democracy even if the state is not in fact democratic.

But a second reason is that elections can serve more purposes for the state than merely the democratic one of allowing the mass of people to help in the selection of leaders and policies. Elections were invented in order to make democracy possible; but once invented, they turned out to have further uses as well. This is an interesting aspect of political institutions that we shall encounter frequently in later chapters. Institutions may be devised in order to serve a particular purpose, but once they are in existence, they may be adaptable to a variety of purposes.

In this case, the thing that recommends elections to the leaders of nondemocratic states is that they can serve *two* main purposes: (1) *the purely democratic purpose of allowing the mass of people to have some direct say in the choice of leaders and policies and* (2) *the more or less universal purpose of allowing the state to mobilize its people and to build up their support for the state by acting it out and participating in the process of government.*

ELECTIONS AS A MEANS OF BUILDING SUPPORT

Let us consider the second of these first. To take one example of a nondemocratic state in which elections figure importantly, consider the Soviet Union. One can make a good case that mass political participation among Soviet citizens has always been as great as it is among citizens of the United States. To quote a study from the 1970s:

Campaign activities draw upon the efforts of millions of Soviet citizens, just as they do Americans. Soviet national election campaigns last about two months, and the campaigning is extremely intensive. The party leadership mobilizes millions of "agitators" and "propagandists," as well as ordinary citizens, to publicize the election, explain the issues and programs which the party considers important, and ensure that the entire population goes to the polls. The weeks preceding the election see the formation of countless study circles, discussion groups, campaign meetings, door-to-door canvassing, rallies, demonstrations and speeches.[1]

Similar comparisons could be made in other areas of political activity, beyond elections per se. For example, about one person out of five in the United States has ever contacted a local government official about some issue or problem. Soviet citizens seem to be about as active in this sphere as Americans, though comparable measures of activity are not available. One study notes that "in the first four months of 1962 some 11,803 citizen demands poured into the offices of the Kirov raion of Moscow. In the first half of 1963 officials of a single raion in Leningrad received over 15,000 letters and visits from the populace involving demands of various sorts."[2] On another front, a recent study found that 8 percent of Americans belong to some sort of political organization. By way of comparison, 10 percent of Soviet adults are members of the Communist party.

In elections specifically, a similar comparison can be made. While only about 50 to 60 percent of Americans vote regularly in presidential elections, about 99 percent of Soviet citizens have generally voted in their national elections. There is great social pressure to vote in Soviet elections, and turnout is high:

> The network of agitators is fully activated during the ten days preceding the election. Agitators must visit each voter in the precinct, explaining the virtues and qualifications of the sole candidate. The mass media publicize the biography of each candidate to the larger soviets and urge a resounding vote of confidence for the regime. The candidate spends no money campaigning but holds meetings with voters.... Refusal to vote is regarded as an unpatriotic act. Even the sick are expected to vote and ballot boxes are brought to the bedsides of hospital patients. Voting occurs on ships that are at sea on election day if there are at least twenty-five voters aboard; the votes are added to those cast in the ship's home port. Passengers on long-distance trains vote in special precincts while in transit.[3]

The election takes up a great deal of time and costs a lot of money. Over two million candidates are elected each time—better than one adult out of a hundred—and they must invest a great deal of time and energy in the campaign. Millions more are engaged in agitation, in serving on electoral commissions, and so on. It is an expensive business.

And yet, until Gorbachev's tentative democratic reforms of 1989, there was never any suspense over the outcomes. Only a single candidate was nominated

---

[1]Richard D. Little, "Mass Political Participation in the U.S. and the U.S.S.R.: A Conceptual Analysis." *Comparative Political Studies* 8 (January 1976): 439.

[2]James Oliver, "Citizen Demands in the Soviet System." *American Political Science Review* 63 (June 1969): 467. Cited in Little, op. cit., n. 1.

[3]John S. Reshetar, Jr., *The Soviet Polity*, 2nd ed. (New York: Harper & Row, 1978) p. 196.

Pro-democracy demonstration in Bulgaria calling for competitive elections.
(AP/Wide World)

for each position. Voters could vote *against* that candidate by crossing out the name, and if a majority of those voting did this, the candidate was not elected. But that happened only rarely. Of the 2,200,000 candidates for election to local soviets in 1977, only 61 were dumped in this way, and almost all of these were from small villages.[4] Clearly the purpose of all this electoral activity was not to choose who would govern the Soviet Union, but it must have had *some* purpose else the authorities would not have invested so much in it.

The most reasonable guess is that the main purpose of elections in the Soviet Union has been to renew the people's enthusiasm and support for the regime. Elections provide a recurring opportunity for the newspapers to pour out praise for the leaders of the state and for citizens, through their actions, to feel that they are a part of it. As all behavioral therapists know, a good way to ingrain a particular point of view in a person's consciousness is to act it out. This would be reason enough for the Soviet Union to put its population "through their paces" at regular intervals.

The Soviet Union is not unusual among nondemocratic states in investing a great deal of time and energy in elections. Nazi Germany's election extravaganzas were famous, and approximately 99 percent of the German people regularly proclaimed their loyalty to Adolf Hitler in this way. In modern times,

[4]Ibid., n. 3, p. 197.

Table 8–1   Percent Agreeing That Ordinary People Have Little "Say" in Government

		1968	
	Voters	*Nonvoters*	*Total*
Before the election	71	83	74
After the election	37	58	42
Change	−34	−25	−32
		1972	
	Voters	*Nonvoters*	*Total*
Before the election	34	58	40
After the election	29	54	36
Change	−5	−4	−4

SOURCE: Recalculated from Benjamin Ginsberg, *The Consequences of Consent: Elections, Citizen Control, and Popular Acquiescence* (Reading, Mass.: Addison-Wesley, 1982), pp. 167 and 170.

such states as Guatemala, Egypt, Romania, Algeria, Chile, both North and South Korea, Paraguay, Hungary, Czechoslovakia, Cuba, the Ivory Coast, and many others have staged elaborate elections of which the outcome was never in doubt. The obvious reason for such elections is to strengthen the people's attachment to the state.

While we do not normally think of elections in democracies as functioning to build support for the system, it can be shown that they serve this purpose just as much in democracies as in nondemocracies. A recent study of presidential elections in America highlighted this fact quite well.[5] At both the 1968 and 1972 presidential elections, a sample of American adults were asked both before and after the election whether they agreed or disagreed with the statement "People like me don't have any say about what the government does." Before the 1968 election, most people, whether or not they ended up voting in the election, agreed with the statement, as can be seen in Table 8–1. The electorate in 1968 was quite disillusioned and had lost a great deal of its faith in the nation's leaders. Conflict over civil rights and American involvement in the Vietnam War had soured people on politics, and the American public had just seen the Democratic nominating convention in Chicago torn apart by demonstrations and by the reaction of the police to the demonstrations. Of those who voted in that election, 71 percent initially agreed that ordinary people do not have any say in government, as did 83 percent of those who ended up not voting. But over the campaign and the election, this outlook changed considerably. After the election, only 37 percent of those who had voted agreed with the cynical view of government, for a drop of 34 percentage points. Among those who did not vote but who experienced the period of campaigning and

[5]Benjamin Ginsberg, *The Consequences of Consent: Elections, Citizen Control, and Popular Acquiescence* (Reading, Mass.: Addison-Wesley, 1982), pp. 166–170.

election, the figure also dropped, but by somewhat less—25 percentage points.

The circumstances in 1972 were different, but there again the election apparently served to reassure the public about the political system. The preelection public in 1972, in contrast to that of 1968, was not turned off to politics. The incumbent Nixon administration was popular (Nixon would get 61 percent of the vote), and the Vietnam trauma had passed. Only 34 percent of those who eventually would vote and 58 percent of those who would not initially agreed with the cynical view of government. The campaign was not one to inspire confidence in the system. It was marked by the forced withdrawal of Thomas Eagleton as the Democrats' vice-presidential nominee because it became known that he had a history of mental illness; by a great deal of personal vituperation between the candidates; and by rumors of corruption and "dirty tricks" that would later produce the painful Watergate scandal.

In spite of this, the campaign period and election of 1972 produced small moves toward greater support of the system, even among an electorate who were already rather supportive before the election. After the election, 5 percent fewer of voters, and 4 percent fewer of nonvoters, agreed with the cynical view.

In Chapter 6 we examined the state's need to maintain sufficient support among its citizens that its authority would continue undiminished. For democracies and nondemocracies alike, elections apparently furnish a potent tool to help ensure this popular base of support. At regular intervals, people's acceptance of the system is reinforced as citizens act out their identification with the state and its leaders.

ELECTIONS AS A MEANS OF SELECTING LEADERS AND POLICIES

But in many countries, elections are obviously meant to do more than simply bolster support for the regime. They may also be the means by which leaders and (sometimes) actual policies are chosen by the people. For this to be the case, an election must involve a *choice between candidates* or a *choice whether or not a particular policy is to be followed*. In democratic states, elections are set up in this way. And in some states that are not ultimately democratic, elections are allowed to function in this way at least at the local level. In Tanzania, for instance, the Chama cha Mapinduzi party controls the nomination of candidates at the national level, and only one candidate appears on the ballot; but in local elections, voters choose among competing candidates.

In democracies, the choice of political leaders at all levels is made by competitive elections. In addition, some democracies provide for the *referendum*, a device by which the voters choose directly through their ballots whether or not a particular proposal will become law. Controlled referendums are also sometimes used in nondemocracies to exhibit and stimulate support in the same way as other elections do. The referendum is discussed in a later section of this chapter.

ELECTORAL SYSTEMS

If elections are to be used to choose political leaders, there must be some rule for translating people's votes into a particular selection of leaders. This is not as simple a matter as one might think. For instance, one might state simply that the candidate who gets the most votes will win the election and take office. But what of the people who voted for a losing candidate—should their votes simply count for nothing? And what if there were a dozen candidates and the one who got the greatest number of votes still had only about 20 percent of the vote— would we want that person to take office? Because of these and similar problems, there is no single obvious way to translate the votes cast by the electorate into the people who will take office. States need to design rules determining what person wins office as a result of any particular result in the voting; these rules are called the *electoral system* of the state.

Obviously rulers of states could, if they wished, write many detailed differences into their electoral systems. At one or another time and place, for instance, a party has been required to win at least 5 percent of the vote to get a seat in the legislature, owners of businesses have been given double votes in order to increase their weight in the electoral choice, some seats in a legislature have been reserved for members of one or another race, and votes have been counted separately and weighed differently for rich people and poor people. The possibilities are limited only by the imagination of those in charge of the state.

In general, however, two broad types of electoral system are used in almost all democracies today—*single-member-district plurality* systems, and *proportional representation* systems. For convenience, they will be referred to from this point on by their initials, SMDP and PR.

SMDP and PR Systems

In the SMDP system, the state is divided into a set of districts, usually having roughly equal populations; one representative is elected from each district to be a member of the legislative body of the state; and whoever gets a plurality of the votes wins the seat. (A "plurality" is the largest number of votes cast for any candidate; note that if there are many candidates running, the plurality may be less than a majority of all votes cast.) Hence the name: A *single member* is elected form each *district* by a *plurality* of votes.

This arrangement is familiar to U.S. and Canadian students, since both countries use versions of the SMDP system. In Canada, the members of Parliament are elected by the SMDP system. In the United States, members of the House of Representatives are elected by an SMDP system and members of the Senate by a variant of SMDP. (There are two senators from each state of the United States, but they are elected in separate years by a plurality so that, in effect, the senatorial electoral system is SMDP.)

Britain is an SMDP system, and these systems are in fact more or less limited, worldwide, to Britain and such· of her former colonies as the United States, Canada, India, New Zealand, and South Africa.

Most electoral democracies of the world use versions of proportional representation (PR). PR is really very simple. Though various formulas and methods are used to calculate the proportional result, the basic principle of PR is that political parties' representation in the legislative body is set roughly proportional to their strength in the electorate. That is, if the Fundamentalist Neopejorative Party got 18 percent of the votes cast in the election, it would get roughly 18 percent of the seats in the legislative body; if it got 30 percent of the votes, it would get roughly 30 percent of the seats.

This may not seem an unreasonable result, but PR was invented precisely because SMDP generally does *not* give such a proportional result. Instead, SMDP generally favors large parties and hurts small ones. This is because a small party, if its voters are spread at all evenly geographically, will have only a small number of voters in each district and may, in fact, not have enough in any one district to achieve a plurality and win there. This is illustrated in Figure 8–1. The hypothetical country of Aksala is divided into twenty districts, each having 50,000 voters. In its most recent election, the Prudential Improvidence party polled 450,000 votes, or 45 percent of the total; the Protection of Artifacts party polled 350,000 votes, or 35 percent of the total; and the Revolutionary Inaction party came in third with a still substantial poll of 200,000, or 20 percent of the votes. As you can see from the map, the PIP won 14 seats with its 450,000 votes, the PAP won 5 seats with its 350,000 votes, and the poor RIP got only 1 seat for its 200,000 votes. That is, 45 percent of the vote got 70 percent of the seats, 35 percent of the vote got only 25 percent of the seats, and 20 percent of the vote got only 5 percent of the seats.

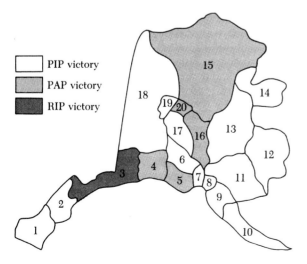

Figure 8–1   A hypothetical SMDP result.

☐ PIP victory

▨ PAP victory

■ RIP victory

This is a fairly typical result of SMDP. Although the example is made up, it was not deliberately constructed to produce this result beyond stating the initial condition that the three parties were of those sizes and had a more or less even distribution of their voters across the country. Most "real life" examples of SMDP fit the same pattern. In the British election of 1987, for instance, the Liberal–Social Democratic Alliance polled 23 percent of the votes but won only 3 percent of the seats in the House of Commons.

In their early elections, most European states used electoral systems similar to SMDP. It was at the urging of small or new parties that felt unfairly discriminated against that most states changed to PR systems in the early part of the twentieth century. Why, you may ask, do any states retain SMDP as an electoral system when it is so unfair? The reason is that there is a practical benefit to the distortion in favor of large parties, which many observers think compensates for the unfairness to smaller parties. Since small parties are disadvantaged by SMDP, there is a tendency for them to disappear or to merge together over time; as a result, SMDP electoral systems tend to encourage the emergence of two large parties rather than a variety of smaller parties.[6] With only one major exception—Canada—SMDP systems have only two major parties, which generally makes it easier to govern the state. With only one possible exception—West Germany—PR systems have more than two major parties, which may make it difficult to govern the state. (We will discuss the relative merits of having just two parties in Chapter 9.)

The trade-off between the two systems is generally one of fairness to minorities and small parties, on the one hand, versus simplifying the party system by weeding out small parties, on the other. Two other issues that may enter into a choice between the two electoral systems are these:

- Electoral participation is likely to be higher under PR then under SMDP. Under SMDP, voters who are in the minority in their district (a Republican in Boston, a Conservative in Quebec City, a Democrat in San Diego) may feel there is no sense even in voting, since their candidates cannot win in any case.
- SMDP provides all legislators with a tie to a particular locality, with a particular set of constituents, while most PR systems do not make this kind of connection.

Two Conditions for the SMDP Bias.   The bias of SMDP in favor of large parties is a function of two conditions: *First, if a small party has most of its strength concentrated in just a few districts, it may not be hurt at all by the SMDP system,* because it may have enough strength in those few districts to win there. Consider if a Southwestern Autonomy party had appeared in Aksala and had polled 60,000 votes in the four southwestern districts. Depending on how its votes were spread among the four districts, it might well have won in one or two of them. (It would have averaged 30 percent

---

[6]The standard statement on the effects of electoral systems is Maurice Duverger, *Political Parties* (New York: Wiley, 1954). See also Douglas Rae, *The Political Consequences of Electoral Laws*, rev. ed. (New Haven, Conn.: Yale University Press, 1971).

of the vote in the four districts and the rest of the vote would have been spread among three parties.)

Again, there are plenty of "real-life" examples of this exception to the rule of SMDP bias. One is the Scottish Nationalist party of Britain, which in October 1974 polled only 3 percent of the vote nationally but, by concentrating that vote in Scotland, won 11 of the 635 seats in the House of Commons. Another good example is Canada itself, which as noted above is the major exception to the rule that SMDP electoral systems tend to limit a country to two major parties. Five major parties are active in Canadian politics, but each of them has a distinct regional identity, so that there is no selective pressure on them from the SMDP system.

Second, the smaller the number of districts, the more likely it is that small parties will be hurt by SMDP. If the state is divided into a small number of large districts, there is less chance that a small party will happen to have enough votes to win in a particular district.

This is illustrated in Figure 8–2, in which the districts of Aksala have been grouped by fours, so that there are now just five larger districts. Under this arrangement, the largest party (PIP) expands its share of the seats from 70 to 80 percent; the PAP drops from 25 to 20 percent; and the "small" RIP (with 20 percent of the vote) disappears.

To carry this to an extreme, if there were only one seat in the legislative body, the whole country would represent a single-member district, with a plurality winning. In this case the ultimate distortion would occur, with the candidate of the PIP winning 100 percent of the "seats" (i.e., the one seat), even though PIP had gained only 45 percent of the total vote.

This last extreme possibility is mentioned because it does, in fact, occur in

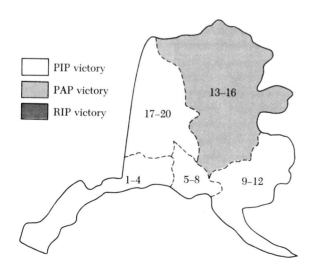

Figure 8–2 A hypothetical election by SMDP, with Aksala divided into only five districts.

the real world. If a state has a president who is popularly elected by all the voters, the election functions, in effect, as a legislative election with one seat under SMDP. (Most democracies do not have a powerful president, but some do—the United States, France, Mexico, and others. Presidential government is discussed at length in Chapter 12.) Where there is a presidency, small parties are driven out of contention, and there is very strong pressure indeed for the system to evolve into one with two large parties. A notable example of this is France, which in 1962 shifted to a popularly elected presidency. Since that time small parties have been gradually declining, until today there are four parties arranged by pairs in loose alliance into a bloc of the Left and a bloc of the Right, plus a fifth party off on its own dimension of opposition to immigrants. The conclusion is unavoidable that the institution of the presidency has forced France's quarrelsome parties to coalesce into something like two large parties.

To summarize the point of this section dealing with electoral systems: *The SMDP system tends to drive out small parties and ultimately to produce an arrangement consisting of two large parties. This effect is less strong if the parties have geographic concentration of voters and may disappear altogether, as in the case of Canada, if the parties' strength is very concentrated by region. The effect is heightened by reducing the number of districts and is especially strong when the state is simply a single district, as in presidential elections.*

REFERENDUMS

Generally, democracies restrict their citizens' involvement in the affairs of state to participation in elections, where, as voters, they may express their choice of potential political leaders. State policies are then set by the elected leaders, without any direct input from the voters. A few democracies, however, allow voters under some circumstances to choose directly, in an election, whether a given policy should be followed. Such an electoral choice is called a *referendum*. The United States does not have any provision for national referendums, but many localities and states do provide for them. California is particularly noted for their use, as in the famous "Proposition 13" referendum in which the state's voters chose to limit property taxes in California communities to 1 percent of the value of the property. Outside the United States, a few democracies provide for the regular use of national referendums. France and Switzerland are two examples, the latter relying on them rather heavily.

Beyond these few instances, many democracies that would not accept the regular use of referendums *do* use them for decisions of great gravity, where it is felt that all the people should be involved in the decision, if only by voting. Spain, for instance, when it initiated its new democratic constitution in 1978, held a referendum so that the constitution could be ratified by the people. Similarly, in the early 1970s, when Norway and Great Britain were deciding whether or not to give up a portion of their national sovereignty and join the

European Community, both put the choice to their people in referendums. (The British voted yes, the Norwegians no.)

Why are democracies so reluctant to give "power to the people" by using the referendum to make laws? The main objection is that a proposed law cannot get the sort of careful consideration and detailed examination in an election campaign that it would get in a legislature or parliament. Voters typically do not have the time or resources to inform themselves about the intricacies of a bill. In a sense, that is "what they hire politicians for." Especially when many bills are voted on in a single campaign, as in California, where twenty or more may appear on a single ballot, only one or two will have been widely discussed among the voters. The other bills will be decided by chance factors such as how enticingly they are worded or where they appear on the ballot, or by the small number of people who may stand to gain from them in special ways and therefore take a special interest in them.

ELECTORAL PARTICIPATION

Let us now shift from elections and electoral systems, per se, to examine how voters act in elections. We shall confine our attention here to voters in democratic elections.

First of all, it is evident that not all of those who are entitled to vote do vote. In the 1984 American presidential election, for instance, only 59 percent of those who were eligible to vote did so; in most elections for local office, the turnout is even less than this.

There is great variation from one place to another, and among different sorts of people in any one place, as to how active people are in elections. At roughly the same time as 50 percent of eligible Americans voted in the 1988 presidential election, the following percentages of the eligible electorate voted in a variety of European elections: Great Britain, 75 percent; Netherlands, 86 percent; West Germany, 83 percent; Italy, 89 percent; Sweden, 90 percent; Austria, 89 percent. It is generally true, as in these cases, that European democracies exhibit higher levels of electoral participation than the United States does. But even within the United States, electoral turnout varies a good deal by geography. In 1988 Georgia had the lowest turnout among the 50 states, only 39 percent; the highest, 66 percent, was Minnesota's.

Beyond geographic variation, certain types of people seem especially likely to vote. Table 8–2 lists various sorts of people who seem especially likely or especially unlikely to vote.

What is it that leads some people to vote more regularly than others? Partly it seems to be a matter of cultural traditions. The high electoral turnout of a state like Minnesota, for instance, seems likely to be a result of the general tradition of constructive citizenship that was strong among the Scandinavian immigrants who made up a large part of Minnesota's early population.

Partly it is a function of practical, almost mundane questions—whether

Table 8–2   Who Is Likely or Unlikely to Vote?

Groups Unusually *High in Participation*	*Groups Unusually* *Low in Participation*
Suburban residents	Young people
Well-educated people	Women (Third World)
Well-off people	Blacks (U.S.A.)
Farmers (U.S.A.)	Blue-collar workers (U.S.A.)
Blue-collar workers (Europe)	

polling day is on a working day (as in the United States), which is less convenient than a Sunday; or whether registration to vote is a cumbersome procedure or an easy one. (In some countries, registration is automatically done by the local authorities and requires no specific action by the person being registered.)

Partly it is a function of the difficulty of making political decisions. This may help explain why well-educated people are more likely to vote than are people with less education; those with less education presumably find politics more puzzling and confusing than those who are better educated do. This problem surely helps to explain why voting turnout is generally low on referendums, which demand more from a voter than simply choosing a party or a candidate.

Finally, it is partly a function of the political circumstances under which the election is held. A close election generally stimulates greater turnout than one that promises to be a walkaway for one side. National elections, because of the great stakes of war and peace that are involved, generally get a higher turnout than they probably deserve as compared with local elections. As noted above, elections conducted under a PR electoral system generally get higher participation than those under SMDP, because under PR no one need worry about "wasting" a vote on a candidate who has no chance to win. And finally, blue-collar workers in Europe participate more faithfully than those in the United States partly because unions in Europe are more active than American unions in mobilizing their voters. And in all European states—unlike the United States—there are present explicitly working-class, socialist parties that draw blue-collar workers into political activity.

THE PARADOX OF PARTICIPATION

We might also flip the question of participation around, and instead of asking "Why doesn't everyone vote?" ask "Why are all these people voting?" Looked at in one way, it is irrational to take the trouble to vote. Seeing how unlikely it would be for a single vote to decide a U.S. presidential election, one might consider it hardly worthwhile to spend a half hour and 8 cents worth of gasoline to get to the polling place. (The odds must be less than one in a trillion

trillion that the other 80 million voters would split exactly even, so that one vote could decide the outcome.) We met the cynic of Skinner's *Walden Two* earlier:

> The chance that one man's vote will decide the issue in a national election is less than the chance that he will be killed on his way to the polls. We pay no attention to chances of that magnitude in our daily affairs. We should call a man a fool who bought a sweepstakes ticket with similar odds against him.[7]

This is what we call the "paradox of participation."[8] It is paradoxical because, if things are considered rightly, *no one who is sensible should vote*, for the reason given above (that, in a large election, it would be extremely unlikely for a single vote to change the result). And if the result of the election is virtually certain to be the same whether you vote or not, why should you take the time and go to the expense? To put it in the concrete terms alluded to in the quote from Skinner, over the years more people are hit by trucks and killed on the way to the polls than change the results of national elections by their single votes. On the average and over the long run, voting is apparently a dangerous and unproductive act.

Paradoxes generally have solutions, and we can try two possible solutions here. First, this paradox obviously holds only for voters taken one at a time. If a large group of voters chose to sit out an election, it is quite possible that their absence could change the outcome. In fact, most politicians spend more time and effort in their campaigns in trying to make sure that the right people get to the polls than in trying to change the minds of people who are planning to vote for their opponents. Politicians certainly recognize the importance of turnout rates in determining elections. Thus, the paradox of participation is a paradox only for voters taken individually. This might resolve the problem for us except that a voter's decision whether or not to vote is taken individually. That is, groups do not decide whether to vote, *voters* decide whether to vote. So the paradox remains.

A second way of addressing the issue is to note that it looks at voting solely as an act to provide benefits or costs to the individual voting. The paradox arises only if we think that voters vote solely because of their wish to exercise their own power in making the government's policies. While it is true that this is the democratic justification for holding elections, we must realize that it casts voting as essentially a *selfish* act in which voters participate only in order to increase their own individual political power. Yet we saw at the beginning of this chapter that in many countries, high electoral turnout occurs even though the voters have no choice of candidates. Clearly voters in those countries are voting for some reason other than to exercise their individual political power, because *their* votes represent no individual political power whatever. They are

---

[7]B. F. Skinner, *Walden Two* (New York: Macmillan, 1948), p. 221.

[8]William H. Riker and Peter C. Ordeshook, *An Introduction to Positive Political Theory* (Englewood Cliffs, N.J.: Prentice-Hall, 1973), pp. 45–68, esp. pp. 57–58.

What Is the Best Level of Participation?

A major argument among political scientists in the 1960s and 1970s turned on this question: Is more participation always better, or is there some optimal level of participation that is lower than 100 percent? Among others suggesting that more was not always better, Gabriel Almond and Sidney Verba expressed the opinion, in *The Civic Culture* (Boston: Little, Brown, 1965), that the ideal citizen participated up to a point but then sat back and trusted government officials to take things from there. This guaranteed an attentive citizenry, but one that would also give its government trust and support. Seymour M. Lipset also fueled the distrust of excessive participation by his finding, in *Political Man* (Garden City, N.Y.: Doubleday, 1960), that the high turnout in the German elections of 1932 and 1933 had had a great deal to do with Adolf Hitler's victories.

Of the several responses, that of E. E. Schattschneider—*The Semisovereign People* (New York: Holt, Rinehart and Winston, 1960)—suggested that nonparticipants were like a time bomb waiting to disrupt the system. Since they were not building patterns of support for the existing system by participating, they could, if they suddenly flooded in as the German voters for Hitler did, cause dangerous results. Schattschneider concluded that we should try to get everyone to participate as much as possible. Carole Pateman, in *Participation and Democratic Theory* (Cambridge, England: Cambridge University Press, 1970), drew an argument straight from classical liberal theory. A main purpose of participation was to help people improve themselves by exercising their judgment and by informing themselves of what was going on. Whether or not instability results, more participation is in and of itself a good thing; the more there is, the better.

The argument seems to have been resolved for now in favor of the defenders of participation. Today, one does not often hear arguments against full and extensive participation. But this argument has been going on sporadically since the time of the ancient Greeks. We may anticipate that it will come up again.

voting out of a desire to do their duty, out of a love of country, and often because of a good deal of social pressure from those around them. In other words, voting for them may be more of a communal act than an individual one.

There is no reason to think that these communal aspects of voting are absent in a democracy. This would certainly help to explain what is otherwise unexplainable—the fact that millions of people vote in elections even though it can easily be demonstrated that voting is of no individual benefit to them. This seems an attractive resolution to the paradox partly because it elevates our discussion of voting above selfish calculations of individual costs and benefits. Love of country is a noble sentiment, and if electoral participation is based partly on it, all the better for elections.

"HOW BINDING ARE CAMPAIGN PROMISES MADE ONLY IN PRIMARIES?"

(Sidney Harris)

THE BASES OF ELECTORAL CHOICE

For whatever reason, then, a great many people vote in elections. How do they choose which party or candidate to vote for? Any number of things may serve as the basis for voting choice in one country or another.

We can distinguish usefully between short-term factors in voting choice and long-term factors. Short-term factors are things about a particular election that may lead a person to vote one way or another. The general state of the economy usually operates in this way, for instance. If times are bad, a number of people will vote against whoever is in office as a way of showing their unhappiness. Professor Edward Tufte has calculated that a 2 percent increase in real disposable income, compared with a 2 percent loss, should make a difference of about 2.5 percent of the vote for the president's party in midterm congressional elections in the United States; this would generally mean that about twenty to thirty more seats would go to the president's party in the good year.[9]

[9]Edward R. Tufte, *Political Control of the Economy* (Princeton, N.J.: Princeton University Press, 1978), p. 112.

Other short-term factors may include the particular appeal (or lack of same) of a candidate. This appears to be particularly the case in the United States and Canada, where the personalities of possible presidents and prime ministers sway large numbers of votes. In most European countries, on the other hand, the voters seem to weigh primarily the various political parties as whole organizations, with less emphasis on the personal characteristics of a party's leading candidate. In 1979, for instance, polls in Britain showed that Margaret Thatcher, the Conservative candidate for prime minister, was less admired and respected personally than James Callaghan, the candidate of the Labour party. But the British electorate did not hesitate to defeat Labour soundly and put the Conservatives—and Mrs. Thatcher—in power. In general, as will be seen in the next chapter, political parties in the United States and Canada are weak organizations compared with those in most countries; as a result, individual candidates in American or Canadian elections carry more personal weight. In countries with strong parties, the focus of the electorate is more on the parties, per se, and individual candidates do not count for as much.

Short-term factors such as a particular candidacy, the state of the economy, an international crisis, or whatever can be potent in deciding an election. But most elections most of the time are determined largely by things that do not change much or that change only very gradually.

One such long-term factor is the identification of some people with a particular political party. We all know some older person who has been a Democrat (or a Republican, or a Conservative, or a Liberal, or a Labour voter, or whatever) "since I was a young child." To such a voter, a particular candidacy or the state of the economy makes less difference than to other voters. Most of the time this person is going to vote by party no matter what is going on. Political scientists call this sort of continuing tie *party identification*.[10] It adds a good deal of stability and predictability over time to election results. We will discuss party identification in more detail in the next chapter.

Another long-term factor that adds stability over time is the commitment of various social groups to one or another party. As we see in Table 8–3, the basic commitment of the working class and the less religious to the Social Democratic party of West Germany was fairly stable from 1953 to 1972; the flip side of this is that the middle class and the religious were rather consistent in *not* supporting the Social Democratic party.

We have noted that long-term factors are things that do not change or that *change slowly*. In this table we see that the effect of religion did not change over the twenty years, since the difference between those who are religious and those who are not stayed about the same. But notice the gradual change in the effect of social class. The difference between the two classes was considerably greater at the beginning of the twenty-year period than at the end. In 1953, there was a 30-percentage-point spread between the two classes, but this had narrowed to a 17-point spread by 1972.

[10]Angus Campbell, Philip Converse, Warren E. Miller, and Donald Stokes, *The American Voter* (New York: Wiley, 1960), Chaps. 6 and 7.

Table 8–3   Social Bases of Support for the Social Democratic Party of West Germany, 1953–1972

	1953	1957	1965	1969	1972
Percent voting socialist of:					
Working class	58	60	57	58	70
Middle class	28	23	31	46	53
Those who never attend church	63	64	64	77	74
Those who occasionally attend church	48	39	48	45	61
Those who frequently attend church	17	19	17	32	28

SOURCE: Calculated from Kendall Baker, Russell Dalton, and Kai Hildebrandt, *Germany Transformed* (Cambridge, Mass.: Harvard University Press, 1981).

In other countries, the following social differences have functioned importantly as bases for voting distinctions:

- Region (The "solid Democratic South" of the United States, for example; or the regional basis of all the Canadian parties)
- Language (The Swedish People's party of Finland, for example)
- Farming (Many countries have had Agrarian parties; Norway and Sweden are two examples.)
- Country of origin (Irish and Italian voters in the United States tend to be Democrats, German and Anglo-Saxon voters tend to be Republicans.)
- Race (Blacks tend strongly to vote Democratic in the United States; the politics of Guyana has been almost totally determined by conflicts between blacks and East Indians.)
- Gender (Women in many countries favor conservative parties, though this may be an indirect effect of religion rather than a direct effect of differences between men and women; in recent years a "gender gap" has opened in the United States, with men disproportionately voting Republican.)
- Age (In 1972, for instance, 63 percent of Germans under nineteen voted for the Social Democrats; only 34 percent of those over eighty did so.)

EXAMPLE: PROPORTIONAL REPRESENTATION ELECTIONS IN ITALY

The most important election in Italy is the election of the Chamber of Deputies, a parliament consisting of 630 members who serve a five-year term.[11] Members of the Chamber of Deputies are elected by proportional representation in the following way. The country is divided into thirty-two electoral districts, from each of which a number of deputies is elected; the number of deputies elected from each district is determined by the population of the district.

Before the election, each party registers with an election commission a list of candidates for that district. The ballot does not list the candidates by name but simply asks voters to choose a party. However, if they wish to do so, voters may write in preferences for up to four candidates of the party they are voting for. This last act is crucial in Italian elections; but as one might imagine, given that it requires that the voter remember the name or number of a candidate, relatively few voters (about 20 percent of the electorate) avail themselves of this opportunity to choose among candidates of their party.

Once the votes have been cast, the electoral commission awards seats to each party proportionally to the party's share of votes cast by the electorate. For instance, if 18 seats are to be filled from a district and the Christian Democratic party received 33 percent of the votes in that district, then the Christian Democrats would receive 33 percent of the 18 seats available, or 6 seats from that district. In this way, nationally across the thirty-two districts, each party gets roughly its fair share of the seats.

Once a number of seats has been assigned to each party, the electoral commission goes to the individual preferences that were written in by the voters. Candidates on a party's list are ranked by the commission in order of the number of preferential votes they have received, and the party's seats are assigned to the candidates at the top of the list. In the example above, the six Christian Democratic candidates who received the most write-in votes in the district would go to the Chamber of Deputies and the rest of the Christian Democratic candidates would not.

In this curious way, Italy combines both a general election, in which voters choose a party, and a primary election, in which they determine the order of priority for the party's candidates. It is a biased system in that the utterly important act of ranking candidates is made so difficult that only politically active people, or those who have been mobilized by an interest group, take part in it. Interest groups and factions within parties have been known to provide their supporters with stencils of the identification numbers of candidates they wished to support, so that even illiterate members could vote correctly. The preference system has also produced a flamboyant, "folksy" style of politics, especially in the southern part of the country, in which politicians kiss babies in the best American style so as to establish a personal following. One athletic performer wrote over 100,000 letters of recommendation annually for voters in his electoral district and sent xeroxes of the letters and the answers he had received to the people he had recommended.[12]

Turnout in Italian elections is high, always over 90 percent in elections for the Chamber of Deputies and generally over 80 percent even in local elections. This may be partly due to that fact that it is against the law not to vote, but that cannot be the full explanation, since there is no penalty attached to the law. All that happens if one does not vote is that a notation is made on

---

[12]John Clarke Adams and Paolo Barile, *The Government of Republican Italy*, 3rd ed. (Boston: Houghton Mifflin, 1972), p. 1984.

one's official record. The high participation may more likely be due to the PR electoral system, which means that no one's vote is wasted, and to the wide variety of parties available to the Italian voter (seven major parties in the last election).

As is often the case in PR systems, the representation of various parties has been very stable. Italy has two main parties, the Communists and the Christian Democrats. From 1963 through 1979, the Christian Democrats received between 38 and 39 percent of the vote in each election, with the Communist vote varying between 25 and 34 percent. Even tiny parties that might otherwise disappear can maintain a stable life under PR, since they are not penalized for their smallness; a good example is the Republican party, which from 1948 to 1979 varied between 1 and 3 percent of the vote.

The 1983 election produced a sudden shock to the system when the Christian Democratic party, which had had such stable support until then, dropped from 38 percent of the vote to 33 percent, only a bit above the 30 percent registered by the Communists. This was widely interpreted as a delayed effect of a loss in credibility the Catholic church had suffered in the mid-1970s, when it led an unpopular attempt to make divorce more difficult. The fact that the Communist party was viewed as rather weak in the early 1980s, so that voters did not feel so compelled to vote for the Christian Democrats in order to block the Communists, may also have contributed to the Christian Democrats' losses. Christian Democratic weakness continued into the 1987 election, in which they received only 34 percent of the vote. It appears that the party system may have undergone a lasting change in 1983.

EXAMPLE: ELECTIONS IN NIGERIA

In 1979 Democracy was reestablished in Nigeria after thirteen years of military rule. Because democracy had broken down in 1966 over conflicts between the regions, new electoral laws were set up to minimize regional rivalry. The country was divided into nineteen "states"; in order to win the key office of president, a candidate had to win more votes nationally than any other candidate *and* receive at least one-quarter of the vote in at least thirteen of the nineteen "states." If no one filled these conditions, a runoff was to be held between the two leading candidates. This system guaranteed that only a person who could draw support from more than a single region could win. Elections were held in 1979 under military supervision and again in 1983 after four years of democracy.

Holding an election in Nigeria is a difficult, cumbersome task. It was at that time a country of 80 million or so people, spread over a large area with often primitive communications. The 1983 elections were held in five weekly installments. First the president was elected; then, a week later, governors of the states; a week later, the senate was elected; then the house of representatives; and finally the state assemblies. The first task facing the government in setting up the election was to draw up a roll of eligible voters. Throughout the country, 158,000 voting stations were established, and men and women were asked to go to the stations to register themselves for the election. The problem of security that this involved is indicated by the fact that with 90,000 policemen in Nigeria, there were nearly twice as many voting stations as there were police.

Campaign style in the election was enthusiastic and aggressive, although all candidates took some pains in their speeches to restrain their followers from violence. The following reportage gives some sense of the campaign:

> Travelling at 100 miles an hour with a Nigerian rent-a-crowd is a memorable experience. We were following President Shehu Shagari as he campaigned in Kano for re-election this Saturday, August 6th. There was a cavalcade—more a chariot race— of over 100 buses, cars and vans, weaving from one lane to another and bursting at the windows with fervid supporters of Mr. Shagari's National party of Nigeria.
>
> People had been brought by the party organisation from all over the state and beyond. Some of them were paid about £5 for "expenses." The crowds at the rallies were large, even in small towns, and the enthusiasm infectious. But this did not mean much electorally, said the experts in the press bus. They agreed that President Shagari would almost certainly be re-elected, but his party was unlikely to win Kano state, which at the last election in 1979 supported the People's Redemption party. As the chariots hurtled past a bus that had veered off into a ditch, a commentator compared the accident with NPN's campaign: "It builds a momentum, but is also liable to crash."
>
> The rally oratory was mostly a crudely revivalist shouting of slogans with one finger raised in the air. The finger symbolises the NPN's slogan, "One nation, one destiny." Followers of Chief Obafemi Awolowo's Unity party of Nigeria raise two fingers for "UP Nigeria." Followers of Mr. Nnamdi Azikiwe's Nigerian People's party raise a fist for "power."
>
> The president himself speaks calmly and is at times gently humorous. He is also a politician who does not scruple to play on religious prejudices. Referring to the question of whether voting should be allowed to interfere with pilgrimages to Mecca, he said: "Chief Awolowo is not worried about the Haj. He worries only about his trips to Israel." (The chief is a Christian who has frequently advocated closer relations with Israel.) But on the whole the president gave forth an air of tolerance and always spoke out against violence. The absence of security around him says something. The crowds swarmed everywhere, with the police ineffectually swinging canes.[13]

The two main concerns of most observers were violence and the possibility of rigged results. Violence did break out—scores of people were killed, and the last three waves of elections had to be canceled in two states because of rioting. But all in all, the violence did not reach levels that made it impossible to respect the elections. Fraud, or the suspicion of it, was a far greater problem. The published roll of registered voters was particularly suspect, because it

[13]*The Economist*, August 6, 1983, p. 32.

listed 65 million people. In a country of approximately 80 million, there simply could not be that many adults, and it was thought that many fraudulent entries had been made. When the incumbent President Shagari won more strongly than anyone had expected he would and his party succeeded surprisingly well in the further elections, the other parties cried foul. There were plenty of examples of fraud for them to point at. The village of Modakeke, for instance, cast 170,000 votes for Shagari, about 500 votes per household.[14]

At the same time, at least elections had been held, and several different parties had succeeded in establishing themselves in one place of power or another. The campaign had been conducted in a constructive way by most candidates, and a president was reelected who was generally considered to be personally honest and temperate. There is a risk of being patronizing here, of saying "For a Third World country, Nigeria did well enough." But in truth, given its history and the growing pains it had suffered through rapid economic growth, Nigeria did do fairly well.

The story has a sad ending, however. On December 31, 1983, military officers overthrew the democratic state, arresting President Shagari. The coup was justified by pointing to corruption, which had been tolerated under Shagari, not only the questionable election results of 1983 but widespread economic corruption as well. However, declines in Nigeria's economy in 1983 probably had as much to do with the coup as did the problem of corruption. Journalists in Nigeria and others interviewing Nigerian students abroad were surprised to see how little regret there was for the passing of the short-lived democracy.

FURTHER READING

Barnes, Samuel H., Kaase, Max, and Allerbeck, Klause. *Political Action: Mass Participation in Five Western Democracies*. Beverly Hills, Calif.: Sage, 1979.

Campbell, Angus, Converse, Philip, Miller, Warren, and Stokes, Donald. *The American Voter*. New York: Wiley, 1960.

Duverger, Maurice. *Political Parties*. New York: Wiley, 1954.

Flanigan, William H., and Zingale, Nancy H. *Political Behavior of the American Electorate*, 5th ed. Newton, Mass.: Allyn & Bacon, 1983.

Huntington, Samuel P., and Nelson, Joan M. *No Easy Choice: Political Participation in Developing Countries*. Cambridge, Mass.: Harvard University Press, 1976.

Nie, Norman, Verba, Sidney, and Petrocik, John. *The Changing American Voter*. Cambridge, Mass.: Harvard University Press, 1976.

Pierce, John C., and Sullivan, John L., eds. *The Electorate Reconsidered*. Beverly Hills, Calif.: Sage, 1980.

Powell, G. Bingham, Jr. "American Voter Turnout in Comparative Perspective." *American Political Science Review* 80 (March 1986): 17–44.

Rae, Douglas. *Political Consequences of Electoral Laws*, rev. ed. New Haven, Conn.: Yale University Press, 1971.

---

[14]*The Economist*, August 20, 1983, p. 38.

Riker, William H., and Ordeshook, Peter C. *An Introduction to Positive Political Theory*. Englewood Cliffs, N.J.: Prentice-Hall, 1973.

Taagepera, Rein, and Shugart, Matthew S. *Seats and Votes: The Effects and Determinants of Electoral Systems*. New Haven, Conn.: Yale University Press, 1989.

Wolfinger, Raymond E., and Rosenstone, Steven J. *Who Votes?* New Haven, Conn.: Yale University Press, 1980.

Chapter 9

Parties:
A Linking and Leading
Mechanism in Politics

In preceding chapters we have talked a good deal about "political parties." The political party is an invention that first developed in the nineteenth century in response to the appearance of elections involving large numbers of voters. Politicians developed the political party as a device to help themselves and like-minded friends get elected, but the party proved to have many other uses as well and has become a ubiquitous feature of modern politics.

We shall explore this theme below, but first let us deal with questions of definition.

THE POLITICAL PARTY

A political party is a group of officials or would-be officials who are linked with a sizable group of citizens into an organization; a chief object of this organization is to ensure that its officials attain power or are maintained in power.

The latter part of this definition distinguishes the political party from the "interest group," which is discussed in the next chapter. In most countries there are many interest groups—such as the American Medical Association, the American Dairy Farmers' Organization, the Natural Gas Supply Association, Friends of the Earth, and so on—who band together to try by way of lobbying, campaign contributions, and other tactics to make sure that the government's policies will be in tune with their wishes. Interest groups are distinguished from political parties in that the former simply try to influence which policies are chosen without actually taking power or setting policies; parties, on the other hand, have as their central purpose the acquisition of power and the direction of policy.

Note that there is nothing about the above definition that says political parties are restricted to democracies and to electoral activity. Revolutionary parties may be organized not to win elections but to seize control of the government by force; totalitarian parties—such as the Nazi party of Germany in the 1930s—may oversee the machinery of a nondemocratic state.

Finally, note that a party joins people together in a more or less formally organized structure. U.S. political parties surely fall at an extreme in the looseness of their organization, but in most countries the parties are clearly delineated, with formal membership that sets those who are "in the party" apart from the rest. For instance, the Conservative party of Britain has about 3 million dues-paying members. The Communist party of the Soviet Union has about 17 million members, who must pass a probationary period of a year before they are accepted for full membership.

The party's nature as a structure, tying together a large group of officials and citizens, provides an avenue by which one part may control or communicate with another. It is this that has made it such a versatile tool of modern politics. We shall explore this in more detail below.

ORIGINS OF THE MODERN PARTY

Although the party has turned out to be useful for a variety of tasks that require control or communication, it was first invented for more limited and self-serving purposes. Long before the coming of electoral democracy, the state had had a varied structure of public officials—mayors, members of parliament, ministers for defense, and so on. Before democracy arrived, people attained these offices in a variety of ways: by being born into them, by buying the office (much as we might today purchase a fried-chicken franchise), by bribery, by appointment.

Once democracy was introduced, however, many of these positions were filled by election. This was different from all the old ways of choosing officials in one important respect: In all the old ways, the person who wished to have the office dealt with a single king or perhaps with a few people who could be bribed; under democracy, the would-be official had to seek the votes of a thousand or more people.

It did not take long for politicians in the new democracies to see that some sort of club or organization that bound them together with large numbers of voters would help them to attain and hold office. Further, large national clubs binding together a whole set of officials with voters throughout the country could function more effectively than a local club built around a single official. With a nationwide organization, voters were not "lost" to the club as they moved from one place to another; a popular official could go from place to place, helping to convince the voters to choose other candidates of the organization; and there would be enough money to hire professional staff who could help with the job of organizing thousands upon thousands of voters. Thus the political party was born.

In Britain, 1867 marks the first year in which there was a reasonably widespread extension of the vote. As of that year, 10 percent of the population was entitled to vote. Directly as a result of this expansion of the electorate, the first modern party organization Britain had known was established in the city of Birmingham:

[In 1867] the Registration Societies, the Reform or Liberal Associations which had sprung up since 1832, were groups of subscribers, of amateurs, and were in the hands of traditional leaders incapable of getting at the masses who had just been brought on the political stage by the extension of the franchise. Birmingham received 30,000 new electors. The [Liberals] believed that to ensure the victory, the party organization ought to reach all these voters, to make them feel that they were about to fight *pro aris et focis*, that the Liberal party was their own party, the party of each one of them. To meet these views, one of the Radical leaders, Mr. W. Harris, architect, man of letters, and secretary of the Birmingham Liberal Association, proposed a plan of organization according to which all the Liberals of the locality were to meet in every ward, and elect representatives to manage the affairs of the party.[1]

In fact, the possibility that an expanded suffrage would lead to the development of political parties was one of the arguments raised by some members of Parliament against expanding the suffrage in 1867:

> ...with a widely enlarged suffrage the candidate would find himself less and less able to come face to face with his constituency, and would be compelled in consequence...to rely more and more on the aid of the election agent, and, as in America, of that of committees and canvassers whose mouthpiece and delegate he would have to make himself.[2]

In the United States, suffrage had been expanded earlier than in Britain, and it was in the United States that, in the first decade of the nineteenth century, the first modern parties had appeared. Similarly, all over Europe, whenever a reasonably large and varied electorate was established with the coming of democracy, the political party appeared.

Like elections themselves, political parties have been widely copied and are now found in many countries that are not electoral democracies. The Communist parties of most eastern European states are obvious examples of this, but many another nondemocratic state has a political party that functions importantly in its politics. Egypt, for instance, is governed by the National Democratic party, Guinea by the Democratic Party of Guinea, Rwanda by the National Revolutionary Movement for Development, Syria by the Ba'ath party. Many more examples could be noted, for many regimes that do not require parties in order to win elections have found that the modern political party—with the links it creates between masses of people and a set of political leaders—is useful to them. One of the wonders of modern politics is that this invention, which was originally devised in order that some officeholders could keep their jobs, has proved adaptable to all sorts of other purposes. The political party has become a "miracle glue" of sorts for politics. Whenever one group of people is to be controlled by another group or even just kept in contact with them, the party has turned out to be a useful tool.

Let us look at some of the ways in which the political party has been used

---

[1]M. Ostrogorski, *Democracy and the Organization of Political Parties*, vol. 1 (Garden City, N.Y.: Doubleday, 1964), p. 80.

[2]Ibid., p. 78.

to do these things. Parties provide all of the following: a basis for the mobilization of masses of citizens; a means of recruiting and socializing political leaders; structured political identity, at both the mass and elite levels; and a method of control within a government structure. We shall look at each of these in turn.

POLITICAL PARTIES AND THE MOBILIZATION OF THE MASSES

We argued in Chapter 8 that one of the main effects of holding elections was to involve the masses of ordinary citizens in acting out their support for the state and, by so doing, strengthening that support. In order for this to happen, millions of voters must be stimulated to go out and actually take the trouble to vote. Governments themselves cannot easily get people out to the polls, so how to reap this particular advantage of elections poses them a bit of a problem. The problem is particularly great where only one slate of candidates is allowed, so that there is no suspense whatever about the outcome of the election. How can the voters be mobilized to get out and vote under these circumstances? A political party is a handy instrument with which to stir up the electorate and get them to the polls. It is controlled by its leaders, who are at the same time the rulers of the state; and it may have a membership that extends down into every village, so it is strategically placed to turn out large numbers of people.

In the United States, political parties make great efforts to get out the vote. They do this not to bolster support for the regime, though that is a side effect, but to help themselves win elections. It is well known that more votes are to be gained by making sure that the people who support you actually turn out to vote than in trying to change the minds of those who oppose you. In the Soviet Union the Communist party has no such motive for stirring up the electorate, but its leaders are anxious to generate a good show of support, so the party does much the same things as American parties do at election time.

Aside from elections, many political parties serve to mobilize the people for special purposes or to meet crises. When President Anwar Sadat of Egypt was assassinated in 1981 and was succeeded by Vice President Mubarak, over a million people joined a demonstration in Cairo to show their support for Mubarak. The demonstration was partly organized by the government apparatus itself but also, in large part, by the ruling National Democratic Party. When the regime of Charles de Gaulle was threatened in France by a general strike in 1969, the turning point at which his opposition was defeated came when his Union of Democrats for the Republic party organized a massive demonstration in Paris for which hundreds of thousands of supporters were bused in from the countryside.

A party may also mobilize masses of people *against* a regime. Many of today's political parties in Third World states—the Congress party in India, for example, or the National Front for Liberation in Algeria—were initially orga-

Menaka Gandhi addressing a party rally, India.
(Baldev/Sygma)

nized in order to carry out a campaign to overthrow a colonial ruler like Britain or France. And when German armies occupied much of Europe during World War II, it was the churches and the political parties that provided the basis for a resistance movement because these were the only structures binding large and widespread groups of people together in ways that made coordinated resistance possible. Today the most important focus of opposition to many regimes lies with political parties.

POLITICAL PARTIES AND THE RECRUITMENT AND SOCIALIZATION OF LEADERS

Another use to which parties have lent themselves, beyond what they were originally designed for, is the recruitment and socialization of leaders. Somebody has to do this in any society, and where there are political parties, they are an obvious choice for the task. What other organization could better seek out promising young people, give them experience at relatively small jobs, and gradually move those who do well to more important jobs, all the while imbuing them with the values that the political leadership wishes to encourage?

In Britain, for instance, an ambitious young woman who was interested in entering politics might work for a while at lesser tasks for one of the major parties, such as the Conservative party. Before too long, if she were interested in standing for Parliament, she might be nominated from a district. To get the nomination, she would have to convince the local selection committee of the Conservative party in that district that she was their best nominee. As a beginner, she would probably be selected in a hopeless district, where no Conservative had much of a chance, but once she had proved that she could campaign well in one or two lost causes, she might get the nomination from a decent district, win, and enter the House. In the House, she would continue to be molded and guided by the party. If she were the sort that party leaders like—witty in debate, hard working, and above all a faithful party voter—she might advance into positions of real responsibility, such as party spokesperson on defense or on health. Eventually, she might aim so high as to be prime minister. To be selected for this position, she would have to win an internal election at which all the Conservative members of Parliament vote to choose their leader. Throughout this career, her advancement would have been primarily due to her support from her party organization, and she would have risen to the top only because she was the sort of person her party wanted and because, in each position she held, she had learned from the rest of the party how to behave in the ways they preferred. This is essentially the only way to make a political career in Great Britain.

In the United States, too, parties are important as devices for the recruitment and socialization of leaders. However, parties in the United States are weaker organizationally than those in Britain, so they do not hold the same monopoly in this regard that British parties do. Most political leaders have worked their way into place through the apparatus of either the Democratic or Republican party, starting at fairly lowly positions. However, primary elections at which a candidate can appeal directly to the voters for nomination, rather than relying on party leaders, can allow a popular celebrity such as the astronaut John Glenn or basketball star Bill Bradley to enter directly into politics at a high level. (The existence of primary elections, which take the selection of candidates out of the hands of party leaders, is often considered the single most important cause of American parties' organizational weakness.) Further, people who have distinguished themselves at some other career are often appointed to a president's cabinet directly without any prior political career and thus without any screening by a party. When John Kennedy appointed his brother Robert as attorney general and when Richard Nixon appointed Harvard professor Henry Kissinger to be secretary of state, no party was involved.

In a one-party state such as Yugoslavia, the single party may serve as the major avenue to any sort of political or economic advancement. The Yugoslav Communist party has actually restricted its membership in order to keep out opportunists who would join simply in order to advance themselves. By strict entrance requirements and by purges, the party is limited to a membership comprising just about 5 percent of Yugoslavia's population. Party leaders have good cause to be concerned about the problem of opportunism. Since all factory directors, all important public officials, and most leaders of institutions such as universities are required to be Communists, there is ample reason for ambitious young people to seek membership no matter what their political beliefs.

POLITICAL PARTIES AS A SOURCE OF POLITICAL IDENTITY

Another unforeseen effect of political parties was the extent to which parties, once one was associated with them, would become an important part of one's identity. Party is probably not the first thing a person would mention when asked "What are you?" A more likely reply would be "I am a Presbyterian," "I am a woman," "I am a student," "I am a Canadian," and so on. But along the way, if you keep prompting, you may well be given the name of the political party with which that person feels associated. As we saw in Chapter 8, this source of identity is called *party identification*.[3] For those who become quite active, the political party may become a vital and central personal concern. What would John Kennedy or Lyndon Johnson have been without the Democratic party? Or Willy Brandt of West Germany without the Social Democratic party? Or Gorbachev of the U.S.S.R. without the Communist party?

One important thing about party as a source of identity is that it can provide continuity in a political world that is otherwise quite fluid. Candidates come and go, wars start and end, political issues arise and fade and are replaced by others, but parties may go on and on and on. The two major parties of the United States are over a century old; the single main party of Mexico is about sixty years old, as is the Communist party of the Soviet Union; Britain's Conservative party is over a century old, and its Labour party is over a half-century old.

By furnishing individuals and politically active people with a lasting political identity, the party can give them a source of political community throughout their lives. Parties may provide an even longer-range continuity in politics than that of a single lifetime if party connections are passed on from parents to children or if local party organizations continue their activity across generations. An ironic instance of the way in which parties can create this sort of continuity is provided by the state of Indiana.[4] Ever since the Civil War, there has been a political split between the southern part of the state and the northern part. There was a good deal of sympathy for the Confederacy in the 1860s in southern Indiana; this translated into support for the Democratic party, which was more sympathetic to the Confederacy at that time. In northern Indiana,

---

[3]The concept "party identification" was first developed fully in Angus Campbell, et al., *The American Voter* (New York: Wiley, 1960), chaps. 6 and 7. For a recent review, see W. Phillips Shively, "The Nature of Party Identification: A Review of Recent Developments," in John C. Pierce and John L. Sullivan, eds., *The Electorate Reconsidered* (Beverly Hills, Calif.: Sage, 1980).

[4]This case was first presented by V. O. Key, Jr., and Frank Munger in Eugene Burdick and Arthur J. Brodbeck, eds., *American Voting Behavior* (Glencoe, Ill.: Free Press, 1959), chap. 15. Their analysis has been updated here.

"WHAT I DON'T UNDERSTAND IS HOW, IN A FEW YEARS, WE'LL BECOME CONSERVATIVE REPUBLICANS."

(Sidney Harris)

abolitionist and Union sentiment ran strong; this led northern voters to support the Republican party. More than a century later, this pattern still holds! As may be seen in Figure 9–1, most of the counties in which the Democratic candidate Jimmy Carter received 40 percent or more of the vote in 1980 fell in the southern fourth of the state. North of this area, Carter got as much as 40 percent of the vote in only a few counties, which is to say that Republican Ronald Reagan got over 60 percent of the vote almost everywhere in northern Indiana.

This distribution of support bears little relation to what we normally think of as the basis for Democratic and Republican voting. Figure 9–2 shows the counties in Indiana in which over 30 percent of the labor force consists of workers in manufacturing industries. Such workers are commonly thought to be the mainstay of the Democratic party, yet a comparison of the two maps shows that whether or not a county is heavily industrial has little to do with whether or not it is strongly Democratic. In fact, there is a slightly negative relationship between the two: While 53 percent of the counties that are "nonindustrial" in Figure 9–2 are heavily Democratic in Figure 9–1, only 34 percent of the "industrial" counties are heavily Democratic.

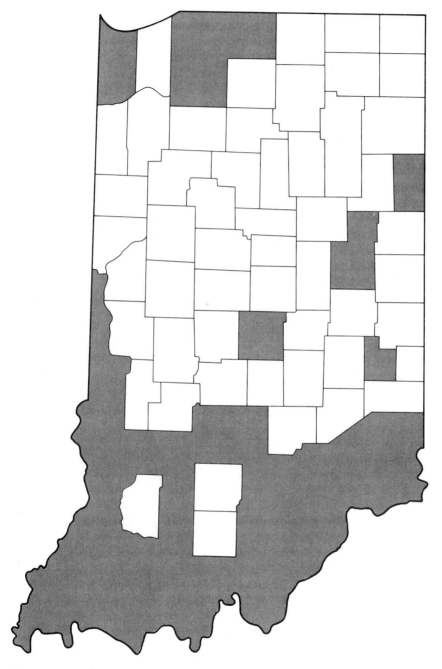

Figure 9–1   Indiana counties 40 percent or more Democratic, 1980.

SOURCE Richard M. Scammon and Alice V. McGillivary, eds., "America Votes 14," Washington, D.C.: *Congressional Quarterly,* 1981.

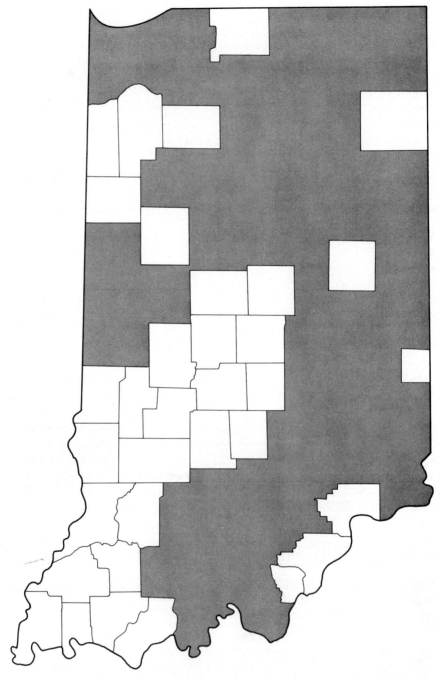

Figure 9–2   Indiana counties with over 30 percent of labor force employed in manufacturing, 1980.

SOURCE U.S. Census Bureau, 1980 Census of Population.

The basic north-south split in the state has been a political fact of life continually since the 1860s. The chief determinant of the geographic distribution of party support is not the economy and not the distribution of industry but events that occurred and were pretty well disposed of 120 years ago. The ability of parties—through their organizational structure and through their grip on people's consciousness—to establish stable lines of conflict is impressive. In this case, the results border on the ludicrous, since it must make little sense that Indiana elections in 1980 are determined by who took what position on slavery and secession in 1868.

POLITICAL PARTIES AS A CHANNEL OF CONTROL

A final unforeseen effect of political parties was to provide some political leaders with a new channel through which to exert control over other leaders. This has been an important factor in politics in the twentieth century.

Remember that a party is an organization that binds a sizable group of political leaders together with a sizable number of ordinary citizens. It is the only sort of organization that regularly does this. Since it spreads so widely both within the set of political leaders and out into the mass of people, it offers an excellent channel for power through which political leaders can control the actions either of other political leaders or of the citizens.

As a channel for controlling other political leaders, the party is important in all sorts of states. The leaders of a party have many punishments and rewards at their disposal—nomination for various offices, support in passing favored legislation, and so on. Perhaps the greatest carrot or stick most of the time is the chance to advance to more powerful positions within the party. Leaders use these inducements deliberately to force obedience on lesser party figures in legislative votes, campaign activity, and so on. Sam Rayburn, who was for many years the leader of the Democratic party in the U.S. House of Representatives, used to caution new members, "To get ahead, get along." That is, to advance within the House hierarchy, obey orders. In the British House of Commons, the party organizations expect such pure obedience in voting that the life of ordinary members is in some ways rather dull, since they are generally just following orders in how they vote.

As we shall see in Chapter 11, this channel of control is crucial in making the parliamentary governments of western Europe and other parts of the world work. But party functions as a channel for power in all sorts of other systems as well. In the communist systems of eastern Europe, the Communist party provides a means by which the apparatus of the state, especially in touchy areas such as the armed forces, is kept under the control of the party leaders. As much as possible, only party members are allowed to serve as high-ranking officers in the armies of the communist countries, and their advancement is strongly affected by their standing in the party.

Parties may also be used as a channel for power by which the leaders of the state control the mass of citizens. This is more common in authoritarian states than in democracies, where direct control of citizens is supposed to be the exception rather than the rule. For example, one particular problem for authoritarian systems is the control of intellectual activity, which might pose a threat to the leaders of the state if it proceeded freely. By placing party members in leadership positions in writers' organizations, universities, professional associations, and the media, the leaders of the state can help to ensure their control over what the citizenry thinks and says. This has particularly been the practice in communist systems, although military dictatorships, the fascist regimes of the 1930s, and other authoritarian regimes have practiced it as well.

PARTY ORGANIZATION

Political parties in the United States are unusual in their organizational structure inasmuch as they are very loose and informal. Any other organization in the country—a savings bank, a bird-watchers' club, a church—would have some sort of formal membership, for which one applies and in return receives a membership card of some sort. Political parties in the United States do not require this of their "members"; in fact, it is often difficult for people to be sure whether or not they are members of a party or indeed which party they are members of. Political scientists have some difficulty specifying just what group of people they are describing when they speak of the "Republican party." Do they mean only the elected Republican officials in Congress and elsewhere? Do they mean the people who run the party's offices? Do they mean just the people who work for Republicans in election campaigns? Do they mean those who are "registered" as Republicans (even if they regularly vote Democratic)? Do they mean those who sympathize with the Republicans? Since there is no formal organization defining those who "belong" and those who do not, anyone is free to define the set as desired.[5]

In other states, however, parties are set up in a more normal way as formal organizations; if one wishes to be a member of the party, one applies for membership, pays some sort of dues, and is formally enrolled with a membership card. As explicit, well-defined organizations, these parties have *organizational structure*, which may greatly affect their political role.

The Conservative party of Great Britain offers a fairly typical example of organizational structure. As we see in Figure 9–3, the party consists of several parts. The key position is occupied by the leader of the party, who is a Conservative member of the House of Commons, elected by the other Conservative members of the House. If the Conservative party is in power, the leader serves as prime minister for Britain; the present leader of the Conservative party is Margaret Thatcher.[6]

---

[5]For a more detailed analysis of this problem, see Frank J. Sorauf and Paul A. Beck, *Party Politics in America*, 6th ed. (Glenview, Ill.: Scott, Foresman, 1988), chap. 1.

[6]This arrangement is discussed in more detail in Chapter 11.

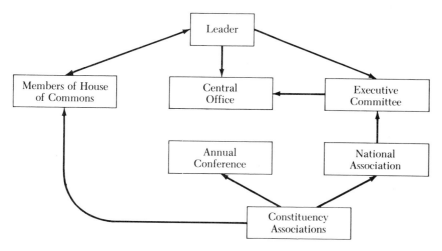

Figure 9–3   Organizational structure of Great Britain's Conservative party.

Notice that one-way arrows (indicating power) go out from the leader to all other units with which the leader interacts except the members of the House. With regard to the latter, power is a two-way street—the members may unseat the leader, and this has occurred several times in the twentieth century; but the leader directs the business of the Conservative party in the House.

Other parts of the party serve as a supporting structure for the leader and the party's members in the House. There are about 3 million dues-paying party members organized into constituency associations. These determine local party policy—including the important question of who will be the party's candidate from that district—but they have very little say in national party policies. Their only influence in this regard is to send delegates to the party's Annual Conference, from which, as seen in Figure 9–3, *no* arrows of power go anywhere. Issues are discussed at the Conference and resolutions passed; these are not binding on anyone, though the party's leaders may treat them as important symptoms of discontent that must be taken seriously.

The National Association is not elected but consists of about three thousand members of Parliament, prospective candidates, party officials, representatives of the constituency associations, and others. It meets annually, and elects an executive committee of 150, which meets several times a year. These bodies consider the direction of the party, organizational questions, and so on, but the fact that they meet so infrequently indicates that what they do is not terribly important.

The Central Office is a large and well financed party bureaucracy that hires regional and local party agents, conducts research on policy, and publishes propaganda. The Central Office is closely controlled by the leader, who directly appoints most of its top officials.

Thus the Conservative party has a complex structure, which is dominated by the members of the House of Commons through their leader. Other parts of the structure are important to the members of the House as a support group, but except for the important power over nominations held by local constituency associations, they have little power over the party's policies. This is not to say that the outside structure is unimportant; if nothing else, the dues paid by its members are the major source of party finance.

Most parties outside the United States have organizational structures more or less similar to this.[7] They may vary in the degree of power given to the outside structure. (The Labour party of Britain, for instance, gives more real power to its Annual Conference than does the Conservative party.) Or, they may vary in how tightly control is exercised. In communist parties, "lower" units in power generally have to toe the line much more precisely than in noncommunist parties; this allows the leader to direct party policies more completely and more efficiently than can leaders of other parties.

PARTY FINANCE

Parties get the money with which to finance their activities from a variety of sources. In the United States, parties generally do not have much money, since most of it is raised directly by candidates from individual contributors and from organized interest groups.

Outside of the United States, *parties* generally raise the money and determine its use themselves.[8] It may come from many kinds of sources:

- *Public finance:* Most states pay a portion of their parties' campaign expenses from public funds. It is always difficult to decide how much money to give to which parties, and established parties generally benefit disproportionately.
- *Individual memberships:* These may provide a good deal of income to a party, especially one with a large membership. Communist parties in the West have been particularly successful in this; in some countries, members pay a percentage of their income as dues to the party.
- *Bribes and kickbacks:* Especially where a single party is associated with a dictatorship, the closeness of the party to government allows it to organize corruption on its own behalf.
- *Interest-group donations:* Business and labor groups, and a few others, may subsidize favored parties heavily.
- *Profits from business enterprise:* Many parties own their own newspapers, banks, and other service firms, which they operate for the benefit of their members. Usually these cost money rather than make it, but some may be quite profitable.
- *Subsidies from foreign countries:* The United States, the Soviet Union, Libya, China, Israel, France, Japan, and other states have subsidized parties in other countries to further their own policies.

---

[7]See Leon D. Epstein, *Political Parties in Western Democracies* (New Brunswick, N.J.: Transaction, 1979).

[8]A general review of party finance (at least political campaign finance) is Khayam Paltiel, "Campaign Finance: Contrasting Patterns and Reforms," in David Butler, ed., *Democracy at the Polls* (Washington, D.C.: American Enterprise Institute, 1981).

Michels's "Iron Law of Oligarchy"

In *Political Parties* (first published in 1915), Robert Michels argues that a political party can never be faithful to the program and constituency for which it was originally founded. In order for the party to vie sucessfully for power, he wrote, it is necessary that it be organized through a specialized division of labor in which certain people become full-time leaders. Once this has happened, however, the leadership group inevitably develops a set of values and perspectives that is different from the original aims of the party. The leaders deal daily with the enemy, sitting with them in parliament, bargaining with them; the party may develop its own stake in the status quo (many European parties, for instance, own banks, newspapers, and other business enterprises) that makes its leaders cautious about rocking the boat; and finally, it is in the leaders' interests for the party to grow as large as possible, and the easiest way to effect this is to moderate the party's positions so as to bring in new groups who had previously not been willing to support it. In short, a political party is caught in a dilemma—it may refuse to develop central leadership, in which case it will probably not attain power; or it may develop central leadership, but at the cost of losing its program.

Political Parties is perhaps the most influential social scientific work of the twentieth century. Michels's theme has been picked up time and again to explain why parties disappoint their followers. It is popular among east European critics of their communist regimes. It provided the theme of George Orwell's novel *Animal Farm*. The Green parties of several west European states (radical environmental protection parties) have taken it to heart, with the West German Greens rotating their leadership at short intervals so that they will not develop a "leadership class."

Whether one regrets Michels's conclusion depends to some extent on whether or not one likes radical parties. But however you feel about the question, it is worth noting two factors that put it in a slightly different light:

1. All the factors that Michels sees at work (contact with the enemy, development of a stake in society, etc.) are things that occur over time. If a movement is successful very quickly, we might expect to see Michels disproved. The Bolshevik seizure of power in Russia in 1917 and the Nazi seizure of power in Germany from 1930 to 1933 are two such cases, and both parties followed their original programs fairly closely. On the other hand, large communist parties have been attempting, since 1945, to gain power in France and Italy, but without success, and both have moderated their positions considerably. This suggests that for the opponents of a radical movement, "buying time" is not a trivial strategy but can systematically help to change the movement.

2. We should also note that even if Michels is right, all is not lost from the radical standpoint. It may be true that every radical party gradually becomes more moderate, yet we might also see party systems in which, over long periods of time, there were always radical parties present, since new parties would replace older parties. This apparent paradox depends on whether we look at things from the viewpoint of the individual party or of the party system. A similar paradox exists with regard to our own lives. We might note that everyone is constantly growing older and conclude, in the style of Michels, that "youth is impossible to maintain." This is true for any individual person, but it is not true for society because new, young persons are continually being born to replace their elders.

POLITICAL PARTY SYSTEMS

So far we have addressed the questions of what a political party does, how it is structured, and so on. All of these questions have involved a single political party, looked at by itself. Another important set of questions revolves around the *pattern* formed by all the political parties in a state. We speak of a "party system" as the set of all parties. Political scientists generally distinguish such systems primarily by the number and relative size of the parties.[9]

A *one-party system* is one in which only a single political party is allowed to be active. The communist states of eastern Europe; Egypt, Algeria, Tanzania, and many other new Third World states; and the right wing dictatorships of Nazi Germany or Franco's Spain are all examples of the one-party system. In such systems, the government and the party are closely identified, since the government generally enforces the rule that other parties are not allowed to be active. The party may closely control the governmental apparatus, as is the case in communist states, or the party may simply have been created by those in charge of government. The party in a one-party system concentrates heavily on the tasks of mobilization, communication, and control. It cannot serve well as an alternative source of political ideas because it is so closely tied to those who are already running the state.

A *dominant-party system* is similar to the one-party system in that a single party holds power all the time, but it differs from the one-party system in that other political parties are allowed to function openly and with reasonable effectiveness.[10]

A good example of a dominant-party system is that of Mexico. A single party, the Party of the Institutionalized Revolution (PRI), has won every presidential election since 1929, usually with 60 to 70 percent of the vote. It is well understood in Mexico that serious politics occurs only within the PRI. Because of this party's long dominance of politics, the whole governmental structure from the civil service on up has very intimate ties to it, and the party has an identification with the system (which it dominates) of the sort that we can observe also in one-party states. Thus the PRI is concerned to raise electoral turnout not because it thinks it would be more likely to win a high-turnout election—it would win in any case—but because the system that it dominates needs high electoral participation in order to build citizen support for the regime.

In many ways, then, a dominant-party system is like a one-party system. But the tolerance of other parties in the system does lead to important differences. For one thing, the existence of alternative parties provides a base for

---

[9]For good discussions of each of the party systems discussed below, see Maurice Duverger, *Political Parties* (New York: Wiley, 1954), and Giovanni Sartori, *Party and Party Systems* (Cambridge, England: Cambridge University Press, 1964).

[10]See Alan Arian and Samuel Barnes, "The Dominant Party System: A Neglected Model of Democratic Stability," *Journal of Politics* 36 (August 1974): 592–614. Also Ariel Levite and Sidney Tarrow, "Legitimation of Excluded Parties in Dominant Party Systems: A Comparison of Israel and Italy," *Comparative Politics* 15 (April 1983): 295–327.

criticism of the government and guarantees that there will be more open debate about politics than in a one-party system. Alternative points of view must
inevitably be openly present in a dominant party system. For instance, the
largest opposition party in Mexico has for many years been the National Action
party, a party of the middle class that has been opposed to the PRI's emphasis
on labor and the poor. In 1982, for the first time, a group of socialist parties to
the left of the PRI figured significantly in a presidential election, gaining about
10 percent of the vote then, and again in the 1988 election.

A frequent pattern associated with dominant party systems in the Third
World is for the independence movement and its leaders to form a political
party once independence has been achieved. They will have generally been
more or less united in the movement for independence, so it is easy for them
to come together in a single party. Furthermore, the problems facing a new
state are so awesome that its leaders often agree that it would be better if the
state were spared internal disagreement for some time. However, once the
dominant party that results from this has ruled for a few decades, it may well
begin to lose its dominance. Corruption may set in with a group of entrenched
officials; the state, now better established, can more easily afford internal disagreements; and the issues of independence fade while new issues that may
divide the old ruling group arise.

Two examples of this pattern are provided by India and Israel. For three
decades after attaining independence in 1945, India was dominated by the
Congress party, which represented Mohandas K. Gandhi's independence
movement. Elections during this period were sure to provide a Congress majority in Parliament, and the important political maneuvers all occurred within
the Congress party. In 1977 however, Congress slipped below 50 percent of
the vote and a coalition of many small, opposed parties came into power. Since
then Congress has held power most of the time, but its dominance has not
been assured in the way it was in the decades after independence.

Israel provides another example. After the state of Israel was established in
1948, the Labour party (which was formed by the mainly European leaders of
the Zionist movement) held virtually unchallenged power until 1977. It was a
great surprise to everyone when, in that year, a coalition of opposition parties
called Likud, led by Menachem Begin, defeated Labour at the polls. In this
case the usual problems of a party that had been in power too long were mag-
nified by demographic change. In the 1950s and 1960s there had been massive
immigration into Israel of Jews from other parts of the Mideast, and by 1977
the country was split about evenly between voters of European origin and
those of non-European origin. The almost exclusively European-led Labour
party had drifted badly out of touch with about half of the electorate.

The point of these examples is that, while a dominant party system is similar in important ways to a one-party system, the availability of other active
parties does guarantee that there will be fairly open discussion and debate, and
it also provides for possible long-term flexibility and adjustment in the system.

A third variant is the *two-party system*. This is typified by the fact that no
one party can count on always holding power but that only two parties can nor-

mally expect to have a chance at doing so. In a two-party system, the two major parties will typically receive over 90 percent of the votes cast, but neither party will very often receive more than 55 or 60 percent of the vote. A prime example is the U.S. party system, in which only the Republican and Democratic parties are normally serious contenders for power. Note that a two-party system does not necessarily *have* only two parties; a dozen or so parties run regularly in a U.S. presidential election, including the Vegetarians, the Prohibitionists, the Libertarians, and the Socialist Workers' party. But only the two major parties have any expectation of winning. Other examples of two-party or nearly two-party systems are those of Great Britain and Austria.

In contrast to a dominant-party system, a two-party system offers somewhat more regular variety and choices in policies and candidates. At the same time, a single party generally wins an election cleanly and is able to govern by itself without forming a coalition with other parties. Thus two-party systems are typified by a certain amount of choice combined with fairly stable and straightforward governance.

The final type of party system dealt with here is the *multiparty system*. This system consists of more than two major parties. A good example is Norway, whose Parliament in 1989 consisted of representatives from the following parties:

Labour party	63 seats
Conservative party	37 seats
Progress (anti-tax) party	22 seats
Left Socialists	17 seats
Christian People's party	14 seats
Centre (Agrarian) party	11 seats
Independent	1 seat

Since there are 165 seats, 83 are required to control the parliament, and no one party had enough seats to rule by itself. As it happened, in this case no coalition could readily be formed, partly because no other party wished to be allied with the Progress party. The Labour party formed what is called a "minority government" (one without enough votes to pursue major initiatives), but the situation was unsatisfactory to almost everyone.

Most democratic systems are multiparty systems. The one factor that seems strongly to determine whether a given state will have a two-party or a multiparty system is its electoral system. If a state uses a form of plurality electoral system, it will almost surely have a two-party system. If it uses a proportional representation system, it will almost surely have a multiparty system. The reason for this should be clear from the discussion in Chapter 8—under a plurality system, large parties have such an advantage that small parties are driven out, until only two major parties are left.

As compared with a two-party system, a multiparty system offers the voter a wider range of choice. Not only are there *more* choices, but the parties are able to be more distinctive than they could be in a two-party system. In a two-party system, since a party must command half or more of all votes cast in the election to succeed, there is great pressure on parties to appeal simultaneously to many different groups. A party may not stake out a clear appeal to farmers, for instance, because it might alienate its supporters in the cities; it cannot appeal clearly to the East because it might lose votes in the West, and so on. Parties in a multiparty system do not have this problem. Since the formation of a coalition is likely in any case, a party does not *have* to be huge to get some share of the power. In the Norwegian example given above, the Labour party represents the special interests of the labor unions, fishing crews, and various other groups; it is a bit bland. The Conservative party represents especially the urban middle class, who want taxes kept down and do not want moralistic constraints imposed by the state. The Christian People's party represents devout Lutheranism and favors prohibition of liquor, religious instruction in the schools, and a ban on abortion. The Centre party represents especially the interests of farmers. The Left Socialists have a variety of programs but are most noted for their opposition to Norwegian membership in NATO. The Progress party is a right-wing party sharply opposed to the welfare state and to immigration. What a "smorgasbord," compared with any existing two-party system! Surely the voter has a greater range of choice in multiparty systems than in two-party systems.

However, there is a balancing advantage to the two-party system. Since most of the time multiparty systems require a coalition government to operate smoothly, a government cannot be set up unless two or more parties agree to cooperate by forming a coalition. Now this may be fine. Sweden, Norway, Finland, West Germany, and other countries have been ruled by stable coalitions of one sort or another through most of their postwar history. But if the need for a coalition coincides with a great deal of animosity among the political parties, there may be trouble. Under this combination of circumstances, it may be difficult to put together a coalition of parties in the first place; or, if one is formed, it may be torn apart by mutual mistrust before it has lasted very long. A prime example of this problem is Italy, which has been governed by forty-four different coalitions since 1945.

CONCLUSION

The disjunction between politics as choice and politics as power has led to some distortion in our view of political parties in a democracy. In general, we have viewed the party much as what Michels wishes it could be—an instrument that expresses politically the unified choice of its members. We have viewed parties as unitary actors and have thought of them, from the standpoint of their members, predominantly in terms of choice. We have not thought of a party as consisting of various groups that may be at odds with each other and that exercise power over one another.

But more often than not, a chief function of a party is to serve as a conduit by which one faction may exercise power over another. It is this that has made the party almost as important to nondemocracies as to democracies, and we have seen that it is also an important function of democratic parties.

Our emphasis on the party as a vehicle for expressing choice has often helped make us insensitive to its importance as a channel for the use of power. Once again, both power and choice are necessary to a full understanding of politics.

EXAMPLE: THE COMMUNIST PARTY OF THE SOVIET UNION

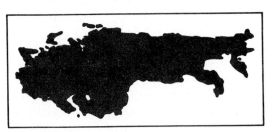
The Soviet Communist party originated in the revolutionary socialist movements of the late nineteenth century. In 1917, drained after three years of fighting World War I, the Russian monarchy collapsed and, in the ensuing confusion, the Communist party seized power and established the Soviet system. This party is intimately tied into the state apparatus that it controls. As stated in chapter 1, article 6 of the Soviet Constitution, "The leading and guiding force of Soviet society and the nucleus of its political system, of all state organizations and public organizations, is the Communist Party of the Soviet Union."

By placing party officials in key positions in the army, the bureaucracy, universities and schools, factories, and so on, and controlling the legislative and executive portions of the government, the party determines public choices in the Soviet Union.

It is a disciplined party. One does not join it casually:

> To be eligible for party membership, an applicant must be eighteen or older, have a good personal record, and know the basics of Marxism-Leninism. Every applicant is required to secure written recommendations from several members who have belonged to the party for at least five years. The application is then considered at a meeting of the entire primary organization, with the applicant present and obliged to answer questions pertaining to his or her political beliefs, private life, personal ambitions, and familiarity with Marxism-Leninism. A favorable decision by the primary organization must be approved by the appropriate upper-level party office. During the first year, the new member, or "candidate," is on probation and may not vote. All members pay monthly dues, ranging from a token fee required from students and pensioners (ten cents per month), to 3 percent of the salary of high-ranking officials. Members are expected to attend periodic meetings of their primary organization, take an active part in various political campaigns, and set an example for nonmembers in work, study, and general conduct. Party members are also expected to do volunteer work in various community projects.[11]

Approximately 17 million Soviet citizens, or 8 percent of the adult population, are members of the party. In return for their service to the party, they receive good jobs and various privileges and may be able to work their way up to positions of power. Those who join the party submit to the discipline of what is called "democratic centralism." Under this rule, all lower levels of the party are unconditionally subordinate to higher levels. Absolute obedience is required, and disobedience is punishable by expulsion. This once meant arrest and exile and still generally means that one is fired from his or her job and blacklisted for future employment. Such discipline is the "central" part of "democratic centralism." The "democratic" side requires that as decisions are in the process of being made, there should be wide discussion of them at lower levels, with communication of the sense of these discussions all the way up to the central level. It is a participatory but tightly disciplined way of organizing the party.

At the national level of organization, the lowest of the important organs of power is the party's Central Committee. It consists of two to three hundred members plus perhaps half as many nonvoting probationary members. The Central Committee meets a few times a year. It does not actively make major governmental decisions—it could hardly do so, meeting so infrequently—but as the "crème de la crème" of Soviet politics, it may function importantly in times of crisis. When a new leader of the Soviet Union must be chosen, for instance, the Central Committee presumably plays an important role. It elects members to the two highest levels of the party, the Politburo and the Secretariat. In fact, however, the Central Committee merely ratifies the nominations it has received from the previous members of the Politburo and Secretariat.

The Politburo is the party's most important body. It is small (fourteen members in 1981) and includes all the chief leaders of the Soviet Union. It meets frequently and deals with all the important decisions of the state. How it functions varies with the power and personality of the party's general secretary, who presides over the Politburo. Stalin presumably was able to dictate to the rest of the Politburo. Recent general secretaries, Andropov and Chernenko, have not been in as strong a position within the party, and Politburo proceedings have presumably been more lively. Mikhail Gorbachev has had greater power in the Politburo than did his predecessors because he has been able to appoint allies to several new positions in the Politburo.

The party Secretariat is nearly as important as the Politburo. Its membership overlaps with that of the Politburo, and the party's general secretary presides over it as well as over the Politburo. While the Politburo deals with all important decisions of the state and many specifically party issues as well, the Secretariat is more specialized. It deals with all the internal affairs of the party—appointment, rules, relations with communist parties in other countries, and so on.

To sum up, the Communist party of the Soviet Union is a large and demanding organization which has intertwined itself with the apparatus of the state to a point at which it is difficult to distinguish the two. We can describe the formal organization of the party, but—because so much depends on informal

[11]Vadim Medish, *The Soviet Union*, 2nd ed. (Englewood Cliffs, N.J.: Prentice-Hall, 1984) p. 87.

political processes within the Politburo, Secretariat, and Central Committee—that still leaves us with large areas of ignorance about how decisions are made.

After seventy years of almost total domination of Soviet politics, the party now finds itself in the late 1980s under fire from reformers emboldened by Mikhail Gorbachev's program of *glasnost*. This has manifested itself in a number of ways. First, a number of party officials who failed to be elected to the Supreme Soviet in the 1989 election were forced by Gorbachev to resign their party posts as well on the grounds that as they had been repudiated by the people, they should not lead the party; this is a radical new doctrine in communist theory. The most dramatic such repudiation was that of Yuri Solovev, the party boss of Leningrad and a probationary member of the Politburo. Though he ran unopposed, he failed to get 50 percent of the vote and was thus not elected; he then had to resign all of his party posts.

Second, a number of party officials in minority republics such as Estonia have had to join in nationalist demonstrations against Moscow's domination of the republic, in order not to be deserted by the people they lead. This has obviously put great strains on party discipline.

More generally, by increasing the status of the Supreme Soviet and other governmental (as opposed to party) institutions, Gorbachev has created a potentially rival center of power. When the country's miners went out on an illegal strike in the summer of 1989 they addressed their demands not to the party, but to the Supreme Soviet. Even though 90 percent of the members of the Supreme Soviet are Communist party members so that ultimate control by the party is not threatened, the elevation of the Supreme Soviet still creates a more complex political structure in which the clear monopoly of power by the party becomes less clear. People have begun to take the party less seriously, and it was thought (as of early 1990) to be losing members. Finally, as of 1990 the Central Committee had voted to recommend to the Supreme Soviet that the Constitution be amended to eliminate the party's monopoly of representation; the motion had not yet been voted on, but surely would be passed, permitting the establishment of multiple parties.

EXAMPLE: MEXICO'S DOMINANT PARTY SYSTEM

Since 1929 when a decade of bloody violence was ended by its establishment in power, the PRI (Partido Revolucionario Institucional) has had uninterrupted control of Mexican politics.[12] It is broadly tied to the population as a whole, but with a special emphasis on peasant farmers and on organized labor. Op-

---

[12]Just how violent this period was can be seen in that about 1 million people, or 1 out of every 15 Mexicans, died violently from about 1910 until order was established. The trauma of this violence may help to explain the staying power of the PRI afterward.

position to PRI was until recently small and not very significant; it has grown quite rapidly, but is still fragmented. PRI power is in any c lenged in a way it had never been before. In the 1982 presidential elec claimed 68 percent of the vote, and it had never done much worse than that in the preceding fifty years. But in 1988, the results (which many questioned as inflated for PRI) were: PRI, 50 percent; a coalition of four disparate parties of the left, 31 percent; PAN (a conservative party), 17 percent. PRI also lost 51 of the 300 Congressional races; in 1982 they had lost (or admitted losing) only one. Change is certainly in the air.

Over the years, since the PRI has been the "only game in town," all players have tended to gravitate to it. Most popularly based organizations in Mexico— farmers' cooperatives, labor unions, youth groups, shopkeepers' groups, and so on—are formally affiliated with the party and provide much of the structure for factional conflict within it. Party leaders find that much of their energy is spent in melding these groups together:

> A particularly difficult case involved the *municipio* of San Martin from which a group had come to protest the preassembly understanding that had been reached with regard to town council offices. Included in the group from San Martin were elements from three affiliated sectors of the party—Popular, Agrarian, and Labor. The most effective spokesmen were from the middle class, or Popular Sector—a primary school teacher and the local doctor. Although these men carried the burden of the argument, there were also representatives from the two other sectors, presidents of local peasant (*ejido*) communities and officers of local unions, who took part from time to time.
>
> The complainants formed a noisy and belligerent semicircle around the chairman. Morales stood facing them. He was taller than most Mexicans and very broad shouldered. When everyone had positioned himself in the office, Morales opened the discussion by asking the nature of the trouble. From somewhere came an angry voice. "We are completely dissatisfied with the situation at San Martin." Morales shrugged his shoulders. "All right, you aren't satisfied. I can't help that. This is no way to further your case." The group became quiet, and the schoolteacher, the doctor, several union officials and some of the *ejido* presidents spoke in turn for their people. They outlined a situation in which the municipal president was the prime offender. He had arranged a convention of the Popular Sector in which he had used outside help to win the endorsement of the assembly for his chosen successor. Neither the peasant leaders nor the union officials had been notified of the assembly. Despite these procedural irregularities the municipal president with his chosen group had proceeded to form the entire list of PRI candidates for municipal office. The list had then been presented to Morales who had given his approval since the minutes of the assembly had made it appear that all was in order. The result was that both labor and agrarian sectors were incensed because of the manner in which their strength had been ignored, and the majority of the Popular Sector also felt cheated.
>
> Morales argued that on the basis of the convening order for municipal assemblies he could not receive complaints until after the official assembly had been held the next day. His general secretary spoke up. "Look here! There are many factors involved in this situation. If you don't like the man your municipal president has selected as his successor, remember at least that he is a well-known businessman and well prepared to talk with government officials about the financial problems of

your *municipio*. Moreover, the present nominee has close ties of friendship with various people in the federal government. It is necessary at least to give such a man a place on the ticket." In reply, the spokesmen for the delegation from San Martin pointed out that they clearly had an "absolute" majority and invited the party officials to come to the *municipio* and see this for themselves. "Don't tell us the party has to wait until after the municipal convention to act on a complaint!" they said. "You can act now if you want to! If you don't we will not have nearly so good a chance." Those from San Martin then pointed out that if the party persisted in the arrangement it would be responsible for putting an undesirable man in the municipal presidency, a man disliked throughout the *municipio*. One spokesman said with conviction, "The *municipio* will be seething with discontent. Do you like that kind of picture? Do you want to be a party to such an arrangement?" Several of the San Martin leaders pointed to sections of the party statutes which supported their argument.

When the delegation showed no signs of leaving until satisfaction had been obtained, Morales capitulated. He gave the following instructions. "Doctor, professor, and other members of the Popular Sector, hold your convention at eight o'clock this evening. I shall be there or shall send a trusted representative. The agrarian and labor sectors will meet beforehand to select nominees for the municipal ticket and delegates to attend the popular sector convention."

After the San Martin episode the excitement became less intense, and the number of people waiting grew steadily smaller. Finally, at four o'clock Morales left the office and took me along with some of his associates to a nearby cafe. There it was decided that the candidate for the state legislature from San Martin should preside over the assemblies that evening. The outcome, as I later discovered, was a victory for the delegation that had visited Morales.[13]

From the standpoint of an ambitious young person, PRI has until recently been the only path into politics. Almost all leaders of factions and groups in the party—even labor and farm groups—are upper-middle-class people with university educations. The route to a political career for young people has been to attach themselves to important party leaders. The young politician offered loyalty and help to the leader, who in return procured jobs for the other and offered help on the way up the career ladder.

In recent years, dissatisfaction with this system has grown. It works to the advantage of monopolies of all sorts—labor unions, producers' associations, professional groups. But it does not provide much scope for individual initiative. New political initiatives can really come only through the party, and then only with the support of leaders who have risen slowly and painfully through the ranks. Young university students are especially impatient with the party's monopoly on political change.

The population as a whole has also begun to show less and less interest in the party and in the elections it contests. Nominations within the party are controlled by an inner circle with little popular involvement. In 1982, the

[13]L. Vincent Padgett, *The Mexican Political System*, 2nd ed. (Boston: Houghton Mifflin, 1976) pp. 5–6.

party was tainted with scandal when the outgoing administration was found to have stolen as much as $3 billion from the treasury, though the new president, Miguel de la Madrid, quickly cleaned house. The 1985 congressional election sparked deep resentment when PRI officials openly tampered with ballots. PAN had expected to win at least a governorship or two and several congressional seats; instead, they won no governorships and lost seats in the Congress. The general disenchantment with the party has been indicated by decreases in participation in Mexican elections over the last twenty years or so. In presidential elections, turnout decreased from 77 percent in 1964 to 65 percent in 1970, and 62 percent in 1976. In 1982, in the middle of an economic crisis, it rose again to 75 percent. Popular dissatisfaction finally led to the PRI's repudiation in the 1988 election, again with increased turnout.

It appears that PRI's monopoly of power is near an end; this, as we have seen in the earlier discussion, is not an unnatural way for a dominant party system to develop. However, the PRI may still enjoy a fairly long period of dominance even if it does not have its old monopoly of power, simply because its opposition is so fragmented and falls partly to the right, partly to the left, of PRI.

FURTHER READING

Burnham, Walter Dean. *Critical Elections and the Mainsprings of American Politics*. New York: Norton, 1970.

Dalton, Russell J., et al., eds. *Electoral Change in Advanced Industrial Democracies: Realignment or Dealignment?* Princeton, N.J.: Princeton University Press, 1984.

Downs, Anthony. *An Economic Theory of Democracy*. New York: Harper & Row, 1957.

Duverger, Maurice. *Political Parties*. London: Methuen, 1964.

Epstein, Leon. *Political Parties in Western Democracies*. New York: Praeger, 1967.

Hendel, Samuel. *The Soviet Crucible*. Boston: Duxbury, 1980.

Janda, Kenneth. *A Conceptual Framework for the Comparative Analysis of Political Parties*. Beverly Hills, Calif.: Sage, 1970.

Janda, Kenneth. *Political Parties: A Cross-National Survey*. New York: Free Press, 1980.

LaPalombaro, Joseph, and Weiner, Myron. *Political Parties and Political Development*. Princeton, N.J.: Princeton University Press, 1966.

Lipset, Seymour Martin, and Rokkan, Stein. *Party Systems and Voter Alignments*. New York: Free Press, 1967.

Loewenberg, Gerhard. "The Remaking of the German Party System." *Polity* 1 (Fall 1968): 86–113.

McCormick, Richard L., ed. *Political Parties and the Modern State*. New Brunswick, N.J.: Rutgers University Press, 1984.

Przeworski, Adam, and Sprague, John. *Paper Stones: A History of Electoral Socialism*. Chicago: University of Chicago Press, 1986.

Rae, Douglas. *The Political Consequences of Electoral Laws*, rev. ed. New Haven, Conn.: Yale University Press, 1971.

Rogowski, Ronald. "Political Cleavages and Changing Exposure to Trade." *American Political Science Review* 81 (December 1987): 1121–1137.

Rose, Richard. *Do Parties Make a Difference?* Chatham, N.J.: Chatham House, 1980.

Sartori, Giovanni. *Parties and Party Systems*. Cambridge, England: Cambridge University Press, 1976.

Sorauf, Frank, and Beck, Paul Allen. *Party Politics in America*, 6th ed. Glenview, Ill.: Scott, Foresman, 1988.

Chapter 10

Structured Conflict: Interest Groups and Politics

In the last chapter we distinguished the political party from the interest group. The former is associated with the process of leadership selection and the organization of government, while the latter is concerned primarily with trying to affect what those in power do. *The interest group is an organized group of citizens one of whose goals is to ensure that the state follows certain policies.*

All sorts of organized groups may function as interest groups. Some are organized solely to lobby governmental officials on behalf of one or another cause. The Sierra Club, a U.S. organization that lobbies for the preservation of wilderness areas, is an example of such an organization. Other groups may be organized primarily for other purposes but take on lobbying and other ways of influencing policy as an important task. Examples of such groups are labor unions, which are primarily organized in order to bargain with an employer but are also usually active politically. Still others focus on other goals but give some attention to politics. An example would be a university, whose first concern is to educate students and conduct research but which may maintain one or two people to lobby the government on bills that concern it.

There are a great many interest groups in a modern state, so many that we generally do not have a good idea of their numbers. There is available a reasonably good census of interest groups in Norway as of the early 1970s; this is presented in Table 10–1.

Over a thousand interest groups in the small country of Norway! And these are only nationwide organizations; all sorts of local groups are not included. No one really knows how many different interest groups a large and diverse country like the United States has, but there must be many thousands.[1]

Interest groups are not confined to democracies or open societies. All states have interest groups. Some do not permit a wide diversity of formally orga-

---

[1] As of July 1987, 4,211 political action committees were registered with the Federal Election Commission. And beyond this there were many local interest groups as well as interest groups that did not organize political action committees to give money to candidates. Edward Zuckerman, *Almanac of Federal PACs: 1988*. (Washington, D.C.: Amward Publications, 1988), p. viii.

10–1   Norwegian Interest Groups, by Type

Category	Number of organizations
Economic	540
Services, industry, finance, etc.	478
Agriculture, forestry, fishing	62
Employers and Unions	274
Noneconomic organizations	388
Cultural	119
Sport, hobbies	94
Humanitarian, social	97
Religious	52
Political	25
Total	1,202

SOURCE: Robert Kvavik, *Interest Groups in Norwegian Politics* (Oslo, Norway: Universitetsforlaget, 1976), p. 42.

nized, politically active groups to exist, since this would seem threatening to their governments. However, even in these, organizations set up for other purposes—the army, universities, natural history clubs, scientific associations, sports clubs, factories—exert political influence to help mold government policies.

In the Soviet Union, for instance, before 1988 only six "social organizations" were officially sanctioned—inventors', athletes', lifesaving, and stamp-collecting clubs; the Red Cross; and an organization for the preservation of historical and cultural monuments—and these were closely monitored.[2] Other social or political organizations outside the Communist party, such as certain religious groups and groups of intellectual dissidents, were harassed and were often either disbanded or forced underground. But at the same time it was well understood that conflict among functionally important groups such as the army, the secret police, the scientific establishment, the industrial bureaucracy—each trying to defend its turf—was a main driving force of Soviet politics, right up to the highest national levels. Under Gorbachev's *glasnost* reforms a wider array of groups has emerged and has begun to contest political issues, especially along cultural and ethnic lines. And of course, conflict among the functional groups (army, etc.) remains intense.

INTEREST GROUPS AND REPRESENTATION

Interest groups are probably the main vehicle in most states for representing public opinion and bringing it to bear in an organized (and therefore effective)

[2]John S. Reshetar Jr., *The Soviet Polity*, 2nd ed. (New York: Harper & Row, 1978), p. 224.

"CHARGE!"

(Reprinted with permission of United Feature Syndicate)

way on the governmental authorities. Political parties cannot do this very well, since they are involved in trying to acquire governmental power for themselves. This quest for power forces parties to incorporate many compromises in their programs in order to appeal to the broadest spectrum of support. If the state is a democracy, this may take the form of an attempt to appeal to a wide range of voters; if the state is not a democracy, it may mean trying to have such a broad appeal that neither the army, the air force, the navy, urban workers, the church, nor any other major group will try to overthrow them. Whatever the case, a political party, by virtue of its most basic goal, cannot serve to articulate and represent people's wishes; it has a different task: to blend various wishes into a larger coalition. The party seeks to make differences fuzzy, but each interest group is free to present its group's wishes clearly and precisely. The task of representing the people's desires, then, falls on the interest group. How well do interest groups do at this?

Generally speaking, interest groups do accomplish this fairly well. Otherwise they would not be the workhorses of political advocacy that they are. However, there are three important barriers that keep interest groups from functioning as well in this area as we might wish:

1. First of all, *not all interests are equally well organized*. Groups whose members have enough leisure to be active in politics are likely to enlist more of their potential clientele than other groups. Similarly, we will see high enrollment from among interests whose members are concentrated in particular localities, rather than spread out; have a basic economic stake in the outcome of policies (a labor union whose members depend on the price of coal for their jobs will organize more thoroughly than a consumer group which might stand

Migrant farm workers, Imperial Valley, California. Moving frequently, working long hours, lacking education and political skills, such workers find it difficult to organize themselves for political action.

(Peter Menzel/Stock, Boston)

to save its members a few percent on their cost of living); are well educated; and so on. Table 10–2, for example, lists enrollment percentages for labor organizations in several different occupational groups.

As a result of such disparities, some interest groups can speak strongly and confidently as representatives of their interest, and they are listened to with respect. Other interest groups, who represent formally only a small percentage of their potential clientele, must speak with a somewhat timid voice. The overall system of interest groups, as a result, does not represent all interests equally well. Those that are easy to organize bulk larger in the system, and their voices are heard more loudly than they should "deserve" on the basis of their numbers.

2. *Similarly, some groups command a disproportionate voice in the interest-group system because they have special advantages*. Consider the following examples:

- In almost all Western countries, business groups have influence beyond what one would expect on the basis of the size of their memberships. They gain added influence because they have a great deal of money to spend on politics; they have a good deal of expertise in advertising and organization, which can be used to political benefit; and the well-being of the country is so closely tied to their own well-being that they must be listened to with respect.

Table 10–2   Percent of Eligible Employees Who Are Enrolled in Labor Organizations, by Industry and Gender, United States

Type of industry	
Agriculture (wage and salary workers)	3
Mining	19
Construction	23
Manufacturing	26
Transportation and public utilities	38
Wholesale and retail trade	8
Finance, insurance, real estate	4
Services	8
Government	43
Gender	
Women	16
Men	24

SOURCE: U.S. Department of Commerce, Bureau of the Census, *Statistical Abstract of the United States 1988*, p. 402.

- In many states whose governments are shaky, large landowners as a group gain exaggerated political influence because of their ties to the army, which may be expected to intervene politically on their behalf.
- In Israel over the past decade, rather small groups of fundamentalist Jewish sects have wielded influence all out of proportion to their numbers because the Labour and Likud parties have been so evenly matched in elections that the small religious parties have held the balance of power.
- In almost all countries with much coastline, the fishing industry has had disproportionate influence because its members are concentrated in what are often key locations politically and because they are willing to go to great lengths to protect their livelihood and their traditional way of life. (It is for this reason, for instance, that it has been so difficult for other countries to get Japan to stop the hunting of whales, even though only a few thousand members of Japan's huge labor force are involved in the whaling industry.)

Such examples could be added to, on and on. Partly because not all interests are equally well organized and also because some have special advantages such as these, the sum total of interest-group representation may give quite a distorted picture of the interests in a country.

3. *Finally, most interest groups are not organized very democratically; their leaders are not closely responsive to the members' wishes*. The leaders of an interest group are usually able to build a base of support within the administrative structure of the group and among its members, which makes it difficult to unseat them. Even where the members of the group elect the leader each year—as is true of most labor unions, for instance—an "inside" group usually dominates the election, so that the same person is elected year after

Table 10–3   Percent of Members Who Would Stay in the Association if It Did Not Lobby at All

Minnesota Farm Bureau	77
Minnesota Farmers' Union	63
Minnesota Retail Federation	57
Minnesota–Dakotas Hardware Association	70
Printing Industries of the Twin Cities	94

SOURCE: Terry M. Moe, *The Organization of Interests* (Chicago: University of Chicago Press, 1980), p. 210.

year.[3] And many interest groups—such as universities, armies, and factories— are not even set up in such a way as to allow periodic elections.

Since the internal structure of interest groups is not very democratic, there is a real danger that their leaders may gradually drift apart from the ordinary members and follow their own political line. Democratic accountability to the membership could prevent this, but in its absence there is little to keep it from happening.

We might expect that the free market would provide a control over this. That is, if the leaders drifted too far away from the ordinary members, the latter would be able to "vote with their feet" and join a competing group. For example there are many different conservation societies, so we might expect that if some members of, say, Friends of the Earth did not like their leaders' positions, they would drop their membership and join some other group, such as the National Wildlife Association.

The trouble with this solution is that a group's political positions are often *not* major factors determining an individual's continued membership in the group. For most union members, the important thing is how skillful their union is in negotiating a good contract with their employer. Another important consideration is the package of extra benefits the union can provide—low-cost group insurance, educational and entertainment programs, low-cost package vacations, and so on. For most members, the union's political activity is a weak runner-up among the things that matter to them.[4]

A survey of several business and agricultural associations asked members whether they would stay in their association if it stopped its political activity altogether but continued to offer them the other benefits they enjoyed. The result is shown in Table 10–3.

These side benefits, which the leaders of groups may manipulate in order to maintain membership in the group, are called *selective incentives*. (They give members an *incentive* for being in the group; they are *selective* in that

[3]Seymour Martin Lipset, Martin A. Trow, and James S. Coleman explore an exception to this rule in *Union Democracy* (Garden City, N.Y.: Doubleday, 1962).

[4]Mancur Olson, *The Logic of Collective Action* (Cambridge, Mass.: Harvard University Press, 1965).

they may be targeted selectively to members of the group.) If the selective incentives available through an organization are sufficiently attractive, they can provide the leaders of the organization with a great deal of leeway in their choice of political positions. Leaders of labor unions have been able to take political positions varying from rather conservative Republican (the Teamsters' Union in the United States) to communist (many French and Italian unions), and their members have not objected strongly as long as their wage settlements and other benefits were good.[5]

Interest groups, then, are not on the whole democratically organized, and their leaders may depart considerably from the members' views. Add to this our two earlier points (that the groups themselves may be rather unrepresentative of the population as a whole, because some kinds of people participate more in groups than others; and that some groups, because of strategic advantage, are able to have more impact than they deserve on the basis of their numbers), and we can see that the overall result of lobbying and other political activity on the part of interest-group leaders may be quite unrepresentative of the wishes of the people.

As a few examples of how the interest-group system may distort public opinion, consider the following:

- In Israel, in deference to small fundamentalist groups, the national airline El Al does not fly on the Sabbath even though it is expensive to have the planes sit idle and most Israelis would prefer to have Sabbath flights.
- In the United States, a majority of those sampled in public opinion polls favor the regulation of handguns, but the National Rifle Association has effectively blocked such laws in most localities.
- In countries with state-run television networks, programming is almost always more "educational" (and dull) than the people would prefer. Leaders of cultural associations are in part responsible for this.

TYPES OF INTEREST GROUPS

We can classify interest groups in all sorts of ways. One of the most frequently used classifications has the added advantage, for this text, of underscoring our point that all sorts of organizations may function as interest groups.[6]

1. Anomic Groups

These are groups with no formal organizational structure and no obvious leaders that come together only temporarily and with the loosest of coordination to their efforts. Typically they are the result of turmoil and excitement, and their

---

[5]An added factor that may hold members in groups and that certainly operates in the case of many labor unions is *coercion*. "Closed shop" contracts often require that a worker must be a member of the union in order to hold a job.

[6]This classification is most fully developed in Gabriel Almond and James S. Coleman, eds., *The Politics of the Developing Areas* (Princeton, N.J.: Princeton University Press, 1960).

The Logic of Collective Action

One of the more interesting works of abstract theory in the social sciences is Mancur Olson's *Logic of Collective Action* (Cambridge, Mass.: Harvard University Press, 1965), which is particularly applicable to the study of interest groups. Olson notes that organized groups will be plagued by the problem of collective goods. (You will recall from Chapter 5 that a collective good is one that no member of the group can be prevented from enjoying.) Even if a business owner does not join the local chamber of commerce, for example, he or she will still benefit from its lobbying activities with the state government.

To Olson, this means that the potential members of the group will each be inclined to save their dues money and not join the group, since they can enjoy the benefits of the group's activity whether or not they join. What is rational for the individual may be tragic for the group, however, since if every potential member did what was rational, there would be no interest group at all and no benefits for anyone.

Olson notes four possibilities that help to explain how one might be able to organize groups in spite of the problem of collective goods:

1. If a group is *sufficiently small*, it may be easier to organize. Each member's contribution is then not trivially small, so all potential members can see that there will be less of the collective good available if they withhold their contribution to the group.

2. The group may offer *selective incentives*, such as life insurance programs or travel packages, that can be withheld from those who do not enter the group.

3. The group may be able to *coerce* members to join whether they wish to or not. The closed shop is an example of this in labor relations. In "neo-corporatist" systems (see below, pages 211–213), the government may require that the group be formed so that it can help to carry out the government's policies.

4. If one member of the group bulks very large relative to the others, then that member may see that the collective good would be impossible to attain without its participation. Therefore that member may join and carry things forward even though smaller members who do not join get a free ride. The largest department store in town, for instance, can hardly avoid joining the chamber of commerce. For a slightly different "group," this helps to explain why the United States figures so importantly in the NATO alliance and provides its smaller allies with a partially free ride.

actions are often violent. Examples of anomic interest groups include lynch mobs, the black urban riots in the United States in 1968, and the student rioters who almost brought down the French government in 1968. When the Canadian premier crossed Canada in a luxurious private railroad car at the height of the recession of 1982, his car was pelted with eggs, bricks, and stones in many towns. The people throwing them functioned as an anomic interest group. Though such groups are not formally organized, they may have a significant political effect.

2. Nonassociational Groups

In a sense, this type contradicts our definition of "interest group" as an organized group of citizens one of whose goals is to ensure that the state follows certain policies. The nonassociational interest group is not organized in any formal way. It consists of some category or another of people who are treated by others *as if* they were representatives of an interest, even though they have not organized themselves formally to act as representatives. It is hard to find examples of nonassociational interest groups in the modern state, where most interests are represented by formally organized groups. In less developed states, the government will often seek out the views of, say, village elders on whether a dam should be built in their region or on some similar question of policy. The elders are not organized in a group to represent their region, but the government *treats* them as if they were.

Perhaps the best example of nonassociational interest groups in the modern state is provided by public opinion polling. In the poll, a randomly selected sample of a thousand or so people of some type—blacks, farmers, high school students, Catholics, or whatever—are asked questions about political issues and their responses are reported publicly. The thousand or so high school students are not organized formally in any way; in fact, they do not know each other or have any way of knowing who else has been contacted by the poll. But what they say is taken by everyone as if it represented the views of high school students as a whole.

3. Institutional Groups

These groups are set up primarily for purposes other than political activity and would certainly exist even if they did not deal with politics at all; these become politically active only in order to defend their own interests in the state's policy decisions. Many examples of this sort of group have been cited above: an army, which is set up to defend the state, may become quite active, even dominant, in the politics of the state in order to further the common interests of its members; a university, which is set up to educate students and conduct research, may find that it must hire lobbyists to procure financial support from the government; and so on.

Institutional interest groups are found in great numbers in all states, but they are of special importance to the politics of closed systems like the Soviet Union, where "associational" interest groups are by and large not allowed.

4. Associational Groups

These are groups that regard political activity as one of their primary purposes. An associational interest group may have some other primary purposes as well;

(Reprinted by permission: Tribune Media Services)

labor unions, for example, exist to bargain with employers as well as to lobby the government, and the National Audubon Society of the United States exists to acquire and maintain its own wildlife refuges as well as to lobby for governmental protection of wildlife. But for all associational interest groups, political activity is *one* of the purposes for which the group was originally set up. This is the "typical" interest group with which we opened our chapter; it is what most people generally have in mind when they speak of "interest groups."

TACTICS OF INTEREST GROUPS

The tactics an interest group will use are determined by the sources of its power and by the opportunities that the political system offers for the use of power.[7] An interest group with many members but little money will concentrate on tactics that take advantage of numbers rather than money, while a group with few members but plenty of money will follow different tactics. And groups that have similar sources of power but find themselves faced with different sorts of political structures may also be expected to follow different tactics. In their political activity, U.S. labor unions, for instance, emphasize electoral activity and campaign contributions to public officials. For Solidarity, the

[7]For a good review of this point, see Norman J. Ornstein and Shirley Elder, *Interest Groups, Lobbying and Policymaking* (Washington, D.C.: Congressional Quarterly Press, 1978), chap. 3.

labor union that transformed the politics of Poland in the 1970s and 1980s in spite of suppression by the Communist government, these focuses of political activity were not available, so it concentrated instead on sit-ins and mass demonstrations.

Let us look specifically at several tactics available to interest groups in a democracy. What leads a group to choose one or more of these?

1. Control of Information and Expertise

Sometimes the members of an interest group control specialized information that is important to the government—information which may, in fact, be required if the group itself is to be controlled by the government. Doctors, for example, are the only people with the necessary expertise to judge medical policy and the quality of medical treatment. Scientists are the only ones sufficiently skilled technically to judge a variety of questions. Oil corporations know more about the oil business than anyone else does. In all these cases a government that wishes to make policy relevant to an interest group must depend on the members of the group for the necessary information and expertise. This gives the group a great deal of power, because the resulting interpretation of things is likely to be slanted a good deal toward the group's prejudices. It does not require that anyone operate dishonestly. Everyone always has a certain slant on things, and if the members of an interest group are the only ones giving the government analysis and interpretation, their slant is inevitably going to enter in.

This tactic requires that relevant information and technical skills be scarce. Labor unions, religious groups, or hobby organizations generally cannot make good use of the tactic for this reason. A dramatic example of this sort of power appeared during the Arab states' oil embargo of the United States in 1977, when it turned out that the only source for information on how much oil was in transit to the United States was the oil companies themselves. The government had no independent source for this.

2. Electoral Activity

This is a different tactic, especially suitable for groups with a large number of members who are at least moderately committed. Such a group may raise money from among its members to contribute to candidates, provide campaign workers to candidates, and deliver its own members' votes for candidates—all in an effort to ensure that people favorably disposed to the group end up in office. If the members of the group are not sufficiently committed to it to choose their vote on the basis of its recommendations, this tactic is of little use; an automobile club, for instance, would not generally be able to deliver its members' votes. Groups that have used this tactic successfully include labor unions, large religious organizations, and ethnic groups. Some other special organizations such as the National Rifle Association in the United States or the wine growers of France have also been successful in this way.

3. Use of Economic Power

An interest group of economic importance to the state may influence the state by threatening to disrupt its economic contribution. Strategically placed unions, such as those of railroad or postal workers, have often been able to enlist the government's help by threatening a strike that would be catastrophically disruptive to the state. At some times, as in France in 1968 or Germany in the 1920s, a *general strike* in which all unions stop working at the same time has been used to try to force an unpopular government out of office. Businesses often threaten communities by telling them that if they don't give them tax advantages or other considerations, they will move their operations elsewhere. Professional sports franchises have been particularly skillful at this kind of threat, forcing communities to provide them with subsidies, build stadiums to house them, and so on. The civil rights movement of the 1960s in the United States gained great impetus when an unknown preacher named Martin Luther King organized a boycott of the city bus system of Montgomery, Alabama, to force the city to allow blacks to sit anywhere they wished on the buses. Similarly, economic boycotts of white businesses have been an effective tool for blacks in South Africa in the late 1980s.

This tactic requires that a large economic stake be maneuverable. That is, the group must be able to turn on or turn off a large enough part of the economy to threaten dire results. This can be accomplished either by a single large corporation, for which it is usually fairly easy, or by a large number of people who, though they are not individually that important to the economy, are willing to coordinate economic disruption (a strike or boycott) so that their combined impact is important. Mass action like this is usually difficult to accomplish, because it requires a large number of people to make an economic sacrifice by stopping work, finding an alternative to riding buses, or whatever. It requires a large and unusually devoted membership.

4. Public Information Campaigns

A group that does not necessarily have a large mass base but which has substantial access to the media may try to change policy by the most indirect of means—by changing the minds of the entire population in the hope that this, in turn, will influence government policy. Institutional interest groups frequently use this tactic, since many other tactics are barred to them. The U.S. Air Force has at times helped to encourage comic strips such as Steve Canyon, which put the Air Force in a good light. Government agencies in all states use "public service advertisements"—giving health advice, moral admonition, and so on—to keep themselves in the public eye as well as to accomplish the direct goal of the advertisements.

This tactic is also useful for an interest with enough money to buy advertising time, especially if other tactics do not look very promising. In the 1970s, American corporations were faced with a new environmental movement that was very difficult to combat. How could a group argue effectively for dirty air?

An expensive and skillfully executed ad campaign on the theme "Businesses don't cause pollution, people cause pollution" helped them to shift the terms of national debate.

5. Violence and Disruption

An interest group may also try to dramatize its case by violent or disruptive activity, or it may try by violence and disruption to convince the leaders of the state that they will pay a high price in turmoil by not yielding to the group's demands. Disruptive but nonviolent protest may be an effective way for an interest group to bring attention to its cause, especially if it has few resources other than a dedicated mass following.[8] But violence is also a frequently used tool. Sometimes it occurs spontaneously in "anomic" interest group activity, as in the urban riots of 1968. Sometimes it is tightly organized, as in campaigns of assassination and kidnapping by terrorist organizations like Italy's Red Brigade.

Terrorism is usually not a very effective technique, as it is simply likely to cost the disruptive group what public sympathy it has, and to call forth strenuous efforts at control by the authorities. A group with a decent chance of accomplishing its goals by other means is not likely to use violence as a tactic. However, there are two circumstances under which groups may resort to it:

a. For a small group of extremely committed people, terrorism is an obviously useful tactic. One must remember that a truly small group (say, fifty to a hundred people) is not likely to be able to bring about major political changes in any case. If no other tactic would succeed anyway, terrorist violence offers them a long-shot possibility. Even a very few people may attract a great deal of attention by way of bank robberies, murders, and kidnappings. They would have little chance of parlaying this attention into the accomplishment of their political goals, but if they were totally committed, they might try despite the odds.

b. The second case in which terrorism might be an effective tactic appears when one region is united in its opposition to the rest of a state and wishes to separate from it or at least to change its legal relationship to the government. A separatist group under these conditions can launch violent attacks on the rest of the state without losing the sympathy of the only "public" that counts for them, the people in their part of the state. In fact, the violence is likely to bring down harsher regulation and police activity in their region, which will serve to strengthen local support for the separatist cause. Many separatist movements— the Irish Republican Army in Britain, the Basque separatists in Spain, Moslem separatists in the Philippines—have used this tactic with success.

6. Litigation

Here an interest group attempts to affect policy by working within the court system. The historic reversal of segregated schooling in the United States was

---

[8]See Michael Lipsky, "Protest as a Political Resource," *American Political Science Review* 62 (December 1968): 1144–1158.

begun in this way when in 1954 the National Association for the Advancement of Colored People (NAACP) sponsored a constitutional test of segregation in the courts. A black student, with the help of the NAACP, sued her school board to admit her to the white school, and she won.

Through court cases, an interest group may hope to change the interpretation of a law or, in some countries, even get it thrown out altogether as unconstitutional. Also, court procedures can be so slow and expensive that the mere threat of tying a governmental agency up in court may get the agency to compromise.

However, litigation is generally a strategy based on weakness. For a group to be successful at litigation, it must depend on the way the law was initially written—something over which it has little control if litigation is its main tactic. And it must depend on finding a sympathetic court, which is also rather chancy. The great appeal of litigation is that it does not require large numbers (all one really has to have is a lawyer) or enormous economic power. Thus it appeals particularly to small, weak groups. Groups that have in recent years depended fairly heavily on litigation in the United States include environmentalists, the handicapped, and groups favoring abortion rights. These are relatively weak groups that have usually been on the defensive.[9]

The history of the civil rights movement in the United States provides varied examples of how circumstances determine strategy. In the 1940s and 1950s the movement for civil rights for blacks was relatively weak. The majority of blacks were still barred from voting in the South, blacks were poor and did not have a great deal of money to contribute, and the movement did not have many white allies, either in public office or outside it. The chief civil rights organization at this time was the NAACP, and its chief tactic was litigation. It achieved several important successes in court, among other things overturning segregated schooling in the South and outlawing the exclusion of black voters from primary elections.

With the increase in support for civil rights in the 1960s and partly as a result of these successes, more money and resources became available to the movement. Blacks had become bolder politically; many more were willing to march in demonstrations to help draw attention to their cause, and they began to acquire significant white allies. At this time new, rival organizations wishing to use different tactics appeared. The Congress on Racial Equality (CORE) and Martin Luther King's Southern Christian Leadership Conference (SCLC) were two new organizations that emphasized, as ways of attracting sympathy and forcing segregationists to yield, the use of economic power and the provocation of segregationists into violence. (Note the clever twist on the use of violence as a tactic—here white officials were goaded into violence so that they would lose public sympathy.) Massive demonstrations, requiring large numbers of dedi-

[9]See for example Susan M. Olson, *Clients and Lawyers: Securing the Rights of Disabled Persons* (Westport, Conn.: Greenwood Press, 1984). In 1989 the abortion rights movement strengthened a good deal in a popular reaction to an unfavorable court decision, and with its increased strength it began to shift its attention from litigation to electoral activity.

cated black and white participants, were held. Violence of their own was never a part of these leaders' strategy, but the provocation of white violence was useful, and the anomic black urban riots of 1965–68, which occurred spontaneously, were used by civil rights leaders as evidence for their claims that blacks had to be treated more fairly.

At this time electoral activity was not especially emphasized, first, because during the 1960s many southern blacks could not vote or were just acquiring the vote and, second, because demonstrations and disruption were proving to be such powerful tools. By the 1970s and 1980s, however, demonstrations began to be less effective. The public was more used to them and thus less impressed by them, and police and public officials had learned not to respond in the picturesquely violent ways that demonstrators had once counted on. At the same time, the electoral importance of blacks had grown. The black percentage of the electorate in many northern cities had reached a point at which blacks could often determine the outcome of mayoral and other elections. In the South, thanks to the gains of the 1960s, most blacks were free to vote and could determine many elections. In the 1970s and 1980s, accordingly, the activity of all black civil rights groups shifted to emphasize more their importance in elections.

We can see in this evolution of the tactics of the civil rights movement a good illustration of our general principle, that interest groups will pick those tactics that best fit the group's resources and the political opportunities offered by those resources.

PATTERNS OF INTEREST-GROUP ACTIVITY

Up to this point we have talked about interest groups primarily from the point of view of the individual group. However, we must also look at the pattern of all group activity in a state. In looking at political parties, we found that the overall pattern formed by the system of parties was important to the state's politics; similarly, we will see that the overall pattern of interest-group activity is also important. Interest-group systems vary in (at least) two important ways.

1. Degree of Organization

In some countries, people are heavily organized by groups; in others, they are not heavily organized at all. Most Third World states are only weakly organized. Institutional interest groups such as the church and the army bulk much larger in the politics of these states than they would otherwise, simply because interest groups of other sorts are weak.

Among industrialized states, there is also great variation. In some, such as the Soviet Union (pre-Gorbachev), the formation of groups is suppressed, and here again institutional interest groups gain in importance by default. But even among open societies, there is a good deal of variation. The Scandinavian countries are probably more thoroughly organized than any others in the world.

For example, about 65 percent of Swedish workers are members of trade unions, compared with about 40 percent for Great Britain and 20 percent for the United States. The percentage of people belonging to political organizations is about twice as high in Norway as in the United States.[10]

2. Degree of Direct Involvement of Interest Groups in Government and Administration

We saw earlier in this chapter that government officials must often depend on interest groups for information and expertise. The way in which governments may tap into this varies from casual arrangements, in which officials occasionally call up interest-group representatives or look up a figure in the group's publication, to quite formal arrangements in which interest-group representatives may sit by right on administrative committees of the government. Under the latter sort of arrangement, which is fairly common in northern Europe, it may be hard to draw the line between interest groups and government.

Two important types of interest-group systems can be identified by variations on these two dimensions. These are *pluralism* and *neocorporatism*. They are important concepts for understanding how interest groups operate in democratic systems.[11]

PLURALISM

"Pluralism" is a system in which all interests organize and compete freely and no one group is able to dominate things. The government is open to pressure from the interest groups, and politics consists largely of the competition among these interest groups to see that the policies they favor are adopted by the government.[12] In terms of our two dimensions above, pluralism is high on the scale of "organization" and low on "direct involvement of interest groups in government"; that is, interest groups are well organized but are quite distinct from the government. There is no state that is perfectly "pluralist"; the term is an abstraction. But the United States approaches the type more closely than most and is often used as a chief example of pluralism at work.

Those who favor a pluralist system of politics point out that with numerous groups operating, there is a good deal of spontaneity to things. It is relatively easy for new ideas to appear from the grass roots, and there is a good deal of flexibility. Further, because the government is simultaneously influenced by many competing groups, negotiation and compromise should be the order of the day. Politics should typically be pragmatic and nonradical.

---

[10]Robert B. Kvavik, *Interest Groups in Norwegian Politics* (Oslo: Universitetsforlaget, 1976), p. 46.

[11]Here, as in our discussion of interest group tactics earlier in this chapter, we shall focus attention on democracies.

[12]The chief source is David Truman, *The Governmental Process* (New York: Knopf, 1951). See also "Pluralism" in *The International Encyclopedia of the Social Sciences*.

Pluralist writers tend to emphasize choice much more than power in their view of politics, and they like pluralism because it seems an ideal way by which to reach the common ground of society. All the various interests in society pull in their varying directions, and the government responds to their pressure by ending up at a kind of equilibrium point where the pressures all balance. With a minimum of distortion, the public choice is reached.

Critics, however, point out that in any real state—as distinct from the idealized abstraction—the set of interest groups cannot represent the people of the state very well, because not all interests are equally able to "organize and compete freely." This was discussed at the beginning of this chapter under "Interest Groups and Representation." If the criticism is true, then a pluralist system might have all the advantages cited by those who favor it, yet we would still have to be suspicious of it because policies based on "pluralist" deliberations could be expected to slant systematically in favor of those groups that can operate effectively and against those that cannot.

NEOCORPORATISM

"Neocorporatism" is another abstraction. It is a system in which all interests are organized and the government deals directly with all affected interests at all stages in the making and administration of policy. Unlike pluralism, under neocorporatism the government does not merely respond to the interest groups' pressure but actively involves the groups themselves in the job of governing.[13] In terms of our two dimensions above, neocorporatism is high on the scales of both "organization" and "direct involvement of interest groups."

Not only does the government draw interest groups into the governmental process in neocorporatism, but parts of the government may also act rather like interest groups. This is not so much a matter of "institutional interest groups" lobbying for their own perquisites and budgets, as it is active engagement in political debate on behalf of certain policies. Parts of the bureaucratic apparatus may take on a greater role of representing popular constituencies and initiating policy demands than is common under pluralism. They are in effect "self-starters" who try to mobilize popular support for their positions. An example is the founding of the European Common Market in 1956; the campaign for unification was spearheaded not by party leaders, but by civil servants. From both sides, then, the boundary between government and interest groups becomes much more fuzzy in a neocorporatist system.

The Scandinavian states approach the neocorporatist model more closely than any others. For instance, in Sweden:

- The government is constitutionally required to send copies of any bill it is drafting to all affected interest groups and to solicit their responses at all stages of the legislative process.

---

[13]A good presentation of the model is Martin O. Heisler and Robert B. Kvavik, "Patterns of European Politics: The 'European Polity' Model," in Marton O. Heisler, ed., *Politics in Europe* (New York: David McKay, 1974), pp. 27–90.

- The drafting of any important bill is preceded by discussions in a special royal commission set up to consider the bill. Representatives of all affected interest groups sit on such a commission.
- Once the bill is passed, its administration will often be turned over to the affected group. For instance, governmental policies on the price of eggs are administered by the egg-growers' cooperative marketing board rather than by a governmental agency.
- Generally, policies are set in a remarkable spirit of cooperation and compromise. There is a reluctance to push any affected group to the wall.

Those who admire neocorporatism point to the cooperative attitude brought forth by such a system. (Sweden, for instance, generally has fewer work stoppages than does the United States. In 1986, some 696,000 working days were lost to strikes in Sweden; in the same year 11,861,000 working days were lost to strikes in the United States.)[14] In fact, for such a system to work at all, there *must* be a cooperative spirit, and putting the system in place may therefore help to call forth the required cooperation.

Also, neocorporatism eases the problem of unequal organization of groups, which flaws pluralism. Simply because groups must be well organized in order to take part in governing, it becomes much more important to interests that they organize their members, and they tend to do so. Indeed, the government sometimes writes a law in such a way that its administration requires the creation of a group that does not yet exist; when this situation has arisen, the government has simply organized the group itself![15]

On the other hand, the neocorporatist system is a fragile one, since it depends so much on cooperation and everyone's willingness to avoid rocking the boat. Since neocorporatism sets up an officially sanctioned set of actors in the system, each with rights to a piece of the pie, no group can go for the jugular of another without endangering the whole system.

This suggests a second important problem in neocorporatism. Because it defines a set of groups with claims on the state and routinizes the process by which the state consults with them, the neocorporatist system tends to petrify the existing line of conflict as of the time it was established. We can expect that lines of conflict will change over time, as old conflicts fade out and new ones arise. It is difficult for the neocorporatist system, with its intricate organizational structure of established and "entitled" interest groups, to adjust to such change. As an example of this problem, one of the most difficult challenges faced by Swedish politics in the last couple of decades has been to find a way of providing political expression to the new concern over the advisability of nuclear power and protection of the environment.

In this section we have considered what one might call "cooperative"

---

[14]In 1987, Sweden lost only 15,000 working days!

[15]This illustrates what is probably the most basic difference between the pluralist and neocorporatist models. Under pluralism, it is assumed that the state apparatus simply responds to the system of interest groups. Under neocorporatism, the state is taken to have a good deal of autonomy; to some extent, it creates the system of interest groups and determines how it operates.

neocorporatism of the sort typified by politics in the Scandinavian states. Neocorporatism of this sort arises from the desires of the government and the interests to develop consensus and minimize conflict in policymaking. Another form of neocorporatism is found especially in Latin America (Brazil and Perón's Argentina) as well as in Mussolini's dictatorship of Italy. This system is imposed on the interests by the state in order to keep them under its control. Though both types of government are "corporatist" in that the government deals directly with groups, the nature of politics is obviously very different in each.

EXAMPLE: INTEREST GROUPS IN FRANCE

France is a system that probably falls somewhere between the pluralist and neocorporatist models of politics. It also shows interesting peculiarities of its own, especially in a certain looseness and unpredictability of structure. French interest groups are rather fragmented; and, compared with groups in other states, they are relatively more likely to engage in provocative violence.

In general, French interest groups have fairly low enrollments from their potential members. Labor unions enroll only about 25 percent of their potential membership, and other sorts of groups have similarly low enrollments.

Further, the organized groups themselves are deeply divided. Frequently several different organizations compete for the same membership, which in other countries would be united behind a single organization. Workers, for instance, are organized in four major, separate unions: the CGT (a communist union with 37 percent of the total union strength); the CFDT (an independent-minded, generally socialist union with 23 percent of organized workers); Force Ouvrier (a reformist union independent of parties with 15 percent of organized workers); and the Catholic Confederation (with 4 percent). Independent unions account for the rest.[16] Farmers' interests, which figure importantly in French politics, are divided among no fewer than five hundred rural defense organizations at the national level.[17]

French politics at all levels is punctuated by sporadic, intense activity against a general background of cynical disengagement, and this holds as true of interest groups as it does of other aspects of politics. This is most notable in the periodic national crises that engulf France. The most recent of these occurred in May 1968, when a dispute between the students and administration of a provincial university flared up into a national confrontation between students on the one hand and administrators and police on the other. It was

---

[16]France. Ministry of the Economy, INSEE. *Donées Sociales 1987*, p. 195.

[17]Henry Ehrmann, *Politics in France*, 4th ed. (Boston: Little, Brown, 1983), p. 187.

marked by the occupation of campuses and pitched battles in the streets. Stimulated by the violence and seeing that the government was floundering in its response to the students, workers all over France went on strike to push their own demands for wage increases and greater control over working conditions. At its height, the strike probably involved half of all employees in France, and it effectively closed the economy down. It was not a tactical move by the union leaders, most of whom opposed the strike, but a spontaneous response by the workers. The combination of battles with the students and paralysis of the economy almost brought the entire system of government down.

It is not only in general crises that groups engage in confrontation. In the events of May 1968, violence and strikes were the result of anomic group activity, but the leaders of organized groups also use violent confrontation from time to time as a deliberate tactic. Extremist farm groups occasionally attract considerable attention by barricading highways or overturning trucks carrying produce they do not wish to see marketed. In 1984, for instance, there were numerous violent incidents involving agricultural imports from Spain. Other groups from which we might not ordinarily expect violence also occasionally tap into it in France. French shopkeepers have engaged in confrontational politics under the leadership of several groups, organizing tax strikes, kidnapping officials, and battling with police.

The incidence of violence on the part of French interest groups should not be taken to suggest that this is the tactic most frequently used by French groups. It is of interest to us because it occurs more frequently in France than in other industrialized states, but most of the time French interest groups spend their energy in less spectacular pursuits—meeting with bureaucrats and elected officials, dealing with political parties, engaging in court actions, and so on.

In their relations with the government, French interest groups are in some instances bound to the government by formal ties of intimacy of the sort we associate with neocorporatism. But more often interest group and government maintain the sort of distance we expect under pluralism. The agricultural sector comes closest to the neocorporatist model. Not all agricultural interest groups are tied intimately to the government, but one group, the Federation Nationale des Syndicats d'Exploitants Agricoles (FNSEA) has become something like the "official" agricultural group for the government. The FNSEA claims to represent about 55 percent of French farmers, which is low for a group that is to play a quasiofficial role in the neocorporatist mode, but it is quite respectable by French standards. During the 1970s, the government turned a number of administrative duties over to the FNSEA, including most of the educational and training tasks carried out in other countries by agricultural extension agents. In most areas the government recognized the FNSEA as the sole representative of farming interests.[18]

But on the whole, interest groups are not this close to the government. In

---

[18]John T. S. Keeler, cited in Ehrmann, op. cit., pp. 188–189.

10–4   Reported Frequency of Interest-Group Actions

	Often (percent)	From Time to Time (percent)	Rarely or Never (percent)
Parliamentary lobbying	32	59	8
Participation in government committees	55	31	14
Formal meetings with government officials	54	32	15
Public relations campaigns	33	44	23
Informal meetings with government officials	47	29	24
Action in the Economic and Social Council	26	26	48
Influencing parties and their leaders	10	37	53
Demonstrations, strikes, direct action	13	20	67
Blocking or sabotaging policy decisions	10	22	68
Legal action	8	20	72

a 1979 survey, 44 percent of group leaders reported that they met with government officials only "sometimes," "rarely," or "never," and only 21 percent reported that they did so "almost daily."[19] When one considers that the job of the interest-group leader is after all to influence government policy, this suggests that modest distance is maintained. Similarly, when asked what was their most effective means of action, only 18 percent named participation in government committees or contacts with civil servants. Table 10–4 lists the percentage of interest-group leaders who stated that their groups used specified tactics "often" or "from time to time." It gives a good overall profile of the activity of French interest groups.

FURTHER READING

Ball, A., and Millard, F., *Pressure Politics in Industrial Societies*. Atlantic Highlands, N.J.: Humanities Press International, 1987.

Bauer, Raymond A., de Sola Pool, Ithiel, and Dexter, Lewis A. *American Business and Public Policy*. New York: Atherton, 1963.

Berger, Suzanne, ed. *Organizing Interests in Western Europe: Pluralism, Corporatism, and the Transformation of Politics*. Cambridge, England: Cambridge University Press, 1981.

Goodman, David S. G., ed. *Groups and Politics in the People's Republic of China*. Armonk, N.Y.: M. E. Sharpe, 1984.

Kochanek, Stanley. *Business and Politics in India*. Berkeley: University of California Press, 1974.

Lehmbruch, Gerhard, and Schmitter, Philippe C., ed. *Patterns of Corporatist Policy-Making*. Beverly Hills, Calif.: Sage, 1982.

[19]The following survey results are drawn from Frank L. Wilson, "French Interest Groups: Pluralist or Neocorporatist?," *American Political Science Review* 77 (December 1983): 895–910.

Loomis, Burdett A., and Cigler, Allan J., eds. *Interest Group Politics*. Washington, D.C.: Congressional Quarterly, Inc., 1983.

Moe, Terry. *The Organization of Interests*. Chicago: University of Chicago Press, 1980.

O'Donnell, Guillermo. *Modernization and Bureaucratic Authoritarianism: Studies in South American Politics*. Berkeley: Institute of International Studies, University of California Press, 1973.

Olson, Mancur. *The Logic of Collective Action*. Cambridge, Mass.: Harvard University Press, 1965.

Ornstein, Norman J., and Elder, Shirley. *Interest Groups, Lobbying and Policymaking*. Washington, D.C.: Congressional Quarterly Press, 1978.

Salisbury, Robert. "An Exchange Theory of Interest Groups." *Midwest Journal of Political Science* 13 (February 1969): 1–32.

Schlozman, Kay Lehman, and Tierney, John T., *Organized Interests and American Democracy*. New York: Harper & Row, 1986.

Skilling, H. Gordon, and Griffiths, Franklyn, eds. *Interest Groups in Soviet Politics*. Princeton, N.J.: Princeton University Press, 1971.

Truman, David B. *The Governmental Process*, 2nd ed. New York: Knopf, 1971.

Walker, Jack L. "The Origins and Maintenance of Interest Groups in America." *American Political Science Review* 77 (June 1983): 390–406.

Wilson, Frank L. "French Interest Groups: Pluralist or Neocorporatist?" *American Political Science Review* 77 (December 1983): 895–910.

Wilson, James Q. *Political Organizations*. New York: Basic Books, 1973.

Chapter 11

National Decision-Making Institutions: Parliamentary Government

In this and the following chapter we shall examine formal arrangements for governing democracies. This chapter will deal with "parliamentary" government, while Chapter 12 will deal with "presidential" government. Parliamentary government is conceptually the simpler of the two and is the form found in most democracies. It will seem unusual to many American readers, however, since the United States is one of the handful of democracies that operates with a presidential system.

The basic principles of a pure parliamentary system are as follows:

1. A parliament of representatives is elected by the citizens of the state. It normally consists of anything from two hundred or so to several hundred representatives. The parliament is the only elected body in the state. Bills passed by the parliament are the law, and no one can overrule them.
2. The executive power of the state (managing the bureaucracy, conducting relations with other states, etc.) is lodged with a *cabinet* of women and men who are selected by the parliament to conduct the affairs of the state. Most or all members of the cabinet are usually members of the parliament who take on executive responsibilities in addition to their legislative chores.
3. The cabinet retains executive power only as long as it has the "confidence" of the parliament—that is, only as long as it can command a majority of the votes. At any time, a majority vote in the parliament may unseat a cabinet and cause a new set of people to be selected as a cabinet. This is referred to as the "government falling." Or, if no vote is actually taken to unseat the cabinet but the cabinet finds that it is unable to put together majorities to pass its important bills, it is expected that the cabinet will resign.
4. Just as the parliament holds the cabinet in jeopardy, the leader of the cabinet (called variously "premier," "prime minister," "chancellor," etc.) normally has the right to have the parliament disbanded, forcing a new election that will lead to a new distribution of power.

This, in a nutshell, is parliamentary government. We shall examine some finer points and some variations below, but these four principles are basic. It is a simpler form than presidential government because it does not allow for any separation of powers. The parliament, and the cabinet that operates only by the support of the parliament, holds all the state's governmental political power.

With this simple concentration of power, political decisions should, in principle, be made clearly and directly, with a minimum of delay. The legislature and the parliament should always be in agreement on important issues—if they were not, presumably the cabinet would fall—and their will cannot be blocked by a court or any other body.

Such a system has two special advantages and disadvantages.

Advantages

1. Because power is unified, the government can respond fairly directly to changed circumstances. For example, parliamentary systems were more successful than fragmented systems such as the United States at developing national energy policies in response to the shortages of oil in the 1970s. In a parliamentary system, all it takes to make a law is a majority of the votes in the parliament, so it is a rather straightforward thing for the party or parties in power to develop a policy and write it into law. In more fragmented systems like that of the United States, many barriers are raised that can slow down or halt the passage of a law. The president may veto the law, the Supreme Court may rule it unconstitutional, states may have proper jurisdiction over it, and so on.

2. A second advantage to a parliamentary system is that the lines of responsibility for policymaking are clear. Elections should mean more, because voters can know exactly whom to blame for their current situation: the party or parties in power. Parties can be held pretty well to their election promises once they are in office, because then there is nothing to prevent them from accomplishing what they had said they would do. In a more fragmented system like that of the United States, this is not so. There are so many independent centers of power that an unhappy policy cannot be blamed on any one of them. The president can say that Congress did it, Congress can point to the Supreme Court, and so on. President Harry Truman was famous for his desk-top slogan, "The buck stops here," but in 1948 he campaigned across the country on the theme that the "do-nothing" Congress, which was controlled by the Republican party, was to blame for his not having accomplished his goals as president. Elections simply can mean more with regard to public policy in a parliamentary system than in a more fragmented system because once election results are in, the party or parties that have won control of the parliament have no excuse for not enacting the policies they had promised.

Disadvantages

1. In a parliamentary system there are few protections for a minority that feels it is being wronged. In a presidential system, a minority may hope that even if it has lost its fight in the legislature, it may retrieve things with the president,

or vice versa. As a result, the support of a bare majority is generally not enough to get a law enacted.

This may be seen either as an advantage or a disadvantage. It is, in fact, the flip side of the advantage noted above, that in a parliamentary system policymaking is straightforward. Though this is in general a good thing, it is clear that there must be some times when we would wish that the government had been slowed down and had been prevented from taking hasty action or action that did not have fairly broad support. A parliamentary system, because of its efficiency, does not do this.

2. A second disadvantage to the parliamentary system is that it *may* produce unstable government. I have spoken above of the "party or parties" that control a parliament. If no one party holds a majority of the seats, then two or more parties must form a *coalition* to control the parliament. In forming a coalition, they will divide up the positions of the cabinet among themselves (party A gets to name the premier, the minister of economics, the foreign minister, and the minister for agriculture; party B gets to name the minister for defense and the minister for industry, etc.). In the parliament, they agree that their combined parties' votes will always be cast on behalf of legislation proposed by the cabinet.

This is fine if the partners of the coalition are in general agreement on most issues. But if the coalition is strictly a marriage of convenience and the parties in it disagree on enough things, it may be hard to keep them together and cooperating for very long. A socialist party may pull out because the coalition has not been able to agree on a program to stimulate employment, a Hindu party may pull out over a question of religious policy, or whatever. At that point the government "falls," and a new coalition must be negotiated.

If this happens only occasionally, it is no problem. Political change obviously must come from time to time. But in a parliamentary system it sometimes happens that the numerical strength of the parties and their relationships with each other are such that it is always difficult to keep a coalition together. This may lead to a paralyzing succession of governmental breakups, in which governmental control is so unstable that people lose confidence in the whole process. Germany suffered from this problem from 1918 till 1933, when Hitler overthrew the weakened democracy. France suffered from it until 1958, when the military intervened and imposed a presidential system. Italy has suffered from it chronically since 1945; in forty-four years (as of 1989) she had had forty-seven different governments. On the other hand most parliamentary systems have not had this problem. The Scandinavian countries, the Low Countries, West Germany, and others have had long histories of generally stable government by coalitions.

CABINET CONTROL

If parliamentary government is to function smoothly, the cabinet must be able to control what goes on in the parliament. If a cabinet could be voted out casually just because the mood of the parliament had changed, no one would find that a satisfactory situation; government would be far too unstable. Particularly if the cabinet is based on a coalition of parties, the basis for bargaining on the makeup of the cabinet is the number of votes each party can deliver. If the cabinet was, in fact, not able to count regularly on the votes of one or another of the parties, the rest of the coalition would feel cheated and the coalition would not last long. As it happens, this is a large part of the problem in Italy; the Christian Democratic party has been an important part of every coalition since 1945, but it is a fragmented party and has never been able to guarantee its parliamentary support very well.

On the basis of this reasoning, we might expect to see, in the many smoothly functioning parliamentary systems, that the cabinets dominate their parliaments. This is indeed the case. The usual situation is that legislation is proposed by the cabinet and is *debated* in the parliament; after all, it is only there that the opposition parties have their innings. But aside from the addition of minor amendments, there is rarely any question but that the legislation will be passed by the parliament. In effect, the parliament is a rubber stamp for the cabinet.

It is ironic that a body that is elected by the parliament and can be brought down at any time by it—a body that is, in effect, created by the parliament—can turn around and control what the parliament does. It is readily understandable that this should be the case, however, if we recall that the members of the cabinet are top leaders of their parties. They are skillful politicians, and they have every reason to find ways to control what happens in the parliament so as to protect the power they enjoy as cabinet members.

In Chapter 9 we saw that a side effect of political parties was that, as organizations, they bind a number of people together and provide a channel by which some of those people can control others. It is by this channel that cabinets control their parliaments. The members of a cabinet participate in parliamentary debates; they vote in parliament; but most importantly, they are leaders or powerful members of their party organizations in the parliament. For the other members, the party provides the avenue for advancement in the parliament. Debate time, committee assignments, the chance of a cabinet post someday—all these are controlled for members of parliament by their party. Those who do not cooperate with their party's leaders generally do not advance. It is by this source of discipline, in their capacity as the leaders of their party, that the cabinet are able to impose their will on the parliament.

WHAT DOES A PARLIAMENT DO?

Because it is so controlled by the cabinet, the governmental role of a parliament is difficult for students from the United States to appreciate. With regard to the passage of legislation, most parliaments are indeed "rubber stamps." From 1945 to 1978, for instance, of bills that the British cabinet submitted to the House of Commons for consideration, 97 percent were approved by

"Delegate" and "Trustee" Models of Representation

An enduring debate in political science centers on what role representatives should assume vis-à-vis their constituents. In the "delegate" model, they should regard themselves as simply speaking for the constituents and should cast each vote as they think the constituents would wish it to be cast. In the "trustee" model, it is assumed that representatives learn more about an issue than any of their constituents could possibly know and have also been chosen on the basis of their superior judgment; we would then expect that on at least a few occasions they would vote differently than their constituents would wish them to vote.

Edmund Burke put the case for the trustee model beautifully in a speech to the electors of Bristol on November 3, 1774, after they had chosen him to represent them:

> Certainly, gentlemen, it ought to be the happiness and glory of a representative to live in the strictest union, the closest correspondence, and the most unreserved communication with his constituents. Their wishes ought to have great weight with him; their opinion, high respect; their business, unremitted attention. It is his duty to sacrifice his repose, his pleasures, his satisfactions, to theirs; and above all, ever, and in all cases, to prefer their interest to his own. But his unbiassed opinion, his mature judgment, his enlightened conscience, he ought not to sacrifice to you, to any man, or to any set of men living. These he does not derive from your pleasure; no, nor from the law and the constitution. They are a trust from Providence, for the abuse of which he is deeply answerable. Your representative owes you, not his industry only, but his judgment; and he betrays, instead of serving you, if he sacrifices it to your opinion.

> My worthy colleague says, his will ought to be subservient to yours. If that be all, the thing is innocent. If government were a matter of will upon any side, yours, without question, ought to be superior. But government and legislation are matters of reason and judgment, and not of inclination; and what sort of reason is that, in which the determination precedes the discussion; in which one set of men deliberate, and another decide; and where those who form the conclusion are perhaps three hundred miles distant from those who hear the arguments?

> To deliver an opinion, is the right of all men; that of constituents is a weighty and respectable opinion, which a representative ought always to rejoice to hear; and which he ought always most seriously to consider. But *authoritative* instructions; *mandates* issued, which the member is bound blindly and implicitly to obey, to vote, and to argue for, though contrary to the clearest conviction of his judgment and conscience,—these are things utterly unknown to the laws of this land, and which arise from a fundamental mistake of the whole order and tenor of our constitution.

the House. And amendments to bills are also tightly controlled by the cabinet in Britain. From 1967 to 1971, the cabinet proposed 1,772 amendments to various bills; of these, 1,770 were approved. By contrast, other members of the House proposed 4,198 amendments during the same period, but only 210 of these passed.[1]

It is apparent that whatever things parliaments do, deciding what legislation is to become·law is not chief among them. In the unified governmental arrangement of a parliamentary system, it is expected that the executive and legislative parts of government will work together to make legislation; and because over the years cabinets have learned to protect themselves by controlling their parliaments, it is by now generally accepted that cabinets call the tune in designing laws.

Is parliament then a useless appendage? No, because it still serves a number of purposes that are similar to those of the U.S. Congress and one further purpose that is peculiar to parliamentary systems.

First, a parliament furnishes a forum for the public debate of bills. The opposition parties have a chance, before a bill is passed into law, to present their position on it and to stimulate public discussion.

Second, a parliament is a place where a bill that the cabinet wants to enact into law is submitted to detailed scrutiny by the friends of the cabinet as well as by its enemies. It may well be that a number of small problems may be uncovered in a complicated bill, problems that the cabinet is happy to have brought to its attention. In the British example above, almost all of the 1,772 amendments introduced by the cabinet were amendments to its *own bills*, since virtually no legislation is considered by the House of Commons except legislation submitted by the cabinet. Most of those amendments were cabinet responses to problems that were brought to their attention in the course of parliamentary consideration of their bills.

Third, a parliament is one of the few parts of the governmental apparatus that has an interest in keeping a critical eye on how the cabinet is administering public policy. The opposition parties are, for obvious reasons, especially eager participants in this, but there is also a general tradition that the cabinet must report regularly to the parliament how it is managing the affairs of the state. This sort of accounting takes many forms. In most parliamentary systems, there is some sort of annual speech made to the parliament describing in broad outlines the state of things and the cabinet's plans for the coming year. In addition, many parliaments use a device called "question time," in which various cabinet members appear regularly to answer questions from other members of the parliament about the way their ministry is being run. The answers they give may spark lively debates.

This third function of parliaments—watching what the executive part of the government does—is not generally met as well in parliamentary as in presi-

[1]Rose, Richard, "Still the Era of Party Government," *Parliamentary Affairs* 36 (Summer 1983): 284–285.

dential systems. The reason is that committees are not generally very strong in parliaments, as will be seen below. Committees in a legislature may provide a powerful site for overseeing the executive. They are groups of legislators who specialize in a particular area of policy and who may become quite expert in it over the years. Furthermore, if they have a good professional staff, they may be able to match the offices of the executive in expertise and in the ability to handle evidence. If the committee can hold hearings and subpoena witnesses, it can provide a strong investigative force. But committees in parliamentary systems are generally weak, so the oversight function devolves primarily on individual members of the parliament, who are usually not much of a match for the experts of the executive office.

From the discussion up to this point, it might seem that a parliament is a poor fish indeed. It has little control over legislation except inasmuch as the cabinet can be persuaded to amend their own bills, and it is not as powerful in oversight of the executive as legislatures elsewhere are. The one thing we have so far noted that it does well is to conduct public debate of bills. All in all, this looks meager as compared, say, with the Congress of the United States. But there is another function of parliaments that is peculiar to parliamentary systems.

The fourth function of a parliament in a parliamentary system is to provide a pool of trained people for service in the executive and a setting in which they operate while serving in the executive; a legislature like the U.S. Congress does not do this. In most parliamentary systems, nearly all members of the cabinet and other political appointments in the executive are members of parliament. In Britain at any given time, about two hundred members of the House of Commons are serving in such positions as prime minister, minister for defense, first lord of the admiralty, other cabinet positions, or lesser executive positions such as parliamentary secretary to the minister for defense, director of the National Health Service, and so on. All of these are members from the party that has a majority in the House, so at the same time something like another two hundred members of the opposition parties are hoping for electoral success that will give *their* parties control of parliament and put them into executive positions. Thus, at any given time, about two-thirds of the members of the House of Commons either hold executive positions or are waiting for them.

The members of the political executive in a parliamentary system are men and women who have been selected by the other members of their party for executive tasks, and that selection is based largely on how well they have performed in debate and other tasks in the House. They are selected after some years of service in the House, which, like any organization, imposes norms of behavior on its members and in many subtle ways changes their behavior and the manner in which they react to things. Once they are in executive positions, these people are still sitting members of the House and take part in its daily business of debate, voting on bills, and so on. Even while they hold executive office, they rub shoulders daily with their colleagues in the House.

Debate in Canadian Parliament.
(Arlene Collins/Monkmeyer Press)

Thus an important task of parliament in a parliamentary system is to produce those who will hold executive office, train them in the ways of politics,
select them, and then serve as the site from which they conduct the executive
functions. In a presidential system, the legislative part of government exercises
its strength in *opposing* the executive, but in a parliamentary system it exercises its strength *through* the executive.

THE LIFE OF A MEMBER OF PARLIAMENT

What is it like to serve in such a body? Consider the situation of a young member of the British House of Commons:

> In the 1974 general election, Mr. Dorrell offered himself as the Conservatives' sac-
> rificial lamb in the solidly Labor dockside district of East Hull. "They want you to
> make your first mistakes in an area where it doesn't matter," he remarks. "But you
> make them all over again where it does."
>   Then in 1976, he was chosen out of 105 applicants for what he saw as the "rea-
> sonably winnable" seat of Loughborough, a pleasantly diversified manufacturing
> and farming district in the East Midlands, about 120 miles north of London. The
> local party organization didn't particularly care for his youth and bachelorhood—he

will be married in September—but his energy and articulateness carried the day. Once nominated, he bought a house in the district.

In a typical parliamentary week, Mr. Dorrell first reads the morning papers in his small apartment a few minutes' walk from Westminster. Most MPs have some quarters, from a shared apartment to an elegant town house, "within the sound of the bells"; when the bells ring for a Commons vote, as they may a dozen times a night, MPs have eight minutes to get to the voting "lobbies."

ROUTINE WORK

After breakfast he is off to the tiny, sparsely furnished office he shares with another Tory freshman, Timothy Eggar, a block from Parliament. His secretary is two floors away in a crowded office shared with other secretaries. Mornings usually go to correspondence and constituent work or research for a magazine or a speech to a private group (junior MPs don't get many chances to speak on the Commons floor). Or there may be a routine committee meeting, where Mr. Dorrell's main role is to vote periodically for government motions to speed a bill along.

Afternoons bring more tiresome committee work, and for the rest of the day he may sit around the House chamber, the tearoom or a dinner table discussing problems with other backbenchers. With the late-night sessions and frequent votes, MPs don't have much of a London social life.

Few members attend the inconsequential Friday sessions, so on most Fridays Mr. Dorrell drives 2½ hours to Worcester, where the family business is, and later another hour and a half to Loughborough "to talk to any group that wants to hear me." After the Saturday "surgery," he stops by a local fair or other social gathering. Sunday he tries to keep free for family or friends.

WHAT THEY'RE PAID

For all this he is paid 11,750 pounds, equal to about $27,570, a year. The salary is up 70% from just two years ago but still far from the $60,662.50 that a U.S. Congressman earns. Ministers get considerably more, but they can't do outside work.

MPs are allowed the equivalent of $18,440 for secretarial help and a part-time researcher. Members of Congress, by contrast, draw up to $308,328 annually to pay up to 18 assistants, and many manage to stash still more aides on committee payrolls.[2]

Why would anyone put up with such drudgery? The obvious reason must be that it is through good soldiering in the supporting role that one may advance to interesting and powerful positions in the executive.

PARLIAMENTARY COMMITTEES

Committees of the U.S. House of Representatives and Senate are well known as independent, bristly bodies that presidents, bureaucrats, and even other

[2]*Wall Street Journal,* August 5, 1980, p. 25.

members of the Congress defy only at their own risk. The State Department quivered in the 1950s when the House UnAmerican Affairs Committee investigated some of its younger personnel. Most bills that are introduced in the U.S. Congress are killed by a committee that refuses to vote them out with a recommendation, or else they die through delay in committees. This is true of many bills originating in the presidential office as well as bills that are projects of individual members of Congress.[3]

Such independent bodies within a parliament would greatly weaken the central unity of parliament with the executive, because as independent sources of power the committees would make it more difficult for the executive leaders to control what happened in the parliament. For a parliamentary system to work well, power must as much as possible be lodged with the leaders of the parties and no one else.

For this reason, committees of a parliament are generally a good deal weaker and less assertive than those in the U.S. Congress. All parliaments must have committees, of course. If hundreds of bills are to be submitted to a parliament in a year, the work of scrutinizing those bills carefully must be divided up among the membership in some way or other; there is simply not time for each member of the parliament to do a careful job on all bills that come down in a year. But care is generally taken that the committees do not operate too independently in doing their work.

As an extreme example of this consider committees in the British House of Commons. Where the U.S. Congress uses "standing committees"—such as the Committee on Foreign Affairs, with a set group of members who serve for years and may become quite expert in the areas of policy that they cover—the British set up an ad hoc committee for each bill as it comes in. The members of this committee are not people who regularly work together, they have been put together just to consider this bill. They have not had years of specialized experience in a particular area of policy. They cannot subpoena witnesses and, in fact, do not hold open hearings on their bill. They have no permanent staff. As one might imagine, their ability to transform legislation and put their own stamp on it is quite limited. The cabinet need not fear that its bill will be stopped or mangled by a committee in the House of Commons.

Other parliamentary systems are not so extreme. It is generally more convenient to use standing committees, so that a new group does not have to be constituted for each bill. Even the British have recently experimented with limited standing committees for the House of Commons. But in smoothly working systems, these standing committees still do not operate with the independence of the committees in the U.S. Congress.

---

[3]For example, see Bruce I. Oppenheimer's analysis of the role of congressional committees in blocking President Carter's attempt to form a new energy policy. Lawrence C. Dodd and Bruce I. Oppenheimer, *Congress Reconsidered*, 2nd ed. (Washington, D.C.: Congressional Quarterly, Inc., 1981), pp. 275–295.

"TODAY THE PRIME MINISTER SIGNED TWO TREATIES, HELPED INCREASE OUR STEEL PRODUCTION, NARROWLY AVERTED WAR, AND SUGGESTED YOU BOTH SIGN UP AT SUNNYVALE RETIREMENT VILLAGE."

(Sidney Harris)

EXCEPTIONS TO PARLIAMENTARY SUPREMACY

We have described here a "pure case" of parliamentarism, which is probably not met with exactly in any country of the world, although Great Britain comes close. Most parliamentary systems have incorporated one institution or another that divides the political power of the state and thus compromises the principle of parliamentary supremacy. For instance, West Germany, Canada, India, and some other parliamentary systems are federal states; this means that important areas of policy are taken out of the hands of the cabinet and parliament. West Germany and some other parliamentary systems tolerate fairly strong and independent committees in parliament. A few parliamentary systems—Austria and West Germany are two examples—have courts that can overrule an act of parliament; we will look at this in more detail in Chapter 12.

In these and other ways, most parliamentary systems incorporate a few exceptions to the basic principles listed on page 217. They are still "parliamentary systems," however.

PARLIAMENTS IN NONDEMOCRATIC SYSTEMS

Many states that are not parliamentary systems as described above still have a parliamentary body. We saw in Chapter 8 that many nondemocratic systems have found it useful to hold elections for a variety of reasons; similarly, many of them find it useful to have a parliament. All a parliament is, after all, is a set of people who are designated to represent other groups of people, usually with some sort of geographic focus to the represented groups. It is not necessary that the parliament be able to operate independently or that it have discretion over laws. It can still sit and do a number of things.

The Soviet Union's parliament, for instance, is the Supreme Soviet. Let me first describe it as it operated for sixty years, before Mikhail Gorbachev's recent reforms:

Governmental decisions were almost all taken elsewhere, within the Communist party, and the parliament was set up so that it could not be a rival to the party. The parliament met only twice a year for just a few days. It spent most of its time hearing long reports from the Central Committee of the party, reports that it ratified unanimously by a show of hands. A sizable number of the members were *not* members of the Communist party, but few of them were repeaters from the preceding parliament. This made it unlikely that they would have the experience or confidence to act independently. Selection to the parliament was generally a token of honor for good citizenship in one's community, factory, or collective farm.

This parliament looks to us like a triviality, yet the Soviet Union made a great fuss about it. It was one of the chief bodies to result from the elections they conducted so enthusiastically, and they set great store by it. It must have been doing something, but what?

One thing it did was to serve as a symbol of a unified nation. As you recall, the Soviet Union sprawls over a vast area in which a number of different languages are spoken. The people of the Soviet Union range from nomadic deer herders in the north to Moslems in the south and very European peoples on the Baltic coast. A parliament that drew individuals from all the regions of the country and was further drawn so as to give extensive play to such groups in the population as women, peasants, and blue-collar workers could serve as a potent symbol of a unified population. This helps to explain the amount of fuss that was made over it as the Soviet authorities advertised this symbol of unity.

The Supreme Soviet also served other purposes. One need of the Soviet regime is to provide means for complaints and suggestions from the population at large to work their way into the decision-making process. We saw in an earlier chapter that the Communist party itself serves this need quite actively, but the members of the Supreme Soviet were also expected to be alert to problems of their constituents, and they could bring these to the attention of appropriate ministries in speeches, if they were able to get the floor, or through less formal means. The Supreme Soviet, like the Communist party itself, served as a useful conduit for popular feeling in a governmental system that did not permit either a free press or the formation of organizations that might serve as rival foci of power.[4]

All this appears to be changing under Mikhail Gorbachev's *glasnost* reforms. In 1989, for the first time, a limited amount of competition was allowed in elections to the Supreme Soviet, the body was allotted several months of meeting time annually, and it was assigned more significant lawmaking powers. The resultant body kicked up its heels a couple of times during its first session. The Communist party still maintained solid control, but a minority of dissident reformers provided lively debate. Most surprisingly, the parliament rejected a number of the premier's proposed ministerial appointments.

CONCLUSION

We have presented here a form of government, parliamentary government, that is closely approximated in a majority of democracies. Its two central principles are that power is unified rather than divided and that it is lodged with a democratically elected parliament and a cabinet that is formed from and works within that parliament.

An irony of parliamentary government is that for members of the parliament who are not serving in its cabinet or in executive posts associated with the cabinet, this unity makes their job rather dull. Unlike a divided system like that of the United States, their main job is not to *decide* whether the cabinet should be doing what it is doing and writing the laws it is writing. That decision has been pretty well taken care of by the basic decision of the parties in the parliament to install this particular cabinet and not to bring it down. It follows that the cabinet's bills must almost always be passed in the end, or else the cabinet would fall. The task of ordinary members of the parliament, then, is to operate on the edges of bills as they come in, to discuss their merits, to suggest amendments that the cabinet may choose to accept, to question members of the cabinet on what they are doing—and, all the while, to groom themselves for eventual participation in cabinets of the future.

EXAMPLE: PARLIAMENTARY GOVERNMENT IN INDIA

The general constitutional arrangement chosen for the new state of India in 1945 was largely drawn from the British parliamentary models, but a few devices were also borrowed from the United States. As is the case with any new state, including the United States itself in the early nineteenth century, India provides an interesting example of the evolution of governmental

---

[4]A good review is Stephen White, "The U.S.S.R. Supreme Soviet: A Developmental Perspective." *Legislative Studies Quarterly* 5 (May 1980): 247–274.

structure through custom and practice. It has taken the first few decades of politics in India to straighten out the relative power of the various parts of the government.

In the general outline of its constitution, India has a parliament consisting of two houses; the lower house is the Lok Sabha, or Council of the People, and the upper house is the Council of the States. A powerful prime minister and cabinet are responsible to the Lok Sabha, and a rather weak president oversees the whole structure. Thus far, India is a fairly standard parliamentary system, but it departs from common practice in two ways: (1) it is a federal system, with state governments which have a good deal of programmatic discretion, and (2) it has a powerful Supreme Court that can overturn actions of the rest of the government.

India is a state that faced grave problems on independence. Its people are among the poorest in the world, with an average annual income per person of $300 in 1987. This places the country among the twenty most impoverished states of the world. At the same time, India's population of about 800 million makes it the second largest state in the world and an important power on the international stage. India is deeply divided internally along lines of religion and language, with three major religions (Hindu, Sikh, and Moslem) and over fifteen major languages.

Until 1945, India was a colony of Great Britain. The pacifist leader Mohandas K. Gandhi and his Congress party led a prolonged movement for independence, which succeeded in 1945. The Congress party dominated early elections in the young democracy, and it was only in 1977 that an opposition coalition was able to break Congress's hold on power. Until 1989 a somewhat changed Congress party ruled under Prime Minister Rajiv Gandhi, but a non-Congress coalition is now in power.

Against this background, let us look at the development of India's governmental institutions and particularly the Lok Sabha. One important issue that had to be worked out in practice over the early decades of independence was the power of the president, who is elected by an electoral college consisting of the members of both houses of Parliament plus the members of the state legislatures. Thus it is conceivable that a president could be of a different party than the party that controlled the Lok Sabha and cabinet. The written constitution initially gave the president broad powers—among others, the power to rule by decree when Parliament was not in session, to declare a state of emergency and rule directly, and to dissolve Parliament or any state government and declare new elections. It might have happened that a strong, independent presidency would have evolved in India.

However, the dominance of the Congress party ensured that this did not happen. Since Congress controlled both houses of Parliament and most state governments, a series of Congress party presidents were selected by electoral colleges. And the prime ministers, who were leaders of the Congress party, made certain that weak and unaggressive people, who would be willing to do what the prime minister told them to do, were put into the presidency. Thus the presidency developed into an office much like that of the queen in Great

Britain. In a formal sense, all of the powers enumerated above are the president's, but the president will exercise them only on the advice of the prime minister. This was formalized in an amendment to the constitution in 1976, stating that the president "shall" act in accordance with the advice of the cabinet and prime minister. The practice was fixed even more firmly during a constitutional crisis the next year. In 1977, the Janata coalition won a majority of seats in the Lok Sabha and put its own cabinet into place. This cabinet asked the president—B. D. Jatti, of the Congress party—to dissolve the legislatures of the nine states which had Congress majorities, and force new elections in those states, He hesitated for a day in doing what the cabinet requested, amid demonstrations and uproar, but finally gave in. Thus the cabinet's supremacy over the president was established by something more dependable than words in a constitution; it was established by practice and precedent.

A second important question that had to be settled during this period was the relative power of Parliament and its cabinet vis-à-vis the Supreme Court. This question came to a point of crisis in 1967, when the Supreme Court ruled that an earlier amendment under which government land reforms were being administered was itself unconstitutional because it violated the Fundamental Rights guaranteed elsewhere in the constitution.[5] (Among other things, the Fundamental Rights guarantee a right against the expropriation of property.) Thus, the government could not constitutionally carry out land reform programs of the sort it wanted, and there was no way in which the constitution could be amended that would allow it to do so. In effect, the Court ruled that the Fundamental Rights comprised a special part of the constitution that was above all parliamentary action.

As one might expect, this ruling caused considerable uproar. Over the next few years, the Court held to its position that the Fundamental Rights occupied a special place in the constitution and struck down various acts of Parliament in their name. A crisis was finally reached in 1971, when Prime Minister Indira Gandhi, frustrated at her inability to pass her reform programs, asked the president to dissolve the Lok Sabha and call for new elections. The single theme of this election was the question of parliamentary supremacy over the Court. When her Congress party swept to victory with 352 of the 518 seats in the Lok Sabha, the prime minister had a popular mandate to establish Parliament as supreme. Parliament amended the constitution with this simple addition:

> Notwithstanding anything in this constitution, Parliament may, in exercise of its constituent power, amend by way of addition, variation or repeal, any provision of this Constitution in accordance with the procedure laid down in this Article.

---

[5]Under the Indian constitution, Parliament is responsible for initiating amendments to the Constitution. Many sorts of amendment can be passed by a simple majority in both houses, while certain sensitive areas require a two-thirds majority in both houses. Ratification by half the states is then necessary for the amendment to become law.

The next year this amendment was challenged in the Supreme Court. After the longest series of arguments ever heard there, the Court gave in and sustained Parliament's right to amend any part of the constitution.

Between these two developments—the establishment of the supremacy of Parliament and its cabinet first over the president and then over the Supreme Court—a basically parliamentary framework similar to that of Britain's was ensured. A third crisis was required, however, to establish firmly the principle of democratic government itself. In 1975, Prime Minister Indira Gandhi was found guilty in a state court of minor campaign irregularities. While her case was pending appeal in the Supreme Court, the opposition parties in Parliament, and some members of her own party, pressed her to resign as prime minister. To forestall such efforts, Mrs. Gandhi struck first. She persuaded the president to declare a state of emergency so that she could rule dictatorially through him. She then had most of the leaders of the opposition arrested, banned a number of opposition organizations, and introduced a considerable degree of censorship for the press. In all, perhaps 50,000 people were arrested for political reasons.[6]

This crisis for democracy was resolved in 1977, when Mrs. Gandhi called for a new election to the Lok Sabha. Presumably, she thought that her party would win this election, but in a massive rejection of her seizure of power, the voters reduced the Congress party to 153 out of the 543 seats in the Lok Sabha. Congress was out of power for the first time since 1945. Though Congress and Indira Gandhi returned to power in 1980 after the opposition parties had proved incapable of governing effectively, the point had been made.[7] The 1977 election was a strong reaffirmation by the Indian people of their desire for democratic government.

To focus more specifically on the Parliament of India, and how it operates, let us first note that the upper house, the Council of States, has less power than the lower house. This is typical of parliamentary systems; another good example is the British House of Lords, whose mainly hereditary members have the power only to delay, not block, bills passed by the House of Commons. The members of the Council of States are not directly elected by voters, which would give them more prestige and legitimacy, but rather are chosen by the state legislatures and are sent to the Council of States to represent their states. Most bills require the Council of States' assent to become law, but there is an important limitation on this power. No money bills, including the annual budget and all tax laws, require the assent of the Council of States. The Council discusses each money bill and may make suggestions to the Lok Sabha, but the Lok Sabha has sole authority to pass the bill. Finally, the most important of all limitations on the power of the Council of States is that the prime minister and cabinet are responsible only to the lower house. This is almost universally true of parliamentary systems. It means that the prime minister and cabinet require the support of a majority of the Lok Sabha to exercise their power (they can be

---

[6]D. C. Gupta, *Indian Government and Politics*, 4th ed. (New Delhi: Vikas, 1978) p. 657.

[7]Indira Gandhi was assassinated in 1984 by her Sikh bodyguards, as a result of tensions with militant Sikhs. Her son Rajiv took her place as prime minister and leader of the Congress party.

ousted at any time by a majority vote on a motion of "no confidence"), but they cannot be ousted by the Council of States.

The Lok Sabha plays a role much like that of the House of Commons in Britain. It has full powers to pass or deny legislation, and the cabinet depends on it for its power. However, because of party discipline, the Lok Sabha is controlled by the cabinet and its members do not feel individually all that powerful. From 1980 to 1984, for instance, of 352 bills introduced by the cabinet, 336 were passed; of 51 bills introduced by individual members, not one was passed.[8]

Aside from the usual informal cabinet domination of Parliament via party discipline, the Indian constitution also gives the cabinet some formal powers that allow it further to dominate the parliament. The most important of these is the power to rule by decree when Parliament is not sitting. This was originally intended to allow for small matters that might need immediate attention when Parliament was not in session, but cabinets have come to use it as a device for taking measures they are not sure they could get through Parliament. Such actions as wage freezes, excise taxes, and rules to regulate smuggling have become law in this way, sometimes just days before or after Parliament was in session.

Still, the Lok Sabha functions importantly as a place for debate and one where the opposition can regularly scrutinize what the cabinet is doing. "Question time" has been borrowed from the British and has taken on a vigorous life in India. During the first hour of each parliamentary day, members of the cabinet are questioned by members of the house and their answers debated. From 1980 to 1984, over 9,000 questions were debated in this way. All in all, though the Lok Sabha has had the usual rocky road of an institution in a new constitution that is being "broken in," the parliamentary system of which it is a part seems to have established itself reasonably well in India.

EXAMPLE: PARLIAMENTARY GOVERNMENT IN WEST GERMANY

West Germany has a parliamentary system that is similar to the general model of parliamentary government presented in this chapter except that, in a number of important ways, the power of the parliament is limited so that the line of power and responsibility is not as clean as in a pure parliamentary system. When the West German system was set up in 1949, the disaster of Hitler's rule was still vivid in everyone's mind. The occupying forces from France, Britain, and the United States were anxious to prevent the rise of another dictator, as were the Germans who wrote the new constitution with

[8]Lok Sabha Secretariat, *The Seventh Lok Sabha* (New Delhi: Lok Sabha Secretariat, 1985), pp. 119–120.

them. Accordingly, power was deliberately fragmented, so that it would be hard for any one person to seize it all. The resulting system of "checks and balances" may seem natural to American readers, but it blends awkwardly with parliamentary government and gives West Germany a rather unusual form of parliamentarism.

Parliament is not wholly supreme in West Germany, as it should be in a "pure" parliamentary system and as it nearly is in India. First of all, West Germany, like India, is a federal system, so there are many areas of governmental activity that are not controlled by the national government. And compared with India, the national government has not devised as many ways of controlling what the state governments do. Further, there is a very active system of judicial review in West Germany, with perhaps the most accessible Supreme Court in the world.[9] Among other things, the Court has, for example, barred national administrations from outlawing the Communist party and from establishing a national television network. Both federalism and the system of judicial review were new constitutional devices for Germany in 1949, inserted into the constitution in order to diffuse and limit the exercise of power.

Another limitation on the power of the lower house and its cabinet is that West Germany's parliament has a powerful upper house that may, if it so chooses, bar the lower house from many actions. We have seen that the House of Lords in Britain and the Council of States in India actually have little power to block a bill. But the upper house of the West German parliament, the Bundesrat, does have the power to block bills of many kinds.

The Bundesrat was strengthened in the new constitution to protect the powers of the newly established states. Its members are not directly elected but are appointed by the governments of the states. Under the constitution, its consent is required for all constitutional amendments and for any law that affects the administrative, tax, or territorial interests of the states. In practice, a series of Supreme Court decisions have established that most bills fall into these categories and require the support of a majority in the Bundesrat to become law. On all other bills, the lower house may override a Bundesrat veto, but it requires more than a simple 50 percent majority in the lower house to do this.

As a result of these provisions, the lower house and its cabinet often do not have the free play to make policy that is theoretically theirs in a parliamentary system. Whole areas of policy, such as education, may be under the control of the states. Or the cabinet and lower house may find that what they wish to do is ruled unconstitutional by the Supreme Court. Finally, if the Bundesrat is controlled by a different party than the lower house, the cabinet may find that it continually has to compromise with the opposition in order to get its bills through. This was the case in the late 1970s, when a cabinet led by the Social Democratic party was faced with a Bundesrat controlled by the Christian Democratic party.

---

[9]Any German citizen may bring a case directly to the Supreme Court by simple petition; it does not even require a lawyer.

The lower house, or Bundestag, is set up along the familiar lines of parliamentary government. The cabinet is responsible only to the lower house, as is standard parliamentary practice, so the lower house controls who sits in the executive. In its turn, the cabinet uses its control of party organization to ensure strict party voting in support of its bills. From 1961 to 1980, there were only fifteen instances in which a member of a party broke ranks and voted against the party position in the Bundestag.[10]

Even within the lower house, however, there are more checks and balances than we generally find in a pure parliamentary system. While party leaders expect total support for their parties' positions, ordinary members have more influence over what those positions will be than is the case in Britain.

First, the parties meet regularly as caucuses to determine their positions on bills. Members actually spend more of their time in meetings of the party caucus than in full meetings of the house. Policies are debated extensively within the party caucus, and the parties have full committee structures within the caucus to give careful and skilled scrutiny to each proposed bill.

Second, unlike the British House of Commons, there are nineteen specialized standing committees with full staffs, which scrutinize bills before they go to the full house. Parties are given strength on the committees proportional to their strength in the house, and each committee selects its own chair. Each bill must be considered twice by one of these committees before it comes before the full house for a vote, and it may be heavily amended by the committee.

The general tone of the Bundestag is businesslike and rather dull, with a strong overtone of interest-group neocorporatism. The members are highly skilled (about one-third hold doctorates) but tend not to be politically combative. In a recent survey, 47 percent of the members were civil servants who had gone on leave to serve in the parliament, while a further 13 percent were officials of interest groups.[11] Full sessions of the house do not provide ringing rhetoric. For example, the Bundestag, like many parliaments, has a "question hour," but answers are generally provided in writing by the minister rather than in person and are read to the Bundestag by an assistant.

The end result of this is that West German parliamentarism does not provide the clean line of responsibility we generally expect from parliamentary government. Even a defeat of the cabinet on a major bill in the lower house does not necessarily lead to the fall of the cabinet, since the Constitution provides for the ouster of a cabinet only under carefully specified conditions.[12]

---

[10]Tony Burkett, "Developments in the West German Bundestag in the 1970s," *Parliamentary Affairs* 34 (Summer 1981): 302.

[11]Ibid., p. 305. Interest-group officials generally take a special interest in their group's concerns, seeking positions on useful committees and in general binding the parliament and the interest-group system tightly together. This helps to produce a "neocorporatist" blending of interest groups and government.

[12]The only way a cabinet can be brought down is for the opposition to propose a motion of no confidence, including a statement of who the new chancellor would be; the motion requires a majority to pass. The cabinet are not required to resign if one of their major bills fails to pass.

The ruling parties cannot necessarily be held responsible by the electorate for the state of public policy, because the policy may actually not have been their choice. It may have been forced on them by the Bundesrat or the Supreme Court, or it might be policy of the "states" rather than of the central government. West German parliamentarism, while it retains the general form and most of the flexibility of parliamentarism in general, lacks the usual advantage of a clean line of responsibility.

FURTHER READING

Abraham, Henry J. *The Judicial Process: An Introductory Analysis of the Courts of the United States, England and France*, 5th ed. New York: Oxford University Press, 1986.

Birch, Anthony H. *Representation*. New York: Praeger, 1971.

Crossman, R. H. S. *The Myths of Cabinet Government*. Cambridge, Mass.: Harvard University Press, 1972.

Jennings, Ivor. *Cabinet Government*, 3rd ed. New York: Cambridge University Press, 1969.

Kommers, Donald P. *Judicial Politics in West Germany*. Beverly Hills, Calif.: Sage, 1976.

Kornberg, Allan, ed. *Legislatures in Comparative Perspective*. New York: David McKay, 1973.

Loewenberg, Gerhard. *Parliament in the German Political System*. Ithaca, N.Y.: Cornell University Press, 1967.

Loewenberg, Gerhard, and Patterson, Samuel C. *Comparing Legislatures*. Boston: Little, Brown, 1979.

Parker, Glenn R., ed. *Studies of Congress*. Washington, D.C.: Congressional Quarterly, Inc., 1984.

Pitkin, Hanna Fenichel. *The Concept of Representation*. Berkeley: University of California Press, 1967.

Welsh, William A. "The Status of Research on Representative Institutions in Eastern Europe." *Legislative Studies Quarterly* 5 (1980): 275–308.

Parliamentary Affairs and *Legislative Studies Quarterly* are useful specialized journals relevant to this chapter.

Chapter 12

National Decision-Making Institutions: Presidential Government

Presidential government is a democratic system in which the legislature and the executive exist independently and are elected independently of each other. Since both parts of the governmental apparatus are responsible for the making and carrying out of law yet are independent, it often happens that they compete and find themselves in conflict. The executive and the legislature are not forced into the kind of cooperation that tends to be ensured in a parliamentary system, where the two depend closely on one another.

Just as the political party provides a glue that allows the parliament and its cabinet to function in intimate cooperation, so, in a presidential system, the political party may operate to soften the natural competition between independent executives and legislatures. In the United States, for example, the president, as head of one of the two great parties, is always guaranteed a large number of friends in the Congress. The system does not force the sort of unity on the president and his party's members of Congress that we would see in a parliamentary system, but still the bond of party allows for a good deal of coordination and cooperation.

However, note two things about presidential-legislative cooperation via party ties:

1. Parties may often be more loosely unified in presidential systems than in parliamentary systems. In parliamentary systems, the premier and cabinet hold over the heads of ordinary members of parliament the threat that they may not advance into executive office if they do not cooperate with the leadership. In a presidential system, the president has little control over the careers and advancement of members of the legislature and thus cannot force unity on them. Even when the president's party has a majority of the seats in the legislature, the president will usually not be able to control what happens in the legislature as closely as most cabinets can control their parliaments in parliamentary systems.

2. Also, there is no guarantee that the party that holds the presidency will also control the legislature. Since the two parts of the governmental apparatus are elected independently, it may well happen that one party will have prevailed in

the presidential election and another in elections for the legislature. For instance, throughout the 1980s, the Republican party held the U.S. presidency and at times controlled the Senate, but the Democratic party controlled the House of Representatives. When this happens, cooperation between the two branches of government is even more fragile.

The most famous presidential system in the world, of course, is that of the United States. A number of Latin American states also use versions of the presidential system, as do several other states around the world, including France and Turkey. In some of these, unified parties provide for more coordination than is found in the United States. In Mexico, for instance, the huge Party of the Institutionalized Revolution has held the presidency and controlled the Chamber of Deputies continually since 1929. Mexico's Constitution also provides the president with a great deal of independent power; under these circumstances, it has not been difficult to provide coordinated policymaking. But as a rule, presidential systems exhibit a good deal less coordination between the executive and the legislature than we see in parliamentary systems.

Since the legislature is a coequal body to the executive in a presidential system, how is the legislature organized and how does it function? In a parliamentary system, the cabinet organizes the business of the legislature, but in a presidential system the legislature must organize itself. How is this done? The U.S. Congress provides a good example.

The U.S. Congress consists of two equal houses, the House of Representatives and the Senate. Each house is governed by leaders who are elected by the party that has a majority in the house and by strong, independent committees whose chairs are appointed from among members of the majority party. Seniority—the length of time one has served in the house—is the dominant factor in deciding who will chair committees. For instance, as of 1989, the Democratic Party had majorities in both the U.S. Senate and House of Representatives. The Majority Leader of the Senate was George Mitchell of Maine, and the Speaker of the House was Thomas Foley of the state of Washington. These two men exercised considerable influence over the business of their two houses, partly through their ability to persuade and partly through formal powers, such as the power to influence appointment to committees, assign bills to committees, and preside over debate.

However, the leaders cannot dominate their houses. Any bill must first be considered by a committee, and these committees operate independently and put their own considerable mark on bills that they bring to the full house. Power in each of the houses is so diffused—among leaders, committees, the minority party, and so on—that no one can be said really to control what happens in either one.

The absence of control is heightened by the fact that voting in Congress is much less a party affair then it would be in a parliament. As we have seen, in a parliamentary system, regular failure by members to support their party's position would lead to collapse of the cabinet; for this reason, among others,

(Reprinted with permission of United Feature Syndicate)

members generally vote tightly along party lines. In the Congress, this incentive for discipline is lacking, so members of Congress choose their votes more individually. Through the 1970s and 1980s, fewer than half of bills passed by the House of Representatives were "party votes" even in the very modest sense that over half the Democrats voted on one side and over half the Republicans on the other.

PRESIDENTIAL AND PARLIAMENTARY SYSTEMS COMPARED

What difference does it make whether a state is a parliamentary or a presidential system? Some differences include the following (we will expand on each of these in the next several sections):

- Policy leadership is often more clearly lodged with a president than with a parliamentary cabinet.
- Responsibility for policy is more difficult to identify in a presidential system.
- Comprehensive policy is more difficult to accomplish in a presidential system than in a parliamentary system.
- Recruitment of executive leaders differs in the two systems.
- There are special problems for review and control of the executive in a presidential system.
- The symbolic and political aspects of the executive are unified in a presidential system, split in a parliamentary system.

- Constitutional review of some sort seems to be more necessary in a presidential system, as is true in general of divided systems of power.

Let us first consider the question of policy leadership. Because presidents have a personal mandate from the voters, they are able to take more direct personal charge of policy than the cabinet can do in a parliamentary system. A parliamentary cabinet owes its position to its parties' members in the parliament, and it must operate with them as a team. The president, on the other hand, is personally elected by all the voters of the nation, and this is true of no other public official. This personal mandate focuses attention on the president, who is accordingly thrust into a position of policy leadership.

Unlike the cabinet in a parliamentary system, the presidential cabinet does not consist of party notables whose appointments are generally obligatory. Rather, presidents appoint a group of cabinet officials who will be beholden to them personally. Often, these officials come from positions in which they have had little political exposure—in recent years, presidential cabinets in the United States have included college professors, lawyers, auto company executives, a president's brother, and other relatively nonpolitical figures as well as politicians. In general, prominent political figures are *not* included, and this helps to focus attention directly on the president and the president's staff.

In most presidential systems, the president is constitutionally designated as the commander in chief of the state's armed forces and is personally charged with the responsibility to direct the affairs of the state, dictatorially if necessary, in the event of war or emergency. The president is also generally given personal responsibility for the direction of foreign policy.

Finally, in the making of laws, the legislative branch in a presidential system habitually puts itself in a passive stance, simply waiting to respond to proposals that the president is expected to put forward.

A presidential system, then, provides for a coherent and unified policy leadership that may be lacking in a parliamentary cabinet, especially if that cabinet is formed of a coalition of parties and most especially if the state suffers from cabinet instability.

GOVERNMENTAL RESPONSIBILITY

A presidential system provides a clear focus for *leadership*, but—ironically—it blurs the final *responsibility* for policies. In a presidential system, no one part of the governmental apparatus can be held responsible for any particular policy or any particular lack of policy. If the president proposes a new energy tax and the tax is defeated in Congress, who is responsible for the lack of tax reform? Is the Congress obstinate? Should the president have proposed a tax that would have been more liable to pass? Should the president have lobbied harder for the bill? It might also happen that the bill would pass, but with amendments that changed it substantially. Is it now the president's bill? Congress's? No one's?

Since they do not present a clear picture of the responsibility for policies, presidential systems exhibit two important weaknesses. First, when voters cannot pin the responsibility for policies on any particular official, their electoral choices become less significant. Should a voter in the United States in 1948 who was upset at inflation vote Republican? That would have been a vote against the party of President Truman, who should perhaps have been held responsible for the inflation. But what if the "do-nothing" Republican-controlled Congress were at fault, as Truman claimed? Faced with a choice like this, the poor bewildered voter must vote on less policy-related criteria, such as candidate's personality or personal favors that an incumbent candidate has been able to do while in office. Eventually, elections come to function less and less as vehicles by which voters can affect the making of policy.[1]

A second weakness of presidential government caused by its blurring of responsibility, is that when public officials do not have clear responsibility for a policy, they may literally begin to behave irresponsibly. If Congress is not directly held responsible for producing a balanced budget, it is easy for members of Congress to vote simultaneously to cut taxes (which will look good to their constituents) and to build highways (which will also look good). "Through the fault of no one in particular," the government usually spends more than it takes in.

Campaign platforms of U.S. parties provide another example of the chronic irresponsibility of presidential systems. Because a party's president cannot be blamed for failing to act into law the party's promises—after all, Congress might not cooperate—it becomes easy for the parties to promise in their campaign platforms whatever they think the voters would like to hear. With power as fragmented as it is in a presidential system, the party will never lack for an alibi if the voters should take them to task for not delivering on their promises.

PRESIDENTIAL SYSTEMS AND COMPREHENSIVE POLICY

It is generally more difficult to make comprehensive policies in a presidential system than in a parliamentary one. Policies are more likely to be patched together of varied compromises or perhaps not to be put together at all. The United States is one of the few democracies that lacks a national energy policy, though this has not been for want of trying. Presidents have proposed energy policies to Congress but have never been able to get agreement on anything recognizable as a policy.

Because of the many points in a fragmented system at which a bill can be

---

[1]A large body of literature has long urged that the United States should try to accomplish "responsible party government" similar to that of Britain. Generally, the argument has been that U.S. parties should become more tightly disciplined, not that the constitutional division of power should be changed. A good example is E. E. Schattschneider, *Party Government* (New York: Holt, Rinehart and Winston, 1942).

blocked, it is generally not enough that a mere majority of the people want something done; considerably more than a majority is required if all the defensive positions provided by a fragmented system are to be overrun. Handgun control, prayer in the schools, and the equal rights amendment are all examples of policies that a majority of the U.S. population want but which have been impossible to enact into law.

If you are suspicious of majorities, as many of the authors of the U.S. Constitution were, this may be seen as a good effect of the fragmentation of power. But there is no denying that it makes the government slow to respond to change.

RECRUITMENT OF EXECUTIVE LEADERS

There is a significant difference between the sorts of leaders who emerge in parliamentary and presidential systems. In a parliamentary system, all or almost all the leaders in the executive have emerged from careers in parliament; indeed, they continue to serve in the parliament while they hold executive office. This means that they will all have had fairly similar lives before they entered the executive. For a decade or two or three, their jobs will have consisted of the wording of bills and of service to the voters in their constituency. They will have had a long period of exposure to the wide range of issues facing the state in diplomacy, tax policy, education, defense, and so on.

The similarity of these executive officers is made greater by the fact that they are mostly selected from among the members of the parliament on the basis of a common set of criteria. Members who move up to executive office are those who do a good job of being a member of parliament—they debate well, they keep their noses to the grindstone, they do not make waves.

Recruitment in a parliamentary system has the virtue that officials are chosen *by those who know them and their work* (their fellow members of parliament) *during a career that has made them familiar with most of the issues they will have to face.* It has the disadvantage that *there is not much variety among the types of people chosen, that they have by and large had little experience in managing things* (legislators spend most of their time responding to initiatives of others), *and that there are few "mavericks" or adventurers included.*

In a presidential system, recruitment into executive office is fairly independent of the legislative parts of government. While a president may have started off with a legislative career, this is by no means necessary. Consider the last eight presidents of the United States:

PRESIDENT	BACKGROUND
Dwight D. Eisenhower	Army general
John F. Kennedy	Senator
Lyndon B. Johnson	Senator
Richard M. Nixon	Senator; vice president
Gerald Ford	Member of Congress

Jimmy Carter	Governor of Georgia
Ronald Reagan	Film actor; governor of California
George Bush	Appointee to various foreign policy positions; vice president

Half of these men had established themselves with the public by something other than service in one of the houses of Congress.

Further, the recruitment of other officials to staff the executive does not draw heavily on Congress in the United States or in most other presidential systems. Only a minority of the membership of recent U.S. presidents' cabinets have been drawn from careers in the Senate or House. Many of the most distinctive and interesting cabinet members have been drawn from careers that were far from Congress, careers that gave them interesting points of view of their own. Two examples are Robert McNamara, secretary of defense under Kennedy and Johnson, who had been a Ford Motor Corporation executive, and Henry Kissinger, secretary of state under Nixon and Ford, who had been a university professor.

This sort of selection has the advantage that it brings varied talents and backgrounds to the task of executive and that, through the introduction of new blood, problems may come to be seen in a new light. New points of view and the zeal of amateurs may thus be brought into policymaking at a high level, as in Jimmy Carter's campaigns on behalf of human rights.

On the other hand, selection is often haphazard, since it is not generally done by those who have worked directly with the candidates; candidates may have little previous experience in important areas (neither Carter nor Reagan,

(Dana Summers/The Orlando Sentinel)

for instance, had had any experience with foreign policy before they became president); and inappropriate choices are more likely than in a parliamentary system.[2]

In short, in a parliamentary system you know much more what you are getting than in a presidential system. Executive officials are not going to surprise you in a parliamentary system, but they will not disappoint you, either.

REVIEW AND CONTROL OF THE EXECUTIVE

Most organizations have some sort of plural board to which the executive leader is responsible and reports regularly. The president of a business corporation must report regularly to a board of directors, the president of a university reports to the board of trustees of the university, a superintendent of schools reports to a school board, and so on.

In a parliamentary system, the parliament serves this purpose. The prime minister and cabinet regularly report to the parliament on the conduct of their business, questions are asked, and so on. There is regular and frequent contact between the cabinet and the parliament regarding the conduct of government.[3]

In a presidential system, however, the members of the executive operate in relative isolation. The press looks over their shoulder constantly, of course, and there is occasionally contact between them and the legislature regarding a particular bill or investigation. But there is no broader body to which the president or other members of the executive regularly report.

This isolation of the presidency often leads to an inward-looking presidential office, with "inside" staff persons accused by those on the outside of arrogance and insensitivity. More seriously, the lack of some regular device for review and control of the president made the Watergate crisis a good deal more traumatic for the United States than it might otherwise have been. When President Nixon was implicated in petty crimes at the Watergate office complex and it became apparent that some airing of the question was needed, there was no regular stage available for this, and extraordinary procedures for impeachment were required. Had he been a prime minister, he would have been called to task in the parliament as a matter of ordinary business.

THE SPLIT EXECUTIVE OF PARLIAMENTARY SYSTEMS

Oddly enough, given that in general parliamentary systems are based on the principle of unifying power, the executive itself is generally split in parliamen-

---

[2]An argument for the desirability of recruitment in the parliamentary mode is made in Harold W. Chase, Robert Holt, and John Turner, *American Government in Comparative Perspective* (New York: Franklin Watts, 1980), chap. 2.

[3]For further comparison along these lines, see William S. Livingston, "Britain and America: The Institutionalization of Accountability," *Journal of Politics* 38 (November 1976): 870–894.

tary systems into the prime minister and cabinet, on the one hand, who are responsible for political and administrative leadership, and some other office that is responsible for the symbolic leadership of the state. In a presidential system all of these functions are united in the president.

In Britain the prime minister and cabinet are responsible for political and administrative leadership, but it is the queen who carries on all the ceremonies and personifies the state. It is she who opens new hospitals and bridges, it is her health and that of her family that the press subjects to ghoulish scrutiny, it is she at whose death the nation will go into deep mourning. Like the president of the United States, she is greeted by a special song when she enters a room, and crowds press in on her wherever she goes. The prime minister remains much more a mundane figure, one who goes about the daily business of governing but does not personally represent the state.

It is clear why the two kinds of executive function are united in one person in a presidential system. The executive is weakened in a presidential system by virtue of the fact that its legislature is not under its control; in order for strong leadership to be available to the state, almost everything that *can* be done to strengthen the president's hand *must* be done. One such thing, an important one, is to give the presidents an aura of majesty that they can use to bolster their political power. More than one member of Congress has gone into the White House and walked out shaken, muttering, "When the president of the United States asks you to vote in the country's interest, what can you do?"

In a parliamentary system there is no need to add to the power of the cabinet in this way, since the cabinet is capable of providing effective leadership without it. If it is not necessary to combine the two faces of the executive in a single office, as is done in presidential systems, there are some obvious advantages to separating them.

First, the symbolic representation of the state in a person appears to fill a deep need of a modern people. The devotion people feel for those who personify their state is real. Consider the following examples. At John F. Kennedy's assassination in 1963, many Americans felt what they later reported as an almost religious experience. In Britain the most disturbing political event of the twentieth century, with the sole exception of the two world wars themselves, occurred when Prince Edward VIII left the throne in order to marry a divorced American. Norwegians credit King Haakon VII with having almost singlehandedly kept the government from surrendering to Germany in 1941, taking his family into exile and making it possible for Norwegians to fight on in the Resistance. Finally, consider the heart-wrenching difficulty with which Americans faced what would have been a fairly simple task if they had not revered the presidency so much—the ouster of Richard M. Nixon in 1974 when he had been implicated in petty crimes.

If modern peoples need a person on whom to focus their reverence for the state, it seems obvious that this had best be someone who has little involvement in day-to-day politics. The queen of Britain, the king of Sweden, the emperor of Japan, the "president" of West Germany (not a president as the term is used in this chapter, but an almost purely ceremonial figure)—these people have virtually no political power and are not involved in routine decision making. This allows them to serve as unblemished objects of national affection. Presidents of the United States, in contrast, must excite mixed feelings among the many people who find themselves in political disagreement with them. On the one hand, these people want to revere the president, but on the other hand, they find themselves faced with a political leader whose policies they may despise. Corporation executives and Republicans in general were in many ways deprived of an object for national reverence during the presidency of Franklin Delano Roosevelt, as were welfare recipients and Democrats in general during the presidency of Ronald Reagan.

Thus, one problem of blending the political executive and the symbolic executive in a single office is that the symbolic function cannot be performed as well when it is located in an office that is inevitably involved in controversy.

The flip side of this problem is that political leadership does not operate as cleanly when reverence for the state gets mixed up with it. A president of the United States gains unfair political advantage from serving as the symbol of the state. Franklin Roosevelt, Lyndon Johnson, Richard Nixon, and Ronald Reagan are presidents who were quite adept at taking positions that had questionable public support, appearing on radio or television with all the sober attention that a president can command, and selling that endangered program to the public. After all, this man is the president of the United States! Whom can we trust more than him?

We may welcome this as a way to cut through the confusion of the divided powers of a presidential system, but it is still unfortunate that, on any public issue at a given time, only one side is able to take advantage of this reverential response. In a parliamentary system, the cabinet and the opposition operate on more even terms in seeking public support for their political positions.[4]

CONSTITUTIONAL REVIEW AND THE FRAGMENTATION OF POWER

Wherever power is fragmented, in a presidential system or a federal one, there seems to be a need for some institution that can operate as a referee to adjudicate disputes among the various holders of power. If a president has part of the power and a legislature has another part, how do we resolve the kind of dispute that must inevitably occur when the legislature says to the president "You've just done something that's supposed to be left up to us"—or vice versa? The obvious solution is to have some third institution that is empowered to serve as a referee. In the United States, this is the Supreme Court.

Over the last two centuries the U.S. Supreme Court has established that it

---

[4]Related arguments may be found in Edward Shils and Michael Young, "The Meaning of the Coronation." *Sociological Review* 1 (December 1953): 63–81, and in Lewis Lipsitz, "If, As Verba Says, the State Functions As a Religion, What Are We to Do Then to Save Our Souls?" *American Political Science Review* 52 (June 1968): 527–535.

Presidential Character

Presidents have not been studied as much as have members of cabinets or parliaments simply because there have been so few of them. In over two hundred years of presidential government, the United States has had only forty-one presidents; in almost thirty years of presidential government, France has had only four. Across so few cases it is difficult to trace any patterns of behavior. The picture is dominated by the personal idiosyncrasies of the relatively few people who have so far filled the role of president. As a result, scholars have analyzed the office of president a good deal in the abstract, thinking about what presidents should be or might be; but few have looked at what presidents *are*.

One exception is James David Barber, who, in his book *The Presidential Character,* 2nd ed. (Englewood Cliffs, N.J.: Prentice-Hall, 1977), draws on the tradition of psychoanalysis, in which people are in any case usually analyzed one at a time.

Barber presents a twofold typology that, he asserts, is useful in understanding the performance of American presidents. He examines the degree to which each president has been active or passive in his role and the extent to which each is positive or negative (likes it or dislikes it) about his work. This typology produces four types of presidents: *active-negatives,* whose basic motive is to obtain and maintain power and who engage in compulsive activity because of a lack of personal self-esteem; *passive-negatives,* who are motivated by a sense of civic duty and citizen virtue and who do not work very hard at being president but agree to do it because they feel a duty to serve the people; *passive-positives,* who are motivated by a need for love and affection and feel that they can meet this need by obtaining the approval of others through their political activities; and, finally, *active-positives,* who are problem solvers, are flexible and productive, and have high self-esteem.

Barber characterizes recent presidents as follows: Eisenhower, passive-negative; Kennedy, active-positive; Johnson, active-negative; Nixon, active-negative; Ford, active-positive; Carter, active-positive. His analysis has been widely criticized simply because it is so very subjective. One person's "active-positive" might well be another's "active-negative." At the very least, though, setting out these categories organizes the way we look at presidents and offers insights into their careers we might not otherwise have gained.

---

has the right to annul acts of presidents and laws passed by Congress whenever it deems either body to have exceeded its proper powers. Although there is occasional grumbling about the Court and its power, it is striking how readily this essentially undemocratic arrangement is tolerated. Think of it! Nine people who are appointed by the president and the Senate and thereafter serve for the rest of their lives without ever being subject to popular election—these nine people wield huge power in our otherwise democratic system. The only explanation for Americans' ready toleration of this is their recognition that the fragmentation of power requires something like this to make their system work.

Constitutional review is found in almost all systems that fragment power and is rare in those that do not. In Table 12–1, the states of western Europe and North America are divided according to whether the governmental system is parliamentary or presidential and whether power is unified geographically or fragmented federally; we then note for each state whether or not it has a system of constitutional review. Switzerland is the only system with fragmented power that does not provide for judicial review. While most unitary, parliamentary systems do not provide for constitutional review, a substantial minority of one-third *do* do so.

The main exception to this rule of thumb (that fragmented power is the reason for constitutional review) is that constitutional review has also had some popularity since World War II as a means of protecting individuals from the arbitrary use of state power. That is, constitutional review has been seen as a tool of "constitutionalism," in which a relatively nonpolitical court can help to place limits on the authority of the government.[5] This helps to explain the popularity of constitutional review in West Germany after the Nazi dictatorship,

12–1   Constitutional Review, Federalism, and Presidential Government: Western Europe and North America

	Constitutional Review	
States with a federal system and/or presidential government		
Canada	Yes	
France	Yes	
Mexico	Yes	
Portugal	Yes	
Spain	Yes	
Switzerland		No
U.S.A.	Yes	
West Germany	Yes	
Unitary states with parliamentary government		
Austria	Yes	
Belgium		No
Denmark		No
Great Britain		No
Iceland		No
Ireland	Yes	
Italy	Yes	
Luxembourg		No
Netherlands		No
Norway		No
Sweden		No

[5]See the discussion of constitutionalism in Chapter 7.

though the federal system there probably would have required it in any case. More to the point, it also helps to explain the institution of constitutional review in Austria, Ireland, and Italy, which have neither federal systems nor presidential governments.

WHY AREN'T ALL DEMOCRACIES PARLIAMENTARY SYSTEMS?

Let us review for a moment what we have looked at so far in this chapter. We first described fairly simply how presidential government operates, and we noted the main difference between a parliamentary system and a presidential system: that the one unifies power and the other divides it. We then examined several aspects of presidential government that result from this difference:

- Concentration of policy leadership with the president
- Difficulty of locating responsibility for policies
- Difficulty of making comprehensive policy
- A different pattern of recruitment for executive leaders
- Special problems for review and control
- A merger of the symbolic and political aspects of the executive in a single office
- A need for constitutional review

While not every one of these differences showed the presidential system to disadvantage, most did. Overall, you have probably been left with the impression that parliamentary systems are better than presidential ones. The parliamentary system is a simpler, more direct, and generally more efficient way of making public choices. Why aren't all democracies parliamentary systems?

The main reason lies in the very faithfulness with which a parliamentary system transposes political divisions into the policymaking machinery. Policy is set and administered in a parliamentary system by a party, or a cooperative coalition of parties, that controls a majority of the votes in the parliament. This makes for straightforward policymaking if a stable majority is possible in the parliament. But if the country is divided into numerous parties that are intensely hostile to each other, it may be impossible to find a large enough number of members of parliament who can work together cooperatively as a governing coalition. It may be that no working majority is available.

Under these circumstances, a parliamentary system may limp along with an unstable government, as Italy has done since 1945, or the country may prefer to use some system that divides power but is more stable than what parliamentarism could provide.

France after World War II was plagued by parliamentary instability similar to that of Italy. The Communists could not cooperate with any of the other parties, Catholic parties had trouble cooperating with Socialists, and so on; in 1958, the regime was overthrown by a military coup and the new constitution written by Charles de Gaulle replaced parliamentary government with a version of presidential government. Similarly, after bloody civil wars among the various linguistic and other factions in Switzerland were settled, the Swiss set up not a parliamentary system but a radically fragmented *federal* system in which the central government has little power.

In much of the Third World, too, democracies, whether or not they started out as parliamentary systems, have often found that they must provide a more stable base for executive leadership than is possible under parliamentarism, even at the cost of fragmenting and complicating public decision-making processes. Many Latin American democracies, under the influence of the United States, used presidential systems from the start; Mexico and Cost Rica are good examples. But many African and Asian democracies—faced with the political stresses of poverty, modernization, and ethnic diversity—have had to modify what started out as parliamentary systems. Nigeria, for example, abandoned parliamentarism when democratic government was reestablished in 1975 and set up a federal system with an independent presidency rather like that of the United States.[6] Turkey has established a presidential system similar to that of France.

Perhaps the message of this chapter, in the end, is that a parliamentary system is the best form of democracy *if* a country is sufficiently unified to cooperate in parliamentary politics.

A NOTE ON CONSTITUTIONS AND POWER

Having looked at formal governmental arrangements in this chapter and the preceding one, we should note an important principle of constitutions that is well illustrated by the development of some of the governmental institutions we have examined.

We saw in Chapter 7 that written constitutions are not static but change and develop as they are put to use. One predictable way in which constitutions change is this: *If power is given constitutionally to a body that lacks the resources to exercise it, informal mechanisms usually develop, leading to the de facto loss of that power* even though the formality of power remains.

One excellent example of this principle at work is the domination of parliaments by their cabinets. Parliaments are vested with supreme authority in the constitutions of parliamentary systems, but a parliament is too large and diverse a group to actually take charge of governmental policy by itself. Over the years, cabinets have developed ways to bully parliaments through the informal mechanism of the disciplined political party. This has shifted actual power from the parliament to its cabinet, which allows policy to be made coherently; but the parliaments remain *formally* supreme. Political parties are rarely even mentioned in the constitutions of democracies, but they have obviously become an important part of living constitutions.

A second example of this general principle is the problem of "localism" in the French parliament before 1958. France had long had a tradition of central governmental dominance over towns and regions. If a town wished to build a

---

[6]This, in turn, succumbed to a military coup in 1983.

new school or pave a new set of streets, it generally needed to get the permission of the government in Paris to do so. These arrangements gave the central government great formal power, but its exercise involved such a huge number of minuscule decisions that it was simply impossible for any central operation to do a good job of making them. In self-defense, over the late nineteenth and early twentieth centuries, town governments devised ways in which they could get special treatment from the Paris government. Because the members of the parliament were elected from local districts, parliament was a special target of these efforts. Town governments tried, with a great deal of success, to convince the local members of parliament to take as one of their chief tasks in Paris the furthering of local causes. Members of parliament eventually spent much of their time and effort in making deals—trading votes with other members so that their towns could get the necessary permission and funds to build town halls or install streetlights. Party discipline declined, and many members' votes were heavily influenced by the deals they had cut with other members, so that the directions of party leaders were often ignored. This trend was a major cause of the increasing instability of the national government. (France had twenty-five different cabinets in the thirteen years from 1945 to 1958.) Thus the formal power over localities' decisions, which was supposed to *strengthen* the central government, in fact helped to weaken it.

A third example is provided by the Bundesrat, the upper house of the West German parliament, which was described in the previous chapter. The

John F. Kennedy sworn in as president.
(Camera Press Limited)

Bundesrat, you will recall, was established in the constitution in order to protect the independence of the new "states" from the central government. If West Germany was to be a federal system, it was reasoned, the states needed a lever in the central government itself to allow them a veto over actions that would take away their rights. Therefore the Bundesrat was established. It consists of representatives from the state governments and must give its consent to any action affecting their tax, administrative, or territorial interests.

Ironically, setting up the Bundesrat and giving it these powers has made it, and the states that appoint its members, sufficiently important to national political leaders that they now try to control what goes on in state politics and have undermined the independence of state leaders in important ways. Elections for state governments often turn on a national issue rather than on those of the state. Figures from the central government campaign hard in the state, not for local figures or for the local party but in terms of national political questions. And once a state election is over, national leaders often put pressure on local leaders to form a particular sort of coalition in the state parliament solely because of the effect the nature of the local coalition will have on the state's votes in the Bundesrat.[7] The existence of the Bundesrat has arguably had an effect just the opposite of what was intended by the framers of Germany's constitution. The states' prerogatives would have probably been protected adequately by the Supreme Court if the Bundesrat had never been set up, and local political leaders would operate more independently of national leaders than is now the case.

In all three of these examples, actual power relationships—the living constitution—have fit themselves to the power of groups in ways quite different from what was intended by those who designed the formal document. Such mismatches between reality and formal rules generally result from a failure to appreciate fully the "power" in "power and choice." If one thinks of politics primarily as a question of working out choices for the state, it will seem that an appropriate set of procedures should do that, and the choice making will follow from the procedures. This ignores the necessities of power and can lead to surprises for those who write rules.

EXAMPLE: PRESIDENTIAL GOVERNMENT IN FRANCE

After World War II, France set up a fairly standard parliamentary system. It was immobilized, however, by the hostility of various parties to each other and by weak discipline within many of them, which made it difficult for coalitions to form and hold together. The average life of a cabinet was about six months, and because ministers did not stay in place long enough to get full control of their offices,

---

[7]For an early example, see Arnold J. Heidenheimer, "Federalism and the Party System: The Case of West Germany," *American Political Science Review* 52 (September 1958): 809–828.

France was, in effect, governed by its bureaucracy rather than by its elected leadership.[8] There was a sense of drift, and in 1958, when tensions associated with Algeria's war for independence were added to the mix, things fell apart. The military took over, and Charles de Gaulle, the hero of World War II, was brought in to set up a new system.

De Gaulle and his advisers designed a new kind of democracy with elements of both presidential and parliamentary government in which, however, the presidential elements have gradually come to dominate things. As first designed, the system consisted of a cabinet responsible to the National Assembly (the lower house of parliament) and of a rather powerful but nonpolitical president. The president, indirectly elected by an assembly of parliament and of mayors, was, in turn, to designate the premier and to preside over the affairs of government, especially foreign affairs and defense policy. The president could bring issues before the French electorate in the form of a referendum and could, if necessary, declare a state of emergency and take over all power for up to six months at a time.

Although this obviously was a powerful position, it did not actually provide much more than what is implicit in the powers of the queen of England or what was implicit in the powers of the French president from 1945 to 1958. The key question was whether the French president would act as a primarily symbolic figure, performing these functions only on the advice of the cabinet, or would realize the full potential of the office's powers. De Gaulle himself served as the first president under the new system from 1958 to 1969. He exercised his potential power strongly and added to that power in three important ways:

- In 1962 he had the constitution changed so that the president was directly elected. The president has since then carried great prestige as the only official elected by all the people of France.
- He set up an executive office with a structure that paralleled the ministries of the cabinet. Any bill that a ministry wished to submit to parliament had to be cleared by its counterpart bureau in the executive office. Eventually many important policies began to be set in the executive office even without the knowledge of the minister involved.
- He established the principle that a president could dismiss a premier at will. The constitution states that the president "designates" the premier but says nothing about dismissal. In 1962, de Gaulle asked his first premier, Michel Debre, to resign, and Debre did so. From that point on, another important element of presidential power had been established.

Today, the premier and cabinet function as agents of the president, conducting much of the day-to-day business of the state and representing the president in relations with the parliament.

The new constitution included a large number of constraints on the inde-

---

[8]Ironically, France was actually governed rather well. During this period, France pioneered in establishing the European Economic Community, and its per capita income grew at a rate of 3.5 percent annually in real terms throughout the 1950s.

pendence of the parliament, which were intended to prevent the immobility that had characterized French government before 1958. An absolute majority of members is required to overthrow a cabinet, so that abstentions or absent members in effect count as votes in favor of the cabinet on a motion of confidence. When the cabinet submits a bill to the parliament, the cabinet has the right to list the priority within which the bill will be debated as well as the rules of debate; thus the cabinet is given considerable power in scheduling the work of the parliament. (Among other rules, the cabinet can require that a bill be voted on as a whole, rather than having a separate vote on any amendment; this frequently used device makes it difficult to amend a bill.) Members of the parliament are constitutionally barred from offering amendments to a bill that would have the effect of either adding to state expenditures or decreasing state revenues; an amendment requiring new expenditure, for instance, must include within itself either a compensating cut in some other expenditure or an increase in taxes. Finally, the independence and power of parliamentary committees was decreased by the simple device of limiting their number to six. This assured that they would be large bodies (the average size of committees is over a hundred members) with broad areas of policy and that they would never again be able to develop into tight-knit groups of specialists.

In effect, by laying down these rules, the new French constitution brought about executive supremacy of the sort that in most parliamentary systems is achieved informally through the political party. Since parties had failed to establish the necessary discipline, constitutional design was used to e· ure executive supremacy. One could argue that the informal device is better because it is more flexible, but the constitutional devices appear to have worked well in France.

These rules established executive domination over the parliament, and—as things have developed in France—"executive" generally means the president. Overall, the French system today may be characterized as a fairly ordinary system of presidential government except for two important things:

- The balance of power is tipped much more to the president vis-à-vis the parliament than is the case, say, in the United States.
- The president governs through a cabinet, which can be turned out of office at will by the National Assembly. This carries obvious seeds of deadlock if one party should hold the presidency and another party the National Assembly. It is at least theoretically possible that the president could name cabinet upon cabinet, which would be voted down by the National Assembly as quickly as they were named. The president could not rule under these circumstances. From 1958 to 1985 the presidency and National Assembly were controlled by compatible parties, so the problem did not arise. In 1985 conservatives won a majority in the National Assembly, and President Mitterand, a Socialist, had to appoint Jacques Chirac, a Gaullist, to the premiership. No one really knew how this would work, but it turned out that when the premier and the president are of different parties, more of the executive power rests with the premier than with the president, though both are then powerful. In all sorts of ways the constitution of France (constitution with a small "c") changes abruptly when different parties come to control the

National Assembly and the presidency. It is almost as if France has two constitutions, which switch on and off like light bulbs.

The period of split control, dubbed "cohabitation" by the French, lasted only three years. In 1988 a newly reelected President Mitterand took advantage of the flush of enthusiasm at his victory and dissolved the National Assembly, calling for a new election of its members. The Socialists regained control, and the old constitutional system of presidential dominance reestablished itself.

EXAMPLE: PRESIDENTIAL GOVERNMENT IN MEXICO

 The present Mexican system arose out of a decade and a half of chaos, from 1910 to 1925. In a swirling tumult of banditry, revolutionary battles, and civil war, approximately a million Mexicans starved or were killed. The period of violence ended in the establishment of the dominant Party of the Institutionalized Revolution, which we examined in Chapter 9. By the 1930s the rule of the party had come to be centered on a very strong presidency, and that regime has continued to the present time.

The president of Mexico dominates all of politics. Although the constitution provides for an independent Congress and Supreme Court much like those of the United States, neither of these bodies is truly independent of the president. The Congress, in particular, is quite subservient. Almost all of its members are members of the party, and the president is de facto leader of the party. Most bills pass unanimously; when opposed votes are cast, they usually total only 5 to 10 percent of the membership. Since 1917, presidents of Mexico have had to use their power of veto only twice, and then on minor matters.[9] Of course, with the growing strength of the opposition parties (which won 51 of the 300 seats in 1988), it seems likely that at some time in the future the relationship between Congress and the president may change.

The Supreme Court is somewhat more insulated from the power of the president and has not infrequently ruled in favor of citizens who were suing the presidential office on minor technical matters. But the Court has always avoided confrontation with the president on important questions of policy. Like the U.S. Supreme Court, the Mexican court refuses to hear cases that it considers "political"; but unlike the U.S. Court, it has interpreted this stricture broadly to include almost any important area of presidential activity.

A president in office has great power. What has saved the system from an

---

[9]Robert Scott, *Mexican Government in Transition* rev. ed. (Urbana, Ill.: University of Illinois Press, 1964), p. 263.

unbearable concentration of power is the firm tradition that presidents must step down after a single six-year term. For six years, a single person rules, but then the party (influenced strongly by the incumbent president) chooses another person to serve the next six years.[10] At this point not only the holder of the presidential office changes, but most other executive officers change as well, as the new president finds jobs for the members of his faction. The holder of a job under one president has only a 30 percent chance of holding a job under the next president.[11]

Such concentration of power, even if it is temporary, does encourage corruption and personal gain, which is a chronic problem of Mexican politics. Mexico appears to go through alternate waves of corruption and reform. The administration of President Alemán from 1946 to 1952 was marked by large-scale corruption, as was that of López Portillo from 1976 to 1982. Various officials of the López Portillo administration are widely thought to have taken $3 billion or more from public funds; his successor, President Miguel de la Madrid Hurtado, came to office pledged to a clean government and prosecuted some of the offenders of the previous regime. Although the corruption is obviously costly and broad, some have speculated that it has the hidden virtue of making possible the regular six-year transition in power. If it were not for the illicit wealth on which they could retire, so this reasoning goes, some officials would by now have devised a way of subverting the six-year rule so that they could stay in office.

FURTHER READING

Abraham, Henry J. *The Judicial Process*, 5th ed. New York: Oxford University Press, 1986. Chapters on judicial review.

Andrews, William G. *Presidential Government in Gaullist France*. Albany, N.Y.: State University of New York Press, 1982.

Brichta, Avraham, and Zalmanovitch, Yair. "Proposals for Presidential Government in Israel," *Comparative Political Studies* 19 (October 1986): 57–68.

Cronin, Thomas E. *The State of the Presidency*, 2nd ed. Boston: Little, Brown, 1980.

Dibacco, Thomas V., ed. *Presidential Power in Latin American Politics*. New York: Praeger, 1977.

Kommers, Donald P. *Judicial Politics in West Germany*. Beverly Hills, Calif.: Sage, 1976.

Neustadt, Richard E. *Presidential Power: The Politics of Leadership*, rev. ed. New York: Wiley, 1976.

Nwabueze, Benjamin O. *Presidentialism in Commonwealth Africa*. London: Hurst, 1974.

---

[10]Again, with increasing competition from opposition parties, the party's nomination may never again confer the office as automatically as it did through and including the 1988 election. By the next election in 1994, this aspect of the presidency may have changed.

[11]Peter H. Smith, "Does Mexico Have a Power Elite?" in Jose L. Reyna and Richard S. Weinert, eds., *Authoritarianism in Mexico* (Philadelphia: Institute for the Study of Human Issues, 1977), p. 139.

Pious, Richard M. *The American Presidency*. New York: Basic Books, 1979.

Rose, Richard. *The Postmodern President*. Chatham, N.J.: Chatham House, 1989.

Rose, Richard, and Suleiman, Ezra N., eds. *Presidents and Prime Ministers*. Washington, D.C.: American Enterprise Institute, 1980.

Rossiter, Clinton. *The American Presidency*, 2nd ed. New York: New American Library, 1964.

Schlesinger, Arthur M., Jr. *The Imperial Presidency*. Boston: Houghton Mifflin, 1973.

Wills, Gary. *Cincinnatus: George Washington and the Enlightenment*. Garden City, N.Y.: Doubleday, 1984.

Chapter 13

Nondemocratic Government

In the last two chapters we have looked at two democratic systems for national decision making: parliamentary and presidential governments. Most of you are familiar with democratic government from your own experience, but in fact the majority of the world's states are not democracies. Democracy requires an implicit agreement by all the conflicting groups in a state to accept the possibility that they will lose out in the making of policy. In effect, it requires an agreement among labor unions, corporations, farm groups, environmentalists, vegetarians, motorcycle enthusiasts, and all other groups to take their chances on the outcome of a general process of policymaking in which the population as a whole gets the deciding voice. Each group accepts the fact that it must abide by the end result and hopes that it will be able to get enough of what it wants out of the process.

When we look at it in this way, it is easy enough to see why democracy is a fragile thing. All that is needed to make a democracy collapse is for one or more important groups to reject the results of the democratic process and to have access to enough power to overthrow the system. Many parts of the world are beset by problems of overpopulation, poverty, and chancy positions in world trade—problems so fierce that it becomes difficult for powerful groups to face policy defeats philosophically; the stakes are just too high. And military forces or popular movements may lie close at hand, willing and able to fight against the existing system.

As one might suspect, under these circumstances only a small number of the world's states are stable democracies. Of the 122 states that have been independent for at least twenty-five years, only 29 have had an uninterrupted record of electoral democratic government during that time. Most of these are prosperous industrialized states whose people can afford to compromise on the "democratic lottery." However, it is worth noting that such poor, small states as Jamaica, Malta, Botswana, and Costa Rica also have steady histories of democratic government.

What of the majority of the world's states that are not democratic? The nondemocratic alternatives are by no means all of one piece. Consider this sampling:

- **The Union of Soviet Socialist Republics** From the Russian Revolution (1917) until recently, power in the Soviet state was lodged clearly with the Communist party. It was self-sustaining, recruiting new young members who could progress through it to build careers. Although Stalin's rise to power in the 1930s was bloody, after Stalin the party saw five peaceful, orderly transitions of leadership. As far as we know, decisions are made more or less collectively within the party, with strong leadership by the party head and a great deal of influence from such groups as the army. Ordinary people have not had a great deal of personal freedom but—compared with the bloody past—laws are at least predictable and dealings with the governmental apparatus are generally orderly. In recent years Mikhail Gorbachev's *glasnost* reforms have opened up politics somewhat. There is still only one legal party, the Communist party; but organized dissident groups have been tolerated, the parliament has been given modest power, and elections have been opened to competing candidates. The new openness has unleashed an outpouring of nationalist sentiment among minority nationalities, to the point of movements for secession (especially in the Baltic republics), and the challenge this poses to the state could possibly lead either to a reversion back to greater state control, or to at least a partial break-up of the Soviet Union.

• **Bolivia** Transitions of power in Bolivia are frequent and generally occur by military coups. Bolivia has experienced 191 coups in her 165 years of independence. At the same time, there have been recurrent attempts to establish democratic government. For example, in 1973, the military group then in power announced a return to civilian government and set elections for 1974. After two attempted coups (which failed) the president, Colonel Hugo Banzer, announced that elections were postponed till 1980. Widespread strikes in 1976 led him to move the election date up to 1978. Elections were held then, but there were so many charges of fraud that the election was declared void. General Juan Asbun, the government-sponsored candidate, thereupon staged a successful coup and took over the government. He himself was deposed four months later by a left-wing officer, General David Aranciba. Elections were held in 1979 but led to a split result, another coup, and another election in 1980, but again a coup followed an inconclusive result. A civilian government was reestablished in 1982, with a promise to hold elections, a promise that was honored in 1985. The parliament elected in 1985 survived without overthrow until the election of 1989, which came off as scheduled. However, the 1985–1989 government was marked by turmoil caused by the worldwide collapse of the price of tin and the rising influence of illegal cocaine manufacturers. In those four years there were three major changes of cabinets, and the nation underwent a national hunger strike and two general strikes by the trade unions, which twice prompted the government to impose a national state of siege.

• **Madagascar** From its independence in 1960 until 1975, Madagascar experienced a troubled democracy, with a good deal of French intervention in its politics (it had been a French colony) and a couple of threatened coups. In 1975, a left-wing military group staged a successful coup and set up a socialist government, with a single national party and a good deal of civilian.participation. By 1976 the party had established its dominance over the military and set up a civilian government, militantly socialist. After elections in 1977, the left wing of the party (which had not done well in the election) withdrew from the party. The party then moved to include more moderates from earlier parties and shifted somewhat to the right. After widespread rioting in 1981 and 1982, the party moved back toward the left to restore order, expelling some of its moderates. A coup attempt in 1982 failed. A presidential election between two leaders of the party was held in that year, and the more moderate candidate, now President Ratsiraka, won. Despite the machinery of elections, Madagascar is a one-party state. However, elections do allow for sparring among factions of the ruling party.

- **Saudi Arabia**   Saudi Arabia has been an absolute monarchy for most of the twentieth century, with power lodged in the Saud family. This is a large, extended family that provides not only the king but also most of the council of ministers and other high governmental officials. It appears that while the king figures very importantly in the making of decisions, this is a genuinely collegial effort in which the council of ministers (including the king) discusses issues and decides on policies. The Saud family are conservative in religious matters and enforce strict Muslim standards of behavior, though they have been enthusiastic about economic modernization.
- **Brazil**   Brazil experienced military government for twenty years starting in 1964, when a left-oriented president was overthrown by a coup, ending a twenty-year period of democratic government. The new military government was repressive, with widespread censorship, political arrests, and torture. After 1964, transitions of power within the military leadership were orderly, by choices negotiated within a government party. Starting in the mid-1970s, the military leadership began an "opening toward democracy," in which repressive measures were gradually relaxed; by 1979, open party competition was once again allowed. In 1982 fairly open elections were held, but under rules that gave the government party many advantages. The opposition parties made many gains—the government held an absolute majority of seats in the Senate but fell short of an absolute majority in the House. The rules the government had written assured them of a majority in the presidential electoral college. In 1984 the country was swept by a massive movement in favor of direct elections for the presidency, with equal access for all candidates. The movement for direct elections further weakened the military government, which acceded to the demands and held an open presidential election in November 1984. The newly elected President Sarney (actually, he was vice-president but had succeeded on the death of his party's presidential candidate) led the country in writing a new democratic constitution, a difficult process which was only completed in 1988. Aside from the political problem of writing a constitution, the country was plagued during this time by an economic crisis brought on by its massive international debt. In 1988, for instance, the government went through three different Ministers of Finance in just nine months. By the end of this period President Sarney was largely discredited, so a search for new leadership in the 1990 presidential election took up much of the country's political energy.

These examples are roughly representative of nondemocratic systems as a whole. It is worth noting, first of all, that they are quite varied politically; they range from conservative Saudi Arabia through the bureaucratic Soviet Union to experimentally socialist states like Madagascar. Second, note that many of the nondemocratic states are not organized all that stably. Of these examples, Bolivia has had an incredibly turbulent history and is currently experiencing a period of democratic government, Madagascar has been through many varied regimes since it attained independence, and Brazil moved fairly systematically from 1974 to 1984 toward a relaxation of its military rule. Saudi Arabia, on the other hand, appears to have a rather stable system. Finally, note that the idea of democracy is alive in most of these states, even if they are not themselves democracies; it has shown new vigor in recent years, with both Bolivia and Brazil establishing democratic regimes and with internal pressure for the Soviet Union to open up its political process.

Of 132 states with more than 1 million inhabitants surveyed as to their politics (as of about 1989), 46 were democracies, 44 had one-party governments, 13 were ruled by military groups, and 9 were monarchies. It was difficult, in many cases, to decide what to call a regime. "Democracy," for instance, may range from open, established democracies like Sweden to a state like Algeria which has only recently opened up its one-party state to some limited competition from other political parties. Mexico's oppressively dominant-party state might be included. And it is difficult to place a state like Thailand, which has from time to time experimented with elections and civilian governments, but whose politics, as most observers agree, have consistently been dominated by the military. What of South Africa, where whites practice democracy among themselves but deny participation to the black majority? The boundary line between "one-party state" and "military government" is also a bit hard to apply in some instances, as military groups may set up skeletal "party" structures to help legitimize themselves. An enumeration such as this is not meant to suggest a false clarity but rather to sketch the rough outlines of the distribution of regimes in the world.

MILITARY GOVERNMENT

The most dramatic alternative to democratic government is *military government*, in which a group of officers use their troops to take over the governmental apparatus and run it themselves. This is called a "coup," from the French coup d'état (strike at the state). About one-tenth of the world's states are under military government.

Why is military government so common? A better question might be why it is not even more common. The military in any state control more armed power than anyone else. If they choose, as a group, to oust the existing government—or even if only a part of the military choose to do so and the rest decide to sit it out—there is no one who can stop them. Civilian governments must obviously depend for their safety on the military's satisfaction, disunity, or reluctance to take over the government. While each of these protective shields is evident in many military groups, it must not be so very unusual that all three would from time to time fail and that the military would break out in a coup. This is particularly likely in a new state, where a tradition of civilian government has not yet had time to take hold. It is not surprising that military coups occur with some frequency around the world.

In a few states, coups have become so routine that they have almost been institutionalized as the normal method of governmental change. In such cases, other political forces have come to be involved informally, much as they would under other arrangements. Key groups such as labor unions may be sought out by one or another military faction as potential allies, and—even though they do not themselves bear arms—their weight is felt.[1]

In Bolivia, for instance, factions of the armed forces regularly depend on other political groups when they are attempting a coup. In 1978, a right-wing government was overthrown by the army, who were aided by left-wing allies in the unions and political parties. After an attempt at an election in 1979, a right-wing coup was tried, but it failed because its leaders were not able to get the support of Congress. And in 1982 yet another military group was forced out of office by a general strike led by the unions. In a bizarre way, coups under these circumstances become a system that involves a fairly wide range of people in the political process. Generally, however, they are more isolated events.

Military governments vary greatly in their political role. In Paraguay, General Alfredo Stroessner seized power in 1954, and secured his position with repression and torture until he was deposed by a military coup in 1989. It is estimated that in 1982 one-quarter of the Paraguayan people were in exile outside the country's borders.[2] In Nigeria, a series of military governments ruled from 1966 to 1978. During much of that time, there was considerable civilian support for the military regime. Although democracy was reestablished peacefully by general consent in 1978, the democratic regime fell once again to a military coup in 1983. Greece was ruled by a right-wing group from the army from 1967 through 1973; this government maintained itself by harsh repressive measures. It broke up in 1974, and democracy was reestablished. In Turkey, the military have taken over the government three times since World War II—in 1960, 1971, and 1980—each time when Turkey's democratic government was verging on chaos. The Turkish takeovers have all been broadly supported and have been followed by a return to democracy after stability was restored.

Military governments vary widely in the one thing in which we might have expected that they would be similar: in their political direction. They are not all of the political right or of any other direction, even though we have a stereotype of the right-wing officers' coup. Of the 13 military governments noted on page 261, a few are of the political right and a few of the left, but the majority are not clearly either of the left or right. Studies that have compared fairly large numbers of military regimes with civilian regimes conclude, on the whole, that whether or not a state has a military regime has little effect on the state's rate of economic development. That is, as a group, military governments are neither especially good at guiding their states' economies nor especially poor at doing so.[3]

These two aspects of coups—the fact that they frequently become incorpo-

---

[1] Martin C. Needler, "Political Development and Military Intervention in Latin America," *American Political Science Review* 60 (September 1966): 616–626.

[2] *Europa Yearbook 1983*, vol. 2, p. 1228.

[3] See especially Robert Jackman, "Politicians in Uniform," *American Political Science Review* 70 (December 1976): 1098–1109.

"Good news. The 'Times' has upgraded us from a 'junta' to a 'military government.'"

(Drawing by Joe Mirachi; © 1984, The New Yorker Magazine)

rated in the broader political process and that they have no clear political complexion, of the left or of the right—have made political scientists a bit cautious in assessing them. As one scholar has noted:

> I would still affirm the general correctness of the position I took on this question ten years ago [that military coups are a repressive move backwards, thwarting necessary social change]. However, subsequent events have suggested that I underestimated the extent to which apparently democratic political processes could in fact be manipulated by elite economic interests to its advantage. This means that interruption of those processes by military seizures of power could, at least in some cases, be a force for promoting development instead of retarding it.[4]

WHY AREN'T THERE MORE MILITARY GOVERNMENTS?

Good or bad, though, it is still surprising that more countries are not governed by the military. There are not as many coups as we might expect, and most

[4]Martin C. Needler, "The Logic of Conspiracy: The Latin American Military Coup as a Problem in the Social Sciences," *Studies in Comparative International Development* 13 (Fall 1978): 31.

Are Military Coups Contagious?

A number of observers have noticed that military coups cluster at certain times. Suddenly a rash of coups will break out in a region such as Latin American or southern Africa, and then coups will once again decrease. Statistical tests have shown that this is not coincidental. Coup makers apparently watch each other's success, and if they have seen a number of their neighbors succeed, they are likely to have fewer qualms about undertaking a coup themselves. Furthermore, if a number of coups have recently occurred in the neighborhood, this lessens the problems of legitimacy. If coups are a frequent thing in the region, initiating a coup will not seem as flagrantly illegitimate as if yours was the only army doing it.

Beyond considerations in any one state, then, coups appear to involve broad, wavelike regional processes. Statistical analysis to measure these processes has proven to be complex and challenging. A good example is Richard P. Y. Li and William R. Thompson, "The 'Coup Contagion' Hypothesis," *Journal of Conflict Resolution* 19 (March 1975): 63–88.

military governments stay in power only a few years. Partly, this may be because most states take pains to imbue their military officers with inhibitions against political intervention. Adolf Hitler required all officers to swear oaths of personal allegiance to him, for instance, and in the training of its officers, the U.S. government assures in many ways that they will understand their proper role to be nonpolitical.

However, more important than such inhibitions are a series of important problems faced by military governments—problems that make officers somewhat reluctant to take and hold power. A uniquely serious one for them is that of *legitimacy*, which was discussed as a general problem of all governments in Chapter 6. Since a military government itself takes power through no regular process but simply seizes it, how can it claim that no other group should similarly displace it? A democratic government is legitimized by the electoral process that produced it, a monarchy is legitimized by the rules of succession on which it is based, a communist government is legitimized by Lenin's theory that the Communist party must lead the revolution. But no process of selection legitimizes the military government. Those who live by the sword shall die by the sword, they say, and a military government must always be concerned to justify its existence. To this end, many military governments add civilians to their governing apparatus or set future dates for a return to democracy. Others try to rally the people through wars and appeals to nationalism.

Another problem of most military governments is that while their leaders *may* be skilled politically, there is little in the profession to which they have been trained that makes this likely. Military organization is usually marked by a fairly orderly passage of commands from higher officers to lower officers, without a great deal of argument in between. This orderliness should not be exaggerated, but many military officers are clearly frustrated by the jabber of daily political requests and arguments with which they must deal once they have taken power.

Finally, many military governments are themselves fairly shaky alliances, united primarily by their opposition to the regime they have displaced and likely to fall apart as new issues that may divide their members arise.

As a result of these problems, military governments are actually rather fragile. Unless they set up the institutions to transform themselves into one-party states, there is a good chance that they will eventually yield to the establishment of democracy. If a military regime is internally divided or has problems generally in governing and if enough of the key figures concerned feel that the uncertainty of the outcome of democratic choice is preferable to the certainty of any other particular group being in control, the stage is set to introduce democracy—or reintroduce it, as the case may be.[5] In the last twenty years, fully nineteen states have switched at least for a time from military government to democracy.[6]

ONE-PARTY STATES

Most nondemocratic systems are not straight military governments, however, but *one-party states*. The one-party state is distinguished by the fact that the government is based on and supports a political party, which is the only party allowed in the state. One-party arrangements have often had their origins in military coups. For example, in Libya, Colonel Muammar Khadaffi seized power in a coup in 1969 and established the Arab-Socialist Union as the sole political party; its general congress, chaired by Khadaffi, is in effect the chief governing body of the state. Other one-party arrangements originated in national independence movements, which were then institutionalized as the single party. In Tanzania, for example, Julius Nyerere led the movement for independence, and his independence movement, the Tanganyika Africa National Union, won 70 of the 71 seats in the first election to the National Assembly. Four years later, a constitution was written that established it as the state's sole party.[7] A number of one-party states originated in socialist revolutions, either indigenous, as in the cases of Cuba, China, or the U.S.S.R.; or imposed by the U.S.S.R., as in the cases of (pre-1989) East Germany, Czechoslovakia, and other East European states.

[5]For an expansion of this argument, see Adam Przeworski, *Some Problems in the Study of the Transition to Democracy*, in Guillermo O'Donnell, Philippe C. Schmitter, and Laurence Whitehead, eds., *Transitions from Authoritarian Rule: Prospects for Democracy*. (Baltimore: Johns Hopkins University Press, 1986), pp. 47–63.

[6]Argentina, Bolivia, Brazil, Burkina Faso, Chile, the Dominican Republic, Ecuador, Ghana, Greece, Honduras, Nigeria, Pakistan, Peru, the Philippines, Portugal, South Korea, Thailand, Turkey, and Uruguay.

[7]Though there is only one legal party, there are still many contests between *individuals* in elections. A majority of the seats in the National Assembly are filled by election, the rest being appointed. In the 1980 election, for instance, about half of the incumbent elected members were defeated by challengers.

What distinguishes these states from other nondemocratic systems, especially from straightforward military governments, is the existence of a reasonably large national political party that both bolsters the government and provides an institutional basis for it. Compared with military rule, the one-party state offers a more stable and responsive form of government. The military government is necessarily limited by the field of vision of the officers who hold power. There is little provision for dealing with broad factional conflict or for the intrusion of diverse opinions. And since the government itself came into being by irregular means, there exists no regular set of arrangements to provide for the replacement of old leaders by new. These are things that may be provided for by the single political party.

A national party is likely to embrace at least a reasonable range of the social groups in a state—labor leaders, industrialists, and intellectuals as well as military leaders. Not all of these may be equally happy with the party; however, they have little choice but to cooperate with it if asked. The party, on its side, needs to involve them if only to keep tabs on potential troublemakers. As a result, the single party as an organization is generally able to have a better feel for opinion in the countryside than a simple group of officers will have. It provides institutional links between the government and the population.

Second, the party can provide an arena in which varied political positions can develop into factions. In this way new conflicts may develop within an existing system rather than arising outside it and posing a threat to it.

Finally, the single party may provide a set of arrangements by which a transition of leadership can be accomplished. A recent example of this capacity was the fairly easy transition from Chernenko to Gorbachev in the Soviet Union after Chernenko's death in 1985. During Chernenko's illness, there had obviously been some process at work by which the Communist party leadership decided who would take over from him.

The one-party state must be distinguished from a democracy with a dominant-party system.[8] A few democracies have party systems in which a single party has dominated government over a long period of time. Mexico is one of the best examples. Since 1929, the Party of the Institutionalized Revolution has won every election with at least 70 percent of the vote. What distinguishes Mexico from the one-party states, however, is that other parties are able to organize and, in fact, do so; despite widespread electoral fraud, it is generally recognized that other parties should win elections if enough people vote for them.

To sum up our treatment of one-party systems: This is the most frequently seen form of nondemocratic government. It may originate in all sorts of ways—military coups, movements for national independence, socialist revolutions, and many others. Distinctively, the one-party state has one (and only one) political party that is fostered by the government. This party adds to the government's capacities and helps to make these regimes more stable than straight military governments are.

---

[8]See above, pp. 184–185.

Muammar Khadaffi, military leader of Libya.
(Reuters/Bettmann Newsphotos)

"COURT POLITICS"

A characteristic of many nondemocratic systems—especially of monarchies and of personal dictatorships like that which the Duvalier family exercised in Haiti from 1957 to 1986, but also of many military governments and one-party states—is that a single person may hold almost all ultimate power in the system and that politics revolves around that single person. It must be emphasized that this is not true of all nondemocratic systems; many have plural institutionalized bodies for decision, as in the central committee of a communist state or the officers' councils that guide some military governments. But it is frequently the case. Extreme examples are the great power held by Hitler in Nazi Germany, Stroessner in Paraguay, Duvalier in Haiti, and the apparently undisputed preeminence of the Ayatollah Khomeini in Iran from 1977 to 1989.

Politics revolving heavily around one person in this way is called "court politics," after the courts of the great European monarchs. Court politics are usually marked by:

- *Less emphasis on the rule of the law and more on the arbitrary whim of the ruler:* In a more plural system, politics is based on competing forces, which may need to agree on the relatively neutral devices of laws and legality to settle their disputes rather than confronting each other directly. In a system dominated by a single person, that person's wishes are likely to dominate over legal considerations.
- *Heavy competition by all other figures for access to the leader:* Access to the

leader's ear may be a major factor in political outcomes. Lower officials may not dare to take vacations, for instance, for fear of missing such a chance.

- *Unusual importance of even apparently nonpolitical figures who necessarily have access to the leader by virtue of their other roles in the leader's life:* Doctors, hairdressers, and even childhood friends may all turn up as important political figures. Martin Bormann, Hitler's personal secretary, was probably the second most important political figure in Germany toward the end of the Third Reich; doctors, astrologers, and others also had some political influence.
- *Flattery, and attempts to shield the leader from unpleasant reality[9]:* A graphic illustration of court politics follows this chapter, in the excerpt from Albert Speer's *Inside the Third Reich*.

"POWER AND CHOICE" AGAIN

To return to the theme of our text, these governments—especially the military governments—might appear to embody a rather pure strain of politics as power. After all, when political control depends on who has the guns, it is hard to deny that power is at work. On the other hand, it is a common mistake to think of nondemocratic governments simply as raw examples of power at work.

One-party governments often see themselves as pursuing communal objectives and develop organizational mechanisms for bringing a wide spectrum of opinion to bear on the government's decisions. Even military governments usually portray themselves as heeding the country's call, and there is often broad support among the people for a military coup. We shall deal with governments such as these more wisely if we remember that the picture is not all black or white but that politics in these states—as in democracies—consists of power *and* choice.

CONCLUSION

To sum up, the nondemocratic alternative is quite a diverse thing and not necessarily very stable. A number of nondemocratic states have set up institutions of politics, especially through a single party or through a monarchy, that provide for politics to be conducted over the long haul; straight military governments, however, have not. There is a good deal of flux among regimes, with rather few stable democratic regimes, not many more stable nondemocratic regimes, and a great many states that are likely to shift among regimes of different sorts. We who live in a stable democracy tend to think of democracy as something that a state either has permanently or does not have at all. It is probably better thought of as a mode of government that is used by many states some of the time but to which relatively few states are permanently com-

---

[9]Actually, aspects of "court politics" (especially this and the preceding one) can be seen wherever great political power is held by a single person. The American presidency has sometimes shown signs of it.

mitted. Even ancient Athens, the birthplace of democracy, moved in and out of democratic government and dictatorship from time to time. Such a perspective helps us not only to view democracy as less than a permanent attribute of states but also to see the alternatives to democracy in the same way.

At present democracy is certainly on the upswing, demonstrating its resilience and its enduring appeal. On the right, over the past ten or fifteen years dictatorships have been eliminated in Spain, Greece, and the Philippines. Argentina, Brazil, and Pakistan have moved from military government to democracy, and Chile is moving in the same direction. The oppressive regime of South Africa is under increasing pressure to extend political rights to blacks. On the left, Czechoslovakia, East Germany, Hungary, and Poland in 1989 ended their Communist parties' monopolies of power; Czechoslovakia and East Germany in particular seem about to institute true, competitive democracy. Other one-party states such as Algeria and Egypt, or military governments like South Korea's, have grudgingly begun to allow limited political competition.

This has been a period of breathtaking change, with a great opening up of politics worldwide. It would probably be a mistake to read finality into it, however. One author, noting these events, has declared that capitalist democracy has won the great ideological debate of the nineteenth and twentieth centuries, and that history as we have known it has now ended because there are no important things left to fight about.[10] Well, the end of history has been declared several times over the past century, but history does not stop. The road to open politics is not easy, and it is also not a one-way street. China has been moving in the opposite direction since the events at Tiananmen Square in 1989, for instance, and it may be that ten years from now I will be writing of an upsurge of religious or ethnic tyrannies, or of something else as yet unimagined. Still, it is good to pause at this point in history and take note once again of the enduring power of the democratic idea.

EXAMPLE: CIVILIAN PARTICIPATION IN NIGERIA'S FIRST MILITARY REGIME

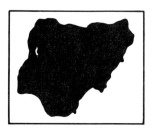

Professor Henry Beinen has studied the nature of the military government that ruled Nigeria from 1966 to 1974.[11] Although this regime included some civilian politicians, the military leaders always had the ultimate last word, a not uncommon pattern for military governments. Professor Bienen studied this regime from the

[10]Francis Fukuyama, "The End of History?" *The National Interest* 16 (Summer 1989): 3–19.

[11]This presentation relies heavily on his study. Henry Bienen, "Military Rule and Political Process: Nigerian Examples," *Comparative Politics* (January 1978): 205–225. See also Henry Bienen with Martin Fitton, "Soldiers, Politicians and Civil Servants," in K. Panter-Brick, ed., *Soldiers and Oil* (London: Cass, 1978), pp. 27–57.

standpoint of the civilians by interviewing a large number of politicians from the Western Province of Nigeria.

About a year after the 1966 coup, the military government brought a number of civilian politicians into the cabinet. At that time a civil war was raging in Nigeria, as the eastern provinces were trying to secede, and the military apparently thought they needed help to mobilize the population and to keep in touch with the grass roots. In the Western Province, General Adebayo, the governor, consulted with local party leaders before he appointed civilian commissioners to the provincial government. The military also set up advisory bodies called Leaders of Thought, in which military and civilian leaders met regularly on an informal basis.

The commissioners to whom Professor Bienen spoke disagreed as to how much real influence they had over the actions of the government, but in general they thought that while the military held ultimate control, the cabinet had considerable power over day-to-day decisions:

> Adebayo said the cabinet was purely advisory. We told him we have an executive council. A Governor in Council. The Secretary Odumosu (civil service head in the state) told him we were right. The attorney general did the same thing. He ignored this often, particularly where the profit margin was involved....

> To some extent I would agree that commissioners did not have the old ministerial powers. Legally speaking we did, but not practically speaking. As a military regime [sic], the governor is the final authority. A commissioner is his advisor. In practice he of course cannot see to everything. He allows you to take decisions on consultation. He invariably approves....

> The cabinet was an executive body; that's a correct view. It was not just advisory. Only once or twice did Adebayo try to assert his position as military governor, and then he reconsidered and took the consensus advice. There were no votes.[12]

The bureaucracy apparently had greater leeway under the military regime than they had had under democracy, and there was a technical rather than political air to decision making. Of the political leaders who were interviewed, 60 percent thought that most of the bureaucracy would not welcome a return to democratic government, while only 10 percent thought that the bureaucracy would want such a return.[13]

If the governmental machinery operated somewhat more smoothly under military rule, this was offset by a lack of communication between the population and the government. It was to address exactly this problem that civilians were added to the government. In the Western Province, the government was severely pressed when widespread rioting by farmers broke out in 1968 and 1969. Farmers attacked the federal prison in daylight in September of 1969, freeing all its occupants; many police were ambushed or disappeared; tax collections nearly ceased. The military were caught unprepared for the level of grass-roots discontent because they had not had enough contact with the villages

---

[12]Bienen, op. cit., p. 213.

[13]Bienen and Fitton, op. cit., p. 42.

to sense what was building up. The civilians in the cabinet gained somewhat in power during this period, as the military leaders depended on them to help assess the farmers' discontent and rebuild a coalition of support for the regime.

How did the civilian politicians rate the military rulers? Though they were, for obvious reasons, predisposed to be critical of the military, they distinguished among the military government's strengths and weaknesses.

The greatest criticism of the military was that they failed to represent and take into account the various groups in the population.

> Those cabinet members who felt that the [civilian] cabinet was politically strong, that its members had grass-roots support, did not see the military as having local links. Individual members mentioned many times how "little people" were afraid to go and see military officers, because to do so they had to pass a series of armed soldiers. Nigerian politicians were often outraged that although the officers and soldiers became rich they spent money only on themselves and their close relatives. The money did not trickle down.[14]

Of the politicians, 81 percent thought that the military had been less successful than civilians in representing the people.[15]

On the other hand, the politicians generally credited the military with creating national unity more successfully than the civilians (by a margin of about 3 to 1) and with bringing stability (by a margin of 2 to 1). They split on whether the military had been more successful in promoting economic development than the civilians, and by about a 2 to 1 margin they thought the military had been less successful than civilian governments at developing health and educational services.

EXAMPLE: "COURT POLITICS" IN NAZI GERMANY

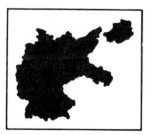

Albert Speer was the relatively nonpolitical coordinator of industrial production for Adolf Hitler during the latter part of World War II. He offers the following accounts of politics in Hitler's inner circle. These provide good examples of the peculiarities of the "court politics" described above.[16]

> In the winter of 1942, during the Stalingrad crisis, Bormann, Keitel, and Lammers decided to close their own ring around Hitler more tightly. Henceforth, all orders to be signed by the Chief of State had to be cleared through these three men. This would supposedly prevent the unconsidered signing of decrees and therefore put a stop to the command confusion caused by this practice. Hitler was content so long as he retained the final decision. Henceforth, the divergent views of various branches of government would be "sifted" by this Committee of Three. In accept-

---

[14]Bienen, op. cit., p. 219.

[15]Bienen, op. cit., p. 220.

[16]Albert Speer, *Inside the Third Reich* (New York: Macmillan, 1970), pp. 300–306, 389–393.

ing this arrangement Hitler counted on objective presentation and a nonpartisan method of working.

The three-man committee divided up its jurisdictions. Keitel, who was to be in charge of all orders relating to the armed forces, came to grief right from the start, since the commanders in chief of the air force and the navy utterly refused to accept his authority. All changes in the powers of the ministries, all constitutional affairs, and all administrative questions were supposed to go through Lammers. As it turned out, however, he had to leave these decisions more and more to Bormann, since he himself had little access to Hitler. Bormann had reserved the field of domestic policy for himself. But he not only lacked the intelligence for these matters; he also had insufficient knowledge of the outside world. For more than eight years he had been little more than Hitler's shadow. He had never dared go on any lengthy business trips, or even to allow himself a vacation, for fear that his influence might diminish. From his own days as Hess's deputy, Bormann knew the perils of ambitious deputies. For Hitler was all too ready to treat the second men in an organization, as soon as they were presented to him, as members of his staff and to make assignments directly to them. This quirk accorded with his tendency to divide power wherever he encountered it. Moreover, he loved to see new faces, to try out new persons. In order to avoid raising up such a rival in his own household, many a minister took care not to appoint an intelligent and vigorous deputy.

The plan of these three men to surround Hitler, to filter his information and thus control his power, might have led to an abridgement of Hitler's one-man rule—had the Committee of Three consisted of men possessing initiative, imagination, and a sense of responsibility. But since they had been trained always to act in Hitler's name, they slavishly depended on the expressions of his will. What is more, Hitler soon stopped abiding by this regulation. It became a nuisance to him, and was, moreover, contrary to his temperament. But it is understandable that those who stood outside this ring resented its stranglehold.

In fact Bormann was now assuming a role which could be dangerous to the top functionaries. He alone, with Hitler's compliance, drew up the appointments calendar, which meant that he decided which civilian members of the government or party could see, or more important, could not see, the Fuehrer. By now, hardly any of the ministers, Reichsleiters, or Gauleiters could penetrate to Hitler. They all had to ask Bormann to present their programs to him. Bormann was very efficient. Usually the official in question received an answer in writing within a few days, whereas in the past he would have had to wait for months. I was one of the exceptions to this rule. Since my sphere was military in nature, I had access to Hitler whenever I wished. Hitler's military adjutants were the ones who set up my appointments.

After my conferences with Hitler, it sometimes happened that the adjutant would announce Bormann, who would then come into the room carrying his files. In a few sentences he would report on the memoranda sent to him. He spoke monotonously and with seeming objectivity and would then advance his own solution. Usually Hitler merely nodded and spoke his terse, "Agreed." On the basis of this one word, or even a vague comment by Hitler, which was hardly meant as a directive, Bormann would often draft lengthy instructions. In this way ten or more important decisions were sometimes made within half an hour. De facto, Bormann was conducting the internal affairs of the Reich. A few months afterward, on April 12, 1943, Bormann obtained Hitler's signature to a seemingly unimportant piece of paper. He became "Secretary to the Fuehrer." Whereas previously his powers, strictly speaking, should have been restricted to party affairs, this new position now authorized him to act officially in any field he wished.

[Speer developed an infected knee and was hospitalized.]

Dr. Gebhardt, SS Group leader and well known as a knee specialist in the European world of sports, ran the Red Cross's Hohenlychen Hospital. It was situated on a lakeside in wooded country about sixty miles north of Berlin. Without knowing it, I had put myself into the hands of a doctor who was one of Heinrich Himmler's very few intimate friends. For more than two months I lived in a simply furnished sickroom in the private section of the hospital. My secretaries were quartered in other rooms in the building, and a direct telephone line to my Ministry was set up, for I wanted to keep on working.

Sickness on the part of a minister of the Third Reich involved some special difficulties. Only too often Hitler had explained the elimination of a prominent figure in the government or the party on grounds of ill health. People in political circles therefore picked up their ears if any of Hitler's close associates was reported "sick." Since, however, I was really sick, it seemed advisable to remain as active as possible. Moreover, I could not let go of my apparatus, for like Hitler I had no suitable deputy at my disposal. Though friends and associates did their best to give me the opportunity to rest, the conferences, telephone calls, and dictation conducted from my bed often did not stop before midnight.

My absence unleashed certain elements, as the following incident will illustrate. Almost as soon as I arrived at the hospital, my newly appointed personnel chief, Erwin Bohr, telephoned me, quite excited. There was a locked filing case in his office, he said. Dorsch had ordered this case transported at once to the Todt Organization headquarters. I instantly countermanded this, saying that it was to stay where it was. A few days later representatives of the Berlin Gauleiter's headquarters appeared, accompanied by several moving men. They had orders, Bohr informed me, to take the filing case with them, for it was party property along with its contents. Bohr no longer knew what to do. I managed to postpone this action by telephoning one of Goebbels's closest associates, Naumann. The filing case was sealed by the party officials—but the seal was placed only on its door. I then had it opened by unscrewing the back. The next day Bohr came to the hospital with a bundle of photocopied documents. They contained dossiers on a number of my time-honored assistants—adverse reports almost without exception. Most of the men were charged with attitudes hostile to the party; in some cases it was recommended that they be watched by the Gestapo. I also discovered that the party had a liaison man in my Ministry: Xavier Dorsch. The fact surprised me less than the person.

Since the autumn I had been trying to have one of the officials in my Ministry promoted. But the clique which had recently taken shape in the Ministry did not like him. My then personnel chief had resorted to all sorts of evasions, until I finally forced him to nominate my man for promotion. Shortly before my illness I had received a sharp, unfriendly rejection from Bormann. Now we found a draft of that sharp note among the documents in this secret file, composed, as it turned out, by Dorsch and Personnel Chief Haasemann (whom I had replaced by Bohr). Bormann's text followed it word for word.

From my sickbed I telephoned Goebbels. As Gauleiter of Berlin he was head of all the party representatives in the Berlin ministries. Goebbels agreed at once that my old assistant Gerhard Fränk was the man for this post in my Ministry. "An impossible state of affairs! Every minister is a party member nowadays. Either we have confidence in him or he must go!" Goebbels said. But I could not find out who the Gestapo's agents in my Ministry were.

The effort to maintain my position during my illness proved almost too much for me. I had to ask Bormann's state secretary, Gerhard Klopfer, to instruct the party functionaries to stay within their bounds. Above all I asked him to look out for the industrialists working for me and to see that no obstacles were placed in their way. For I had no sooner fallen sick than the district [*Gau*] economic adviser of the party had begun making inroads into my system. I asked Funk and his assistant Otto Ohlendorf, whom he had borrowed from Himmler, to take a more affirmative attitude toward my principle of industrial self-responsibility and to back me against Bormann's district economic advisers.

Sauckel, too, had already taken advantage of my absence to "make a general appeal to the men involved in armaments for an ultimate commitment." Faced with theses effronteries from all sides, I turned to Hitler to tell him of my woes and ask his help. My letters—twenty-three typewritten pages that took me four days—were a sign of the funk I was in. I protested against Sauckel's arrogation of power and against the thrusts of Bormann's district economic advisers, and I asked Hitler for a statement of my unconditional authority in all questions that fell within my jurisdiction. Basically, I was asking for the very thing I had unsuccessfully demanded in such drastic language at the conference in Posen, to the indignation of the Gauleiters. I further wrote that our total production could be carried out rationally only if the "many offices which give directions, criticism, and advice to the plant managements" were concentrated in my hands.

Four days later I appealed to Hitler again, with a candor that really was no longer in keeping with our present relationship. I informed him about the camarilla in my Ministry which was undermining my program. I said there was treachery afoot; that a certain small clique of Todt's former assistants, led by Dorsch, had broken faith with me. I therefore considered myself forced, I wrote, to replace Dorsch by a man who had my confidence.

This last letter, with its news that I was dismissing one of Hitler's favorites without asking him beforehand, was particularly imprudent. For I was violating one of the rules of the regime: that personnel matters must be broached to Hitler at the right moment and by skillful insinuation. Instead, I had bluntly come at him with charges of disloyalty and questionable character in one of his men. That I also sent Bormann a copy of my letter was either foolish or challenging. In doing this I was running counter to all I knew about the nature of Hitler's intriguing entourage. I was probably acting out a certain attitude of defiance, forced upon me by my isolated position.

My illness had removed me too far from the true focus of power: Hitler. He reacted neither negatively nor positively to all my suggestions, demands, and complaints. I was addressing the empty air; he sent me no answer. I was no longer counted as Hitler's favorite minister and one of his possible successors—a few whispered words by Bormann and a few weeks of illness had put me out of the running. This was partly due to Hitler's peculiarity, often noted by everyone around him, of simply writing off anyone who vanished from his sight for a considerable time. If the person in question reappeared in his entourage after a while, the picture might or might not change. It disillusioned me and snapped some of my ties of personal feeling toward Hitler. But most of the time I was neither angry nor in despair over my new situation. Physically weakened as I was, I felt only weariness and resignation.

FURTHER READING

Bebler, Anton. *Military Rule in Africa: Dahomey, Ghana, Sierra Leone, and Mali*. New York: Praeger, 1972.

Collier, David, ed. *The New Authoritarianism in Latin America*. Princeton, N.J.: Princeton University Press, 1979.

Duverger, Maurice. *Political Parties*. New York: Wiley, 1955. Especially pp. 255–280.

Finer, S. E. *The Man on Horseback: The Role of the Military in Politics*. New York: Praeger, 1962.

Huntington, Samuel P. *The Soldier and the State*. Cambridge, Mass.: Harvard University Press, 1957.

Huntington, Samuel P., and Moore, Clement. *Authoritarian Politics in Modern Society*. New York: Basic Books, 1970.

Jackman, Robert. "Politicians in Uniform." *American Political Science Review* 70 (December 1976): 1098–1109.

Jackson, Robert H., and Rosberg, Carl G. *Personal Rule in Black Africa*. Berkeley: University of California Press, 1982.

Johnson, John J. ed. *The Role of the Military in Underdeveloped Countries*. Princeton, N.J.: Princeton University Press, 1962.

Linz, Juan J., and Stepan, Alfred. *The Breakdown of Democratic Regimes*. Baltimore: Johns Hopkins University Press, 1978.

Needler, Martin C. "The Logic of Conspiracy: The Latin American Military Coup as a Problem in the Social Sciences." *Studies in Comparative International Development* 13 (Fall 1978): 28–40.

Neumann, Franz. *Behemoth: The Structure and Practice of National Socialism, 1933–1944*. New York: Oxford University Press, 1944.

Nordlinger, Eric A. *Soldiers in Politics*. Englewood Cliffs, N.J.: Prentice-Hall, 1976.

O'Donnell, Guillermo, Schmitter, Philippe, and Whitehead, Laurence. *Transitions from Authoritarian Rule: Prospects for Democracy*. Baltimore: Johns Hopkins University Press, 1986.

Perlmutter, Amos. *The Military and Politics in Modern Times*. New Haven, Conn.: Yale University Press, 1977.

Rouiquie, Alain. *The Military and the State in Latin America*. Berkeley: University of California Press, 1987.

Sartori, Giovanni. *Parties and Party Systems*. Cambridge, England: Cambridge University Press, 1976. Especially chap. 7.

Chapter 14

Bureaucracy and the Public Sector

In the last few chapters we have reviewed the structure of governments. But a great deal goes into policymaking beyond what government leaders do. The government may establish by law that the speed limit on highways is 55 miles per hour, but what this means in detail is determined by hundreds of thousands of traffic patrol officers across the country. It is they who decide whether this means that you are ticketed if you drive 56 miles per hour or whether there is a "zone of grace" so that you are ticketed only for speeds of 60 miles per hour or above. It is they who decide whether a woman with a bleeding wound in her arm is in bad enough shape that she is justified in speeding to the hospital at 75 miles per hour. It is they who decide whether to treat a well-dressed man in a dark-blue sedan differently from a youth in blue jeans who is driving a red sports car, warning the one and ticketing the other.

The local police officer, the public health inspector, the president of the state university, the teacher in a public school—these are just as much a part of the policymaking machinery as the legislator, judge, or U.S. president. In fact, for most citizens, it is *these* people, and not the legislator, judge, or president, who embody the state and its policies. People receive the policies of the state from police officers, immigration officials, I.R.S. agents, schoolteachers, agricultural extension agents, and members of fire departments, not from the nation's president or members of Congress.

Any state, if its operations are at all complex, must have a large number of people like this—people who are not directly involved in politics in the sense that they share in making major decisions but who are involved in the construction and implementation of the policies that carry out those decisions. These are collectively called the *public administration* of the state. A modern state has a large number of people in its public administration. Figure 14–1 charts the growth of the public administration of the United States since 1950.

The number of public employees in the United States climbed from 6,400,000 in 1950 to 16,200,000 in 1980, almost wholly from increases at the state and local levels. (Federal civilian employment increased over this period by about 1,200,000.) Public employment climbed not only in absolute numbers but also as a proportion of the total civilian labor force. In 1950, 11 percent of all employed civilians were public employees; by 1980, this had risen to 16 percent. In other words, by 1980, 1 out of 6 employed persons was a member of the U.S. public administration.

276

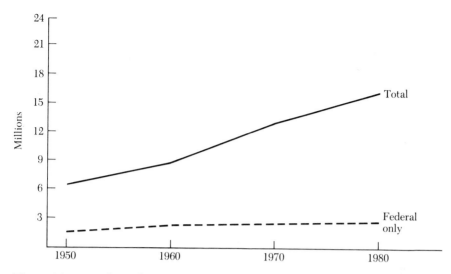

Figure 14–1　Total number of civilian public employees (combined local, state, and federal) in the United States, 1950–1980).

SOURCE U.S. Department of Commerce, Bureau of the Census, *Statistical Abstract of the United States*.

Actually, all this understates the growth of government *operations* by a good deal. Federal operations obviously grew by much more than the growth in federal employment shown in the chart. What happened is that the federal government has tended over the years to expand its operations by contracting jobs out to private research firms and other organizations not directly in the government. The rapid growth of Washington, D.C., over the last few decades has been driven more by the growth of "beltway bandit" firms associated with the government than by growth of the government itself.

PUBLIC ADMINISTRATION AS A POLITICAL PROBLEM

The fact that some part of policymaking is done by such a large number of people poses something of a problem for the state. Public administrators as a group obviously have significant governmental power, yet they are too numerous and individually too unimportant to be controlled very effectively. Thus, *a significant part of the governmental power of any state is necessarily not under close political control*.

Examples of the governmental discretion of administrators are numerous. American police officers have a good deal of discretion, for instance, in whom they stop to search for weapons or illegal substances, and numerous studies of American police in the 1960s and 1970s showed that the rate at which black youths were stopped was far higher than that for white youths under similar

Public employees at work. The state meets a citizen. Woodstock, New York.
(Mark Antman/Stock, Boston)

circumstances.[1] Fortunately, with publicity and a heightened sensitivity to the problem, this practice has diminished; however, it still stands as an example of the extent to which police officers make government policy. As another example, consider the agents of the I. R. S. in the United States who audit taxpayers' returns. Inevitably, given the complexity of our tax laws, interpretation of the laws will vary from one agent to the next. As a result, the outcome of a tax audit depends at least to some extent on which agent handles it. Finally, consider the fact that the teachers of America determine, by their individual actions, the grading system that has such important ultimate effects on students' careers.

These and other examples show that even rather minor administrators make a good deal of governmental policy. The politically responsive part of government (elected officials, party leaders, military juntas, courts, or whatever) must be concerned to make certain that, at least in broad outline, they control the policies implemented by administrators. This control is not easy to design, however. An early study in this area illustrates the problem. In 1948 the U.S. Supreme Court ruled that it was unconstitutional for school districts to schedule certain hours during the day in which religious groups would come to school and provide classes in religion for those students who desired it. (Students who did not wish to have religious instruction were sent to study hall.) The Court ruled that this practice violated the constitutional separation of

[1]For example, Irving Piliavin and Scott Briar, "Police Encounters with Juveniles," *American Journal of Sociology* 70 (September 1964): 206–214.

(Sidney Harris)

church and state. Nearly ten years later, in a survey of Pennsylvania school superintendents, one-tenth of those responding stated that their school districts continued this practice, even though it was unconstitutional. The survey also ascertained that the superintendents understood the Court decision fully; they were acting not out of ignorance, but deliberately.[2]

CHARACTERISTICS OF GOOD PUBLIC ADMINISTRATION

The way in which we organize our public administration should help us to maximize a number of desirable traits. Among these are the following:

1. *Honest, accurate translation of political leaders' decisions into more specifically designed policies:* This addresses the problem referred to above, of making sure that political leaders control at least the broad outlines of policy.

---

[2]Frank J. Sorauf, "*Zorach* v. *Clausen:* The Impact of a Supreme Court Decision," *American Political Review* 53 (September 1959): 777–791.

2. *Flexibility in dealing with special cases at the point of delivery:* While administrators should be obedient to directions from above, they should not be slavishly obedient. If a police officer pulls a driver over for speeding and discovers that the driver is trying to get a child with a gaping wound to the hospital, we do not want the officer to write a ticket.

3. *But this flexibility should not be used arbitrarily:* "Arbitrary" action is action taken capriciously, without regard to the truly important circumstances of a case. Stopping and searching blacks because of their race is an arbitrary act, for example. Another example would be to allow some students to take a makeup examination but to deny the makeup to others who had had the same excuse.

4. *Feedback of expert advice; active imagination, and assertive inquiry on the part of administrators:* We hope that administrators will know more about their areas of work than anyone else and that they will not hang back from sharing their expertise with the public and with their political leaders.

5. *Efficiency:* We hope that all this can be done without costing too much.

Now, we have said that all of these are desirable traits. So they are, but it is important to note that some of them are to a certain extent mutually contradictory, so that all of them cannot be fully met simultaneously. For instance, there is some tension between item 1 (honest, accurate translation) and item 2 (in which we expect administrators to follow their own judgment). Item 3 is difficult in and of itself, since one person's capriciousness is another person's courageous judgment. And item 4 (feedback of expert advice) assumes an independent-minded set of administrators who fit oddly with the task of honest, accurate translation.

It follows that there is no one best way to organize public administration; various modes of organization will emphasize one or another of these good things. Therefore, under varying circumstances, varying modes may be preferred.

"BUREAUCRACY": A REFORM OF THE LAST CENTURY

Bureaucracy is one way to organize the public administration. The word "bureaucracy" is often used in common language simply to mean the public administration, usually with a connotation of distance. But social scientists have a precise meaning for it—a particular mode of administrative organization that was developed as a reform in the nineteenth century and has spread widely to be the most generally used mode today.

Let us first set the stage of the eighteenth and early nineteenth centuries to show how bureaucracy developed as a reform of the systems then in place. Generally at that time, in both Europe and North America, positions in the public administration were treated as pieces of property, to be exchanged among people. In the United States, this took the form of the infamous "spoils system," by which administrative jobs were treated as commodities with which victorious candidates rewarded their party's workers. When the presidency changed hands, for instance, all post-office managers in the country were fired and new people from the victorious party were put in their place. The same thing happened with state highway and surveyor jobs when one party replaced another in a state capital; so also with fire and police jobs when city hall changed hands.

In Europe, positions in the public administration were individually bought and sold more or less as investments. A wealthy family wishing to establish a son in a comfortable life would buy him a position in the customs service, an officer's commission in the army, or some similar position.

Needless to say, such loose arrangements produced inefficient service, and there was little control over the quality of officials. In the United States, for example, some post-office managers could not read. And since for most officials, getting the job in the first place was the only trick (what they did once they were there did not bear consequences for them), controlling officials' acts was difficult.

In the nineteenth century there arose a new method of organizing public administration, one that social scientists have come to call "bureaucracy."[3] Under a system of bureaucracy:

1. Members of the public administration are appointed and promoted on the basis of their qualifications for the job they are to do.
2. Special requirements of training or experience are set for the position.
3. Administrative procedures are standardized, so that relatively little is left to individual officials' biases or passions.
4. Clear lines of command are established, in which an order from a high official goes to a lower official, who then passes the order on to the next level, and so on until it reaches the point of operation. This arrangement is called a *hierarchical command structure*.
5. Finally, public administrators are shielded from day-to-day political pressure, usually with a system of tenure.

This new, cleaner, and more efficient way of organizing the public administration was first used in appointments for procurement officers with the French and Prussian armies in the eighteenth and early nineteenth centuries. It demonstrated its usefulness in this area and spread rapidly. In the United States, the coming of the bureaucratic mode was embodied in the move for civil service reform at the turn of the century, which eventually took most administrative positions out of party control and based them on competitive civil service exams. By the time of World War II, some form or another of bureaucracy was the usual method of organizing public administration throughout Europe and North America. And as new states attained their independence in the Third World, they also generally adopted some form of bureaucracy. It is today the usual mode of administrative organization throughout the world, although there are many variations on its general themes.

---

[3]For the definitive statement, see Max Weber, "Bureaucracy," in H. H. Gerth and C. Wright Mills, *From Max Weber* (New York: Oxford University Press, 1958), pp. 196–244.

BUREAUCRACY VS. FLEXIBILITY

As noted above, there is no ideal way to organize administration. Of the various things that may be desirable in public administration, bureaucracy is particularly strong on the accurate translation of leaders' decisions and on preventing arbitrary behavior. Believe it or not, it is also rather efficient. (Bureaucracy has to some extent been identified in the public mind as wasteful because the public has high expectations for how cheaply one might expect administration to be done. Compared with private businesses, the administrative costs of public agencies are usually not all that far out of line.)

However, the very standardization and clarity of command that accomplish these good things mean that bureaucracy cannot very well provide for local flexibility. Also, though the requirements for training and for decisions based on merit generally produce well-qualified officials, the system of standardization does not encourage independent-mindedness on their parts, so bureaucracy does not especially tend to produce helpful expert advice to political leaders. Administrators under most versions of bureaucracy tend to hold their advice until it is asked for.

This means that the bureaucratic form of organization will fit some sorts of administrative needs better than others. Where standardization and obedience are especially important, bureaucratic organization fits well. Where independent and flexible judgment are especially important, it does not. Military service is one area in which standardization and obedience are important, because if a general is conducting a wheeling motion on a battlefield, everything could be lost if one battalion wheeled in the wrong direction. The bureaucratic model fits military operations well, and indeed the military—with their clean lines of command and their tendency to "do things by the book"—exemplify the bureaucratic model. On the other hand, public enterprises in which obedience is less important and individuality is more so are not as well served by bureaucratic organization. The university or college is such a place—the object here is to put a gifted individual in the lab or in front of a class and let that person do creative things.

It follows that bureaucracy is a better form of organization for some areas of the public administration than for others, depending on the relative needs for smooth obedience and for individualistic judgment. To a considerable extent, these differences are reflected in the organization of various agencies; almost universally the armed forces are the most bureaucratically organized agencies in any state's public administration, and universities tend to be rather decentralized.

However, there is generally a tendency toward bureaucracy, with most operations being organized more bureaucratically than would really be necessary. Most public administrators appear to be tilted toward standardization and away from individual initiative, a natural result of the human desire for safety and security. An official working within standardized procedures, unlike one who is supposed to make independent choices, cannot be blamed for the results. Procedures shelter bureaucracies, so bureaucracies foster procedures. Impressionistic evidence for this, at least, is offered by the fact that there are apparently no armed forces in the world set up in anything but a pretty straightforward bureaucratic mode, whereas universities in many places are hemmed in by tight rules.[4]

THE PROBLEM OF PROTECTED INCOMPETENCE

Another common problem of bureaucratic organization stems from a combination of two factors: (1) the difficulty in *public* administration, as compared with private business, of evaluating how well a person has performed a job, and (2) the requirement in a bureaucracy that administrators be shielded from direct political pressure, usually by a system of tenure.

In private business, a standard yardstick is available to evaluate how well a person has done in a job. If profits have gone up in that person's sector, if sales have been high, or whatever—if the person has made money for the company—then the job has been done well. But how do we evaluate the performance of public administrators? There is no notion of "profit" in the operations of a public school, or of the army, or of a state's department of highways. A professor is supposed to teach well, but there is no dollar figure that can tell us *how* well the professor has taught. A highway superintendent is supposed to maintain the roads well, but there is no dollar figure that can tell us how well they have been maintained.

Combine this with the fact that political intervention against members of the bureaucracy is difficult and unlikely, and you have a situation in which incompetent administrators will rarely be removed from their positions. Few unambiguous standards of their performance are available, and—in the absence of clear-cut evidence—superiors will be reluctant to take action for fear that they will be accused of favoritism or political interference.

As a result, although bureaucracies do not particularly attract incompetent people—and although, by their entrance requirements, they have some success at selecting unusually competent people—those incompetents who do get in are less likely to be removed than they would be in private businesses.

ADJUSTMENTS TO BUREAUCRACY

Though "bureaucracy" is only one way to organize the public administration, it is the dominant mode of organization across the world, as we have seen. Indeed, it is so dominant that the word "bureaucracy" has become almost a synonym for public administration, in much the way that "Kleenex" has come to be synonymous with facial tissues or "Xerox" with photocopies.

As a term loosely signifying public administration, "bureaucracy" has a number of unpleasant connotations. "Bureaucrats" are thought to be lazy, ar-

---

[4]For example, in some European universities there are official limits on the number of pages that students may be required to read. In Norway in 1983, the limit for a fifteen-week political science course was 600 pages.

rogant, inflexible, shortsighted—and too numerous. Partly this derives from the fact that it is impossible to construct an ultimate, best form of organization for the public administration; as we have seen, the various characteristics we would wish to see in a good public administration are to some extent mutually contradictory. Partly, it derives from real weaknesses of "bureaucracy." In various parts of the world, adjustments have evolved or have been invented that can soften bureaucracy when it is excessively "bureaucratic." Some of these are the office of *ombudsman*, provisions for opening government files for inspection, informal interference in the bureaucracy by political leaders, corruption, and—in general—pressure from public opinion.

1. *The office of ombudsman* is a Swedish invention. An ombudsman is a government official whose primary duty is to seek out citizens' complaints of abuse by public administrators and to negotiate changes in the offending practices. The ombudsman idea has been picked up and copied in many other countries. In the United States, it has not been used at the national level; but Hawaii, Florida, and other states have established ombudsman offices. Many nongovernmental institutions have also found it an attractive idea. Universities have established ombudsman offices for their students or faculty, newspapers have set up a "readers'" ombudsman, and so on.

2. *Freedom of information* laws have been passed in many countries, and the United States has been a pioneer in this direction. Under such laws, individuals are guaranteed the right to examine most kinds of "internal" governmental documents, including dossiers that may have been gathered on them personally. The intent of the laws is to allow citizens to find out generally what procedures administrators are following in processes that are of interest to them; more specifically, it allows citizens to check and correct any information the government has gathered about them.

3. *"Interference" in administration by political leaders* may act as a safety valve to help correct abuses. You will recall that, in the bureaucratic mode of organization, administrators are shielded from much direct intervention by political leaders. This was intended to avoid the excesses of a spoils system.

However, it does not compromise the bureaucratic model greatly if political leaders take advantage of their potential power over administrative budgets to seize bureaucrats' attention and get them to deal with a constituent's problem. In the United States, in particular, this has become a major part of the job of a member of Congress and has developed into an important correction of bureaucratic inflexibility. It is well understood that if you are having trouble getting a passport or your social security check has been held up, you should call your member of Congress for help. In 1976, for instance, members of the U.S. Congress each handled an average of 11,954 personal problems for constituents, and the caseload has grown a good deal since then.[5]

4. *Corruption* is a hard thing to argue for. When administrative officials accept bribes for favors and services rendered, this demoralizes people and injures the legitimacy of the whole operation. Bribery ranges from small pota-

[5]U.S. Congress, House, Commission on Administrative Review, *Final Report*, House Document 95-272, 95th Cong., 1st sess., 1977, vol. 2.

toes—a small bribe to fix a traffic ticket or expedite a governmental inspection—up to the sort of bribe on which a governmental minister can get rich. In many states, especially those that are less developed politically, bribery is the normal way of doing business with administrators.

Although corruption is, on the face of it, a bad thing, it does provide adjustments of a sort to the inflexibility of a bureaucratic administration. Like any market mechanism for choice, it allows some discrimination on the basis of how intensely various people want a thing, rather than treating everyone— fairly, but therefore inflexibly—exactly alike. As in any market mechanism, intensities of preference will then be taken into account.

For example, assume that two people are waiting at the customs office and things are going slowly. One of the two is in no rush, but the other has been summoned to the bed of a dying father. In desperation, the one who is in a hurry pays a large bribe to the customs inspector and is whisked through the line. The person who was in less of a hurry prefers to save the money and is delayed. This is a less than ideal solution, but at least the bureaucracy *did* respond flexibly to the differing needs of the two people.

There are many drawbacks to using corruption as a corrective for bureaucracy. For one thing, apart from providing harmless adjustments of the sort described above, corruption can also lead to actions that are directly injurious to the state's policies. It is one thing for a person rushing to the bedside of a dying relative to use bribery, but it is quite another for counterfeiters, dope smugglers, and assassins to do so. Also, as is true of all market mechanisms for choice, it is money that talks. A poor person whose need was objectively greater would receive less flexible treatment than the person who was well off and could afford to pay the bribe.

Still, corruption does function to add flexibility to a bureaucratic system, and this may sometimes be a positive thing.

5. *Pressure from public opinion* can help to correct bureaucratic sluggishness and abuse. Administrators are ultimately dependent on political processes for their offices' budgets, so they must be attentive to public opinion. Also, since they are human, they want to be liked and admired for what they do. Public criticism hurts them and will usually lead to improvements where there have been problems. Agricultural agencies, welfare services, research agencies, the postal service—all are worried by stories in the press about any shortcomings in their operations and all keep in reasonably close touch with their "clients," the groups most affected by their policies.

Perhaps the best evidence that public opinion serves as an important corrective to bureaucracy may be found by looking at an agency that is *not* under much direct pressure from public opinion. In democracies all over the world, immigration services are relatively free from pressures of public opinion because their "client group"—those who wish to enter the country as immigrants—cannot vote in elections and usually lack powerful friends. It is almost universally true that these offices are less responsive to their clients and more inclined to make arbitrary judgments than are other government agencies.

• *Item:* The United States Immigration Service several years ago tried to save about $20 million by setting a rule that no visas could ever be renewed under any circumstances. They would have saved the money by eliminating the positions of clerks who at that time handled applications for renewal. This decision ignored several important things: The hundreds of millions of dollars that would now not have been spent in the United States by visitors who were unable to prolong their stay, the human hardship and ill will that would have resulted, and the fact that there would still have had to be some provision for emergency cases, such as heart attacks and appendectomies on the day of departure. The Immigration Service was eventually talked out of it, as it was a silly idea.

- *Item:* Within the last several years, a German visiting the United States on a valid visa was turned back at the Minneapolis airport and forced to return home because he had a pornographic homosexual magazine in his suitcase.
- *Item:* When the Norwegian government in 1980 decided to reduce the number of work permits they would grant to foreigners by 50 percent, the Norwegian Immigration Service also reduced the staff to deal with those requests by 50 percent. They forgot that though they were going to say yes only half as often, just as many people would be *asking* as before. It was not long before the office had such a backlog that applicants were required to wait nine months to a year for an answer.
- *Item:* In the late 1970s, until they were dissuaded by embarrassing publicity, the British Immigration Service required a virginity test of women who were applying for permission to immigrate to Britain.

SOCIAL REPRESENTATIVENESS OF PUBLIC ADMINISTRATION

Because members of the public administration are not under very direct political control and adjustments such as those described above can go only so far, there has been recurrent concern over how socially representative top bureaucratic decision makers are; that is, there has been a concern that they should not be too different from the population as a whole in such things as class background, race, or gender. There has been some controversy over this. On the one hand, advocates of "representative bureaucracy" urge that if administrators are not politically responsible, we should at least do all we can to assure that they will look at things in the same ways that the common people

Table 14–1   Backgrounds of European and American Senior Civil Servants

	Britain	*Germany*	*Italy*	*Sweden*	*U.S.A.*
Social class origin (percent)					
Upper	35	42	42	42	47
Middle	47	50	49	43	35
Working	18	8	9	15	18
Sex (percent)					
Female	2	1	0	3	2
Male	98	99	100	97	98

SOURCE: Robert D. Putnam, "The Political Attitudes of Senior Civil Servants in Britain, Germany, and Italy," in Mattei Dogan, ed., *The Mandarins of Western Europe* (New York: Wiley, 1975).

would. On the other hand, skeptics have responded that we should not want "common people" in positions of uncommon importance and that we should not expect top public administrators to be any more socially representative than the leaders of corporations, universities, or other large institutions.[6]

Whatever our feelings on this, certainly many governments have made efforts to assure that top public administrators will be reasonably representative. The United States in the 1970s and 1980s has tried by affirmative action programs to increase numbers of minority and women officials. Decades earlier, after World War II, many European countries (France, for example) attempted to increase the proportion of their officials who were from the working class. They did this by changing their entrance procedures and providing for internal promotions from less important administrative posts.

Generally speaking, the effectiveness of such attempts is limited. As Table 14–1 shows, the sex and class backgrounds of senior administrative officials are remarkably similar across a fairly varied set of countries. These figures are based on a study conducted in 1970, however, so that effects of any recent efforts to bring more women in at this level would not show up here; however, it may well be that the same figures today would show little change.

CONCLUSION

The members of the public administration pose a dilemma to a state's political leaders. They are too numerous and individually too minor to control very effectively, yet collectively they have a major impact on policies. We have reviewed in this chapter various ways by which the state may address its dilemma—establishment of the bureaucratic model, adjustments to the bureaucratic model, attempts to achieve "representative bureaucracy"—but none of these can be fully successful. This is a problem of politics in which "half a loaf" may truly be the best one can hope for.

EXAMPLE: THE FRENCH BUREAUCRACY

The "ordinary" bureaucracies of industrialized states do not vary greatly from one country to another. Mail carriers, teachers, agricultural extension agents, and so on are organized and do their jobs in fairly similar ways around the industrialized world. Where there is considerable variation is in how the higher civil service—the managers, diplomats, specialists, and so on—are organized and work. In this

---

[6]See discussions in Samuel Krislov, *Representative Bureaucracy*, Englewood Cliffs, N.J.: Prentice-Hall, 1974; and Kenneth John Meier, "Representative Bureaucracy: An Empirical Analysis," *American Political Science Review* 69 (June 1975): 526–542.

realm the French are quite distinctive; theirs is arguably the best civil service in the world.

In this section we shall address almost solely the higher civil service. First, however, it should be noted that one thing *is* unusual about the "ordinary" French civil service: It is relatively small. In 1980 there were only approximately 2.5 million full-time local and national civil servants in France outside of the military. This compares, for example, with 3.2 million in Great Britain.[7]

The higher civil service of France consists of about four to six thousand highly trained persons. Most of these work within one of the ministries (defense, health, etc.) but at any given time over a thousand of them are working in more independent ways, either as staff advisers to the premier or ministers or in relatively autonomous administrative bodies, which I shall describe below. Further, a certain number of them are at any time on loan to businesses, universities, or local government.

One of the things that distinguishes the French higher civil service is the training and ability of its members, which leads also to a high degree of self-confidence and pride. There are two main routes of entry into the higher civil service. If one wishes to be a specialist, such as a scientist or statistician, one normally receives a university education from one of the "great" technical schools, such as the Polytechnic or the School of Agronomy, followed by more specialized training at an institution such as the School of Mines or School of Statistics and Economic Administration. If one wishes to be a generalist, after university one enters the famous National School of Administration (the ENA). One of the most difficult schools in the world to enter, the ENA gives its graduates a general training in administration and in the social sciences. Whether from one of the "great schools" or the ENA, higher civil servants in France are noted for their verbal skill and for a tendency to abstraction and mathematical reasoning. They are pragmatic rather than ideological and usually emphasize economics over politics.

The second thing that sets French higher civil servants apart is the tradition of "detached service," whereby they may leave the national civil service for periods of time either on personal leave or on loan by the national government to work in business, local government, or the universities or to hold elective office. In the 1970s, for example, about one-fourth of the members of the parliament were civil servants on leave from their administrative posts, and as of 1984 there were twenty-five national civil servants on loan to the city of Paris.

Under these circumstances, the French have developed a more politicized civil service than that of most countries, one that lives on the frontier between "politics" and administration. When François Mitterand became president in 1981, for instance, about four hundred high administrators were replaced with others who would be more compatible with the new regime, although Mitterand took pains to demonstrate that this was not done solely on the basis

[7]Douglas E. Ashford, *Policy and Politics in France* (Philadelphia: Temple University Press, 1982), p. 69.

of party connections. This politicization appears to have added vigor to the higher civil service and has allowed French civil servants to lead aggressively in the development of such new political thrusts as the campaign for a tunnel under the English Channel, the adoption of the value-added tax, and the formation of the Common Market.

It was stated above that the French higher civil service is "arguably" the best in the world. The other side of the "argument" is raised by those who see the civil service as too insulated from the rest of the population, too haughty, and overly given to technical fixes.

> Instead of a homogenous administration equally open to everyone, one sees established an aristocracy of a few thousand young men produced through privileged channels; the isolation of their education easily persuades them that they are destined to retain among themselves (and for themselves) the administration of the state, and above all its best jobs. Less and less are they touched by doubts; the assurance of their elders and their own success convinces them that it is enough to advance confidently under cover of their technique to make obstacles disappear. The sharing of a certain exoticism of language or of modern administrative techniques or of economics; the sense of making up a kind of network between the bosses and dauphins of the great public and private businesses; the exhilaration, still hardly acknowledged, of feeling in their hands such means of action, and such docile underlings; all these make up the psychology of a senior civil servant, young and ardent, certainly devoted to what he considers the public good, but more inclined to define it himself, or to let it be defined by the boss, than to listen on this subject to the aspirations of the country.[8]

EXAMPLE: THE SAUDI ARABIAN BUREAUCRACY

A severe problem facing most Third World states is that their bureaucracies are newly established and often had to be assembled hurriedly as the state was formed. Technical expertise is scarce, and the bureaucracies have also not had time to build up an esprit de corps, with high expectations for performance, such as that seen in France, for example. As a result, Third World states seem to be especially burdened with sluggish, cautious, inefficient administration.

The bureaucracy of Saudi Arabia illustrates these problems. Saudi Arabia is not a poor country, so it is spared the problems of poverty that many other Third World states endure. Like most of the Third World, however, the Saudi government and public administration were established in their present form only in the last few decades; before that, the Saudis had had little experience in modern public administration.

---

[8]"Le Regime des 'Jeunes Messieurs,'" *Courrier de la Republique*, November 1965, quoted in Anthony Sampson, *The New Europeans* (London: Hodder and Stoughton, 1968), p. 345.

A study of the values and attitudes of middle-range Saudi bureaucrats reveals a group of people who are cautious, wedded to routine, and not very ambitious.[9] Table 14–2 presents the bureaucrats' answers to several questions.

Answers to other questions were consistent with the four given in the table. For instance, 78 percent of the bureaucrats would prefer a low-paying job with few risks to a high-paying job with high risks. There is, of course, no "typical" Third World state. Saudi society is a conservative one, in which traditional values are strongly enforced. This may help to explain the bureaucrats' caution about social change, but it should not have much to do with their caution in dealings with their superiors, and in this the Saudi bureaucrats seem to be similar to those in most of the Third World. This caution, of course, may not be wholly a bad thing. It fits the standard bureaucratic model and should ensure the faithful transmission of orders. However, we saw earlier in this chapter that an emphasis on any one virtue in administration is purchased at the cost of other virtues. In this case, flexibility and innovation are lost—virtues that are important to Third World states which, like Saudi Arabia, are undergoing great social and economic change.

EXAMPLE: BATTLING THE BUREAUCRACY IN BRAZIL[10]

Wherever modern government structures are built on an already highly developed legal and administrative system, bureaucracies are bound to multiply. Brazil is no exception. What is exceptional is the degree to which Brazilians have managed to circumvent the more rigid and obstructive bureaucratic rules. In addition, the government has recently had some success in attacking the rules themselves.

Brazilians have described their federal administrative system as excessively centralized, formal, and distrustful of the public. This view dates back at least to the temporary transfer to Brazil of the Portuguese kingdom and its centralized administration in 1808, and perhaps even further, to 1549, when the first governor-general arrived with a framework of laws and regulations even before there were people to conform to them. The formalism embodied the prejudice that documents are more important than facts. The distrust showed in the controls that required endless lists of certificates, attestations, licenses, and other documents. Not many years ago the case was reported of an export license that required 1,470 separate legal actions and involved thirteen government ministries and fifty agencies.

[9]Saud al Nimir and Monte Palmer, "Bureaucracy and Development in Saudi Arabia: A Behavioral Analysis," *Public Administration and Development 2* (April–June 1982): 93–104.

[10]World Bank, *World Development Report 1987* (Oxford, England: Oxford University Press, 1987), p. 73.

14–2   Attitudes of Saudi Bureaucrats

	Strongly Agree (percent)	Agree (percent)	Disagree (percent)	Strongly disagree (percent)	Number Answering Question
It is best to change or cancel programs that cause social conflict.	25	59	14	2	(282)
Social change should not be instituted at the expense of traditional values.	37	53	8	2	(287)
It is best to consult with one's superior before making a decision.	26	57	15	1	(288)
In making decisions, no one should violate rules and regulations.	21	55	21	2	(286)

SOURCE: Saud al Nimir and Monte Palmer, "Bureaucracy and Development in Saudi Arabia: A Behavioral Analysis," *Public Administration and Development* 2 (April–June 1982): 93–104.

The *jeito* was employed to overcome such difficulties. This Portuguese term, corresponding roughly to "knack," "way," or "fix" in English, refers to the varied ways that Brazilians, like people in other countries, get around the maze of regulations and legal requirements. The jeito principle has been remarkably effective. It relies significantly on the *despachante* (roughly, an expeditor), who has counterparts in many countries but has been especially active in Brazil, where the lubrication of sticky administrative processes has been essential for social mobility and rapid economic development.

The despachante is an intermediary who, in return for a commission or fee, purchases and fills out the multiplicity of legal forms, delivers them to the proper persons, and extracts the needed permission or document. The system developed when the simplest transactions, such as obtaining a marriage license or identity card, could take ages or days or hours, depending on whether one used despachantes and how much they were paid. The despachantes are thriving, specialized professionals and have their own union and competitive examinations. Some specialize in police work, naturalizations, auto licenses, marriages, or "legalization of real estate." The despachantes who arrange imports and exports have long enjoyed a legal monopoly. Each typically has several employees, and almost all sizable businesses maintain their own despachantes.

Brazil's rapid economic growth and social evolution demonstrate that a complex bureaucracy need not be a barrier to development. The costs are nevertheless substantial. Moreover, such resourceful adaptations of the jeito may have been too effective and undermined attempts to reform public administration.

The most recent efforts to reform the system, rather than live with it, began in 1979. A National Debureaucratization Program was designed to simplify administrative procedures and, more broadly, to reverse what was seen as the relentless trend toward growth in government, excessive centralization, and abundant regulation.

The results in 1979–84 were impressive. On the basis of a citizens' project (which surveyed all the points of contact of individuals, throughout their lives, with bureaucratic requirements) it was possible to eliminate, or simplify, a long list of documents and procedures ranging from notarization requirements and driver's licenses to passport extensions, university enrollment processes, and income tax returns. Evidence of residence, economic dependence, and so on, could be established with simply a written statement by the interested party rather than legal certificates and third-party attestation. Thus a "presumption of truth" displaced the "rule of distrust." Other legal procedures were simplified. In all, more than 600 million documents a year were removed from circulation. The savings have been estimated at close to $3 billion a year, equivalent to about 1.5 percent of Brazil's GDP.

In the economic field the main achievements were to simplify rural credit procedures, to change commercial registration procedures so that forming a company could take three days rather than three to six months, and to bring relief from bureaucracy to 1.5 million small enterprises. For the time being, however, the program has left many areas of regulation untouched, including some that are important to industrialization and trade.

It is significant that, although a minister of debureaucratization was appointed, no new government department was formed. The program was implemented by an executive secretary and just twelve assistants. At the very least—and on a limited front—some progress has been made in simplifying the rules and changing the relationship between citizens and civil servants.

FURTHER READING

Aberbach, Joel D., Putnam, Robert D., and Rockman, Bert A. *Bureaucrats and Politicians in Western Democracies*. Cambridge, Mass.: Harvard University Press, 1981.

Allison, Graham T. *Essence of Decision: Explaining the Cuban Missile Crisis*. Boston: Little, Brown, 1971.

"Bureaucracy," in the *International Encyclopedia of the Social Sciences*.

Crozier, Michel. *The Bureaucratic Phenomenon*. Chicago: University of Chicago Press, 1963.

Dogan, Mattei, ed. *The Mandarins of Western Europe: The Political Role of Top Civil Servants*. New York: Wiley, 1975.

Gruber, Judith E. *Controlling Bureaucracies*. Berkeley: University of California Press, 1987.

Heidenheimer, Arnold J., ed. *Political Corruption*. New York: Holt, Rinehart and Winston, 1970.

Hood, Christopher C. *The Limits of Administration*. New York: Wiley, 1976.

Kaufman, Herbert. *Red Tape: Its Origins, Uses, and Abuses*. Washington, D.C.: Brookings, 1977.

LaPalombara, Joseph, ed. *Bureaucracy and Political Development*. Princeton, N.J.: Princeton University Press, 1963.

Ostrom, Vincent. *The Intellectual Crisis in American Public Administration*. University, Ala.: University of Alabama Press, 1973.

Riggs, Fred. *Administration in Developing Countries*. Boston: Houghton Mifflin, 1964.

Smith, Bruce L. R., ed. *The Higher Civil Service in Europe and Canada: Lessons for the United States*. Washington, D.C.: Brookings, 1984.

Suleiman, Ezra N. *Politics, Power, and Bureaucracy in France*. Princeton, N.J.: Princeton University Press, 1974.

Part IV

INTERNATIONAL POLITICS

Chapter 15

Politics Among States

In the preceding chapters, we have looked at the manner in which politics—the use of power to make collective choices for a group of people—is carried on within states. But states also carry on politics *among* themselves. For instance, they sign trade agreements setting up special arrangements for the exchange of goods between firms in two or more countries. Or a number of states may agree to coordinate their military activities, as in the NATO and Warsaw Pact alliances. Regular exchanges of scientific information are set up among states. Agreements are drawn up committing all those who sign to such things as a promise not to test nuclear weapons in the open air. Treaties are drawn up to protect wildlife that migrates across state borders. Wars are fought, and are settled. All these are examples of politics among states rather than within any one state. This sort of politics is commonly called "international politics."

THE EVOLUTION OF THE INTERNATIONAL SYSTEM SINCE WORLD WAR II

Before analyzing international politics abstractly, it will be useful to review the development of the international system since World War II.

From the seventeenth century until the twentieth, most of the world's wealth and military power were concentrated in Europe, and various European states used that power to subjugate large populations around the world and form them into colonial empires. By the early twentieth century, European dominance was already weakening, especially because of the increasing power of the United States. The Europeans then hastened their slide from power by squandering their wealth and slaughtering their youth in World Wars I and II. Although other powers such as the United States and Japan were eventually involved in these wars and they *have* been called "world wars," almost all of the fighting and destruction centered in Europe. The European states emerged from World War II in 1945 exhausted, with only enough strength left to reconstruct themselves internally.

Two major changes in international politics resulted from this exhaustion of Europe: (1) two new superpowers—the Soviet Union and the United States—arose to fill the power vacuum and (2) the European states' empires threw off European rule, since the Europeans no longer had the power to hold them in subjugation.

The rise of the Soviet Union and the United States to dominate world politics created quite a different kind of system than what had gone before. When

(AUTH, ©1989 Philadelphia Inquirer. Reprinted with permission of Universal Press Syndicate. All rights reserved)

Europe dominated world politics, a number of substantial powers were involved in the system because Europe itself was so fragmented. Britain, France, Germany, Italy, and to some extent the Soviet Union, Japan, and the United States could figure in alliances. Many varying combinations of states in alliance were possible, and patterns of alliance shifted as states jockeyed for position. In the world after 1945, however, and especially from 1945 to about 1960, the system of politics consisted simply of a bipolar rivalry between the United States and the Soviet Union.

The two superpowers had been allies in the war against Hitler and initially set out into their domination of the world with pledges to cooperate in building a new, peaceful political order. However, they differed widely in political philosophy, and they had conflicting political and economic goals. The Soviet Union, both for economic advantage and in order to insulate itself militarily and politically from west European states such as Germany and France (which had frequently attacked it earlier in the century), used its dominating military force in the region to bring most of eastern Europe under its control. By 1946, Winston Churchill had coined the phrase "iron curtain" in his famous speech at Westminster College, Missouri:

> From Stettin in the Baltic to Trieste in the Adriatic, an iron curtain has descended across the continent. Behind that line lie all the capitals of the ancient states of Central and Eastern Europe. Warsaw, Berlin, Prague, Vienna, Budapest, Belgrade,

Dependency Theory

Over half the states in the world today were colonies of other states forty years ago. An important question for the study of international politics is: How do these new states fit into the international system?

"Dependency theory," which was developed largely in the 1970s, offers insights both into this question and into the problems of economic development in the Third World that were discussed in Chapter 4. According to dependency theory, though *states* in the Third World are formally independent, the economies of these states are dependent on the industrialized economies; as a result, the states do not have true political freedom. Many Third World states depend heavily on exporting a single product extracted in fairly simple ways from the earth, such as coffee, bananas, copper, or tin. This makes these states vulnerable to even slight disturbances in international markets and leaves them in a situation of "dependency" on the industrialized economies. Even Third World states that have accomplished considerable industrialization depend on loans and technology from the industrialized states and are not free to be very adventurous politically.

In its emphasis on the role that economic forces play in determining politics and on the subjugation of weaker parts of the world to industrialized capital, dependency theory is obviously influenced by Marxist theory. It presents quite a different picture of the world from what we see on the map, with many brightly colored independent states varying the colors of Latin America, Africa, and Asia. Most of these states are seen in dependency theory as still not having achieved true independence of their old colonial powers. The international system, for practical purposes, consists of far fewer than the 163 independent actors the map suggests.

A good source on dependency theory is J. Samuel Valenzuela and Arturo Valenzuela, "Modernization and Dependency." *Comparative Politics* 10 (July 1978): 535–557.

Bucharest and Sofia, all these famous cities and populations around them lie in what I must call the Soviet sphere, and all are subject in one form or another not only to Soviet influence but to a very high and, in many cases, increasing measure of control from Moscow.[1]

In 1947 President Harry S Truman announced that the United States was sending economic aid to the embattled anticommunist government of Greece, and the Cold War was joined.

The period of rivalry between the Soviet Union and the United States from 1945 on into the 1960s (and at frequent periods since the 1960s) is called the "Cold War" because, while it has at times involved intense animosity, it has never developed into full-scale "hot" warfare. Various skirmishes have been

---

[1]Randolph S. Churchill, ed., *The Sinews of Peace: Post-War Speeches by Winston S. Churchill* (London: Cassell, 1948), p. 100.

The war and famine in Ethiopia caused this Eritrean mother and child to flee to an intensive feeding clinic in the Sudan.
(Sarah Putnam/The Picture Cube)

fought—the Soviet blockade of West Berlin in 1948, war between the United States and the Soviet client state of North Korea in 1950—but there has never been direct fighting between the two superpowers. There is a clear reason for this. Not only was the international system turned into a bipolar system after 1945 but the two superpowers of that system were armed with a new kind of weapon that made a war between them essentially unwinnable. Nuclear weapons are so destructive that, in an all-out nuclear war, either combatant would be able to ruin the other.[2] As a result, the bipolar system that followed World War II has been marked by a frustrated rivalry in which the two superpowers have chewed on their animosity toward each other but have not been able to do much about it.

---

[2] A new literature has begun to question whether nuclear weapons really prevent war. This literature points out that in the 1920s many people thought that the existence of poison gas, in combination with the development of modern air forces, had made all-out war unwinnable. Any power, even if it were going down in defeat, could launch such deathly attacks with gas canisters that the winner of the war would be destroyed. Therefore, it was agreed, no one would dare to wage war against a power that had poison gas weapons. As it turned out, full-scale war was waged in World War II, but without gas. All the participating powers had chemical weapons, but none ever used them for fear of retaliation in kind. The revisionist literature argues that all-out conventional warfare might similarly occur today without the use of nuclear weapons. See, for example, John Ellis van Courtland Moon, "Chemical Weapons and Deterrence: The World War II Experience," *International Security* 8 (Spring 1984): 3–35.

The other main result of Europe's exhaustion after World War II was the breakup of the old colonial empires. Fully 91 of today's 163 states were colonies of European states at the outbreak of World War II. In other words, there are more than twice as many states in the world now as there were in 1941. These new states find sympathy and support from some of the older states—such as China, Egypt, and the states of Latin America—which, although they were independent before World War II, find that they share a common set of problems with the newer states. Together, these new and older states make up the Third World.

The growth in numbers and importance of the Third World states has changed the international system markedly. The Third World commands many of the world's natural resources and comprises about three-fourths of its population. However, it does not command anything close to a proportional share of wealth or military power. Most of the states of the Third World are individually weak, although some, like India, China, and Brazil, have developed into moderately important powers. However, as a group they account for so much of the world that they cannot be ignored. Many Third World states, as they grow in wealth and military ability, appear to have a great potential as future powers. The United States, the Soviet Union, and the states of western and eastern Europe all court Third World states as important markets for the goods they produce and as important powers for the future.

Through the 1960s, '70s and '80s, the Soviet-American bipolarity came to dominate the world system less than it had in the 1940s, '50s and early '60s. The Cold War is still with us and flares up (or should we say "chills down"?) intermittently, but it does not dominate the international scene as fully as it once did. In part, this has been due to the rise to at least modest power of Third World states for whom the Cold War is less important. Examples are India and Brazil and especially the OPEC association of oil-producing states. In part, too, it has been caused by the spread of nuclear weapons. Through the early 1960s, only the United States, the Soviet Union, and Britain had nuclear weapons. Today China, India, and France have acquired them, and numerous other states are rumored to have them or to be developing them.

Finally, what had earlier been rather tight blocs of East and West have loosened considerably. China broke with Soviet leadership in the late 1950s, distracting the Soviet Union from its confrontation with the West. (Today there are approximately as many Soviet troops stationed on the Soviet border with China as on Soviet borders with Europe.) And various east European states, such as Hungary, Romania, and Poland, have experimented to see how far they could press the Soviet Union in allowing them independent action. At the same time, the western European states have become less dependent on the United States. With France under President de Gaulle leading the way, they have broken out into more independent foreign policies.

Today the world is dominated by two main lines of conflict—the Cold War animosity between the Soviet bloc and the bloc led by the United States; and the "north-south" tension between the Third World and the industrialized states of both blocs. The international political system is becoming more fluid and less rigidly bipolar than it once was. Overall, the world has progressed economically in many ways; people in most parts of the world are better off than they were twenty years ago. But the ill-understood and unmanageable threat of nuclear weaponry still looms over everyone.

INTERNATIONAL POLITICS

Now let us look more abstractly at international politics. We will first consider a few ways in which politics *among* states differs from politics *within* a state, the sort of politics with which we have been concerned so far in this book. It will be necessary, in doing this, to add one new concept, the "fiduciary political role." After we have looked at this question we will conclude by examining the nature of power in international politics and the possibility that the whole system of states operates in some way to balance the distribution of power.

To begin then, how is international politics like that which we have been looking at so far in this book, and how is it different? In its main outlines, politics among states is a good deal like politics within states. The same general sorts of policy questions are addressed in both—regulation of potentially harmful behavior, aid programs for the weak, guarantees of standard weights and measures, and so on. And just like politics within states, politics among states is marked both by the use of force and by appeals to mutual self-interest, that is, by power and choice. Political decisions—decisions on behalf of groups of people—are reached in both kinds of politics. But in important ways international politics differs from politics within a state. *The most important difference is that there is no single central authority to provide ultimate settlement of a dispute among states. Also, political figures are more likely to follow overtly selfish* (selfish on behalf of their states' interests) *strategies in politics among states. And finally, political interchange does not proceed as easily in politics among states as it does in politics within a state.* Let us look at each of these points.

THE ABSENCE OF CENTRAL AUTHORITY

In politics as it is carried on within a state, the various antagonists are all subject to a central authority that has enough power to settle a question firmly. If environmentalists square off in conflict with a mining company, both sides know that ultimately their dispute will be resolved by some higher authority that has the power to make them accept that decision, even if they do not agree with it. In the United States, that authority would be Congress, the president, or perhaps the Supreme Court; in the Soviet Union, it would be the Central Committee of the Soviet Union; in Saudi Arabia, it would be the king. The point is, within any state there is a central authority, more powerful than any single political force, that can enforce decisions on any question that comes up. The only exception to this would be a state involved in a civil war, which is precisely a situation in which there is no clearly established central authority.

In politics conducted *among* states, however, there is generally no central position of authority. Therefore states that become involved in disputes must ultimately settle them themselves, whether by negotiations or through war. Other states may give helpful advice and exert pressure on the disputants, but there is no body of any sort that can impose a settlement.

The United Nations would be a potential body of authority. It is an organization of over 150 states, most of the states of the world, that accepts responsibility for many of the things a government would do within a state. That is, it is concerned to preserve law and order by preventing violent solutions to disputes (i.e., wars); it promotes health programs, education, and research; it tries to see that poorer states are helped.

But while the United Nations tries to do the *things* a government does, it cannot do them *the way a government would do them*. It has no army or police force of its own to enforce its decisions. Rather, it must depend on voluntary help from its member states. And, since few states are going to send their soldiers voluntarily into a place where they are not wanted—and thus risk war with the people on whom they are enforcing the United Nations' decision— this effectively means that the UN can almost never send in a police force unless the disputants all agree voluntarily to accept it. This still allows the UN a helpful role when the nations involved in a dispute want to bring in a neutral group to police their negotiated settlement. For instance, small United Nations forces supervised the initial disengagement of Egyptian and Israeli forces after their 1967 war. This is a far cry from the real policing power that would give the United Nations the authority to force a decision on the parties in dispute, but it has helped on occasion to reduce international violence.[3]

Another potentially ultimate authority in the system of states is the International Court of Justice, headquartered in the Netherlands. The Court is a branch of the United Nations, but the body of "international law" over which it decides goes back far beyond the United Nations, which was founded only in 1945. Since that time, forty-six cases have been tried in the Court, but again, any solution laid down by the Court sticks only if the parties of the dispute voluntarily abide by the Court's ruling. In 1984, for instance, Nicaragua brought suit against the United States for mining its harbors. When the United States refused to admit that the Court had jurisdiction, the Court could do little. Most cases that come to the Court are not of this sort but are cases in which all who are involved have agreed in advance to accept the Court's decision, whatever it may be. In these circumstances, the Court can serve as a useful tool for resolving disputes, but it cannot play the role a government would play.

Since there is no ultimate governmental authority in the world, politics

---

[3]For a good discussion of the UN's role, see Indar J. Rikhye, Michael Harbottle, and Bjørn Egge, *The Thin Blue Line: International Peacekeeping and Its Future* (New Haven, Conn.: Yale University Press, 1974).

among states is in many ways what we might expect politics within a state to be if that state had no government. States that are large and strong are able to bully smaller states, and they usually get what they want. Small states must attach themselves to stronger states, through alliances, for protection. In effect, gangs of states join together for mutual protection just as, in a governmentless state, people would form gangs.

FIDUCIARY POLITICAL ROLES AND INTERNATIONAL MORALITY

Before we consider the second special aspect of international politics, we must define a new concept—*the fiduciary role in politics*.[4] We say that someone acts in a fiduciary role if that person operates as an agent on behalf of another person's interest. A real estate agent acts in a fiduciary role on behalf of a person who wishes to sell a house, or a lawyer acts in a fiduciary role for a client.

The important thing about fiduciary roles for our purposes is that a person acting in a fiduciary role stands in a peculiar moral position. Let us assume that the fiduciary agent is personally upright and moral and that among the agent's "upright" traits is a strong sense of duty toward the person whose interests are being represented. Now let us suppose that the agent is caught in circumstances in which doing the thing that is personally moral will hurt the interests of the person who is represented. Consider the lawyer, for instance, who may sometimes need to browbeat a timid witness in order to defend a client. What is the right thing to do? We hope such a lawyer would never browbeat a timid person on his own behalf, but is it right for him to impose his personal scruples on the client's case, and thereby injure the client's interests?

This sort of situation arises frequently in modern life, because today we have given more and more of our activities over to agents. A university's board of trustees might all oppose apartheid in South Africa and refuse personally to hold stock in South African corporations, but is it right for them to impose their personal convictions in this matter on the university? A corporation president might be generous personally and wish to pay the company's workers more than the going rate, but it is the stockholders who will pay if the company does this, not the president. Is it right for the president to be generous with their money? A real estate agent might not remain silent about that tiny leak in the north gable in trying to sell her own house, but is she right to tell the truth about a client's house? In general, we recognize that a different moral situation exists when people do something on behalf of others than when they do it to help themselves. We feel differently about a prostitute who is in the trade as a normal occupation than we do about a mother who, in dire straits, prostitutes herself in order to get food for her children.

---

[4]William H. Riker presents the concept of fiduciary role in much the way it is used here in *A Theory of Political Coalitions* (New Haven, Conn.: Yale University Press, 1962), pp. 24–27.

How does all this relate to international politics? It is important to international politics because here, more than in the politics within a state, almost all decisions are made by those who see themselves as acting in fiduciary roles, on behalf of the people in the state they represent. In politics as it occurs *within* a state, political figures act to some extent as fiduciary agents (members of Congress, for instance, represent their constituents); but they are largely personal decision makers who represent no clear single interest. Leaders of states, however (and the diplomats and others who help them to construct the state's position in international politics), work on behalf of a single clear "client," the people of that state. It is well understood that a state's leader owes first duty in international politics to the state and its interests, and that anything or anyone else in the world for whom the leader feels affection must run a distant second. We expect George Bush to serve the interests of the United States, François Mitterand to serve the interests of France, Hosni Mubarak to serve the interests of Egypt.

This gives a different and colder moral tone to international politics than we find in politics within states. We expect leaders of states to be more cold blooded in international politics than they would be domestically. And what is regarded as personal virtue in domestic affairs may be seen as perverse and harmful in international politics.

Leaders of states have often been forgiven for official acts that, if done for personal gain, would have blackened their names forever. Harry Truman, for instance, killed many thousands of Japanese civilians when he ordered atomic bombs dropped on Hiroshima and Nagasaki, and Churchill launched devastating firebomb attacks on German cities. But they were judged at least partly in light of their official positions. The fact that leaders of states see themselves as filling fiduciary roles is reinforced by *nationalism*, which generally sees other peoples as being less human, less deserving of justice and mercy, than our own. This makes both the leaders and general populations of states more comfortable than they might otherwise be with their states' amoral behavior.

This case, however, should not be overstated, since the political actions of states are not *solely* based on calculations of cold rationality. Emotions play a role, and some of these may be generous. For instance, U.S. support for Great Britain in World War II was based on more than just rational considerations, though there were certainly elements of rationality involved as well. And clearly, U.S. support of Israel in recent years has involved something beyond rationality. But in its broad outlines, international politics must be distinguished from politics within states by its relatively greater tone of cold calculation.

IMPEDIMENTS TO INTERNATIONAL COMMUNICATION

A third major difference between international politics and politics within states is that communication between leaders is more cumbersome and more vulnerable to misunderstanding than is communication within any one state. Within a state, the various political leaders generally speak the same language. More importantly, they "speak the same language" in that they know each other fairly well, generally have a common fund of experiences and stories, and share the same culture.

In international politics, the people involved must often use interpreters to converse, which makes the proceedings more formal and slow and also leaves a good deal of room for misunderstanding. The problem of interpretation can lead to amusing moments, as when President Jimmy Carter's statement that he was happy to be in Poland was translated as "I lust for Poland." But the formalization of interchanges can produce more important glitches than that.

More serious yet is the frequent lack of shared assumptions and motivations, which may lead to a failure of communication between states. After World War I, U.S. diplomacy was deeply flawed by Woodrow Wilson's inability to understand the motives of its allies, Britain, France, and Italy. The leaders of Britain and France in the 1930s responded to Hitler in what was probably an inappropriately gentle way because they did not understand what he wanted to do. In the postwar period, U.S. and Soviet leaders have had continual trouble dealing with one another appropriately because they approach their mutual interchanges with such different historical and political assumptions.

POWER AND INTERNATIONAL POLITICS

Under these circumstances—with most decisions made by reciprocal bargaining or through conflict, with a relatively naked rationality operating, and with severe difficulties of communication—international politics is a rough game. More simply and directly than in politics within a state, the raw power of the participants determines the outcomes.

On what is this power based? First and foremost, a state's *military power* determines its overall power in international politics. Military power is hard to assess. Different states emphasize different kinds of arms. Czechoslovakia is landlocked, of course, so it has no navy, but it has an excellent small army and air force. How do we compare it with Great Britain, which has an excellent small navy? And how does nuclear capacity figure in our calculations? (Britain has it, Czechoslovakia does not.) Beyond this problem of comparing apples and oranges, there are imponderable questions such as toughness, morale, and battle readiness that must be considered. Israel's armed forces are much stronger than their small size would suggest, simply because of their spirit and their level of training and because they have had frequent combat experience; they are "tried and true." Finally, any armed force will fight better when defending its home soil. A smaller and weaker army may well be able to defend itself successfully against a stronger army under some circumstances.

A good example of this is the tough resistance that Argentina was able to maintain in 1982 against the more imposing and experienced British armed forces in the Falkland Islands war, even though Argentina eventually lost. An even better example is the defeat dealt to the large and powerful U.S. forces by North Vietnam.

Table 15–1 displays a few aspects of the military strength of the dozen states that are probably the strongest military powers in the world.

Population

A state with a large number of people—like India, Indonesia, or Nigeria—gains power just from the mass of its population. Nigeria is the leading state of sub-Saharan Africa primarily because it has the largest population of the region. This large population gives it a sufficient "critical mass" that it is the natural center for cultural and economic activity in the region; it thus becomes a hub of communication.

Another reason why population per se serves as a basis of power is that in wartime, even if a state does not have a powerful army, it may be quite difficult to defeat if it has a large population. Hitler discovered this when he invaded the Soviet Union in 1941. The Soviet army was initially no match for the Germans and retreated rapidly. But the Germans kept going, and going, and going and were still only part of the way into Russia. Their lines of communication stretched over a thousand miles, they were sitting in the midst of a hostile population; winter came on, and still there was a large population left in regions they had not yet occupied. From the remnant of Russia, Stalin was able to build a powerful army that eventually defeated the Germans.

Table 15–1   Twelve Major Military Powers

	Persons in Uniform	Of These, Air Force	Defense Budget (billions of dollars, 1988)	Nuclear Weapons?
China	3,200,000	500,000	$ 12.1 (est.1987)	Yes
France	456,900	104,000	31.88	Yes
E. Germany	172,000	37,000	12.75	No
W. Germany	488,700	108,700	30.31	No
Great Britain	316,700	93,500	33.76	Yes
India	1,362,000	115,000	9.89	Yes
Israel	141,000	28,000	5.71	Rumored
Italy	386,000	73,000	13.85	No
Japan	245,000	57,000	29.63	No
Poland	406,000	92,000	4.36	No
U.S.A.	2,163,200	603,600	289.00	Yes
U.S.S.R.	5,096,000	444,000	*	Yes

*Extremely difficult to estimate

SOURCE: International Institute for Strategic Studies, *The Military Balance, 1988–1989* (London: International Institute for Strategic Studies, 1988)

Of course, population alone will not make a state strong. In the nineteenth century, China, the largest state in the world, was dominated easily by the smaller European powers. Today the two largest states in the world, India and China, are still only intermediate powers.

Economic Power

Even if it is not militarily powerful, a state may figure importantly in international politics if it controls something of economic importance. Saudi Arabia has only a small military force, for instance, but it has often been able to get other states to do what it wishes because they depend on it for their oil imports. West Germany's army is large and effective, but it is primarily oriented to defense against the Soviet bloc and so cannot realistically be used by West Germany as a threat to make other states do what it wishes. Greater leverage for West Germany comes from the fact that, for the last decade, it has had the strongest, most stable economy in western Europe. In many years, it has had surplus funds that it was willing to lend to its friends, sometimes with political strings attached.

That economic position may also *fail* to provide a political tool is illustrated by the various attempts of the United States to use threats of economic punishment to get the Soviet Union to do what it wants. Because the United States cannot credibly threaten the Soviet Union militarily (a war between the two superpowers would be so destructive that no one would dare to start it), the United States has at various times tried to use its economic muscle to influence the Soviets. When the Soviet Union invaded Afghanistan, the United States canceled its exports of grain to the Soviets, promising to start them up again if the Soviets changed their policy. Similarly, in the 1970s the United States tried through economic sanctions to get Soviet and Polish leaders to liberalize the regime in Poland. These efforts did not work, however, because the United States is simply not important enough economically to the Soviet bloc countries, whose economies are rather self-contained, to force them to back down on policies that are important to them.

Geography

Many states are protected by natural formations that render them more secure militarily than their armed power alone would suggest they should be.[5] Great Britain has always benefited from the fact that it is an island, separated from the rest of Europe by the English Channel. It was this which prevented Hitler from invading England during World War II. Similarly, Switzerland has always been rather secure in its rough mountains. Until the coming of air trans-

---

[5]An interpretation of international politics that emphasizes economic and especially geographic sources of power is Harold and Margaret Sprout, *The Ecological Perspective on Human Affairs, with Special Reference to International Politics* (Princeton, N.J.: Princeton University Press, 1965).

portation, the United States was sufficiently isolated from Europe that it could get by with a very small army. Germany has suffered over the centuries from the fact that it sits in the middle of a wide plain stretching from northern France into the Soviet Union, a plain along which armies can move easily. It is generally expected that if conventional warfare were to break out between NATO and the Warsaw Pact nations today, the main battlefield would be Germany.

Leadership

Finally, skilled leadership may make a difference in the actual weight a state carries in international politics. Charles de Gaulle, by skillful diplomacy and a flair for public relations, was able to make France the leading state of western Europe in the late 1960s and 1970s. Woodrow Wilson's leadership probably diminished the influence of the United States at the end of World War I. Hitler and Mussolini led their states into disastrous, overreaching wars of conquest.

POWER AND CHOICE IN INTERNATIONAL POLITICS

It is easy to see the "power" side of international politics, but with no central authority to define common goals for the international system, it is not so easy to see that international politics may also involve "choice." Some theorists think that the international system works toward certain common goals, however, even in the absence of a coordinating authority.

Hans Morgenthau has developed an elegant analysis of international politics based on the concept of the "balance of power," which assumes that the international system has a natural tendency to prevent any one state from dominating the system.[6]

This tendency, which is a characteristic of the system as a whole, results if all of the states within it individually try to maintain their own power. If any one state begins to grow too large, other states become alarmed and combine against it, thus keeping power balanced. In this way the system operates with a "hidden hand" to maintain itself as a multiple set of competitive states. Historic examples of the balance of power at work include the fairly evenly matched alliance structure in Europe on the eve of World War I; the combination of numerous European states to balk an ambitious Napoleon; and the role of Britain over four centuries, throwing its support first to one, then to another European power, always on the weaker side, in order to prevent any one power from dominating the continent of Europe. The Cold War between the Soviet Union and the United States, with their rather evenly matched alliances, may be interpreted as a natural working out of the balance of power.

---

[6]Hans Morgenthau, *Politics Among Nations*, 5th rev. ed. (New York: Knopf, 1978), chaps. 11–14.

Morgenthau credits the balance of power with a number of good things: the maintenance of a varied system of states; in particular, the protection of small states; and, under some circumstances, a decrease in warfare. He also notes numerous problems in the balance of power, however.[7] In particular, since as we have seen international power is difficult to measure, states may never be quite sure where they stand vis-à-vis other states and may start wars because they have improperly assessed the balance of power. The prolonged war between Iraq and Iran in the 1980s started when Iraq undertook simple aggression against a weakened Iran, which it thought could easily be defeated. Iran, fighting on its home soil, turned out to be stronger than anticipated, and the war developed into a bloody stalemate.

At this point, balance-of-power analysis is important for us because it shows that even in the anarchy of international politics, politics may be interpreted as more than simply the exercise of power. As we have tried to show throughout this book, a proper understanding of politics always requires that we remain simultaneously aware of its two sides.

CONCLUSION

The unpredictability and danger of international politics can be awesome, especially now, in the nuclear age. Politics on this level can be analyzed in the same ways that we analyze other kinds of politics, but the high stakes involved put a greater edge on that analysis than we feel in the study of politics within states. In a general text such as this, we can touch only briefly on international politics, but it is hoped that you will have developed a taste for more. We need urgently to build a better understanding of international politics.

A personal note in conclusion: We tend, when analyzing politics, to think of it in the abstract and rather dispassionately. We analyze people's actions according to the resources available to them and to a rational application of those resources to their goals. By and large this analysis works well. We can generally tell which of two countries will be able to impose its will upon another, what sort of people will turn out to vote in greater numbers at election time, how a change in party finance will affect candidates' strategies, and so on. But sometimes passionate belief can cut through all this. Ideas and ideology can take on a power of their own, which transcends all analysis. No political scientists in the early 1960s predicted the tumultuous events of the civil rights movement. And who would have thought that little Vietnam would be able to best the United States in a war? Or that primitive Afghanistan would be able to defy the Soviet Union for years on end?

Just as a small dog, if it is on its home ground, may be able to send a larger one running away with its tail down, so may the weaker side—even a very

---

[7]Ibid., chap. 14.

weak side—prevail in politics if its supporters believe strongly enough that they are right.

As Marshall McLuhan so aptly put it, "Nothing is inevitable as long as one person is aware that it is happening."

FURTHER READING

Chan, Stephen. *Issues in International Relations: A View from Africa*. New York: Macmillan, 1987.

Claude, Inis L. Jr. *Swords into Plowshares: The Problems and Progress of International Organization,* 4th ed. New York: Random House, 1971.

Greenstein, Fred, and Polsby, Nelson, eds. *Handbook of Political Science*, vol. 8: *International Politics*. Reading, Mass.: Addison-Wesley, 1975.

Ikle, Fred C. *How Nations Negotiate*. New York: Praeger, 1967.

Nicolson, Harold. *Diplomacy*, 3rd ed. New York: Oxford University Press, 1963.

Pirages, Dennis. *The New Context for International Relations: Global Ecopolitics*. North Scituate, Mass.: Duxbury Press, 1978.

Rosenau, James N., ed. *In Search of Global Patterns*. New York: Free Press, 1976. Forty contributors discuss the ways in which they have developed their interpretations of international politics.

Russett, Bruce M., and Starr, Harvey. *World Politics: The Menu for Choice*. San Francisco: W. H. Freeman, 1981.

Sprout, Harold and Margaret. *Toward a Politics of the Planet Earth*. New York: Van Nostrand Reinhold, 1971.

Stoessinger, John G. *Why Nations Go to War,* 3rd ed. New York: St. Martin's, 1982.

Triska, Jan F. *Dominant Powers and Subordinate States*. Durham, N.C.: Duke University Press, 1986.

Ulam, Adam B. *The Rivals: America and Russia since World War II*. New York: Viking, 1971.

Appendix

Principles of Political Analysis

There are a number of basic principles of argument and logic that students should learn in an introductory political science course. In part, these should have shown up implicitly in much of the material you have already read and discussed in this course, but is is also helpful to look at them more directly. They are included here not as a tag end or afterthought but because this seems to be the best way to handle them. Some instructors may prefer to use this section at the beginning of a course, some at the end, others at some other point. Locating this discussion in an appendix leaves to the instructor the decision of how to handle it.

FALSIFIABILITY

The most basic principle of political argument is that in order to be useful, any statement about politics must be *falsifiable*. That is, it must be at least potentially possible that the statement is not true and could therefore be falsified. For example, the statement "two-party systems tend to produce less redistribution of income than multiparty systems do" would be falsified if we compared the two-party and multiparty systems of the world and found that there was little difference between the two in the degree of income redistribution they produced. Or the statement "Ted Kennedy has shown little sympathy for blacks" would be falsified if one produced a long list of statements and actions in which Ted Kennedy demonstrated sympathy for blacks.

On the other hand, some statements about politics are true by definition. "Michael Dukakis lost the 1988 presidential election because most of the voters chose George Bush" is one example. "The poor countries of the world are more backward economically than rich countries" is another. Think about it: How would you go about falsifying either of these statements? They are true by definition.

Since these statements could not possibly be demonstrated to be false, they are automatically true. Such a statement does not tell anything about the world that we did not already know before we read the statement. Literally, a statement that is not falsifiable says nothing about the world. Such statements are called *tautologies*.

The two examples given above are fairly obvious, so you might wonder why the importance of falsifiability is emphasized here. Surely, mustn't it be obvious when a statement says nothing new? If so, it wouldn't seem to be much of a problem. As it happens, though, it is not always immediately clear that a statement is a tautology. Consider the following: "A country with a large agricultural sector and a large industrial sector to its economy will tend to have a small service sector." Such a country will not "tend" to have a small service sector, it will *always* have a small one, because this statement is true by definition. To have a large agricultural sector means that a large percentage of the labor force is employed in agriculture; if the country also has a large industrial sector, then another large percentage of the labor force is employed in industry. What's left consists entirely of the service sector. Since the percentages employed in different sectors must always sum to 100 percent, this means that if the first two percentages are large, there cannot be much left for the service sector. Its percentage must by definition be small, so the statement is a tautology—though to most people it would not be obvious, at first glance, that such was the case.

As you become involved in the analysis of politics, you will be surprised at how often statements about politics turn out, on closer examination, to be true by definition.

We have now cleared the underbrush a bit, and know that we are to deal only with statements that are at least potentially falsifiable. Clearly, however, some of these statements will be more interesting than others, and we don't want to waste our time with the uninteresting ones. This leads us to the following question:

WHAT MAKES A STATEMENT INTERESTING?

There are three kinds of statements about politics:

- *Statements of fact:* These state what *is,* they *describe* reality. Examples: "The American president is elected for a four-year term." "There are two major political parties in West Germany." "Somalia has been at war with Ethiopia off and on for several years."
- *Statements of value:* These state *how good* something is; they *evaluate* reality. Examples: "The U.S. Constitution provides the best governmental system in the world." "Sales taxes are not as good as income taxes because they are regressive." "A planned economy provides a better life for people than a free-market economy."
- *Explanatory statements:* These state *why* something is as it is; they *analyze* reality. Examples: "George Bush defeated Michael Dukakis in the 1988 presidential election because most voters were satisfied with the economy." "People whose parents were very interested in politics tend to be especially interested in politics themselves." "The sending of unclear diplomatic signals increases the likelihood that war will break out."

All three types of statement are appropriate areas for political investigation and argument. Whatever sort of statement you make, however, you want it to be an interesting one. A statement will be relatively interesting to the extent that it offers your readers something that (1) is of concern to them and (2) would have been difficult for them to accomplish for themselves. The fact that the statement must be of concern to your readers is obvious and requires no further comment. (Most American readers, for instance, would not be much concerned about the precise arrangements for choosing a king in Sweden, and statements about it would not be especially interesting to them.) However, note the further condition for interest—that the statement should offer your readers something that would have been difficult for them to accomplish for themselves. This is not so obvious.

Consider two descriptive statements about Congress: "Congress has 535 members," and "Three-fourths of the members of Congress have cast a vote at one time or another on direct instructions from a lobbyist." (The second of these is purely imaginary and, one hopes, false!) These two statements would be of equal *concern* to students of Congress, but the second statement would be more interesting to them because it is something that would have been difficult for them to learn for themselves. They could have learned how many members there are in Congress by a quick glance in any encyclopedia, but it would take a clever investigator, working for a long time, to ascertain the truth of the second statement.

Similarly, "justice is good" is not a very interesting statement of value. Presumably, everyone would be able to agree with it without much thought, so it does not provide us with much that is new. However, the statement "discrimination is good" is a challenging statement, one that goes against the grain. It would not automatically occur to most of your readers and would require a good deal of clever argument to be rendered plausible for them. Arguing for this statement requires a lot of thought, which you must provide for your readers, and will thus be proportionately more interesting to them.

As a final example, the explanatory statement, "Rich countries will tend to have bigger armies than poor countries" is not a very interesting explanation of the size of armies, because it is so obvious that coming up with it did not require much thought. "Countries with high unemployment, and therefore cheap labor, will tend to have large armies" is a more interesting explanation of the same thing. A thoroughly obvious, hence uninteresting, explanation is called a *trivial explanation*.

As a general rule, statements of value and explanatory statements require more thought on the part of the writer than descriptive statements do, and they are thus more likely to be interesting statements. Students writing papers are often tempted to write descriptive papers, laying out a set of descriptive statements, simply because this is easier than justifying statements of value or explanation. You should remember that unless you choose a *challenging* descriptive problem, your paper will not be a particularly interesting one. Often you will be given a particular descriptive investigation as an exercise; you might, for instance, be asked to trace the progress of a bill through the legislative process. If so, describe away! But if you are simply asked to "write a term paper about some aspect of the legislative process," you will generally be able to write a more interesting paper if you choose a question of value or of explanation.

CAUSATION AND EXPLANATION

Let us look a bit more closely at explanation. An explanatory statement necessarily involves the notion of causation. We *explain* a certain thing by saying
that another thing *causes* it. For example, we might explain the fact that the
U.S. government has difficulty making broad, systematic policy in areas such
as energy by blaming it on the separation of powers in the American system.
That is, we *explain* the existence of the difficulty by saying that the difficulty is
caused by the separation of powers. (Presumably this would be because there
are many points at which the political power of opponents can be decisive—the
presidency, either house of Congress, or the courts—as a result "difficult" programs are hard to pass.)

In the example above, we cannot conceive of any way to explain the American difficulty except to assert one or another possible cause of the difficulty.
So to explain is to analyze causes.

But what is causation? What does it mean to say that one thing causes another? In general, we think that to cause something is to *bring it about,* to
bring it forth, to produce it. Turning a key causes my car to start. The Soviet
Union's opposition to a proposal causes the defeat of the proposal in the United
Nations. The increasing electoral advantages of incumbents in U.S. congressional elections have caused an increase in the average seniority of members of
Congress. And so on.

We think of causation as working only forward in time. In order for one
thing to produce another thing, the "producer" has to precede the "product"
temporally. So it doesn't make sense to think of Ronald Reagan's electoral victory in 1984 as having caused Walter Mondale to argue for tax increases during
the 1984 campaign; but it does make sense to think of Mondale's position as
one of the causes of Reagan's electoral victory.

However, temporal precedence is not enough to establish one thing as a
cause of another. We do not think of winter as causing spring, for instance,
even though we know that "when winter comes, spring can't be far behind."
Although the seasons unfold together, we do not think of one season as bringing the other about. Similarly, it is probably true that brunettes tend to be
Democrats, since for historical reasons a number of ethnic groups with dark
hair—blacks, Native Americans, Chicanos, southern Europeans—have gravi-
tated to the Democratic party. Yet even though people acquire their hair color
long before they give a thought to which party they will support, we do not
think of hair color as causing people's party preferences. It is only a coinci-
dence that the two tend to vary together.

Political scientists put a great deal of effort into trying to sort out what
things cause the things in which we are interested. Why does the United
States have only two major parties? Why are so few Third World states democracies? Why do communist economies not grow more quickly than they
do? If we could experiment with politics in a laboratory, as chemists or phys-
icists do in their specialties, we could hold all other possible factors constant;
we could allow only the one we wished to examine to vary and then see

whether, when it varied, the thing we were trying to explain also varied. For instance, a physicist may place two identical weights on identical wheelchairs on slopes of different angles and measure the effect of the angle of slope on the speed of descent; since nothing else varies, it is clear in this case that only differing angles of slope can be causing differing speeds of descent. If we could manipulate things in this way, we would feel confident in stating that the one thing was causing the other to vary. However, with rare exceptions, we cannot experiment with the things we are examining in political science. We cannot change the electoral system of the United States in order to see what effect this would have on the number of parties, or change Third World states to industrial states in order to see whether their political regimes would change, or change command economies to market economies in order to see whether they would become more productive.

What we *can* do is observe variations and changes as they occur around us and try to figure out which variations or changes actually cause other things to happen. The challenge in doing this is that no *one* thing ever changes in isolation from everything else, in the way a physicist can arrange it in the laboratory. Everything is always changing at once, and we must use our creative sense to try to sort out *which* changes have caused *which* others.

For example, in 1961, France changed its electoral system to one based on a presidency, which should, in principle, tend to bring about a two-party system. Over the years since then, France has indeed seen a coalescence of its party system into five parties, organized in two well-defined blocs. But did the new electoral system bring about the coalescence? At the same time that France was adjusting to its new electoral arrangements, it was also experiencing unprecedented prosperity, which might perhaps have made people less likely to support small, radical parties. Also, it was at this time that the very popular Charles de Gaulle served as president. He drew a very large political party about himself—something he could probably have done no matter what the electoral system was and which knocked out several smaller parties. What, then, was the effect of the change in electoral arrangements on the number of parties?

Under such circumstances, we cannot be certain of the effects of one thing on another. We can and do use our common sense, asking, for example, what the effects of electoral systems *should* be. And we can look at overall patterns across many cases, asking what has happened after changes of electoral system in other countries. The end result is not a firm, indisputable finding but rather something to be argued about. There is nothing wrong with this.

HISTORICAL EXPLANATION

A natural affinity between the field of history and what we have been discussing here should be apparent to you. Historians follow a series of events as they move forward in time, linking them to one another. This is much like the analysis of causation that political scientists frequently engage in.

There is a difference in emphasis between the two fields, however. Historians are more often concerned to present a single train of events—a biography of Lincoln, a history of negotiations at the Council of Europe, a military history of World War II, and so on—with causal analysis left somewhat implicit. Political scientists, on the other hand, are more likely to be looking for overall patterns (embodied in theories) and less concerned with tracing carefully through any single case or train of events.

The important thing to note is that this is only a difference of degree. Both political historians and political scientists are engaged in the same task—to make sense out of the myriad political events occurring around us—and historians as well as political scientists do this by *explaining* certain things, showing that they are caused by other things.

Remember from our earlier discussion that it is not enough just to show that one thing happened before another. If we are to treat the earlier event as causing the later one, we must also establish some basis for treating it as having brought the other about, or having produced it. *This necessity holds just as much for the historian as for the political scientist.*

This is an important point for students in political science courses, because as you are assigned research papers to write, a deceptively simple route may appear to be a paper that traces the history of something: a history of the arms race between the Soviet Union and the United States, a biography of Senator Dole, a history of the diplomacy leading up to the Camp David peace accords, a description of how the National Security Council developed, a tracing of changes in French fiscal policy since the Socialists came to power, and so on. Any of these could make an excellent topic for a paper, but if you do it right, it will be neither easier nor more difficult than any other topic would be. To do the job right is to try to establish causal relationships among the events as they transpire. If, in attempting to write a paper of this sort, you simply lay out the events—first X happened, then Y, then Z—you will have merely described things. And as noted above, you will not have a very interesting paper. However, if you operate here as all good historians do—that is, if you try to explain why the train of events occurred as it did—you will have an interesting and not necessarily easily written paper.

A FEW COMMON PITFALLS IN ANALYSIS

As you analyze politics, you must think straight. For the most part, common sense will carry you well; and practice, and criticism from your readers, will help to sharpen your abilities. As an introductory help, you may find it useful to consider three common flaws in analysis that you should watch out for both in your own and others' work.

1. *Begging the Question.* Frequently writers answer a question with an answer that simply restates the question. It looks as though it has answered the question, but it has not. It has simply turned the question into another form and does not produce much forward progress. This is called "begging the question."

For example, a person analyzing the victory of North Vietnam in the Vietnam War might state that North Vietnam won because it was more powerful than South Vietnam. But, this does not really answer the question we want to see addressed; it simply changes it slightly into the question: Why was North Vietnam more powerful than South Vietnam? Similarly, an analysis of American voting behavior concluding that people vote for candidates they prefer would not seem to have brought us forward. It would simply leave us with the further question: Why do people prefer certain candidates over others? Questions of value can also be begged. For instance, a paper arguing that socialism is a better system than capitalism because it is more just—unless it expanded on this to show what was meant by "justice"—would simply leave us with the question: What makes socialism more just than capitalism?

These examples may have all seemed rather simple, and you may have wondered why you would need to be cautioned to watch out for a flaw that is so easily avoided. But begging a question is actually easy to do. Not all instances of it are as obvious as the examples used here. For instance, people often argue about policy on the basis of "natural rights," rights so basic to the nature of humanity that they take priority over all else. The Declaration of Independence appeals to "certain inalienable rights, [among which are] life, liberty, and the pursuit of happiness," and argues that because the king of England had violated these rights, his rule was outlaw; hence it was proper to rise in revolution against him. At a later period, administrators in Hitler's Germany were charged with the crime of having obeyed and enforced Hitler's laws. This was a crime because the laws themselves were in violation of natural rights. Basic privacy, the right of a woman to control her own body, and the fetus's right to life are other things that have been defended at one time or another as natural rights.

This sort of argument comes readily to us, and we slip easily into it. It is, in fact, a useful rhetorical device. But we should realize, when we assert the existence of natural rights, that unless we accompany this assertion with an analysis of human nature, we are begging the question in the following way: "X should be defended because it is a natural right." But what makes it a natural right? The fact that it is basic to the very nature of a human being. But how do we know what is basic to the nature of a human being?

2. *Circular Argument*. A circular argument is one in which a person proves A from B, but we know that B is true only because of A. In other words, B implies A, but we believe B only if we first believe A. The argument goes in a circle and does not offer any new reason to believe either A or B.

Suppose, for example, we argued that political influence of the military is a major cause of the size of defense budgets, but that we measured "military influence" by the size of the armed forces. In this case, we would be asserting that military influence is what causes defense budgets to be large, but since our measure of "military influence" is something that itself is a direct result of the size of defense budgets, finding that the two things tend to rise and fall together would give us no new reason to believe the original statement.

3. *Post hoc Explanation*. A post hoc explanation is the "Monday-morning quarterback" of explanation. It consists of taking a set of things that have already happened, showing that one of them plausibly could have resulted from the others, and, on the basis of this, asserting that those others are in general a cause of the thing in question.

For example, many commentators have looked at the sequence of events leading up to World War II and have asserted that it was the appeasement of Britain and France that led Hitler on and resulted in his frantic war of conquest. This is certainly plausible, but it is post hoc.

The danger in post hoc explanations is that for *any* event there will be some set of things that happened at more or less the same time and that may look like a plausible explanation for it. If those same things happen again in the future, they may or may not produce that same result. It is not that a post hoc explanation is *wrong*, but that it leaves us with a greater feeling of certainty than we should have. We confuse the set of events that first suggested an idea to us with verification of the idea. What has suggested that appeasement encourages aggressors? The events leading up to World War II. How do we know that it's true? Just look at Hitler!

The three problems of argument noted here are by no means the only ones you should watch for, but they are three common problems. In the end, these three, and all of the rest, boil down to a matter of simple common sense. If you are endowed with some of that, you won't go wrong.

Glossary

Following each term, the first page on which it is introduced substantively appears in parentheses.

American conservatism (*p. 44*)   The rather loose ideology known in the United States as "conservatism." Since it is really a variant of the more general ideology of liberalism and has relatively little to do with the more general ideology of conservatism, it has been distinguished in this book by the name *American conservatism*. American conservatism is particularly suspicious of governmental intervention to make people more equal but is often willing to entrust government with power in order to maintain codes of moral behavior.

American liberalism (*p. 44*)   The rather loose ideology known in the United States as "liberalism." Since it is only a variant of the more general ideology of liberalism, it has been distinguished in this book by the name *American liberalism*. American liberalism is particularly concerned to make people equal, and it is relatively willing to entrust government with power in order to bring this about; it is also particularly concerned to maintain freedom of expression.

anomic interest group (*p. 203*)   Politically relevant groups with no formal organizational structure and no obvious leaders that come together only temporarily and with the loosest of coordination to their efforts.

arbitrary action (*pp. 88 and 280*)   Action that is taken capriciously. The people affected do not know what to expect before the action and do not learn afterward the grounds on which the action was chosen.

associational interest group (*p. 203*)   The "typical" interest group—an organized group of citizens, one of whose primary purposes is to affect the policies of the state.

authority (*p. 107*)   Power based on a general agreement that the holder of the power has the right to issue certain sorts of commands and that those commands should be obeyed.

balance of power (*p. 309*)   The idea that the international system works in a natural way to keep the power of states balanced so that no one state can ever achieve domination of the entire system.

begging a question (*p. 317*)   "Answering" a question (actually, failing to answer it) by offering a rephrasing of it as an answer. Example: "Why did Britain win the Falkland Islands war?" "Because Britain was more successful militarily than Argentina." (This leaves us with the question "Why was Britain more successful militarily than Argentina?" which just restates the original.)

"behavioralist" political science (*p. 15*)   Political science that emphasizes statistical analysis and abstract theories seeking out basic, essential regularities across a whole set of events.

bureaucracy *(p. 280)* A way of organizing the public administration that emphasizes professionalism, recruitment and promotion on the basis of merit, standardization of procedures, and the smooth flow of commands.

cabinet (in parliamentary system) *(p. 217)* The executive portion of a parliamentary government. It consists of ministers, most of whom are usually members of the parliament. Each minister is responsible for the administration of some part of the government's services, such as health or defense. The cabinet leads the parliament, proposing legislation, conducting the country's foreign policy, and so on. It serves at the pleasure of the parliament and can be ousted by a majority vote of no confidence.

causation *(p. 315)* An interpretation of relations between events in which one event "brings about" or produces another event. Example: "Poverty is a major cause of communist support in the Third World."

circular argument *(p. 318)* An argument in which one proves A from B but in which A itself provides our only evidence that B is true.

coalition *(p. 219)* A tactical combination of varied groups, constructed so that the groups will in combination be large enough to command power that they can then share among themselves. Frequently applied to parliamentary government, in which 50 percent of the votes in parliament are required in order to form a cabinet, but in which it may be necessary to combine two or more parties in order to amass 50 percent of the votes.

collective good *(p. 99)* A thing that benefits all members of the collectivity and which no one can be prevented from using. Because it is difficult to get individuals voluntarily to pay part of the cost of the good, it is usually chosen by governmental authority.

committees (legislative) *(p. 225)* Small group of legislators whose task (usually) is to review carefully a proposed piece of legislation and recommend to the full legislature what action should be taken on it. In many legislatures, bills may be amended by the committee or killed in entirety. Committees may also perform other tasks, such as investigating an area of possible legislation.

communism *(p. 55)* The more militant branch of socialism. Communists generally argue that the only way to build a socialist state is by revolution. Therefore they are sometimes less interested in electoral activity than are the democratic socialists. Since the 1920s, communists have generally acknowledged the leadership of the Soviet Union in the formulation of their goals and strategies. See also *socialism; democratic socialism*.

conservatism *(p. 48)* An ideology positing that the most important goal of politics is to create stable communities based on a hierarchy of power, in which leaders and followers have reciprocal responsibilities and obligations. Unlike liberalism, conservatism is not suspicious of power and does not seek to limit the power of the state. Rather, the point of conservatism is that that power should be in the hands of a traditional class of rulers. See also *American conservatism*.

constitution *(p. 127)* A set of rules by which power is distributed in a political group, such as the state. This generally consists in part of a formal set of rules, but it always contains as well various informal mechanisms, traditions, and understandings by which power is assigned to people.

constitutional review *(p. 246)* A system under which a judicial or quasijudicial part of the government can annul acts of other parts of the government if, in its judgment, those acts violate the constitution of the state.

consitutionalism *(p. 140)* The doctrine that states' constitutions should be designed fairly, not so as to give undue advantage to any particular group, and that the government should then be faithful to that constitution. In this way, individuals are protected against arbitrary governmental action.

coup (p. 261)   The forceful deposition of a government by all or a portion of the armed forces and installation of a new; military government.

court politics (p. 267)   The political process in a state where great power is vested in a single person, as in traditional monarchy or in a personal dictatorship.

democracy (pp. 113 and 258)   A state in which all fully qualified citizens vote at regular intervals to choose, among alternative candidates, the people who will be in charge of setting the state's policies.

democratic socialism (p. 55)   The branch of socialism that supports electoral democracy and holds that the proper way for workers to control society is to win elections. Democratic socialists are also generally more moderate than communists in the goals they set, being more willing to settle for piecemeal progress rather than holding out for a complete remaking of society. See also *socialism; communism*.

dictatorship   A governmental arrangement in which those who hold power did not gain power by any regular, constitutional process and are not responsible in their exercise of power to any formal set of rules.

dominant-party system (p. 184; contrast "one-party system")   A political party system in which various parties are allowed to function openly and with reasonable effectiveness but in which a single party nonetheless holds power all the time.

due process (p. 88)   An expectation that certain set procedures must always be followed in making a policy and that if they were not, the policy should be void.

efficient policies (p. 91)   Policies that produce the greatest good at the least cost.

electoral system (p. 152)   A set of rules by which the outcomes of an election (a set of officers elected, or whatever) is determined from the distribution of votes cast by the electorate.

established church   A church or other organized religion that is established by law as the official church or religion of a state and which has political and legal ties to the government of the state. Examples are the Anglican church, which is established in Great Britain; the Roman Catholic church, which is established in Italy and many other countries; and Judaism, which is established in Israel.

European Community (p. 32)   An organization of twelve western European states that have set up a rather weak common government and have coordinated many of their economic policies.

externality (p. 99)   A situation in which there are social costs or benefits beyond the individual costs and benefits involved in a transaction.

fairness (p. 85)   A situation in which all people are treated as they deserve.

fascism (p. 55)   A political movement that appeared in many countries in the 1920s and 1930s. Fascism stressed militaristic pageantry and a strident nationalism as ways of binding the people to a single dramatic dictator. Franco, Mussolini, and Hitler were fascist dictators.

federal state (p. 135)   A state in which the constitution grants to regional governments a legal monopoly over certain political decisions, such as educational policy. Thus, two different governments will control the same group of people, but with regard to different political questions.

fiduciary role (p. 304)   A role in which one acts as an agent on behalf of someone else's interests. This role often places the agent in problematic positions.

government (p. 108)   The one group in society all of whose power involves authority. At least potentially, there is no limit to the range of activities over which it may exercise authority.

gross national product, or GNP   The total value of all goods and services exchanged in a society. That is, the sum of such things as the value of all food sold, the value of all mechanics' work on automobiles, the value of all educational activity, and so on. The higher the GNP, the greater the total amount of economic activity in the society. Per capita GNP divides GNP by the population, to measure how economically well-off the average person is.

higher civil service *(p. 288)* Specialized and executive members of the public administration, corresponding to professionals and managers in the private sector.

ideology *(p. 42)* A set of ideas that are related and that modify one another; that is, an organized set of ideas about something.

implicit power *(p. 7)* Power in which A does what B desires not because of anything B says or does, but because: (1) A senses that B wants something done and (2) for any of a variety of reasons, A wishes to do what B wants done.

incentive compatibility *(p. 132)* A situation in which those who make decisions on behalf of society benefit personally when their decisions benefit society. When incentive compatibility is present, society does not need to depend on nobility of character in its officials; it can depend on a more reliable force—their concern for their own self-interest.

incrementalism *(p. 94)* A policy of making decisions cautiously and implementing them through small, staged changes rather than in bold sweeps.

institutional interest group *(p. 203)* A group that is primarily set up for some purpose other than political activity but which becomes politically active in order to defend its own interests in the policy decisions of the state.

interest group *(p. 195)* An organized group of citizens one of whose goals is to ensure that the state follows certain policies.

International Court of Justice *(p. 303)* The court that hears cases at law between states. It has no power to enforce its rulings.

international politics *(p. 297)* Politics conducted among states rather than within a single state.

justice *(p. 85)* Rewarding people on the basis of the contributions they make to common efforts, of their need for the reward, or at least approximate equality of treatment. How these three criteria are weighted is important in determining the justice of a policy and will vary from one person to another.

legitimacy *(p. 109)* A belief on the part of large numbers of people in a state that the existing governmental structure and/or the particular persons in office should appropriately wield authority.

liberalism *(p. 45)* An ideology positing that the most important goal of politics is to help individuals develop their capacities to the fullest. To this end, people should be regulated and aided by governments as little as possible, so that they will learn from the experience of being responsible for their own decisions. Liberalism may be summarized by the slogan, "That government is best which governs least." See also *American liberalism*.

manifest power *(p. 7)* Power based on an observable action by A that causes B to do what A wants.

market mechanism *(p. 95)* A mechanism whereby social choice results from choices of all members of the collectivity rather than a decision made by the central governing unit.

mobilization *(p. 172)* The systematic stimulation of concerted effort by large numbers of people, as in elections or demonstrations. This term is used especially in reference to such stimulation conducted on its own behalf by the government.

multinational corporations Corporations like Exxon or ITT, which have become so large and conduct their operations in so many different states that we can no longer realistically think of them as belonging to any particular state.

multiparty system (p. 186)   A democratic system in which there are more than two major parties.

nation (p. 29)   A large group of people who are bound together and recognize a similarity among themselves because of a common culture—in particular, a common language seems important in creating nationhood. Nations often but not always coincide with the political boundaries of states. The Kurdish language and culture is spread across parts of Turkey, Iraq, and Iran; Irish nationalists and British nationalists are mixed together in Northern Ireland, where they are at each other's throats. There are many similar examples of mismatches between national "boundaries" and the boundaries of states. Such mismatches are a potent source of political turmoil.

nationalism (p. 25)   Passionate identification with a state on the part of its citizens.

nationalization of industry (p. 69)   The acquisition of an industrial operation by the government, which then operates it directly as part of the governmental administration.

neocorporatism (p. 211)   A system of government and interest groups in which all interests are organized but—instead of simply responding to groups' pressures—the government actively involves the groups themselves in the job of governing. This active governmental role distinguishes neocorporatism from pluralism.

nonassociational interest group (p. 203)   One or another category of people who are not formally organized in any way but are treated by others as if they represented an interest.

ombudsman (p. 284)   A government official whose primary duty is to seek out citizens' complaints of abuse by public administrators and to negotiate changes in the offending practices.

one-party system (p. 184; contrast "dominant-party system")   A political system in which only a single political party is allowed to be active.

one-party state (p. 265)   A state in which the government is based on, and in turn supports, a single political party. No other party is allowed to function in other than a token way.

paradox of participation (p. 158)   The paradox that no one should really vote if their only reason for voting is that they wish to help their favored candidate win. The odds that all the rest of the voters will produce a tie are incredibly small, and that is the only circumstance in which the person's vote will make any difference at all to the candidate.

parliamentary government (p. 217)   A democracy in which the executive and legislative functions are merged in one institution, the parliament. The parliament is the state's supreme legislature, but it also appoints a committee (the cabinet) to serve as the political executive for the state.

party identification (p. 162)   A personal identification with a political party. Not just agreement with its policies or candidates of the moment, but an enduring identification with the party itself.

pluralism (p. 210)   A system of government and interest groups in which all interests organize and compete freely, with no one group dominating, and in which the government is open to pressure from the groups so that policy is largely the outcome of groups' competing pressures.

political culture (p. 119)   The set of all attitudes and beliefs held communally by a people, forming the basis for their political behavior.

political party (p. 169)   A group of officials or would-be officials who are linked with a sizable group of citizens into an organization; a chief object of this organization is to ensure that its officials attain power or are maintained in power.

political science (p. 14)   The academic field that takes as its sole and general task the analysis of politics, especially the politics of the state.

politics (p. 4) The making of common decisions for a group of people through the exercise of power by some members of the group over other members.

post hoc explanation (p. 319) An explanation tailored to the particular set of events to be explained. ("Post hoc" means "after this.") A danger in this is that mere coincidences may be treated as general relationships in the explanation.

power (p. 6) The ability of one person to cause another to do what the first wishes, by whatever means. (See also *implicit power* and *manifest power.*)

presidential government (p. 237) A democratic system in which the legislature and executive exist independently and are elected independently of each other. Generally the president takes a leading role in forming policy but must have the consent of the legislature if that policy is to be enacted. A presidential system divides power, whereas a parliamentary system unifies it.

progressive taxation (p. 77) A system of taxes that takes a greater proportion of a person's income if the income is high than if the income is low.

proportional representation electoral system, or PR (p. 153) An electoral system in which parties receive a number of seats in the legislature roughly proportional to the number of votes that were cast for them among the electorate.

public administration (p. 276) The set of people who are not involved directly in the making of major political decisions but who construct and implement the policies that carry out those decisions. Examples are police officers, public health nurses, IRS agents, public university presidents.

question time (p. 222) A device, originating in the British House of Commons and since imitated in many parliaments, by which cabinet members appear regularly in the parliament to answer questions from members about the administration of their offices. These questions and answers often spark hot debate.

radicalism (p. 94) Making decisions in bold sweeps and changing policies rapidly, so as not to miss opportunities that might disappear if one moved slowly.

referendum (pp. 151 and 156) An election in which voters choose directly whether a particular proposal will become law; this contrasts with other kinds of elections, in which voters choose among various candidates for a political office.

regional integration (p. 32) A partial merging of the political and economic structures of several states in the same region of the world. The most successful attempt at regional integration to date has been the formation of the European Community.

regressive taxation (p. 77) A system of taxes that takes a greater proportion of a person's income if the income is low than if the income is high.

regulation (p. 68) Direct laying down of rules by the government as to how people may conduct their affairs. This is distinguished from *indirect* governmental direction of choices, as when a government taxes liquor heavily to discourage its use but does not actually make its use illegal. The latter would constitute regulation.

representative bureaucracy (p. 286) The idea that members of the public administration should be similar to the groups they serve in such characteristics as class, race, and gender, so that they will be able to serve them better.

selective incentive (p. 200) Benefits that an organization offers its members in addition to the central purposes of the organization. A trade union, for example, may offer its members such added benefits as low-cost package vacations.

single-member-district, plurality electoral system, or SMDP (p. 152) An electoral system in which the state is divided into geographic subdivisions, each subdivision is represented by a single member in the legislature, and the candidate who attains a plurality of votes in that subdivision is the one who fills the seat.

socialism (p. 51) An ideology positing that society consists of classes (groups of people who are similarly placed economically) which are constantly in conflict. In order to create a just society in which people are equal, the working class should take over the state and direct all industries.

socialization (p. 119)   The process of learning the facts, assumptions, and attitudes that we use in responding to politics. This occurs most rapidly in childhood and youth but continues throughout life.

state (p. 13)   The basic unit by which people are organized politically; often casually called "country" or "nation." States are militarily independent of each other and are guided by governments that typically regulate the economy, set the laws of the state, and so on. States in the twentieth century tend to be relatively large territories with stable boundaries whose populations are bound together by intimate political ties. In marginal cases such as the European Community, it can be a bit tricky to say exactly whether a unit is or is not a "state." In the United States, "state" also has a second meaning, referring to one of the fifty regional divisions (California, Alaska, Florida, Minnesota, etc.) into which the United States is divided.

Supreme Soviet (p. 131)   The parliament of the Soviet Union. It does not meet frequently and does not exercise great power. Its powers have recently expanded.

"traditionalist" political science (p. 15)   Political science that emphasizes legal and historical methods and the complex whole that is being studied.

trivial explanation (p. 314)   An explanation that is obvious to the audience and therefore not very interesting to them. Example: "Why does John eat so much?" "Because he's hungry."

tautology (p. 312)   A statement that is logically true and thus cannot be shown false by an examination of evidence. Example: "All brunettes have dark hair."

two-party system (p. 185)   A democratic system in which two parties regularly receive 90 percent or more of votes cast, but in which it is rare for either of them very often to receive more than 55 or 60 percent of the votes. These two parties will replace each other in office fairly frequently.

unitary state (p. 135)   A state in which no other governmental body but the central government has any areas of policy that are exclusively under its control. In a unitary state, local and regional governments may potentially be overruled by the central government in any political decision they may make.

United Nations (p. 32 and 303)   An organization of almost all of the world's states. The UN provides a forum at which complaints can be aired; it has occasionally helped to cool off conflicts between states; and its specialized committees seek to improve world standards of health, education, and so on.

welfare state   A state in which the government seeks, by a complex set of policies, to ensure that its citizens will not suffer great economic insecurity or grievous want. Such policies may include guaranteed pensions, public provision of health care, public attempts to prevent unemployment, public help in the care of children, and so on. Most industrialized states have established welfare states in the period since World War II.

Bibliography

Aberbach, Joel D., Putnam, Robert D., and Rockman, Bert A. *Bureaucrats and Politicians in Western Democracies*. Cambridge, Mass.: Harvard University Press, 1981.

Abraham, Henry J. *The Judicial Process: An Introductory Analysis of the Courts of the United States, England, and France*. 5th ed. New York: Oxford University Press, 1980.

Adams, John Clarke, and Paolo Barile. *The Government of Republican Italy*. 3rd ed. Boston: Houghton Mifflin, 1972.

Alba, Victor. *Politics and the Labor Movement in Latin America*. Stanford, Calif.: Stanford University Press, 1968.

Alford, Robert R. *Health Care Politics*. Chicago: University of Chicago Press, 1975.

Allison, Graham T. *Essence of Decision: Explaining the Cuban Missile Crisis*. Boston: Little, Brown, 1971.

Almond, Gabriel, and Coleman, James S., eds. *The Politics of the Developing Areas*. Princeton, N.J.: Princeton University Press, 1960.

Almond, Gabriel, and Verba, Sidney. *The Civic Culture*. Boston: Little, Brown, 1965.
———, eds. *The Civic Culture Revisited*. Boston: Little, Brown, 1980.

Anderson, Charles. *Statecraft*. New York: Wiley, 1977.

Andrews, William G. *Presidential Government in Gaullist France*. Albany: State University of New York Press, 1982.

Arian, Alan, and Barnes, Samuel. "The Dominant Party System: A Neglected Model of Democratic Stability," *Journal of Politics* 36 (August 1974): 592–614.

Ascher, William. *Forecasting: An Appraisal for Policy Makers and Planners*. Baltimore: Johns Hopkins University Press, 1978.

Ashford, Douglas E. *Policy and Politics in France*. Philadelphia: Temple University Press, 1982.

Axelrod, Robert, Bobrow, Davis, Eulau, Heinz, Jones, Charles O., and Landau, Martin. "The Place of Policy Analysis in Political Science," *American Journal of Political Science* 21 (May 1977): 415–433.

Bachrach, Peter, and Baratz, Morton. "The Two Faces of Power," *American Political Science Review* 56 (December 1962): 947–953.

Baker, Kendall, Dalton, Russell, and Hildebrandt, Kai. *Germany Transformed*. Cambridge, Mass.: Harvard University Press, 1981.

Baker, Pauline H. "Nigeria: Lurching Toward Unity," *Wilson Quarterly* 4, no. 1 (Winter 1980): 70–80.

Bakvis, Herman, and Chandler, William M. *Federalism and the Role of the State*. Toronto: University of Toronto Press, 1987.

Ball, A., and Millard, F. *Pressure Politics in Industrial Societies*. Atlantic Highlands, N.J.: Humanities Press International, 1987.

Barber, Benjamin. *Strong Democracy*. Berkeley: University of California Press, 1984.

Barber, James David. *The Presidential Character*. 2nd ed. Englewood Cliffs, N.J.: Prentice-Hall, 1977.

Barnes, Samuel H., Kaase, Max, and Allerbeck, Klause. *Political Action: Mass Participation in Five Western Democracies*. Beverly Hills, Calif.: Sage, 1979.

Bauer, Raymond A., Pool, Ithiel de Sola, and Dexter, Lewis Anthony. *American Business and Public Policy*. New York: Atherton, 1963.

Bebler, Anton. *Military Rule in Africa: Dahomey, Ghana, Sierra Leone, and Mali*. New York: Praeger, 1972.

Beer, Samuel. *British Politics in the Collectivist Age*. New York: Knopf, 1965.

Berger, Suzanne, ed. *Organizing Interests in Western Europe: Pluralism, Corporatism, and the Transformation of Politics*. Cambridge, England: Cambridge University Press, 1981.

Bienen, Henry. "Military Rule and the Political Process: Nigerian Examples." *Comparative Politics* 10 (January 1978): 205–225.

Bienen, Henry, with Fitton, Martin. "Soldiers, Politicians and Civil Servants." In *Soldiers and Oil*, edited by K. Panter-Brick. London: Frank Cass & Co., 1978.

Birch, Anthony H. *Representation*. New York: Praeger, 1971.

Brichta, Avraham, and Zalmanovitch, Yair. "Proposals for Presidential Government in Israel." *Comparative Political Studies* 19 (October 1986): 57–68.

Burkett, Tony. "Developments in the West German Bundestag in the 1970s." *Parliamentary Affairs* 34 (Summer 1981): 291–307.

Burnham, Walter Dean. *Critical Elections and the Mainsprings of American Politics*. New York: Norton, 1970.

Cameron, David. "The Expansion of the Public Economy: A Comparative Analysis." *American Political Science Review* 72 (December 1978): 1243–1261.

Campbell, Angus, Converse, Philip, Miller, Warren E., and Stokes, Donald. *The American Voter*. New York: Wiley, 1960.

Chan, Stephen. *Issues in International Relations: A View from Africa*. New York: Macmillan, 1987.

Chase, Harold W., Holt, Robert, and Turner, John. *American Government in Comparative Perspective*. New York: Franklin Watts, 1980.

Chrines, S. B. *English Constitutional History*. London: Oxford University Press, 1947.

Claude, Inis L., Jr. *Swords into Plowshares: The Problems and Progress of International Organization*. 4th ed. New York: Random House, 1971.

Collier, David, ed. *The New Authoritarianism in Latin America*. Princeton, N.J.: Princeton University Press, 1979.

Conover, Pamela Johnston, and Feldman, Stanley. "Belief System Organization in the American Electorate." In *The Electorate Reconsidered*, edited by John Pierce and John L. Sullivan. Beverly Hills, Calif.: Sage, 1980.

Coulter, Philip B. *Measuring Inequality*. Boulder, Colo.: Westview Press, 1989.

Cronin, Thomas E. *The State of the Presidency*. 2nd ed. Boston: Little, Brown, 1980.

Crossman, R. H. S. *The Myths of Cabinet Government*. Cambridge, Mass.: Harvard University Press, 1972.

Crozier, Michel. *The Bureaucratic Phenomenon*. Chicago: University of Chicago Press, 1963.

Dahl, Robert. *Modern Political Analysis*. 4th ed. New York: Prentice-Hall, 1984.

———. *Who Governs?* New Haven, Conn.: Yale University Press, 1961.

Dalton, Russell J., et al., eds. *Electoral Change in Advanced Industrial Democracies: Realignment or Dealignment?* Princeton, N.J.: Princeton University Press, 1984.

Davis, Otto, Dempster, M. A. H., and Wildavsky, Aaron. "A Theory of the Budgetary Process," *American Political Science Review* 60 (September 1966): 529–547.

Dawson, Richard E., Prewitt, Kenneth, and Dawson, Karen. *Political Socialization*. 2nd ed. Boston: Little, Brown, 1977.

Deutsch, Karl. *Nationalism and Social Communication*. Cambridge, Mass.: MIT Press, 1953.

Dibacco, Thomas V., ed. *Presidential Power in Latin American Politics*. New York: Praeger, 1977.

Dodd, Lawrence C., and Oppenheimer, Bruce I. *Congress Reconsidered*. 2nd ed. Washington, D.C.: Congressional Quarterly, 1981.

Dogan, Mattei, ed. *The Mandarins of Western Europe: The Political Role of Top Civil Servants*. New York: Wiley, 1975.

Dougherty, James E., and Pfaltzgraff, Robert L. *Contending Theories of International Relations*. 2nd ed. New York: Harper & Row, 1981.

Downs, Anthony. *An Economic Theory of Democracy*. New York: Harper & Row, 1957.

Duverger, Maurice. *Political Parties*. New York: Wiley, 1954.

Eckstein, Harry, and Gurr, Ted Robert. *Patterns of Authority*. New York: Wiley, 1975.

Ehrmann, Henry. *Politics in France*. 4th ed. Boston: Little, Brown, 1983.

Epstein, Leon D. *Political Parties in Western Democracies*. New Brunswick, N.J.: Transaction Books, 1979.

Evans, P. B., Rueschmayer, D., and Skocpol, Theda, eds. *Bringing the State Back In*. Cambridge, England: Cambridge University Press, 1985.

Fenno, Richard. *Home Style: House Members in Their Districts*. Boston: Little, Brown, 1978.

Finer, S. E. *The Man on Horseback: The Role of the Military in Politics*. New York: Praeger, 1962.

————, ed. *Five Constitutions*. Harmondsworth, Middlesex: Penguin, 1979.

Flanigan, William H., and Zingale, Nancy. *Political Behavior of the American Electorate*. 5th ed. Newton, Mass.: Allyn & Bacon, 1983.

Frears, J. R. "The Decentralization Reforms in France," *Parliamentary Affairs* 36 (Winter 1983): 56–66.

Friedrich, Carl. *Limited Government: A Comparison*. Englewood Cliffs, N.J.: Prentice-Hall, 1974.

Gellner, Ernest. *Culture, Identity and Politics*. Cambridge, England: Cambridge University Press, 1987.

Ginsberg, Benjamin. *The Consequences of Consent: Elections, Citizen Control, and Popular Acquiescence*. Reading, Mass.: Addison-Wesley, 1982.

Goodman, David S. G., ed. *Groups and Politics in the People's Republic of China*. Armonk, N.Y.: M. E. Sharpe, 1984.

Graber, Doris. *Mass Media and American Politics*. Washington, D.C.: Congressional Quarterly Press, 1980.

Greenstein, Fred, and Polsby, Nelson, eds. *Handbook of Political Science*. Reading, Mass.: Addison-Wesley, 1975.

Gruber, Judith E. *Controlling Bureaucracies*. Berkeley: University of California Press, 1987.

Gupta, D. C. *Indian Government and Politics*. 4th ed. New Delhi: Vikas, 1978.

Hah, Chong-do, and Martin, Jeffrey. "Towards a Synthesis of Conflict and Integration Theories of Nationalism," *World Politics* 27, no. 3 (April 1975): 361–386.

Hartz, Louis. *The Liberal Tradition in America*. New York: Harcourt, Brace, 1955.

Harvey, Jack, and Bather, L. *The British Constitution*. 3rd ed. London: Macmillan, 1972.

Heclo, Hugh. *Modern Social Politics in Britain and Sweden*. New Haven, Conn.: Yale University Press, 1974.

Heidenheimer, Arnold J., Heclo, Hugh, and Adams, Carolyn. *Comparative Public Policy*. 2nd ed. New York: St. Martin's, 1983.

Heidenheimer, Arnold J. "Federalism and the Party System: The Case of West Germany," *American Political Science Review* 52 (September 1958): 809–828.

————, ed. *Political Corruption*. New York: Holt, Rinehart and Winston, 1970.

Heisler, Martin O., ed. *Politics in Europe*. New York: David McKay, 1974.

Hendel, Samuel. *The Soviet Crucible*. Boston: Duxbury, 1980.

Herz, John H. *The Nation-State and the Crisis of World Politics*. New York: David McKay, 1976.

Hood, Christopher C. *The Limits of Administration*. New York: Wiley, 1976.

Hunter, Floyd. *Community Power Structure*. Chapel Hill: University of North Carolina Press, 1953.

Huntington, Samuel P. *The Soldier and the State*. Cambridge, Mass.: Harvard University Press, 1957.

Huntington, Samuel P., and Moore, Clement. *Authoritarian Politics in Modern Society*. New York: Basic Books, 1970.

Huntington, Samuel P., and Nelson, Joan M. *No Easy Choice: Political Participation in Developing Countries*. Cambridge, Mass.: Harvard University Press, 1976.

Ikle, Fred C. *How Nations Negotiate*. New York: Praeger, 1967.

Jackman, Robert. "Politicians in Uniform," *American Political Science Review* 70 (December 1976): 1098–1109.

Janda, Kenneth. *A Conceptual Framework for the Comparative Analysis of Political Parties*. Beverly Hills, Calif.: Sage, 1970.

————. *Political Parties: A Cross-National Survey*. New York: Free Press, 1980.

Jaros, Dean. *Socialization to Politics*. New York: Praeger, 1973.

Jennings, Ivor. *Cabinet Government*. 3rd ed. New York: Cambridge University Press, 1969.

Johnson, John J., ed. *The Role of the Military in Underdeveloped Countries*. Princeton, N.J.: Princeton University Press, 1962.

Kaufman, Herbert. *Red Tape: Its Origins, Uses, and Abuses*. Washington, D.C.: Brookings, 1977.

Kochanek, Stanley. *Business and Politics in India*. Berkeley: University of California Press, 1974.

Kommers, Donald P. *Judicial Politics in West Germany*. Beverly Hills, Calif.: Sage, 1976.

Kornberg, Allan, ed. *Legislatures in Comparative Perspective*. New York: David McKay, 1973.

Krislov, Samuel. *Representative Bureaucracy*. Englewood Cliffs, N.J.: Prentice-Hall, 1974.

Kvavik, Robert. *Interest Groups in Norwegian Politics*. Oslo: Universitetsforlaget, 1976.

Lane, Robert E. *Political Ideology: Why the American Common Man Believes What He Does*. New York: Free Press, 1962.

Lange, P., and Garrett, G. "The Politics of Growth: Strategic Interaction and Economic Performance in the Advanced Industrial Democracies, 1974–1980," *Journal of Politics* 47 (August 1985): 792–827.

LaPalombara, Joseph. *Interest Groups in Italian Politics*. Princeton, N.J.: Princeton University Press, 1964.

————, ed. *Bureaucracy and Political Development*. Princeton, N.J.: Princeton University Press, 1963.

LaPalombara, Joseph, and Weiner, Myron. *Political Parties and Political Development*. Princeton, N.J.: Princeton University Press, 1966.

Lasswell, Harold R., and Kaplan, Abraham. *Power and Society*. Yale Law School Studies, vol. 2. New Haven, Conn.: Yale University Press, 1950.

Lave, Charles A., and March, James G. *An Introduction to Models in the Social Sciences*. New York: Harper & Row, 1975.

Lehmbruch, Gerhard, and Schmitter, Philippe C., eds. *Patterns of Corporatist Policy-Making*. Beverly Hills, Calif.: Sage, 1982.

Lenin, V. I. "State and Revolution." In *Sources in Twentieth-Century Political Thought*, edited by Hanry Kariel. New York: Free Press, 1964.

Levite, Ariel, and Tarrow, Sidney. "Legitimation of Excluded Parties in Dominant Party Systems: A Comparison of Israel and Italy," *Comparative Politics* 15 (April 1983): 295–327.

Li, Richard P. Y., and Thompson, William R. "The 'Coup Contagion' Hypothesis," *Journal of Conflict Resolution* 19 (March 1975): 63–88.

Lindblom, Charles. *The Intelligence of Democracy*. New York: Free Press, 1965.

————. *Politics and Markets*. New York: Basic Books, 1977.

Linz, Juan J., and Stepan, Alfred. *The Breakdown of Democratic Regimes*. Baltimore: Johns Hopkins University Press, 1978.

Lipset, Seymour Martin, and Rokkan, Stein. *Party Systems and Voter Alignments*. New York: Free Press, 1967.

Lipset, Seymour Martin, Trow, Martin A., and Coleman, James S. *Union Democracy*. Garden City, N.Y.: Doubleday, 1962.

Lipsitz, Lewis. "If, as Verba Says, The State Functions as a Religion, What Are We to Do Then to Save Our Souls?" *American Political Science Review* 52 (June 1968): 527–535.

Lipsky, Michael. "Protest as a Political Resource," *American Political Science Review* 62 (December 1968): 1144–1158.

Little, Richard D. "Mass Political Participation in the U.S. and the U.S.S.R." *Comparative Political Studies* 8 (January 1976): 437–460.

Livingston, William S. "Britain and America: The Institutionalization of Accountability," *Journal of Politics* 38 (November 1976): 870–894.

Loewenberg, Gerhard. *Parliament in the German Political System*. Ithaca, N.Y.: Cornell University Press, 1967.

————. "The Remaking of the German Party System," *Polity* 1 (Fall 1968): 86–113.

Loewenberg, Gerhard, and Patterson, Samuel C. *Comparing Legislatures*. Boston: Little, Brown, 1979.

Loomis, Burdett A., and Cigler, Allan J., eds. *Interest Group Politics*. Washington, D.C.: Congressional Quarterly, Inc., 1983.

MacIver, R. M. *The Web of Government*. New York: Macmillan, 1947.

Maier, Charles S., ed. *Changing Boundaries of the Political*. Cambridge, England: Cambridge University Press, 1987.

Mandel, Ernest. *Late Capitalism*. London: NLB, 1975.

Marx, Karl, and Engels, Frederick. *Basic Writings on Politics and Philosophy*, edited by Lewis S. Feuer. Garden City, N.Y.: Doubleday, 1959.

McCloskey, Herbert. "Consensus and Ideology in American Politics," *American Political Science Review* 58 (June 1964): 361–382.

McCormick, Richard L., ed. *Political Parties and the Modern State*. New Brunswick, N.J.: Rutgers University Press, 1984.

Medish, Vadim. *The Soviet Union*. 2nd ed. Englewood Cliffs, N.J.: Prentice-Hall, 1984.

Meier, Kenneth John. "Representative Bureaucracy: An Empirical Analysis," *American Political Science Review* 69 (June 1975): 526–542.

Michels, Robert. *Political Parties*. New York: Free Press, 1962.

Miller, Warren E., Miller, Arthur H., and Schneider, Edward J. *American National Election Studies Data Sourcebook, 1952–1978*. Cambridge, Mass.: Harvard University Press, 1980.

Millet, Kate. *Sexual Politics*. Garden City, N.Y.: Doubleday, 1970.

Moe, Terry. *The Organization of Interests*. Chicago: University of Chicago Press, 1980.

Moon, John Ellis van Courtland. "Chemical Weapons and Deterrence: The World War II Experience," *International Security* 8 (Spring 1984): 3–25.

Moore, Stanley W., et al. *The Child's Political World: A Longitudinal Perspective*. New York: Praeger, 1985.

Morgenthau, Hans. *Politics Among Nations*. 5th rev. ed. New York: Knopf, 1978.

Mueller, John. *War, Presidents, and Public Opinion*. New York: Wiley, 1973.

Nagel, Jack H. *The Descriptive Analysis of Power*. New Haven, Conn.: Yale University Press, 1975.

Needler, Martin C. "The Logic of Conspiracy: The Latin American Military Coup as a Problem in the Social Sciences," *Studies in Comparative International Development* 13 (Fall 1978): 28–40.

———. "Political Development and Military Intervention in Latin America," *American Political Science Review* 60 (September 1966): 616–626.

Nettl, J. P. "The State as a Conceptual Variable," *World Politics* 20 (July 1968): 559–592.

Neumann, Franz. *Behemoth: The Structure and Practice of National Socialism, 1933–1944*. New York: Oxford University Press, 1944.

Neustadt, Richard E. *Presidential Power: The Politics of Leadership*. Rev. ed. New York: Wiley, 1976.

Nicolson, Harold. *Diplomacy*. 3rd ed. New York: Oxford University Press, 1963.

Nie, Norman, Verba, Sidney, and Petrocik, John. *The Changing American Voter*. Cambridge, Mass.: Harvard University Press, 1976.

al Nimir, Saud, and Palmer, Monte. "Bureaucracy and Development in Saudi Arabia: A Behavioral Analysis," *Public Administration and Development* 2 (April–June 1982): 93–104.

Nordlinger, Eric A. *Solders in Politics*. Englewood Cliffs, N.J.: Prentice-Hall, 1976.

Nwabueze, Benjamin O. *Presidentialism in Commonwealth Africa*. London: C. Hurst & Co., 1974.

O'Donnell, Guillermo. *Modernization and Bureaucratic Authoritarianism: Studies in South American Politics*. Berkeley: Institute of International Studies, University of California, 1973.

O'Donnell, Guillermo, Schmitter, Philippe, and Whitehead, Laurence. *Transitions from Authoritarian Rule: Prospects for Democracy*. Baltimore: Johns Hopkins University Press, 1986.

Oliver, James. "Citizen Demands in the Soviet System," *American Political Science Review* 63 (June 1969): 465–475.

Olson, Mancur. *The Logic of Collective Action*. Cambridge, Mass.: Harvard University Press, 1965.

Olson, Susan M. *Clients and Lawyers, Securing the Rights of Disabled Persons*. Westport, Conn.: Greenwood Press, 1984.

Ornstein, Norman J., and Elder, Shirley. *Interest Groups, Lobbying and Policymaking*. Washington, D.C.: Congressional Quarterly Press, 1978.

Ostrogorski, M. *Democracy and the Organization of Political Parties*. Garden City, N.Y.: Doubleday, 1964.

Ostrom, Vincent. *The Intellectual Crisis in American Public Administration*. University, Ala.: University of Alabama Press, 1973.

Padgett, L. Vincent. *The Mexican Political System*. 2nd ed. Boston: Houghton Mifflin, 1976.

Page, Benjamin I. *Who Gets What from Government*. Berkeley: University of California Press, 1983.

Paltiel, Khayam. "Campaign Finance: Contrasting Patterns and Reforms," in David Butler, ed., *Democracy at the Polls*. Washington, D.C.: American Enterprise Institute, 1981.

Parker, Glenn R., ed. *Studies of Congress*. Washington, D.C.: Congressional Quarterly, Inc., 1984.

Pateman, Carole. *Participation and Democracy Theory*. Cambridge, England: Cambridge University Press, 1970.

Patterson, Thomas E. *The Mass Media Election*. New York: Praeger, 1980.

Pechman, Joseph A., ed. *Setting National Priorities: The 1984 Budget*. Washington, D.C.: Brookings, 1983.

Perlmutter, Amos. *The Military and Politics in Modern Times*. New Haven, Conn.: Yale University Press, 1977.

Peterson, Paul. *City Limits*. Chicago: University of Chicago Press, 1981.

Piliavin, Irving, and Briar, Scott. "Police Encounters with Juveniles," *American Journal of Sociology* 70 (September 1964): 206–214.

Pious, Richard M. *The American Presidency*. New York: Basic Books, 1979.

Pirages, Dennis. *The New Context for International Relations: Global Ecopolitics*. North Scituate, Mass.: Duxbury, 1978.

Pitkin, Hanna Fenichel. *The Concept of Representation*. Berkeley: University of California Press, 1967.

Piven, Frances Fox, and Cloward, Richard A. *Regulating the Poor*. New York: Pantheon, 1971.

Przeworski, Adam. "Some Problems in the Study of the Transition to Democracy," in Guillermo O'Donnell, Philippe C. Schmitter, and Laurence Whitehead, eds. *Transitions from Authoritarian Rule: Comparative Perspectives*. Baltimore: Johns Hopkins University Press, 1986, pp. 47–63.

Przeworski, Adam, and Sprague, John. *Paper Stones: A History of Electoral Socialism*. Chicago: University of Chicago Press, 1986.

Quinn, Anthony, ed. *Political Philosophy*. Oxford, England: Oxford University Press, 1967.

Rae, Douglas. *The Political Consequences of Electoral Laws*. rev. ed. New Haven, Conn.: Yale University Press, 1971.

Reshetar, John S., Jr. *The Soviet Polity*. 3rd ed. New York: Harper & Row, 1989.

Reyna, Jose L., and Weinert, Richard S., eds. *Authoritarianism in Mexico*. Philadelphia: Institute for the Study of Human Issues, 1977.

Rigby, Thomas H. *Communist Party Membership in the U.S.S.R., 1917–1967*. Princeton, N.J.: Princeton University Press, 1968.

Riggs, Fred. *Administration in Developing Countries*. Boston: Houghton Mifflin, 1964.

Riker, William. *Federalism: Origin, Operation, Significance*. Boston: Little, Brown, 1964.

————. *A Theory of Political Coalitions*. New Haven, Conn.: Yale University Press, 1962.

Riker, William H., and Ordeshook, Peter C. *An Introduction to Positive Political Theory*. Englewood Cliffs, N.J.: Prentice-Hall, 1973.

Rikhye, Indar, J., Harbottle, Michael, and Egge, Bjorn. *The Thin Blue Line: International Peacekeeping and its Future*. New Haven, Conn.: Yale University Press, 1974.

Rogowski, Ronald. "Political Cleavages and Changing Exposure to Trade," *American Political Science Review* 81 (December 1987): 1121–1137.

Rose, Richard. *Do Parties Make a Difference?* Chatham, N.J.: Chatham House, 1980.

————. *The Postmodern President*. Chatham, N.J.: Chatham House, 1989.

————. "Still The Era of Party Government," *Parliamentary Affairs* 36 (Summer 1983): 282–299.

Rose, Richard, and Suleiman, Ezra N., eds. *Presidents and Prime Ministers*. Washington D.C.: American Enterprise Institute, 1980.

Rosenau, James N., ed. *In Search of Global Patterns*. New York: Free Press, 1976.

Rossiter, Clinton. *The American Presidency*. 2nd ed. New York: New American Library, 1964.

Russett, Bruce. *What Price Vigilance?* New Haven, Conn.: Yale University Press, 1970.

Russett, Bruce M., and Starr, Harvey. *World Politics: The Menu for Choice*. San Francisco: H. W. Freeman, 1981.

Sabatier, Paul, and Mazmanian, Dan. "The Implementation of Public Policy: A Framework of Analysis," *Policy Studies Journal* 8 (Special Issue, no. 2, 1980): 538–559.

Salisbury, Robert. "An Exchange Theory of Interest Groups," *Midwest Journal of Political Science* 13 (February 1969): 1–32.

Sampson, Anthony. *The New Europeans*. London: Hodder and Stoughton, 1968.

Sartori, Giovanni. *Parties and Party Systems*. Cambridge, England: Cambridge University Press, 1976.

Schapiro, Leonard. *The Communist Party of the Soviet Union*. New York: Random House, 1960.

Schattschneider, E. E. *Party Government*. New York: Holt, Rinehart and Winston, 1942.

————. *The Semisovereign People*. New York: Holt, Rinehart and Winston, 1960.

Schlesinger, Arthur M., Jr. *The Imperial Presidency*. Boston: Houghton Mifflin, 1973.

Schlesinger, Joseph. *Ambition and Politics: Political Careers in the United States*. Chicago: Rand McNally, 1966.

Schlozman, Kay Lehman, and Tierney, John T. *Organized Interests and American Democracy*. New York: Harper & Row, 1986.

Schulman, Paul R. "Nonincremental Policy Making," *American Political Science Review* 69 (December 1975): 1354–1370.

Scott, Robert. *Mexican Government in Transition*. Rev. ed. Urbana: University of Illinois Press, 1964.

Shamir, Michal, and Sullivan, John. "The Political Context of Tolerance: The United States and Israel," *American Political Science Review* 77 (December 1983): 911–928.

Shils, Edward, and Young, Michael. "The Meaning of the Coronation," *Sociological Review* 1 (December 1953): 63–81.

Shively, W. Phillips. "The Nature of Party Identification." In *The Electorate Reconsidered*, edited by John C. Pierce and John L. Sullivan. Beverly Hills, Calif.: Sage, 1980.

Shonfield, Andrew. *Modern Capitalism*. Oxford, England: Oxford University Press, 1965.

Skilling, H. Gordon, and Griffiths, Franklyn, eds. *Interest Groups in Soviet Politics*. Princeton, N.J.: Princeton University Press, 1971.

Skinner, B. F. *Walden Two*. New York: Macmillan, 1948.

Skocpol, Theda. *States and Social Revolutions*. Cambridge, England: Cambridge University Press, 1979.

Smith, Anthony B. *Theories of Nationalism*. New York: Harper & Row, 1971.

Smith, Bruce L. R., ed. *The Higher Civil Service in Europe and Canada: Lessons for the United States*. Washington, D.C.: Brookings, 1984.

Sniderman, Paul. *Personality and Democratic Politics*. Berkeley: University of California Press, 1975.

Solzhenitsyn, Alexander. *The Gulag Archipelago, 1918–1956*. New York: Harper & Row, 1974.

Sorauf, Frank. "Zorach vs. Clausen: The Impact of a Supreme Court Decision," *American Political Science Review* 53 (September 1959): 777–791.

Sorauf, Frank, and Beck, Paul A. *Party Politics in America*. 6th ed. Glenview, Ill.: Scott, Foresman, 1988.

Speer, Albert. *Inside the Third Reich*. New York: Macmillan, 1970.

Sprout, Harold and Margaret. *The Ecological Perspective on Human Affairs, with Special Reference to International Politics*. Princeton, N.J.: Princeton University Press, 1965.

Stoessinger, John G. *Why Nations Go to War*. 3rd ed. New York: St. Martin's, 1982.

Suleiman, Ezra N. *Politics, Power, and Bureaucracy in France*. Princeton, N.J.: Princeton University Press, 1974.

Sullivan, John L., Pierson, James, and Marcus, George E. "An Alternative Conceptualization of Political Tolerance," *American Political Science Review* 73 (September 1979): 781–794.

Taagepera, Rein, and Shugart, Matthew S. *Seats and Votes: The Effects and Determinants of Electoral Systems*. New Haven, Conn.: Yale University Press, 1989.

Tilly, Charles, ed. *The Formation of National States in Western Europe*. Princeton, N.J.: Princeton University Press, 1975.

Triska, Jan F. *Dominant Powers and Subordinate States*. Durham, N.C.: Duke University Press, 1986.

Truman, David. *The Governmental Process*. 2nd ed. New York: Alfred A. Knopf, 1951.

Tuchman, Barbara W. *A Distant Mirror: The Calamitous Fourteenth Century*. New York: Alfred A. Knopf, 1978.

Tufte, Edward R. *Political Control of the Economy*. Princeton, N.J.: Princeton University Press, 1978.

Ulam, Adam B. *The Rivals: America and Russia Since World War II*. New York: Viking, 1971.

U.S. Senate, Committee on Governmental Operations. *Confidence and Concern: Citizens View American Government*. Washington, D.C.: Government Printing Office, 1973.

Valenzuela, J. Samuel, and Valenzuela, Arturo. "Modernization and Dependency," *Comparative Politics* 10 (July 1978): 535–557.

Verba, Sidney, Nie, Norman, and Kim, Jae-on. *Participation and Political Equality*. London: Cambridge University Press, 1978.

Verba, Sidney, and Nie, Norman H. *Participation in America*. New York: Harper & Row, 1972.

Walker, Jack L. "The Origins and Maintenance of Interest Groups in America," *American Political Science Review* 77 (June 1983): 390–406.

Wallerstein, Immanuel. *The Capitalist World Economy*. Cambridge, England: Cambridge University Press, 1979.

Weissberg, Robert. *Public Opinion and Popular Government*. Englewood Cliffs, N.J.: Prentice-Hall, 1976.

Welsh, William A. "The Status of Research on Representative Institutions in Eastern Europe." *Legislative Studies Quarterly* 5 (1980): 275–308.

Wheare, K. D. *Federal Government*. 4th ed. London: Oxford University Press, 1963.

White, Stephen. "The U.S.S.R. Supreme Soviet: A Developmental Perspective," *Legislative Studies Quarterly* 5 (May 1980): 247–274.

Wiarda, Howard, ed. *New Directions in Comparative Politics*. Boulder, Colo.: Westview Press, 1985.

Wildavsky, Aaron B. *Speaking Truth to Power*. New Brunswick, N.J.: Transaction Books, 1987.

Wills, Gary. *Cincinnatus: George Washington and the Enlightenment*. Garden City, N.Y.: Doubleday, 1984.

Wilson, Frank L. "French Interest Groups: Pluralist or Neocorporatist?" *American Political Science Review* 77 (December 1983): 895–910.

Wilson, James Q. *Political Organizations*. New York: Basic Books, 1973.

Wolfinger, Raymond E., and Rosenstone, Steven J. *Who Votes?* New Haven, Conn.: Yale University Press, 1980.

Wrong, Dennis. *Power*. New York: Harper & Row, 1979.

Index

Aberbach, Joel D., 292
Abraham, Henry J., 236, 256
Adams, Carolyn, 83
Adams, John Clarke, 165n
Alford, Robert R., 83
Allerbeck, Klause, 167
Allison, Graham T., 292
Almond, Gabriel, 118, 125,
    160, 201n
Ambler, Eric, 26
amendability of constitutions,
    131
analytic political philosophy, 60
Anderson, Charles, 85n
Andrews, William G., 256
anomic interest groups, 203
Aquinas, Thomas, 61
arbitrary policy, 88, 280
Argentina, 141
Arian, Alan, 184n
Aristotle, 60
Ascher, William, 103
Ashford, Douglas E., 288n
associational interest groups, 203
Augustine, Saint, 61
authority, 107–109
Axelrod, Robert, 103

Bachrach, Peter, 9
Baker, Kendall, 123, 163
Baker, Pauline H., 36n
Bakvis, Herman, 146
Balewa, Abubakar, 36
Ball, A., 215
Bangladesh, 31
Baratz, Morton S., 9
Barber, Benjamin, 125
Barber, James David, 247
Barile, Paolo, 165n
Barnes, Samuel H., 167, 184n
Basque "nation," 30, 31
Bather, L., 144
Bauer, Raymond A., 215
Bebler, Anton, 275
Beck, Paul A., 180n

begging the question, 317
"behavioral" political science, 15
Berger, Suzanne, 215
Berlin, Isaiah, 62
Berry, William D., 70
Biafra, 36
Bienen, Henry, 270–271
bipolar international system, 298
Birch, Anthony H., 236
Blake, William, 54
Bobrow, Davis B., 103
Bolivia, 259
Brandt, Willy, 130
Brazil, 260
    bureaucracy, 291–293
Briar, Scott, 278n
Brichta, Avraham, 256
Bronowski, Jacob, 62
bureaucracy, 280–286
Burke, Edmund, 49, 221
Burkett, Tony, 235n
Burnham, Walter Dean, 193

Cameron, David, 70
Campbell, Angus, 162n, 175n
Canada, 135
Catholic Church, 128–129
causation, 315
Central Committee, 189
Chan, Stephen, 311
Chandler, William M., 146
Chase, Harold W., 244n
China, 131
Chrines, S. B., 142n
Churchill, Winston, 94,
    298–299
Cigler, Allan J., 216
circular argument, 318
Citrin, Jack, 125n
class, 52
Claude, Inis L., Jr., 311
Cloward, Richard A., 84
coalition, 219
Cold War, 299–300
Coleman, James, 200n, 201n

collective good, 99, 202
Collier, David, 275
Combs, James, 111n
Commission (of European
    Community), 39
committees of parliament,
    222–223, 225–226
communism, 55
Communist Party, U.S.S.R.,
    188–190
Congress, U.S., 238–239
Conover, Pamela Johnston, 43n
Conradt, David, 122, 123
conservatism, 48–52
    "American," 44
constitution, 127
constitutional review, 246–249
constitutionalism, 140–141
Converse, Philip E., 62, 162n
corruption, 284–285
Coulter, Philip B., 84
Council of Ministers, 39
coup d'état, 261
court politics, 267–268
Cronin, Thomas E., 256
Crossman, R. H. S., 236
Crozier, Michel, 292

Dahl, Robert, 8–9, 16, 62, 125
Dalton, Russell, 123, 163, 193
Dante, 22
Dawson, Richard E., 119n
defense policy, 70–73
DeGaulle, Charles, 253–254
delegate model of
    representation, 221
dependency theory, 299
Deutsch, Karl, 41
Dexter, Lewis A., 215
dialectic (Marx), 54
Dibacco, Thomas V., 256
Dodd, Lawrence C., 226n
Dogan, Mattei, 292
dominant party system, 184, 266
Doughterty, James E., 33n
Downs, Anthony, 193
Duchacek, Ivor D., 146
due process, 88
Duverger, Maurice, 154n,
    184n, 275

ENA, 280
Ebenstein, William, 62
Eckstein, Harry, 120n
economic development, 78–80

education policy, 73–74
efficiency of policy, 91–93
Egge, Bjørn, 303n
Ehrmann, Henry, 213n
Eisenhower, Dwight, 129
Elder, Shirley, 204n
elections, 147 ff.
Electoral College, 128
electoral systems, 152–156
electoral turnout, 157
Engels, Frederick, 59
Epstein, Leon D., 182n
Estonia, 135
Eulau, Heinz, 103
European Community, 32, 37–41
European Court of Justice, 40
European Parliament, 39, 40
Evans, P. B., 27
experimentation and causal
    inference, 315–316
externality, 99

fairness, 85–91
falsifiability, 312–313
fascism, 55–56
Federal Register, 68
federalism, 135
Feldman, Stanley, 43
Fenno, Richard, 16
fiduciary role, 304
Finer, S. E., 146, 275
Fiorina, Morris P., 68n
Fitton, Martin, 270n
Flanigan, William H., 167
Fogelman, Edwin, 62
France:
    bureaucracy, 287–289
    constitution, 129
    constitutionalism, 141
    interest groups, 213–215
    presidency, 252–255
Franco, Francisco, 56
Frears, J. R., 139n
freedom of information laws, 284
Friedrich, Carl, 146
Fukuyama, Francis, 269

Gandhi, Indira, 232
Garrett, G., 84
Gellner, Ernest, 126
Germany, 131
    Basic Law, 129
    federalism, 136
    parliamentary government,
        233–236

political culture, 121–123
Germany (Nazi), elections, 149
Ginsberg, Benjamin, 150
glasnost, 57, 128, 146, 190, 196, 229
Goldwin, Robert A., 146
Gonzalez, Felipe, 57
Goodman, David S. G., 215
Gorbachev, Mikhail, 57, 128, 146, 190, 196, 229
government, 27, 107–108
Gowon, Yakubu, 36
Graber, Doris, 126
Greens, 57
Greenstein, Fred, 311
Griffiths, Franklyn, 216
gross national product, 65
Gruber, Judith E., 292
Gupta, D. C., 232
Gurr, Ted Robert, 120n

Hah, Chong-do, 26n
Harbottle, Michael, 303n
Hartz, Louis, 49n, 59
Harvey, Jack, 144
health policy, 74
Heclo, Hugh, 83
Heidenheimer, Arnold J., 83, 103, 252n, 293
Heisler, Martin O., 211n
Hendel, Samuel, 193
Henry II, 7
Herz, John H., 25n
hierarchical command structure, 281
Hildebrandt, Kai, 123, 163
historical explanation, 316–317
Hitler, Adolf, 56, 110–111
Hobbes, Thomas, 62
Holt, Robert, 244n
Hood, Christopher C., 292
Hunter, Floyd, 8
Huntington, Samuel P., 167, 275
Hyman, Herbert H., 120

ideology, 42, 43
Ikle, Fred C., 311
implicit power, 7
incentive compatibility, 132–134
incremental decision-making, 94, 96
India, 30, 135
    dominant party system, 185
Indiana, electoral division, 175–179

Inglehart, Ronald, 57, 126
institutional interest groups, 203
interest group, 195
International Court of Justice, 303
international law, 303
Israel, dominant party system, 185
Italy:
    coalitions, 187
    elections, 163–165

Jackman, Robert, 262n
Jennings, W. Ivor, 146, 236
Johnson, John J., 73n, 275
Jones, Charles O., 103
judicial review, 246–249
justice, 85–88

Kaase, Max, 167
Kaplan, Abraham, 16
Kaufman, Art, 146
Kaufman, Herbert, 293
Keeler, John T. S., 215n
Key, V. O., Jr., 175n
Khadaffi, Muammar, 265
Khomeini, Ayatollah, 112
Kim, Jae-on, 117
King, Martin Luther, 206
Kochanek, Stanley, 215
Kommers, Donald P., 236, 256
Kornberg, Allan, 236
Krislov, Samuel, 287n
Kurdish "nation," 30
Kurds, 135
Kvavik, Robert B., 196, 210n, 211n

Landau, Martin, 103
Lane, Robert E., 126
Lange, P., 84
LaPalombaro, Joseph, 193, 293
Lasswell, Harold D., 16
Latvia, 135
Lave, Charles A., 16
legitimacy, 109–112, 264
Lehmbruch, Gerhard, 215
Lenin, V. I., 25
Levite, Ariel, 184n
Li, Richard P. Y., 264
liberalism, 45–47
    "American," 44
Lindblom, Charles, 96, 98
Linz, Juan J., 275
Lipset, Seymour Martin, 160, 193, 200n

Lipsitz, Lewis, 246n
Lipsky, Michael, 207n
litigation, 207–208
Little, Richard D., 12n, 148
Livingston, William S., 244n
Loewenberg, Gerhard, 193, 236
Lok Sabha, 232–233
Loomis, Burdett A., 216
Lowery, David, 70
Luther, Martin, 61

McCloskey, Herbert, 126
McCormick, Richard L., 193
Machiavelli, Niccolo, 61
MacIver, R. M., 11n, 16
McLuhan, Marshall, 311
Madagascar, 259
Maginot Line, 129
Magna Carta, 142
Mandel, Ernest, 25
March, James G., 16
Marcus, George E., 115, 126
Maier, Charles S., 16
manifest power, 7
Mao Tse-tung, 141
market mechanisms, 95
Martin, Jeffrey, 26n
Marx, Karl, 52
Marxist theory of the state, 25
Mazlish, Bruce, 62
Mazmanian, Dan, 103
Medish, Vadim, 189n
Meier, Kenneth John, 287n
Mexico, presidency of, 255–256
Michels, Robert, 183
military government, 261–265
military power, 306–307
Mill, John Stuart, 46, 47
Millard, F., 215
Miller, Arthur H., 117, 124n
Miller, Warren E., 16n, 117
Millet, Kate, 13
Mitterand, François, 139
mobilization, 172–173
Moe, Terry M., 200
Monnet, Jean, 38
Moon, John Ellis van
        Courtland, 300n
Moore, Clement, 275
Moore, Stanley W., 119n
Morgenthau, Hans, 309–310
Mueller, John, 126
multiparty system, 186–187
Munger, Frank, 175n
Mussolini, Benito, 56

NAACP, 208
Nagel, Jack H., 16
Napoleon, 129
nation, 29
nationalism, 25–26
NATO, 41
Needler, Martin C., 262n, 263n
Nelson, Joan M., 167
neocorporatism, 211–213
Nettl, J. P., 41
Neumann, Franz, 275
Neustadt, Richard E., 256
Nicholson, Harold, 311
Nie, Norman H., 116–117, 126,
        167
Nigeria, 30–31, 35–37
    elections, 166–167
Nimmo, Dan, 111n
nonassociational groups, 203
Nordlinger, Eric, 275
Norway, 81–82
Nwabueze, Benjamin O., 256
Nyerere, Julius, 111, 265

Obasanjo, Olusegun, 37
O'Donnell, Guillermo, 216, 275
Oliver, James, 148
Olson, Mancur, 200n, 202
Olson, Susan M., 208n
ombudsman, 284
one-party system, 184, 265–266
Oppenheimer, Bruce I., 226n
Ordeshook, Peter C., 159n
Organization of American
        States, 32
Ornstein, Norman J., 204n
Ostrogorski, M., 171
Ostrom, Vincent, 293

Padgett, Vincent, 192
Page, Benjamin I., 84
Palestine Liberation
        Organization, 31
Palmer, Monte, 290
Paltiel, Khayam, 182n
paradox of participation,
        158–159
Parker, Glenn R., 236
parliamentary government,
        217 ff.
party identification, 162, 175
Pateman, Carole, 160
Patterson, Samuel C., 236
Patterson, Thomas E., 117–118,
        126

Pechman, Joseph A., 84
perestroika, 57
Perlmutter, Amos, 275
Peterson, Paul, 84
Petrocik, John, 167
Pfalzgraff, Robert L., Jr., 33n
Pierce, John C., 167
Piereson, James, 115, 126
Piliavin, Irving, 278n
Pious, Richard M., 257
Pirages, Dennis, 311
Pitkin, Hanna F., 60n, 236
Piven, Frances Fox, 84
Plamenatz, J., 62
Plato, 59
pluralism, 210–211
Politburo, 189
political culture, 119
political parties, 169–183
political party systems,
    184–187
political science, 14–16
political socialization, 119
  agents of, 120–121
politics, defined, 4–6
Polsby, Nelson, 311
Pool, Ithiel de Sola, 215
post hoc explanation, 319
Powell, G. Bingham, Jr., 167
power, 6, 306–309
power and choice perspectives,
    11–13
presidential government, 237
PRI, 191–193
progressive taxation, 77
Prohibition, 130
proportional representation, 153
protected incompetence, 283
Prussia, 22
Przeworski, Adam, 193, 265n
public administration, 276
Putnam, Robert D., 286, 292

Quebec, 31, 135
question time, 222
Quinton, Anthony, 60n

radical decision-making, 94
Rae, Douglas, 154n
recruitment, 173–175, 242–244
redistribution of income, 77–78
referendum, 151, 156–157
regional integration, 32
regressive taxation, 77
regulation, 68

representative bureaucracy,
    286–287
research and development, 74
Reshetar, John S., Jr., 128n,
    145, 148n, 149n, 196n
Riggs, Fred, 293
rights, basic, 89–90
Riker, William H., 62, 135n,
    159n, 304
Rikhye, Indar, 303n
Rockman, Bert A., 292
Rogowski, Ronald, 193
Rokkan, Stein, 193
Roosevelt, Franklin, 129
Rosberg, Carl G., 275
Rose, Richard, 193, 222n, 257
Rosenau, James N., 311
Rosenstone,, Steven J., 168
Rossiter, Clinton, 257
Rouiquie, Alain, 275
Rueschmayer, D., 27
Russett, Bruce M., 84, 311

Sabatier, Paul, 103
Salisbury, Robert, 216
Sampson, Anthony, 289n
Sani, Giacomo, 115n
Sartori, Giovanni, 184n, 275
Saud al Nimir, 290
Saudi Arabia, 260
  bureaucracy of, 289–290
Schambra, William A., 146
Schattschneider, E. E., 160,
    241n
Schlesinger, Arthur M., Jr., 257
Schlesinger, Joseph, 146
Schlozman, Kay Lehman, 216
Schmitter, Philippe C., 215, 275
Schneider, Edward J., 117
Schulman, Paul R., 103
Scott, Robert, 255n
Scott, Walter, 26
Secretariat (Communist Party),
    189
selective incentives, 200–201
Shagari, Sheliu, 37
Shamir, Michal, 115
Shils, Edward, 246n
Shively, W. Phillips, 175n
Shonfield, Andrew, 74n
Shugart, Matthew S., 168
Sibley, Mulford Q., 62
single-member district,
    plurality electoral
    system, 152–153

Skilling, H. Gordon, 216
Skinner, B. F., 20, 159
Skocpol, Theda, 27, 41
Smith, Anthony B., 41
Smith, Bruce L. R., 293
Smith, Peter H., 256n
Smith, W. Rand, 57n
Sniderman, Paul, 126
social security, 77, 92–93
socialism, 51–55
socialization, 119
Solidarity, 204–205
Solzhenitsyn, Alexander, 141
Sorauf, Frank J., 180n, 279n
Spain, 134
Speer, Albert, 271–275
split executive of parliamentary
        systems, 244–246
Sprague, John, 193
Sprout, Harold, 308n, 311
Sprout, Margaret, 308n, 311
Sri Lanka, 82–83
Starr, Harvey, 311
state, 13, 29
    autonomous, 27
Stepan, Alfred, 275
Stoessinger, John G., 311
Stokes, Donald, 162n
Strauss, Leo, 62
Stroessner, Alfredo, 262
subsidies, 67
Suleiman, Ezra N., 257, 293
Sullivan, John L., 115, 126,
        167
Supreme Soviet, 127–128, 131,
        190, 228
Sweden, 211–212
Switzerland, 30

Taagepera, Rein, 168
Tanzania, 151
Tarrow, Sidney, 184n
tautology, 311
tax expenditures, 68
Teich, Robert, 74n
Thatcher, Margaret, 57
Third World, 35, 66, 301
Thomas à Beckett, 8
Thompson, William R., 264
Tierney, John T., 216
Tilly, Charles, 24n
"traditionalist" political science,
        15
transfer payments, 67
Triska, Jan F., 311

trivial explanation, 314
Trow, Martin, 200n
Truman, David, 210n
Truman, Harry S, 218
trustee model of representation,
        221
Tuchman, Barbara W., 21
Tufte, Edward R., 161n
Turner, John E., 244n
two-party system, 185–186

Ukraine, 135
Ulam, Adam B., 311
Union of Soviet Socialist
        Republics, 135, 258–259
    constitution, 127–128,
        144–146
    elections, 147–149
unitary state, 135
United Kingdom, 128–129, 134
    constitution of, 141–144
United Nations, 32, 303
United States of America:
    constitution, 129
    constitutionalism, 140
    political culture, 123–125

Valenzuela, Arturo, 299
Valenzuela, J. Samuel, 299
Verba, Sidney, 116–117, 118,
        125, 160, 167

Walker, Jack L., 216
Wallerstein, Immanuel, 41
Weber, Max, 281
Weiner, Myron, 193
Welsh, William A., 236
Wheare, K. D., 146
White, Stephen, 229n
Whitehead, Laurence, 275
Wiarda, Howard, 16
Wildavsky, Aaron B., 103
Wills, Gary, 257
Wilson, Frank L., 215n
Wilson, James Q., 216
Wolfinger, Raymond E., 168
Wolin, Sheldon S., 62
Wrong, Dennis, 16

Yonng, Michael, 246n
Yugoslavia, 30

Zalmanovitch, Yair, 256
Zingale, Nancy H., 167
Zuckerman, Edward, 195n